D0161119

Death and Religion in a Changing World

Kathleen Garces-Foley, Editor

M.E.Sharpe
Armonk, New York
London, England

Death and Religion in a Changing World

Cover photo by Bob Bednar, "US Highway 285-North, south of Roswell, New Mexico, August 2003."

Library of Congress Cataloging-in-Publication Data

Death and religion in a changing world / Kathleen Garces-Foley, editor.
p. cm.
Includes bibliographical references and index.
ISBN 0-7656-1221-6 (hc : alk. paper)
1. Death—Religious aspects. I. Garces-Foley, Kathleen, 1972–

BL504.D363 2006
202'.3—dc22 2005009185

Printed in the United States of America

The paper used in this publication meets the minimum requirements of
American National Standard for Information Sciences
Permanence of Paper for Printed Library Materials,
ANSI Z 39.48-1984.

BM (c) 10 9 8 7 6 5 4 3 2 1

Contents

Acknowledgments

This volume would not have been possible without the support of many people. Most especially, I am grateful to the contributors for taking on the challenge of writing to both an introductory and specialized audience and for putting up with my eager editing. At M.E. Sharpe, I want especially to thank acquisitions editor James Ciment, who worked with me on the project from its inception, and Cathy Prisco, who took care of all the details. Thanks are also due to University of California, Santa Barbara colleagues Leslie Smith and Brian Cooper, who provided editorial assistance on some of the chapters, and Wade Clark Roof, Paul Spickard, and David Machacek, who gave me advice at various stages of the project. Tony Walter of the University of Reading, UK, provided very helpful feedback on the overall project. Much gratitude goes to my partner, Anthony Garces-Foley, for his steady support in seeing the project through. I dedicate this book to my parents, Drs. Marie and John Foley, who instilled in me a love of learning and teaching. They taught me how to think, how to write, and the importance of telling a joke on the first day of class.

Introduction

Kathleen Garces-Foley

This book is a study of the intersection of death and religion in contemporary societies. Students of religion have long found this intersection fruitful for understanding the social behavior and worldviews of human beings. In the nineteenth century it was believed that the origin of religion could be found by studying ancient death practices. While the search for the origin of religion has been replaced by new questions, today scholars continue to be fascinated by the variety, complexity, and vitality of religious responses to death. The intersection between death and religion is revealing, for in the face of death humans have long expressed what we value most and what we believe to be the nature of reality and the meaning of human life. But death is not only an opportunity for an expression of beliefs and values; it is also an arena for making meaning, community, ritual, and myth. As David Chidester explains, "*Homo religious* is *Homo symbolicus*—the religious person is a symbol-using, -owning, and -operating person," and it is through the symbolic forms of religion—symbols, myths, rituals, and traditions—that the finality of death is transcended.[1] Rather than something people turn to in the face of death, religion is enacted or lived out as they, in the words of Robert Orsi, "make something of the worlds they have found themselves thrown into."[2] Faced with a death, expected or unexpected, the living must respond.

What people do in the face of death figures centrally in the following chapters. Death sets in motion a flurry of activity surrounding the body of the deceased as well as the social body. Something must be done with the physical body if for no other reason than that its presence will soon become unbearable. Something must be done about the people who are mourning. Something must be done about the dead person's stuff. These are quite practical concerns that may or may not be imbued with religious significance, but the practice of religious rituals and the reliance on religious frames of meaning in some form in the wake of death continues to be extraordinarily widespread. While religion maintains its primary place in human responses to death, how it is enacted varies considerably over time and space. As the reader will discover in each of the following chapters, religious traditions are not static systems of beliefs and rituals separable from culture, but dynamic, evolving, contested terrain deeply imbedded in social context. How one enacts religion, which beliefs and which rituals are appropriated from those available in a particular space, time, and circumstance, is the crucial question at the intersection of death and religion.[3]

The purpose of this volume is to look intently at the intersection of death and religion in order to understand how human beings enact, revise, and improvise religious practices in a rapidly modernizing world. It is commonly thought today that the continuing relevance of religion in modernity lies in its therapeutic benefits. This relegation of religion to such a diminished, conciliatory capacity is progressively more untenable as we recognize the continuing power of religion in the modern world. While the therapeutic function of religion is widely accepted in the West, it is clear from the following studies of religious responses to death that religion often fails to fit into its designated therapeutic role. For example, belief in a paradisiacal afterlife may assuage grief, but fears of punishment and the unsettled dead provide no consolation to grievers. Prescribed rituals for mourning and the disposition of the dead can serve as a useful guide, but these expectations may be unclear and contested, not to mention quite onerous to comply with, creating additional stress for the mourners. From the vantage point of death, one becomes keenly aware that religion, and its place in modernity, is far more complicated than first thought.

Within these chapters the reader will find many terms used to describe the formal religious actions that surround death. *Death rites* serves as the most inclusive of these terms since it includes both predeath rites and postdeath rites, those rituals focused on the deceased and those focused on the mourners. Often, the authors use more specific terms, such as *funeral* or *funerary rites, mortuary rites, burial rites, funeral protocols, bereavement* or *mourning rites,* and *memorial rites.* These terms are nowhere strictly defined in this volume and some are used interchangeably, presumably because no single term adequately captures the complex array of religious responses to death. Ritual studies scholar Ronald Grimes distinguishes formal religious rites from the gestures surrounding them, such as weeping or publishing a death notice. In practice, trying to separate what is social custom from religious ritual is quite difficult. The chapters in this book focus on formal, explicitly religious rites—that is, those actions that are intentional and socially recognized as such; however, in doing so the chapters also elucidate the porous boundaries between custom and religion, ritualized action and formal rite.[4]

For our purpose of understanding religion as it is enacted, the category of "practice" is especially useful. In contrast to the rites that are prescribed by God, tradition, or religious authorities, religious practices are what people actually do. Religious historian David Hall explains, "Practice always bears the marks of both regulation and what, for want of a better word, we may term resistance. It is not wholly one or the other."[5] The focus on practice reveals an incongruity between what is prescribed and what is performed. As Juan Campo brings forth so clearly in his chapter on Islam, this incongruity reveals not only the limited ability of religious authorities to define and control religious practice but the ways in which the physical and social circumstances of death constrain religious practice. Practice also reveals the challenge of identifying what is "prescribed," given that there are always competing claims for the legitimacy of religious authority. Enacting religion means wading through the array of voices—including religious elites, funeral specialists, media experts, and family members—claiming authority to define the appropriate religious response to death. For the religious practitioner, practice involves sorting through the competing versions of how one ought to respond to death in light of the immediate needs and limitations of the particular social context.

Religion is enacted by particular people in particular places at particular times. There is no "religious approach to death" separate from its context. Over time, religious practices change: the way Jews buried their dead at the time of Jesus is not the same as it is today. Across cultures, religious practices vary: Muslims in Indonesia cremate their dead and Muslims in the United States bury their dead. Within religious traditions, doctrinal and ritual differences are copious: Protestant Christians may cremate but Orthodox Christians do not. Culture, class, ethnicity, education, lineage, and gender may all influence how people enact religion in the face of death. Trying to make sense of all these variations is a daunting task. Some would argue that with so much diversity it is erroneous to even speak of unified religious traditions: there is no such thing as Buddhism—only Buddhisms, no Christianity—only Christianities, and so forth. The authors of this anthology take the contextualization of religion very seriously, but they still speak of religious traditions and what binds adherents together. Some religious peoples are bound together through religious authority, some by practices, and some by reverence for scripture, while others do not cohere tightly at all. For example, it makes much more sense to speak of "Hinduisms" than it does to speak of "Sikhisms." In the following chapters there is no easy solution to the incongruity between the categories in which we talk about religion and the way religion is actually lived out. The need to oversimplify in order to relay complex ideas in a small number of pages and the need to resist the misleading neatness of such generalizations coexist in a dissatisfying truce.

While fascinating books have been and will be written on the death practices of past eras, this book is about the present. It is about how the present social context affects the way individuals enact religious traditions that have been practiced for hundreds and, in some cases, thousands of years. In varying degrees around the world, humans have been confronted with significant social changes that we lump together under the name of modernity. Technological and scientific advances, secularization, urbanization, commodification, shifting gender roles, changing family structure, environmental degradation, globalization, and individualism all profoundly shape how we live and die in contemporary societies. A few decades ago electric crematories were unheard of in India, and Muslim cemeteries did not exist in the United States. Religious traditions are inherently conservative, but change they do, and our focus on the contemporary presents a fascinating opportunity to watch how such change occurs through the everyday enactment of religion in the face of death. At the intersection of death and religion, we find a vital tension between tradition and modernity out of which contemporary people fashion a response to death. This vantage point sheds light not only on the tension between religious tradition and modernity but on the ways in which people have always been forced to make something of their worlds "in, with, through, and against the religious idioms available to them in culture."[6] Those who believe that tradition cannot survive in the modern world will be surprised to learn in the following chapters the tensile strength and adaptability of religion.

This book began in the classroom; at least, that was where I first imagined it. As a doctoral student at University of California, Santa Barbara, I was first given the chance to teach the religious studies department's lower-division course, Religious Approaches to Death, during summer school in 2001. My first foray into teaching made me all the more passionate about the study of lived religion. Unfortunately, while there are several excellent books on religious beliefs regarding the afterlife and prescribed funeral rites, there are few introductory texts that consider how religion and death intersect in social context.[7] In order to teach the course with a focus on lived religion, I needed a text that would contextualize religious approaches to death and update the existing scholarship to account for our rapidly changing world. Developed with pedagogy in mind, the chapters in this book aim to introduce students to the study of death practices, as well as make theoretically rich and original contributions to the field that will be useful to scholars.

There are many ways a book on this topic could be organized, and I have chosen the most obvious: by religious tradition. This choice provides in a single book a comprehensive study of contemporary death practices within the major world religions. The chapters in part I, Religious Approaches to Death, examine how Hindus, Jews, Buddhists, Christians, Muslims, and Sikhs respond to death. In addition, while it would be impossible to take account of the many ethnoreligious traditions that fall outside the boundaries of world religions, I chose to begin the book with a chapter on one indigenous community, the California Chumash. Many religious studies textbooks begin with such a chapter, and this practice has been rightly criticized for relegating native peoples to a historical past tense.[8] Making quite the opposite point, Dennis Kelley shows how the Chumash use death practices to proclaim publicly their continued presence in California and to reclaim traditional practices in ways that respond to the exigencies of death in contemporary America. Kelley's chapter provides a theoretical framework for understanding the tension between the traditional and the modern that resonates throughout this volume.

All the chapters in part I share a similar structure in order to facilitate comparative discussion across religious traditions. To aid the introductory student, they begin with a concise introduction to the religious tradition and its historical death practices and beliefs before turning to the contemporary situation. In looking at the contemporary death practices of religious people, the contributors were asked to turn their attention beyond the West. Several authors were able to use their own field research to do this, and others drew upon existing scholarship. To the extent possible given their expertise, they have shown the diversity within religious traditions by contrasting death practices in two or more regions of the world. The reader may be surprised to find two chapters on Christianity when the other religious traditions are covered in a single chapter. This decision reflects the dominance of Christianity among the intended audience of the book, namely students in North America, Europe, and Australia. The choice was also a pragmatic one based on the scarcity of scholars able to write on Christianity as a whole. In keeping with the focus on lived religion, all the authors have contextualized their scholarship through the stories of real people. These stories, as Lizette Larson-Miller reminds us, are much more than quaint accessories to scholarly writing. There are no religious approaches to death outside of their lived embodiment in the lives of real people facing real death. Their stories reveal much about the continuing significance of religion, which can be easily missed when scholarship strays too far from the people religion matters to most.

There are many issues arising at the intersection of death and religion in contemporary societies that impact religious traditions in general. In part II, Death in Contemporary Societies, a series of essays examines how death practices in the West have been strongly influenced by widespread social changes such as secularization, individualism, spirituality, public religion, and the prevalence of the media. These chapters provocatively explore the areas of greatest change in death practices in the West and consider their implications for the future of religious response to death. In the concluding epilogue, Evan Berry examines the tension between modernity and religious tradition as it runs through all the chapters and highlights their theoretical contributions. Despite the breadth of this volume, there is much that is not covered. For example, the dying process and the conflicts that have arisen between lifesaving technologies and religious understandings of death deserve much more treatment. The growth of the hospice movement around the world is another area that awaits further study, as does the relationship between belief and practice and changing visions of the afterlife. The reader will undoubtedly add other neglected areas to this list. It is our hope that this study will stimulate much more discussion and research on the complex ways religion is enacted in the face of death in the modern social context.

NOTES

1. David Chidester, *Patterns of Transcendence: Religion, Death, and Dying,* 2nd ed. (Belmont, CA: Wadsworth, 2002), 5.

2. Robert Orsi, "Everyday Miracles: The Study of Lived Religion," in *Lived Religion in America: Toward a History of Practice,* ed. David D. Hall, 3–21 (Princeton: Princeton University Press, 1997), 7.

3. Ibid.

4. Ronald L. Grimes, *Deeply into the Bond: Re-inventing Rites of Passage* (Berkeley: University of California Press, 2000), 219.

5. David Hall, "Introduction," in *Lived Religion in America: Toward a History of Practice,* ed. David D. Hall, vii–xiii (Princeton: Princeton University Press, 1997), xi.

6. Orsi, "Everyday Miracles," 7.

7. Books on afterlife beliefs include Hiroshi Obayashi, ed., *Death and Afterlife: Perspectives of World Religions* (New York: Greenwood Press, 1992), and Christopher Jay Johnson and Marsha G. McGee, eds., *How Different Religions View Death and Afterlife* (Philadelphia: Charles Press, 1991). Books that address both beliefs and practices include David Chidester, *Patterns of Transcendence:*

Religion, Death, and Dying, 2nd ed. (Belmont, CA: Wadsworth, 2002); Colin Murray Parkes, Pittu Laungani, and Bill Young, eds., *Death and Bereavement Across Cultures* (New York: Routledge, 1996); and Authur Berger et al., eds., *Perspectives on Death and Dying: Cross-Cultural and Multi-Disciplinary Views* (Philadelphia: Charles Press, 1989).

8. Michael D. McNally criticizes textbooks on religion in America for confining Native religions to the first chapter, but the same pattern can be found in textbooks on religion and death; see McNally, "Religion and Culture Change in Native North America," in *Perspectives on American Religion and Culture,* ed. Peter W. Williams, 270–285 (Malden, MA: Blackwell, 1999).

I

RELIGIOUS APPROACHES TO DEATH

Chapter 1

The Politics of Death and Burial in Native California

Dennis F. Kelley

Having received some of my best postgraduate training among Native American communities, sitting around the dinner table, playing with the kids and dogs out in the yard, driving an elder to the grocery, and so forth, I find it important to begin (as one always should) with a story. This story comes in two parts.

> **Part One**—On August 3, 1992, a pipeline owned and operated by Union Oil Company of California (Unocal) just off the California coast at Avila Beach sprang a leak, sending some 600 barrels of oil into the ocean. During the cleanup operations, heavy equipment and helicopters were brought in, using the bluff overlooking what is now called Pirate's Cove as a staging point. In less than a week of operations, the already fragile topsoil of the bluff was eroded at an alarming rate, weakening the cliffs along some of the most beautiful and uncluttered coastline in San Luis Obispo County. The work was also literally uncovering what was once a closely guarded secret: on this small piece of private property sits a space known by the Chumash Indians of San Luis Obispo as *Sextápu*—special for many reasons but primarily because of the presence of ancestral remains.
>
> Over the years, Chumash people had been coming to this place in relative secrecy. Owned by a private landowner but in a "flashpoint" (the no-build zone surrounding the nearby oil storage facility), it is completely void of the trappings of the modern California coast. The no-build zone means no condos, no houses, no structures of any kind could be built here, but also that neither the state nor the county would take over the maintenance or policing of the stretch of beach that lay below the bluff. After years of wrangling, the owner stopped trying to prevent people from descending the trail to the shore, and it became a popular "clothing-optional" beach where dogs were free of leash laws, campfires could be built, and alcohol consumed. There had been an uneasy détente

established between various factions that assumed ersatz ownership of the area, with a loosely organized group of sunbathers and vagabonds forming in order to maintain a modicum of propriety.

However, with the spill and subsequent cleanup damage to the area, the one group for whom this détente had to be reevaluated was the Chumash community. Rapid topsoil loss had exposed the area's true nature, and an unfortunate piece in the local newspaper brought pothunters (individuals who illegally dig for artifacts) and an increased, albeit unwanted, curiosity from regular beachgoers. The subsequent battle between the Chumash and virtually everyone else who had any vested interest in the area brought to light a very uncomfortable fact, namely, that even this decidedly left-leaning, Sirrah-and-Volvo mecca was united in its opinion that the area should not be closed off to foot traffic, regardless of Native concerns. In fact, once the large equipment was gone, the bluff became even more conducive to automobiles, beyond the occasional four-wheel drive trucks that dared to venture off the main road leading to the area, and regulars created a de facto parking area through regular use on the most damaged portion of the site.

It was during my involvement in some of the various attempts at settling the issue that I received a crash course in the application of the legislative quagmire known as the Native American Graves Protection and Repatriation Act (NAGPRA). It was also at this time that I heard Chumash elder Pilulaw Khus utter the phrase "the whole damn state is a site!" in response to a contract archaeologist who was given the task of determining the level of Unocal's responsibility for site cleanup. This archaeologist (ill-advisedly, as anyone who knows Pilulaw would attest) took a condescending stance with regard to the boundaries of the "sacred" area, attempting to mitigate his employer's responsibility by claiming that the area damaged by the actual spill was not "site," a sort of academic border-designator between the sacred and the profane. It was, therefore, the portion of the property that contained the human remains that was of archaeological significance, and the sacrality of the area was for the law to decide.

After much wrangling, some of it quite confrontational, San Luis Obispo County requested that Unocal repair the damage to the site. The company agreed (the worst for Unocal was yet to come, as the state ordered it to essentially move the nearby town of Avila Beach, clean up yet another oil spill, then replace the town, which it did to the tune of several million dollars), and the area was covered in fill dirt, boulders placed in order to block vehicle traffic onto the most sensitive portions, and native vegetation planted. The path down to the beach was moved so that it skirted the site, and the circles formed at regular intervals for memorial rituals at Sextápu have several new faces, both Indian and non.

Part Two—A Chumash elder, María Torres[1] passed away on February 13, 2001. Grandma María had become increasingly interested in her Chumash heritage late in life, as many of her generation were underexposed to it as young people due to the stigma attached to being Indian in the nineteenth and early twentieth centuries. As she grew older, she gladly participated in the revival of the Chumash maritime culture via the community's unique plank canoe and its associated traditions. The canoe, called a *tomol,* had become the catalyst for the increased cultural awareness of her children's and grandchildren's generations, and whenever the paddlers went to sea or there were repairs to be made and ceremonies to be observed, Grandma María was there to give the blessings. Upon her passing, a distinct split in family comfort level with regard to Native burial and funerary practices arose. The key factions were the devout Roman Catholics, for whom their Chumash ancestry was virtually irrelevant, and those more sharply invested in their Chumash heritage to the level of an absolute rejection of Catholicism. The Roman Catholic mission system, after all, had brought misery to the Native population in the area and perpetrated the near demise of the entire culture.

The night before the funeral, the Rosary was said at the funeral home. At this ceremony, traditionally a small, intimate mourning ritual that includes a recitation of the Holy Rosary, there was a brief, unnerving, but also extremely interesting incident. Some family members who identified closely with their Chumash heritage attempted to bring Native elements into the ritual in the form of white sage, both burnt as incense and placed in bundles in the casket. These relatives also attempted to sing traditional songs, make offerings of tobacco, and place handmade objets d'art in the casket prior to burial. Other, more devoutly Catholic family relatives openly objected, and the tension almost developed into open physical confrontation. However, a compromise was reached. The Native elements of Grandma María's mourning ritual were done in private, away from the Rosary Mass, and herbal medicines and burial items were allowed to be placed in the casket.

The following day, at the actual funeral, the rift was out in the open again. The funeral was held at the local mission church, clearly one of the acknowledged battlegrounds with regard to Chumash religious culture, and again, an uneasy compromise was struck. While many attendees very pointedly remained outside the church in the parking lot, the funeral Mass was said inside, with members of the *tomol* crew accompanying the casket both into and out of the church, bearing tomol paddles aloft. Those who were unaware of the discomfort surrounding the whole process were delighted by the way in which both the Native and Catholic spiritual practices were acknowledged. However, beneath the surface lay the real tensions that often pit family members against each other and maintain a level of discord within the Chumash communities—a discord used to justify the lack of a Chumash voice in regional politics.

An interesting contradiction lives between the lines of these stories, and not one that can easily be divided into the cultural differences between Natives and non-Natives. What I see, rather, is the inherent difference between the "modern" and the "traditional." Though this dichotomy is often (and I think mistakenly) seen as merely "ancient versus contemporary," I would argue that it is inherently possible to be both traditional *and* contemporary. However, modernity is, among a great many other things, suspicious of tradition in that traditional culture focuses primarily on values that have been handed down from generation to generation, while modernity tends to privilege the new, the innovative, and the topical. What I will attempt here is an analysis of the very different meanings that death and burial practices have in contemporary Native communities that attempt to live a traditional culture and in their "modern" counterparts by placing the traditional approaches toward death and burial in a modern political context. This context can be seen in the various issues surrounding California's Chumash Indians. These communities, for there are several distinct regional identities under the common name *Chumash,* have been engaged in an ongoing struggle for cultural integrity since the first arrival of Europeans in the sixteenth century.

For the Chumash, the issues surrounding death and burial operate at deep existential levels. This is true for Native American communities all over this continent and indeed for indigenous peoples everywhere. While it would be wrong to assume that there is a "Native American Religion" (singular) that can be compared to "Christianity" or "Buddhism," it is in the realm of the "modern versus traditional" comparison that broad relative categories can be utilized to make comparative arguments. For our purposes, then, the rituals surrounding death and burial in an inherently traditional community, the Chumash, will provide the backdrop for a discussion of the meanings traditional communities associate with death, the ritual practices that emerge from those meanings, and their implications within the history of Chumash interactions with Western modernity. It is in ritual practices that contemporary Native communities can establish their "nonmodern" credibility, and in religious practice that traditional cultures continue their connection to place ("place" here refers to the larger concept of embeddedness).

RITUAL AS PRACTICE

In a recent article, Michael McNally challenges scholars to shift toward a practice-centered approach to American Indian religious traditions rather than focusing on the "beliefs" that usually take most of our attention. More than merely "theory-speak for its own sake," he suggests that this different perspective will clarify the role that practice plays as Native communities navigate their way through modernity. He also implies that the academic treatment of Native spirituality has thus far been centered on a search for ethnographic authenticity, sifting through the contemporary activities of Indian communities that have been sullied by modern ideas in search of the "purer" elements associated with precontact cultures. McNally finds that an attempt to "recalibrate our analysis in terms of practice rather than belief" would open up the dialogue to include the growth and dynamism inherent in these communities and bring us closer to an understanding of the role that modern ideas and Western cultural influences have played in the continuity of Native American culture.[2] McNally's work focuses, in part, on the role that Christian hymn singing has played in the maintenance of Ojibwe cultural integrity. He finds that, once the hymns had been translated into the Ojibwe language and learned by the community, the singing of them maintained some of the protocols that accompany Ojibwe singing—an important aspect of traditional Ojibwe culture. Thus, when the community sang these hymns, they were, in fact, maintaining traditional Ojibwe cultural patterns regardless of the content of the hymns themselves. To this cogent argument I would add that the refocus on issues of practices, such as song protocol, can also shed light upon Native religious practices generally, and it can clear the way for an appreciation of contemporary traditions and ongoing ritual construction within the context of modern Native America.

This sentiment echoes my own work with my cousins in the Chumash communities of central California, for whom missionization and colonization continue to affect the ways in which they negotiate the contemporary religious environment. That environment has been polluted by the stark, absolutist categories set out by early anthropologists of the region and reified by cultural evolutionism, which persists in the kind of old-school, structuralist anthropology that dominates Chumash scholarship at present. It is my view that this outdated position presents real pitfalls to those struggling to establish and maintain their identity as Chumash people.

This situation revolves around two main points. First, that the undue focus on beliefs that McNally addresses also exposes an unnaturally sharp and erroneous distinction between issues of practice and belief, actions and concepts, ritual and myth. These distinctions serve the interests of the dominant culture by allowing it, through the use of specialized, rigid categories, to establish and maintain control over the discourse, rendering an inequitable distribution of what Pierre Bourdieu, among others, has called "symbolic capital."[3] As can be seen in Part One of the above story, this control can have real consequences for those who reckon their identity and ancestral connection differently from the prevailing "expert" opinion. The focus upon religion as a system of "belief" and culture as a system of "meaning,"[4] and the interrelated assertion that Indian communities have either died out or become watered down by adopting Western aspects of both culture and religion, set up Western scholars as the experts whose theory of knowledge possesses the capacity, via symbolic power, to impose the principles of the construction of reality—in particular, social reality—a major dimension of political power. This control over the ways in which Native people are understood in terms of their spirituality, religiosity, and contemporary sacred practices serves to reify, and promulgate, the myth of the "vanishing Indian," a myth that is only recently being unraveled by contemporary scholars of Native American religion, the delay due, in part, to its ongoing use as a tool for the genocidal practices of colonialism. This situation as it manifests itself in Indian Country has been discussed by such thinkers as Vine DeLoria, Ward Churchill, and Wendy Rose.[5] In this chapter I will provide a case in point with the Chumash communities and their attempt to establish control over the parameters of the discourse surrounding their dead, which is vital to their drive toward cultural revitalization.

The Spanish Mission System

Spain's excursion into what is now California was a foray into what would be the absolute outskirts of an already overextended empire. An abject inability to deal with much resistance among Indians of the interior part of the state gave Spain the impetus to allow the Roman Catholic Church to establish missions as a means of "converting" various Native communities with the hope of turning these missions into pueblos, or towns, with which the Spanish crown could then establish control over the territory. Hence, the colonization process for Alta California differed greatly from Spain's earlier, and much more violent, colonization of Mexico and Central and South America. This new method, however, was no less insidious and devastating to the Native populations of the region.

The missions of Alta California were organized and overseen in the latter part of the eighteenth century by a Franciscan with Inquisition experience and a severe personality, Padre Junipero Serra. A man who had designs on martyrdom among the "savages" since childhood, this astute and driven administrator planned and directed the establishment of twenty-one missions in California, reaching along the coast or at a short distance inland from San Diego in the south to Sonoma, beyond San Francisco Bay, in the north.[6]

In spite of somewhat romantic visions of kindly padres ushering docile Indians into the modern world, California missions were essentially religious plantations designed to benefit Spain and its ruling elite. The imposition of nonnative crops and animals made it difficult for those Indians (and there were many) who initially resisted the loss of their economic autonomy to maintain traditional plant and animal management schemes. Soldiers that accompanied the padres intimidated the populations, who were used to dealing with their neighbors in more sophisticated ways, such as financial contracts and intermarriage, and the diseases brought by the Europeans made the maintenance of communal systems difficult, to say the least.

Epidemics can be considered the most effective tool of the colonizers in California. Diseases such as smallpox, measles, diphtheria, and syphilis brought Indian communities to a standstill as enormous drops in population, and the intense suffering that these diseases caused in their victims, meant that aid to the sick and obligations to the dead became the main preoccupation. For most mission-area Native communities, the situation demanded that they view the padres as allies. Certainly, the rise of these unknown maladies coincided with the Spaniards' arrival; therefore, they must know how to treat them properly. Baptism of dying infants and their parents became the first major break for the padres' conversion plans. In fact, the mission lifestyle, such as the practice of forcibly separating Indian children from their parents and placing them in disease-ridden quarters, most likely increased the spread of the diseases as well as the suffering experienced by the victims. Pioneering demographer Sherburne F. Cook conducted exhaustive studies and concluded that perhaps as much as 60 percent of the population decline of mission Indians was due to introduced diseases.[7]

In addition to desperate parents of dying children, many others eventually sought out mission living as a way of mediating the loss of personnel and traditional economic activity that the missions themselves had caused. The plan was to convert the Indians over a ten-year period, after which they would be given the mission lands, crops, and livestock to work on their own, thus creating pueblos ready for participation in Spain's already impressive trade scheme with the Far East via the Philippines. The padres, however, never realized this ultimate goal. Instead, they greedily kept control over the stolen lands and the economic wealth that they represented. The argument frequently used by the padres was that the Indians were like simple children who would be unable to survive without the help of the missions. In reality, as settlers moved into the area from Mexico, the missions were a key provider of manual labor for the new ranchos, even to the point of creating a completely idle landed upper class, to whom the padres were beholden. It is no wonder that the padres were reticent to give up this source of free labor, and the mission wealth, in both hard currency and valuable land and resources, reached a peak at around the time the peasant class became fed up with the same arrangement to the south. Mexicans revolted and won independence from Spain in 1821, and the missions were pressured by the new authority to "secularize"—turn over all lands but for the missions themselves to private ownership—and release all Indians who wished to leave the control of the mission padres.

In considering the religious effects of the mission system, it must first be noted that California, in precontact times, supported a vast number of relatively independent, village-oriented tribal groups. Unlike what missionaries encountered elsewhere on the continent, there were very few large-scale political systems overseen by councils or single leaders. Instead, some two dozen language stocks were divided into separate linguistic and cultural groups that were intensely regional in nature, and the first issue to be overcome by the padres was understanding these divisions. Dialects would change frequently as the missionary process moved through the state, and cultural differences from region to region were marked. Of course, since the goal for the colonists was to erase all non-Spanish Catholic practices, the variety of sacred practices was of little consequence. However, broad regional similarities, managed and maintained as part of an overall interregional trade relationship, meant that, from the Native perspective, the sacred activities of the padres did not look so foreign as to make inclusion impossible. For missionaries on the eastern U.S. coast, by way of contrast, the systems were so significantly and diametrically opposed as to make the conversion process a considerable struggle. In California, regional sharing of ceremonial practices was common, and all villages had individuals well-versed in the languages and practices of their neighbors, all the better to facilitate cooperative resource management and intermarriage. Thus, when the Roman Catholic ceremonies were shown to the Indians, they most likely recognized enough of the postures, actions, and seasonal markings to make the transition easier. In addition, the goals of the empire were paramount, so the padres were loath to deny participation by willing congregants because of such trivial issues as complete lack of adherence to the Roman Catholic worldview. Baptize and "civilize" first, indoctrinate later.

California religious philosophies tend to be extremely different from Western, Judeo-Christian sacred narratives, tending toward codified behavioral protocols designed to facilitate proper responses to the world as it exists in the present, rather than in a distant afterlife. Many California tribal traditions employ a host of other-than-human participants, from plant, animal, and environmental spirits to heroes, deities, and sacred beings of human origin. It can be said, then, that Roman Catholic doctrine, with its saints, angels, and martyrs, made for relatively easy translation, such that many contemporary California mission Indians inherited the stories of the "before time," Coyote and his adventures, and ceremonial practices and seasonal observances from their ancestors despite the seemingly total disruption by the colonial process of missionization.

Even today, many Native Californians see no sharp distinction between their Native traditional ways and their Catholic upbringing. While many modern California Indian people do reject the church due to its bloody and oppressive history, it is nevertheless true that you are as likely to find the elders of these former mission Indian communities at Mass on Sunday as not. For the younger generation, applying the worldview handed down to them from time immemorial to information gathered from a variety of contemporary sources is fueling a resurgence in traditional practices within which the original victims of the mission system would most likely feel right at home.

Raising the Living

For many contemporary Westerners, the key function of burial rituals is to foster "closure" among the living and therefore mitigate the difficulties of the loss of loved ones. However, in traditional cultures, burial also marks the transfer of the deceased from one status to another, marking a whole new set of responsibilities to that person. For the contemporary West, this relationship is not at all unknown, with regular visitations to gravesides and mausoleums a well-established practice, as is the regular invocation of the deceased as remaining active in one's life. However, it would seem that this practice, limited as it is in contemporary culture, is widely acknowledged as unidirectional. In other words, the living are doing it for their own therapeutic benefit, to help them through difficult times by calling upon their dead relatives for support. In traditional cultures, however, the responsibilities to the dead are undertaken to promote the happiness and health of the deceased, as well. Whether it be Hindu household shrines or Ndembu ancestral meals, the dead rely to some degree upon the living for their sustenance. To neglect these duties is a severe breach of one's responsibilities as a good person. When American Indian burial places are disturbed, therefore, the ancestral spirits of the dead relatives are likewise disturbed. Much of the sadness felt by the Chumash, who have experienced loss of control over land and resources and massive cultural disruption at the hands of the Spanish, Mexican, and finally American interlopers has this fact at its core. The ancestors are invoked at all ceremonies and gatherings, and a return to the important responsibilities to the dead is paramount for many who seek a deep renewal of their cultural connections.

When Grandma María died, or "crossed over" as the Chumash say, several very important practices that the Chumash community is bringing back into regular use were not undertaken. Chumash passings are now often accompanied by the ritual preparation of the body. Two main funeral homes on the central coast have become aware that this ritual may be called for and make every effort to facilitate it. The ritual primarily involves washing the body with water gathered from the land; it is accompanied by singing and the use of herbal medicines, both applied as ointments for the body and burned as incense, and finishes with the placement of a pair of California poppies on the eyes of the deceased. The emerging regularity of this set of rituals that is bound up in the burial practice provides an important opportunity for contemporary Chumash people: the communal participation in a Chumash tradition. Certain families in the area that have participated in this ritual are consulted and involved, the family of the deceased provides a meal for the participants, and additional families are asked to contribute in various ways, for example, by providing the physical elements of the washing ceremony—local freshwater springs are visited for the water, herbal medicines gathered—all with their own accompanying rituals and protocols.

The participation in the many practices surrounding death rites frames opportunities for identity maintenance, which I see as a combination of reckoning, development, and assertion. Reckoning refers to a sort of assessment, a calculation of where people are situated vis-à-vis their sense of "Indianness." Development can be seen as the ongoing growth process, usually oriented around language acquisition, community involvement, and ritual participation. Assertion, with which I will be most concerned from here on, is the overt display to the outside world of what people have come up with via the other two. To refer back to my story from the beginning, while much of what was accomplished with regard to the disposition of Sextápu as a sacred place was motivated by deeply held feelings about the places where ancestors are buried, I believe that those involved due to their Chumash heritage were also engaged in the important task of being seen *as Chumash.* For too many Americans, and especially Californians, American Indians are like the Bengal tiger: there are more in captivity than there are in the wild. Many contemporary American Indian political activists merely transgress this assumption, placing themselves incongruently in strategic issues. Similarly, for the members of Grandma María's family and the Chumash community, it was an important gesture of the continuing presence of the Chumash in California to participate ritually in her burial preparations. As it was, the priest who officiated at her funeral Mass remarked about the tomol crew and Grandma María's Native heritage in his homily. And for the first time in recent memory, her obituary did not include the phrase "death of the last Chumash Indian." For people who are raising their children to know themselves as Chumash, this is an important step in helping them reckon their identities.

For indigenous people, the tendency is toward fluidity with regard to personal identity, but a unity with regard to place. In other words, it is often difficult for the Native people with whom I work to see themselves as a complete individual apart from others. Who they are as individuals is inherently situational. However, they see world, and indeed the universe, most often as a coherent tapestry that is impossible to parcel. Maintenance of a collective identity (most Indian nations' names for themselves simply mean "people" in their languages) is therefore dependent upon maintaining a connection to the constant universe. For Euroamericans, on the other hand, there seems to be a trend in the opposite direction. They begin from a place of absolute ego; the establishment and maintenance of individual identity is paramount, and though they obviously change as people over time, they are always that same individuals moving through various aspects of time and space. But they see the world as particulate in nature, a machine made up of separate components that can be pulled out of context and understood on their own terms, in a constant and inexorable state of flux.

The indigenous sense of identity and space, then, carries a fixed connection to places on the landscape. This fact has many implications, but the most important for this discussion regards the interring of the dead. The kind of approach to one's responsibilities regarding the ancestors described above assumes free access to those places, as well as their remaining undisturbed. These practices, then, are key to the process of identity development. While one may reckon oneself to be in the Chumash ancestral chain, what that might entail in terms of community participation and ceremonial obligations is a group learning process.

Within the area of American Indian religious traditions, the key data sets with regard to revitalization movements continue to be the Handsome Lake Tradition, the Ghost Dance, and the Peyote Religion, the foundations of the Native American Church. What these all have in common is the assertion by the practitioners that their participation in these rituals would bring about a radical change in the situation in which the Indians found themselves. In the case of the Ghost Dance, they claimed that these changes would affect the whole continent, while in the Handsome Lake movement, the entire world would be transformed in an apocalypse in the true sense of that term. The narrow scholarly focus on these radical shift systems has colored the way in which analysts have approached the issue of revitalization among contemporary American Indian communities, rendering a skewed version of the on-the-ground attempts made by many involved in this process today. Many analysts look to the attempts at revivalism among Native Americans as a vast transformation of current circumstances, and indeed, that is the case in some examples.[8] However, in the majority of American Indian communities since the turn of the last century, I would argue, what is viewed as a revival movement is the manifestation of a process that I call "reprise," which will be discussed in more detail below. This sense of the revitalization process assumes that the core elements of the worldview never went anywhere. Like a seasonal waterway, Native traditions continue, though often below the surface. The motives that once gave rise to rituals that went unpracticed after contact were maintained in communal relationships and approaches to the universe, and the process of identity reckoning involves merely taking the proper clothes out of storage and donning them once again.

This process of reprise is behind some of the demographic puzzles provided by recent census figures addressed by Joane Nagel.[9] Nagel examines the interesting conundrum arising out of the 1990 national census, in which people claiming American Indian ancestry jumped from half a million (in 1960) to 2 million people. Interestingly, a full five times more respondents reported American Indian as their "ancestry" than identified it as their "race," even though American Indian was not listed as a possible ancestry. Of those who did claim American Indian as their "race," 22.4 percent did not provide a tribal affiliation. The respondents who proclaimed their "race" to be American Indian are neither the entirety of those who believe themselves to be at least part Indian genetically nor those who legally qualify for federal entitlement programs due to blood quantum and/or tribal enrollment status, which, according to available figures, was approximately 800,000 people in 1980.[10]

Noting these ambiguities, Nagel then casts about among sociological and political science categories for a theoretical explanation for the increase in the number of Americans choosing American Indian as at least part of their self-identity. Combining the aforementioned analysis of census figures with archival research into newsworthy mention of American Indians between 1960 and 1980, along with correspondence and telephone interviews (including one with an incarcerated Leonard Peltier), she makes a fairly persuasive case for "ethnic mobilization"—ethnic groups organizing to litigate, lobby, and protest—as a suitable explanation for this phenomenon. Nagel also points to political and economic transformations that grew out of the civil rights movement, such as Lyndon Johnson's war on poverty, Richard Nixon's push for Indian self-determination, and the Reagan-era explosion of reservation casinos, as examples of Red Power joining similar black and Chicano-American movements of the post–Martin Luther King era.

Nagel notes the decade between 1969 (the year of the Alcatraz Island occupation) and 1980 (the massive defunding of social services during the Reagan years) as a time when there was a 72 percent increase in the number of Americans who identified themselves as American Indian. She asserts that it was "the federal government [that] promoted an Indian ethnic revival . . . by funding Indian organizations and by providing increased incentives for Indian ethnic identification and activism," from $345 million in 1960 to $1,979 billion in 1980.[11] She argues that the termination policies of the 1950s, which forced many American Indians into an urban working class away from reservation communities, were the impetus for the pan-Indian "powwow" culture that the dispossessed young people of American Indian descent produced after the cultural renaissance of the 1960s. The Alcatraz "Indians of All Tribes" takeover, therefore, was emblematic in that its leaders were essentially all enrolled in the first Native American Studies course at San Francisco State University, learning to become educated, enculturated activists in the mold of Gandhi, Martin Luther King Jr., and the Nigerian leader Nnamde Azikewe.[12] These leaders, then, were the ironic product of government assimilationist policies, rendering an Indian Country diaspora that was nonetheless marginalized vis-à-vis the dominant culture due to the unique nature of American Indian history. However cogent Nagel's findings are, she nearly falls into the same trap as the scientific rationale does by assuming a complete break in the continuity of American Indian culture after the turn of the twentieth century.

What I propose is a view that sees the true elements of culture as traveling below the surface of overt behaviors and practices and that points to a lifeway capable of adapting itself to new and changing circumstances. Like the Salinas River where my grandmothers drew water, the dry season of the dominant culture did not cause evaporation, but rather drove the flow underground. The musical term *reprise,* therefore, is a much more fitting term than *revival* in that it alludes to the rearticulation of an earlier theme whose basic elements remained present throughout the piece. Nagel's take, important and informative as it is, depends on the assumption that repression of specific practices associated with American Indian "religiosity" and the eclipse of "traditional beliefs" by those of the dominant culture (Christianity, market capitalism, primogeniture, etc.) was total. This understanding is evident in the anthropological and historiographic use of the specific theological term *conversion* when referring to both religious and social adaptations by Indian communities over time, and especially within the discourse surrounding Chumash culture and history, as it is set within the Spanish mission system, for which the conversion of the natives was ostensibly the primary goal. However, as evidenced by the continuing presence of ritual practice among perhaps the most aggressively missionized people on the continent, this "conversion" was as much a conversion of

Christianity into an Indian framework as vice versa. Rituals such as burial and memorial ceremonies, then, provide opportunities for communal reprise via the development and assertion of identity.

In the process of learning the behaviors and skills required for proper ritual practice, the Chumash have also begun to fashion a rhetorical system within which protocol and the actual requirements for acceptable community member behavior are transmitted to others, especially the young people. This body of information ranges from practical concerns, such as who does what and when, to ontological statements of emotive quality that go to the very nature of the Chumash worldview. This worldview itself is somewhat cobbled together from recollections of elders and ethnographic information gathered around the turn of the last century. Often, the ideas therein are at odds with what ethnographers assert is "authentic" Chumash religion. However, given the dynamic nature of culture, the role that religious action plays in mediating historic change provides the Chumash with opportunities to assert their contemporary identity. The presence of these ritual activities is all the contemporary Chumash require to authenticate that identity, and they place themselves in situations that require ceremonies and rituals in order to participate in their own religious and historic development. Therefore, in the reprise of Chumash culture, ritual, such as the death practices we are looking at here, provides an opportunity to express what it is that constitutes the Chumash ethos, as well as assert the continuing presence of Chumash culture via the specific employment and manipulation of symbolic elements relevant to ritual action.

In the analysis of this process of symbolic definition and employment in the case of death practices, it will first be necessary to shed light on the way in which I understand the operational qualities of symbols. For this I borrow heavily from the work of Sherry B. Ortner, who has articulated what I believe to be a clear and utilitarian category of symbol, namely the "key symbol."[13] Ortner orders this category of symbol into a continuum with two ends labeled "summarizing" and "elaborating." Summarizing symbols, as the name implies, are those that sum up, expressing and representing to the participants what the system means to them.[14] I would identify this category as the broad sense of sacred symbol—objects of reverential emotion (e.g., the cross, an eagle feather, the flag). Ortner sees elaborating symbols as working in the opposite direction, rendering complex and undifferentiated feelings, ideas, and emotions comprehensible and giving participants the ability to communicate these to others. In addition, elaborating symbols are seen as acting in either the conceptual or action spheres.[15] This symbolic representation provides categories for action and, I would add, the important category of protocol. It is within the responsibility to one's ancestors that the issue of protocol, the assertion of identity, and practice merge.

The ritual reprise in which the Chumash communities are engaged serves as a clear example of what J.Z. Smith has termed the "'gnostic' (knowing) dimension to ritual"[16] in that the Chumash are aware of the incongruity between traditional burial practices and memorial ceremonies and those of the dominant culture, and therein lies the point. In addition, an important element of this ritual reconstruction is the conscious creation of protocol—protocol that speaks to what the Chumash see as a traditional (read "non-Western") and ethical way to live—with these practices providing a vehicle in which important lifeways can be transported to the next generation.

This process is not without controversy in that there are politically and economically situated elements, land developers, county supervisors, anthropologists, and so forth, who criticize the Chumash on the grounds that their endeavors lack "authenticity" and who openly question the seeming incongruity between the "contemporary and constructed" and the "traditional and authentic." In the dissemination of this viewpoint by anthropologists and others I see the reification of the "vanishing Indian" tale occurring. Somewhat ironically, this is also where a practice-centered approach could be employed in order to clarify these seemingly diametric positions. Both McNally and I draw upon the work of Pierre Bourdieu in his unpacking of the approach to practice.

Bourdieu responds to what he calls the "gnoseological problems" that Émile Durkheim raises with regard to traditional society, as revealing the political nature of the interaction between traditional cultures and contemporary social structures.[17] Specifically, Bourdieu states that "forms of classification are forms of domination" and that a sociology of knowledge rests upon "symbolic domination."[18] In other words, when Durkheim comments on traditional cultures using categories derived from modern discourse, it reveals such questions as "How do we know what we know?" Furthermore, to assume that the modern categories are the correct ones to use places traditional ways of knowing (and therefore ways of being) in a position of inferiority. American sociology of the 1950s and 1960s, Bourdieu claims, took on the character of an orthodoxy, a *communis doctorum opinio* that is inappropriate for the sciences and served the demands of those in power by insisting that any discourse on the social world should be "kept at arm's length and neutralized."[19] On a perusal of sociological reviews of the period, Bourdieu found "empty academic rambling about the social world, with very little empirical material . . . [using] . . . concepts that are only understandable if you have some idea of the concrete referent in the mind of the people using these concepts."[20]

It is my view that American anthropology turned to Native American culture with what has been called "salvage ethnography," a sense that the beliefs and behaviors of Native cultures needed to be ascertained and categorized before their inevitable disappearance. This motive rose from the same social and cultural milieu that informed the sociology of the time, one that places the industrial West, in particular American-style free market industry, at the apex of human culture. The scientific exploration, classification, and archival of the nonindustrial, "primitive" cultures, therefore, needed to be done before their inevitable demise "like the snow before the noontide sun," to quote one early archaeologist of Chumash sites.[21] Thus, the social sciences of the 1950s and 1960s were being informed by the same cultural stimulus described by Bourdieu. Scholars relied upon a set of reified categories for social behavior above which the analyst can hover and observe, aware of them in ways that escape the simple minds of the Natives. In addition, scholars have argued that the "primitive mind" can be seen as a window into our own human past, thus erecting some difficult barriers to the free expression of contemporary American Indian religiosity via the biases inherent in this ethnocentric position. The notion that we can draw a linear progression beginning with our earliest human origins and ending with the scientific method employs a hierarchy wherein Native traditions are below *real* "religions" of the Judeo-Christian variety, which are themselves less intellectually developed than Western science.

One example of these continuing biases is the ongoing, uncritical use of terms such as *conversion* when discussing the missionization of American Indian tribes and communities. This term is so misused as to be virtually worthless when attributed to the California mission Indian experience. The implication is that the Spanish completely transformed all the "neophytes" in their control into Christians in the fullest sense of that (also problematic) term. Nonetheless, it is the continuing position of the anthropologists widely considered to be the experts in Chumash culture that, by the 1820s, all Chumash had been converted.[22] The very serious political and economic implications of this position are clear: people claiming Chumash identity will have the authenticity of their "beliefs" questioned due to charges of cultural construction and will have difficulty pressing their claims to any part of the territory once attributed to the Chumash, rising from the perceived break in the continuity of religious tradition due to their "complete" missionization. Continuity, of course, remains a large factor in any official—county, state, or federal—action with regard to Indian land-use claims.

Dem Bones

With the possible exception of fishing rights, there exists no more contentious issue between institutionalized state and corporate forces and American Indians than the protection and repatriation of burial items and ancestral remains. While the foundations of strongly held Native positions on the fishing debates are beyond our scope here, more germane are the issues surrounding the protection of the final resting places of Native people and the opposition to such protective measures. Certainly, in California, motives in the form of lucrative condo, strip mall, and highway construction contracts factor heavily into this opposition. Nonetheless, one would expect some degree of understanding on the part of the developers as to why Indian people would like their ancestors' graves left undisturbed. But often quite the opposite is true. As I myself have encountered, some developers hold these places, and these remains, in no more esteem than the dirt in which they reside, and I have heard horror stories of skulls being kicked into backfilled trenches in order to keep from disrupting the project.

Prior to the recognition of the legal rights that Native communities possess in caring for the places of interment, there were few obstacles to archaeological appropriation of American Indian burial-related items, including the remains of the dead. However, vigorous activism on the part of Natives and their allies resulted in legislation at both the state and federal levels, culminating in the passage of the Native American Graves Protection and Repatriation Act (NAGPRA) in 1990. NAGPRA addresses three broad areas: terminology, museum collections, and archaeological excavations. The law overtly protects the disposition of human remains, sacred objects, including those associated with burial rituals, and materials of cultural significance, both in situ as well as in museum collections. NAGPRA established a process designed to assist federal agencies and museums in determining the appropriate Native American community responsible for decisions regarding the disposition of ancestral remains and sacred objects and materials that the act places in the category of "impending cultural patrimony." All museums, state, and federal agencies in possession or control of these remains and objects were required to make a complete inventory of these items and, where possible, to identify their cultural affiliation with the goal of their repatriation into the possession of those relatives for reburial. Inventories were to be completed by November 1995, and their completion required these institutions to involve and consult with tribal governments and traditional religious leaders. Museums and federal agencies were, from the implementation of the act, to provide the appropriate documentation of these materials and to participate in their repatriation upon request from a tribal entity. NAGPRA also established a seven-member review committee and provides grants for both tribes and museums in order to implement the act.[23]

The significance of this convoluted system of regulations and mandates becomes clearest in the fine print. NAGPRA clearly supports Natives' claims to their deceased relatives and the objects associated with those burials, but only when a definite lineal connection can be verified by Western academics in the persons of archaeologists and cultural anthropologists. In other words, it is the Indians who must convince the scientists that their claims are valid—that their sacred places are indeed *actually* sacred to them and not merely a means to the end of their own individual validation.

According to ethnographic details quoted by many scholars of California's mission period, the padres of the later mission era made careful note of the traditions surrounding Chumash mourning and burial rituals. Every village encountered in Chumash territory by Spanish mission fathers had a specific designated cemetery with grave markers and signs of ongoing grave visitation. Chumash cemeteries were usually close to, or at times within, the village boundaries proper, and there is archaeological evidence that some dwellings contained burials beneath their floors.[24] Johnny Flynn proposes that the relationship of the Chumash to the bones of their ancestors was similar to the relationship between the world of the living and the other worlds perhaps mirroring it but also perhaps facilitating passage between them.[25] For the Chumash, the universe is organized around three distinct realms: this world we live in, called *Itiashup;* the world above, called *Alapayashup;* and another realm, sometimes said to be below this one, sometimes said to be parallel, called *Coyinashup.* The boundaries between the realms are permeable, and the denizens of the realms can move between them. However, there are proper protocols for the movement from this world to the next, while the inhabitants of Coyinashup, generally considered malevolent, can pass between their world and ours at will (although usually they do so at night). What is most pertinent is the passing of the dead on to what seems to be a division of Alapayashup called *Shimilaqsha,* a land which the Chumash consultants told the early ethnographer J.P. Harrington was a fiesta (the Chumash of that period spoke mostly Spanish), an eternal party where all needs were provided for and everybody was happy, dancing and singing.[26] For all intents and purposes, then, the evidence available with regard to Chumash approaches to death indicates not morbid fear, but acceptance of the inevitable and necessary movement on to the next realm.

Before Spanish intervention, a special society of women served as the undertakers, with ceremonies of initiation accompanying entrance into this group. The undertakers washed and anointed the body and placed poppies over the eyes. The placement of the poppies derives from the tale of the journey of the deceased to Shimilaqsha, which began with Raven removing the eyes of the dead and replacing them with poppies. A male relative was then designated to carry the deceased to the cemetery. At the graveside, the carrier stood with legs akimbo and all the mourners crept between his legs to the graveside on all fours. The burial pit was large enough for the deceased to be interred in a sitting posture, though some archaeological evidence contradicts this posture in certain areas. The pit was lined with stone slabs or wood planks, and ethnographic data suggest that tomol planks were used for some burials, even in inland areas. Items of practical use, such as hunting tools, bowls, mortars and pestles, and shell bead money, were placed in the pit with the body. This practice seems to resonate with the belief that the dead have all they need in Shimilaqsha. Rituals varied, but involved the priests, whom the Chumash call *'antap,* and attendees singing songs of mourning and lament, and the 'antap blowing smoke from a pipe into the grave and then toward all directions. The family of the deceased then paid all who helped in the burial with shell bead money, and a feast was held in their honor. Every two or three years, a larger, more general mourning ceremony was held, consisting of processions, dances, songs, and a large central fire into which all who had lost relatives in the previous period threw images representing their dead relatives. In some regions, these images took the form of a human body and were stuffed with silk, glass beads, and even food during the mission period.[27]

For the San Luis Obispo Chumash today, Sextápu is one of the places where there is certainty that mourning rituals were, and still are, appropriate. Although piecing together proper ritual elements from the memories of elders, ethnographic texts, and au courant senses of nature and the cosmos has provided a decidedly loose and emergent set of protocols within which memorial ceremonies are held there, the act of *doing* ceremony at all, and doing it *there* rather than elsewhere, are incredibly important in the ongoing Chumash communal development. The details may vary from what one of the aforementioned "experts" might find as an authentic representation of Chumash religious beliefs. I remember singing "Will the Circle Be Unbroken?" at a memorial ceremony held at Sextápu one starry solstice night. The real measure of authenticity is the role that these practices play in the maintenance of Chumash communal boundaries. Herbal medicines accompanied Grandma María on her journey because a key element of the memorial ritual is the placement of herbal medicines such as sage, sweetgrass, and tobacco, along with culturally relevant materials such as acorns, shell bead money, and hand-carved steatite effigies (small "charms" fashioned out of a soft stone to resemble orcas, dolphins, pelicans, and the like), at specific areas corresponding to known remains, as well as to the cardinal directions. At the same time, in both the Sextápu memorials and in the reprise of burial practices, sage is burnt and tobacco smoked in accordance with known Native ritual practices from around the country. Again, exactly how these things were done in antiquity and their exact replication are less relevant than the presence of culturally connected people doing ceremony meaningful to them.

Remembering the ancestors, maintaining proper relationships with the spirits of those who have gone ahead to Shimilaqsha, and recognizing that they are often as present with us now as they were before their death are all ways that contemporary Chumash people can participate in the cycle of life, thus ensuring the continuity of the universe. For the Chumash, then, as for many Native communities, the disposition of the dead, both at the time of burial and in perpetuity, requires careful adherence to the ritual provisions of care and remembrance. The permeability of the boundaries between worlds goes both ways, after all, and to neglect the ancestral remains in this world has a direct impact on their ability to experience fully the happiness of the next. Children must never be allowed to forget those who have gone ahead of them, lest they lose sight of where they themselves are going.

CONCLUSION

After Grandma María's funeral, several family members who felt threatened by the Indian ways seemed to have softened somewhat, and one man came to where the tomol crew members were still gathered with their paddles. He shook their hands, thanked them for being there, and then said, "I remember Grandma talking about Indian stuff when I was a kid, especially the canoes. I always liked boats and the ocean back in the day . . ." As he trailed the comment off, the tomol captain asked if he would come to a gathering sometime and share what he remembered with the children. He responded in the affirmative and he did in fact participate in a subsequent canoe activity.

Some years ago an elder from the Santa Ynez band of Chumash Indians who had driven up to a Sextápu protest grabbed a young, long-haired dissident, took him aside, and told him that it was up to his generation to make people *understand* Native American issues, not just learn about them. That kid was me. I'm still unsure what he meant exactly, but in any case, my sense of responsibility to the cause of knowledge has taken me into very odd places, not least of which has been a tomol in the middle of the Santa Barbara Channel. The activities to which I have been exposed that fall under the realm of "ceremony" have been far too numerous to mention. The thing Chumash ceremonies all seem to have in common is the importance of remembering those who have gone before from the most ancient ones in the before time to those that have died within our own personal memories. No matter how bad a relationship is between two Chumash community members, when there is a death in a family, all bitterness is set aside and they mourn together. In the larger discussion of what is "authentic" tradition that the Chumash often find themselves in, surely there can be few better testaments to the continuity of their traditions.

It has been my position that those elements that fall under the general term "belief" can be seen as the clothes that are hung upon the body of practice. As McNally has shown with the Ojibwe hymn singers, and I with the Chumash tomol, such vehicles as Christian hymns and power tools can provide the form, not for assimilation, but for "negotiating culture change in the realm of historical time," suggesting ways to enact important cultural constructs and providing contemporary Chumash people with strategies for maintaining cultural continuity.[28]

In the contemporary realm, adherence to traditional religious practices is a double-edged sword. On the one side, the beliefs that ostensibly underpin these practices are deemed arcane in the extreme when compared to the deeply held precepts of the modern world. Even a modern religious "ashes to ashes, dust to dust" approach to death fits into the scientifically correct format. On the other side, the established scientific priesthood of archaeologists and ethnographers are free to gauge the levels of acculturation and assimilation to which even the smallest variance between the academic canon and the activities of contemporary Native people seems to point. However, it is the presence of these practices in contemporary contexts, as well as their dynamic nature, that attests to the continuity of communal identity and makes for viable Native presence in the modern world.

But perhaps more important is the act of training McNally's "refocused" lens on our modern systems of death, burial, and mourning. In what ways does *avoiding* the places where our relatives are buried constitute ritual activity? What sort of ceremonial role is played by professional undertakers and funeral directors? According to Arnold Van Gennep,[29] ritual practice is a way to mediate the passage between here and there, this existence and that one, and placing the bodies of our dead loved ones into the hands of strangers, having others inter them in cemeteries seldom visited, and not taking time to ceremonially remember those who have gone before us surely speaks volumes about the devaluation of human relationships in modernity.

In the realm of modern intellectual discourse, there is another ritual obligation: to see that the terms we use to describe traditional cultures and their lifeways (terms like *spiritual, sacred, religious, belief*) are kept honed like surgical instruments, lest they be used as sledgehammers. In the field of popular opinion, which is the manifestation of these competing discourses, political motives may be overtly declared or remain hidden, but the control over the arena in which this game plays out has serious ramifications for those among us who fight every day to hold on to those things that are important to our identities as Indian people. As Nagel has pointed out, there is much to be learned by the self-identification practices of contemporary Native Americans, and viewing this process through the lens of standardized census forms can amount to attempting to measure the master's house using the master's yardstick. For contemporary American Indian communities, the process of authentication comes not in measuring the external hue of the cloth against a pristine, ancient swatch, but rather in noting how the weight and durability of the threads combine in various ways to render a garment capable of support and protection in an ever-changing climate.

It was highly significant that the issues surrounding the endangered sacred place Sextápu were brought both to public and official notice and alerted many people to the fact that there was a Chumash community in the region at all. But the communal reprise experienced by San Luis Obispo Chumash people, both from the defiant act of protest and the ritual acts in the frequent memorial ceremonies that now take place, is the greater sum. Chumash people from all over the state read of the conflict in their local papers and came to join the protests, staying to adhere to ritual obligations and protocols, bringing along the children who will make up the next generation, and for whom regular trips to honor those who have gone before will be routine. And when the people who asserted Grandma María's desire to experience the smooth transition from this world to the next with the promises of eternal fiesta, despite resentment from some family members, make their own crossover, there will be an expectation among their children and grandchildren that this time will be accompanied by familiar and ancient rituals of death and mourning, within which the knowledge of their ancestors will once again be shared with the community.

While visiting the places where relatives are buried and indeed the very act of their interment are things most people tend to take for granted, I have seen that for Native people, these are essential, culturally bonding acts for which they still struggle. And it is in the struggle, whether confronting bulldozers at archaeological sites or intransigent family members on church steps, that the assertion of identity draws the water from below the surface to quench the people's thirst on their journey to Shimilaqsha.

NOTES

1. It is both the wish of the family and Chumash tradition not to use the name of a person who has died. In order to both honor the tradition and maintain the privacy of the family involved, I have used a pseudonym.

2. Michael D. McNally, "The Practice of Native American Christianity," *Church History,* December 2000, 834–859.

3. See Pierre Bourdieu, *The Logic of Practice* (Stanford: Stanford University Press, 1980) 112–121.

4. McNally, "Practice of Native American Christianity," 836.

5. See, for example, Vine DeLoria's *God Is Red* (New York: Grosset & Dunlap, 1973); Ward Churchill, *Indians Are Us? Culture and Genocide in Native North America* (Monroe, ME: Common Courage Press, 1994; Wendy Rose, "The Great Pretenders: Further Reflections on Whiteshamanism," in *The State of Native America: Genocide, Colonization, and Resistance,* ed. M. Anette James, 403–422 (Boston: South End Press, 1992).

6. For further information on the mission system and its implications for Native Californians, see Lisbeth Haas, *Conquests and Historical Identities in California, 1769–1936* (Berkeley: University of California Press, 1995), and Robert H. Jackson and Edward Castillo, *Franciscans and Spanish Colonization: The Impact of the Mission System on California Indians* (Albuquerque: University of New Mexico Press, 1995).

7. Sharburne F. Cook, *The Population of the Californian Indians, 1769–1970* (Berkeley: University of California Press, 1976).

8. See, for example, the transformation of Alkalai Lake Reserve, Canada.

9. Joane Nagel, *American Indian Ethnic Renewal: Red Power and the Resurgence of Identity* (New York: Oxford University Press, 1996).

10. Ibid., 84–101.

11. Ibid., 123–124.

12. Ibid., 142.

13. Sherry B. Ortner, "On Key Symbols," in *Reader in Comparative Religion,* ed. William A. Lessa and Evon Z. Vogt, 92–98 (New York: Harper & Row, 1973).

14. Ibid., 94.

15. Ibid., 95.

16. Jonathon Z. Smith, *Imagining Religion: From Babylon to Jonestown* (Chicago: University of Chicago Press, 1982), 63.

17. Pierre Bourdieu, *In Other Words: Essays Towards a Reflexive Sociology* (Stanford: Stanford University Press, 1980), 24.

18. Ibid.

19. Ibid., 38.

20. Ibid.

21. Stephen Bowers, quoted in Arlene Benson, *The Noontide Sun: The Field Notes of the Reverend Stephen Bowers, Pioneer California Archeologist* (Menlo Park, CA: Ballena Press, 1997), 23.

22. See, for examples of this, John Johnson, "An Ethnohistoric Study of the Island Chumash" (master's thesis, University of California, Santa Barbara, 1988); John Johnson, "Chumash Social Organization: An Ethnohistoric Perspective" (PhD diss., University of California, Santa Barbara, 1988); Chester D. King, "The Evolution of Chumash Society" (PhD diss., University of California, Davis, 1991); Jeanne E. Arnold, "Cultural Disruption and the Political Economy in Channel Islands Prehistory," in *Essays on the Prehistory of Maritime California,* ed. T.L. Jones, 129–144 (Center for Archeological Research at Davis #10. University of California, Davis, 1992).

23. For information on NAGPRA and its implementation, see the NAGPRA page of the National Park Service's Web site at www.cr.nps.gov/nagpra/index.htm.

24. Chester D. King, "Excavations at Parker Mesa" (Lan-215), in *Archaeological Survey Annual Report for 1961–1962,* 91–155 (Los Angeles: University of California, 1962).

25. Johnny Flynn, "From Three Worlds to One: An Analysis of Chumash Religious History" (PhD diss., University of California, Santa Barbara, 1991); John Peabody Harrington, "1933 Field-work Among the Mission Indians of California," in *Explorations and Fieldwork,* 87–90 (Washington, DC: Smithsonian Institution Press, 1991).

26. Edward D. Castillo, "An Indian Account of the Decline and Collapse of Mexico's Hegemony over the Missionized Indians of California," *American Indian Quarterly* 13, no. 4 (1989): 391–408.

27. King, "Excavations at Parker Mesa." See also Thomas Blackburn, *December's Child* (Berkeley: University of California Press, 1976), and Fernando Librado, *The Eye of the Flute: Chumash Traditional History and Ritual,* ed. Travis Hudson (California: Santa Barbara Museum of Natural History, 1977).

28. Dennis F. Kelley, "'The World Is a Canoe': Tradition, Identity, and Symbolism in the Reprise of Chumash Religious Orientation" (master's thesis, University of California, Santa Barbara, 2002).

29. Arnold Van Gennep, *Rites of Passage* (Chicago: University of Chicago Press, 1961).

CHAPTER 2

Contemporary Hindu Approaches to Death

Living With the Dead

MARK ELMORE

Arriving in northern India for a year of fieldwork, I settled in a house outside of Shimla with Vijay Thakur, a retired government official.[1] We spent our first night together chatting over Indian whiskey and sulfur-salted peanuts. When it was my turn to explain why I had arrived at his house with a van full of digital equipment and heavily accented Hindi, I began by telling him that I was interested in how death was understood in India today and how technological and ideological changes had influenced approaches to death. He took a deep breath, and as the blood rushed to his cheeks, he began a three-hour lecture on the "fraudulent character" of traditional death rites. He argued that these rites could be explained in terms of the material needs of the mourners and fundamentally as a form of exploitation by greedy priests. For him the priests performed neither spiritual nor social functions. He was questioning and rejecting the approach to death that his ancestors had taken for hundreds of years. While his lecture was filled with anger, revolutionary metaphors, and Western scientific terminology, none of these things prevented him from adorning his otherwise austere walls with garlanded photographs of his relatives. Though he rejected the external rites of ancestor veneration, he continued to live with his dead relatives. Their photographs filled the walls of his rooms and served as a material reminder that his parents were the source of his inspiration and ethical strength. Vijay's attitude highlights the hybridity of contemporary Hindu approaches to death. While traditional approaches to death are being challenged in many spheres of life, the ancient rites and beliefs continue to live on amid photographs of the dead, electric crematoriums, and cybermemorials.

It would be wrong to assume from his rejection of traditional death practices that Vijay had adopted a skeptical, materialist approach to death. Rather he, like almost all other Hindus with whom I have worked, believes that the dead and the living continue to influence each other. The space between this world and the next, between life and death, is not as great as it is in many other religious traditions. The dead and the living often inhabit the same spaces and interact with each other visually, ritually, and emotionally. Homes are filled with ritual photographs of the dead, ghosts inhabit crossroads, and dead parents continue to exert influence on their children's behavior long after death. Even for individuals skeptical of traditional rituals, the dead continue to wield inexorable force.

To begin to comprehend what death means for contemporary Hindus, we must first understand some of the complexities of Hindu traditions. Hinduism is not a religion like other "world religions." It has no founding figure, no absolutely authoritative text, no single deity, and no official institutional hierarchy. Indeed, all the common criteria used to define religions are absent here. Moreover, while many facets of Hinduism can be traced back more than 3,000 years to the period when its first texts were being compiled, the term did not assume its current meaning until the nineteenth century, when much of South Asia had come under the control of the colonial British administration. Like other religious traditions, "Hinduism" is more appropriately thought of as "Hinduisms" or "Hindu traditions" because it varies greatly across time and space and according to social location. Contributing to this diversity is the caste system, a system of social stratification that divides people into three or four hereditarily and hierarchically ordered classes that are often subdivided into innumerable others. Despite efforts to eradicate it, the caste system, which developed from the ancient South Asian *varna* system, continues to strongly impact how religion is understood and practiced in South Asia. Individuals at the top of the hierarchy generally perform more elaborate ritual duties and often perform rites for other people. They are also generally conservative with regard to the preservation of traditional values and practices. Those at the lower end of the caste hierarchy are often less concerned with ritual perfection or purity, which is not to say that they are any less interested in religion or any less devout. The types of rituals people perform, the temples they visit, and the offerings they give to deities are highly specific to the different castes. For these reasons and many more, we will refer to Hinduism in the plural.

Attempting to represent or explain this diversity is a bit like trying to contain an afternoon monsoon in a test tube. From the fire sacrifice rituals of the earliest periods to renunciate traditions, beliefs and practices regarding death are extraordinarily varied. The goal of this essay is to understand how most Hindus today approach death—that is to say, how "ordinary" Hindus think about death and respond to it on a daily basis. Since there is such tremendous diversity among Hindus in this regard, at best we can try to identify some general patterns of beliefs and practices that resonate in the lives of many, though never all, Hindus. To do this, I will draw on extensive ethnographic fieldwork completed in the remote regions of Himachal Pradesh in northern India. Working from this example, I will show how the world of the living is intimately tied to that of the dead as well as explore the personal, familial, and sociological implications of these relations. I will also give examples from other areas—including Tamil Nadu, Gujarat, England, and Benares—that add to our understanding of both the variability and interconnectivity of Hindu traditions globally.

The chapter is divided into six sections, each addressing a different aspect of the relationship between the living and the dead. We will begin with a brief discussion of the personal implications of maintaining intimate relations with the dead. From there we will see how Hindus care for the dead from the moment of death and how this care provides a space where the living can connect with the dead. We will then examine the material artifacts that are used to connect the living to the dead, looking not only to ancient traditions of memorial making, but also how these practices are being altered by photography in contemporary communities. These material artifacts and other modes of communication are used to connect not only with the peacefully dead, but also with the untimely dead, the dead who have not been transformed into ancestors and who wander the hinterlands of existence, making demands on the living. Thus we will look at different types of ghosts and the various modes of communicating with and pacifying these troubled spirits. But death does not simply link the living with the dead; it also connects the living to the living. To understand this, we will examine how death and its attendant rites can bring together families and communities even as it physically takes them apart. Finally, we will examine how the relationship between the living and the dead is changing in the Hindu diaspora, paying particular attention to the difficulties faced by immigrant communities in maintaining relationships to traditional practices while living in the modern Western world.

APPROACHING DEATH

For someone raised in a Western setting, the most striking thing about death in South Asia is its paradoxical status. While it is visible on the banks of rivers, on the roadside, and on the edges of cities, it does not occupy such a prominent position in the minds of Hindus going through their daily lives. I have been continually amazed how death fails to worry people in Himachal Pradesh, where I conducted interviews in 2002 and 2003. Its inevitability and uncertainty are simply not cause for concern. In hundreds of interviews, I almost never heard anyone express anxiety about her or his impending death.

Rather, when discussing death and its impending reality, people tend to laugh. I have found no other topic that can so powerfully elicit laughter and warm humor, except perhaps the fumbling failures of foreigners. This is particularly true of people who are near to death. When I asked a series of questions about what types of rituals are done after someone dies, the most common response I received was a soft smile and a joke. Once, while interviewing a group of four elderly Rajput women (the youngest of whom was seventy-five) deep in the hills of the Pabbar River basin, they responded with waves of laughter, saying, "What else can we do? We take the body, throw it on the fire, and forget about it. That is it. *Bas.*" This remark, which seems so callous on the surface, eloquently summarizes one of the most pervasive approaches to death in Hindu traditions: people accept their fate, but their acceptance is not framed by anxiety, fear, or melancholy. It is framed by humor.

The mediation of mortality by laughter offers the people of Himachal some degree of freedom from the vicissitudes of death. In a discussion of the role of humor in traditional

Sanskrit versions of the destruction of the universe, Lee Siegel observed a similar strategy: "The mortality which defines life, the end inherent in all living cells, is extracted, exorcised, and objectified in jokes about death. The laughing one makes an effigy 'out there' of his own death and, as if in some ancient apotropaic rite or festive carnival, death is mocked with brazen shows of excoriating laughter to keep it at bay."[2] But this laughter is more than a psychological mechanism for creating distance. It is made possible only by a set of beliefs and practices that brings death close and allows people to see it in less than apocalyptical terms. Death is not so utterly other that it is uncontrollable. Rather, death is funny because it is positioned at the incongruous space between what we can know (the death of others) and what we cannot know (our own death). Death is something that we live with daily and yet, as the people of Himachal continually reminded me, we never know the time of our own death.

This humorous acceptance of death is premised on an intimate relationship between the living and the dead. It is made possible by a series of beliefs and their ritual performances that bring the dead into continual contact with the living. Understanding this relationship, we cannot overestimate the importance of karma, the cycle of transmigration (*saṃsāra*), personal duty (*dharma*), and fate (*kismat, bhāgya*). These concepts meld into each other as people explain death, personal tragedy, misfortune, social position, and good luck, serving as the conceptual background against which individual approaches to death are lived.

The concept of transmigration or saṃsāra, which literally means "to wander or to pass through a series of states," signifies the stages that the Self (*ātman*) traverses as it moves from birth to death to rebirth to redeath. Everything in this world, even the gods, is subject to the laws of saṃsāra. Though the origins of this concept are somewhat obscure, it is at the center of not only Hindu but also Buddhist and Jain relations to death. While some scholars locate its origins in the Vedic belief in redeath (*punarmṛtyu*), others contend that it was a belief held by the original, non-Aryan tribes of the Gangetic plains, while still others claim it was developed by wandering or anti-Vedic groups. The truth of its origins may never be known, but the concept of transmigration continues to forcefully shape how people relate to death. Here, death is a transitional phase to be traversed before one is reincarnated.

Reincarnation, however, is not the final goal. Reincarnation is a temporary state that is ultimately to be overcome. The final goal is liberation (*mokṣa*) from the cycle of transmigration (saṃsāra). Mokṣa is of central concern to the Hindu textual tradition and has even been called the central goal of Hindu religious thought and practice by textual scholars both inside and outside the tradition. Although most Hindu villagers do not often spend time struggling toward this goal, it is worth considering briefly if for no other reason than to contrast the philosophical traditions with the widespread ritual traditions of Hindus.

The possibility of liberation from transmigration is present not only throughout the corpus of early speculative texts called Upaniṣads (eighth to fifth century BCE), but also throughout the later literature, which reaches a high point in the nondual (*advaita*) philosophy of Sankara (eighth century CE). Mokṣa here is generally achieved by turning inward, away from mundane life. To turn inward in this way is to search for knowledge of the Self (ātman), by which everything else is known. To know the Self is to know all that there is to know. The essential Self is of the nature of pure consciousness and is not any particular consciousness. It is not consciousness of something or even consciousness of the act of cognition. Rather, it is the space of "pure" consciousness consciousness without any subject or object. The fundamental step in this process is the equivalence of the essential Self, the basis for all of subjective reality, with the ground of all Being—of all objective reality (Brāhman). Thus, the Upaniṣads develop a system of equivalence wherein the inner Self, the fundamental ground of all subjective consciousness, *is* the objective ground of the world (Brāhman). To know this, to realize the equivalence of the inner and the outer, to understand the Self as Brāhman, is to be free from the ties that bind a person to the world of birth and death, the world of saṃsāra. While such a goal appeals to a minority who become renunciates, it is too abstract and too distant for most Hindus to even consider. When thinking about death and what happens afterward, they are often more concerned with their reincarnation, a process that is heavily dependent upon the fruits of actions from this and earlier incarnations, or one's karma.

In the earliest "Hindu" textual sources, karma originally meant properly performed ritual action that had the power to harmonize the earthly and heavenly realms. It could thereby produce benefits for the performer in this life and after death. However, this concept gradually evolved to denote an impersonal ethical system whereby one's current situation was understood as the ripening of previous seeds sown by earlier actions and dispositions. This concept has a massive array of understandings. For Jains, the entire material universe is itself karma. Nothing in this universe exists without karma. For Buddhists, karma is something more subtle that travels from birth to birth. Whereas in Hindu traditions karma adheres to the soul (ātman), for Buddhists there is no soul to which karma can adhere. While these different traditions may disagree about the specifics of karma, they all agree on a doctrine of causation in which the past and the present make an indelible impression on the future. Most importantly for our purposes here, the doctrine of karma fundamentally shapes how people approach death. Within the highly stratified caste system, one's material, familial, and emotional circumstances are considered a direct product of one's earlier actions. They are the ripening of seeds that were planted by earlier actions. Reflexively, one's actions in this life will directly impact the next birth, as will the difficulties that one will be forced to endure in the afterlife as the soul travels through various hells and heavens before being reborn.

The astute reader will notice an apparent contradiction here. If the doctrine of transmigration is operational, and karma is an impersonal system of cause and effect, reaping its results as the soul travels from birth to birth—changing bodies like a person changing clothes—how can there be an afterlife at all? Moreover, why would it matter if the living continued to perform ritual activities on the behalf of the dead if their position were determined by their own previous actions and the laws of a universal impersonal force? While scholars both inside and outside of Hinduism have yet to come to consensus on these questions, perhaps the best way to understand how the ideas of transmigration and karma, on the one hand, and afterlife and ritual obligation to the dead, on the other, fit together is to understand them as two different levels of responses. In my own fieldwork, I have found that people tend to use both explanations and find little discrepancy between them. In general, it can be said that when people talk about karma and saṃsāra, they are generally talking about issues of ultimate significance (cosmic creation, the development of humankind, etc.). These concepts do not easily find themselves in everyday conversation. However, when people are discussing dead ancestors, the afterlife, heavens, or hells, they are usually discussing more worldly issues of health and sickness, ritual obligation, or familial duty. These are concepts and practices that are analogous to and intertwined with the pragmatics of daily life. While these two approaches to death and the afterlife appear to be mutually exclusive, in practice they blend into each other. Some creative interpreters have even melded them into a single system, as we shall see later.

To eliminate the negative effects of karma, one is admonished to do "good action." This action has a dual effect. While it dissolves the stains of past negative action, it also has a positive effect of creating seeds that will ripen into beneficial fruits. Doing "good action" is a rough translation of the concept of dharma. Dharma is itself a word with many faces. It can mean simply "religion," but in the context of *Pahāṛī*[3] culture it most often means performing actions that benefit others. In her book on Himalayan foothill folktales, Kirin Narayan tells a story that illuminates the relationship between karma, dharma, and the problem of death.[4] In this story, a man dies and travels to the court of *Dharmarāj,* the lord of death who judges the value of one's life. The lord of dharma asks the man whether he wants to experience heaven or hell first. The man chooses heaven, thinking that at least he will have had a small experience of heaven. He is allotted only a short time in heaven, because he has done only a small amount of "good action." While in heaven he begins to give gifts and to sponsor religious rites. Because of these "good actions" he progressively extends his time in heaven until all the "good action" that he has performed erases all of the negative deeds of his previous life and he does not have to serve his time in hell.

This story illuminates at least two important concepts. The first is that the afterlife is not ontologically different from this manifest world; it operates according to the same principles. "Good deeds" are powerful both in this world and the next. These "good deeds" are the only thing that can eliminate one's time in hell and alter one's karma. Once altered, positive karma assures one a place in heaven and, subsequently, an excellent rebirth. This story also highlights the central refrain of this chapter, which is that the world of the living and that of the dead are intimately intertwined. One's actions in this life directly affect what happens in the afterlife and later what will happen in one's next life. The performance of "bad deeds" in this life or in the afterlife has direct negative effects.

When one comes before Dharmarāj (or *Yama*), a judgment on one's life is made. Often one is forced to spend time in one of the many different hells. It must be noted that there is no consistent understanding of all the different hells. Rather, these vary considerably with time, geography, and caste. The most common versions of these hells derive from the Garuḍa Purāṇa. This text is the one most commonly associated with death. Many of the mantras used in the cremation ceremonies are drawn from this text, and it is read aloud both when a person is dying and during the mourning process. The sections of this text that directly address death and its complexity—the greatest part of the text—are set as a dialogue between the gods Garuḍa and *Kṛṣṇa.* Garuḍa has just returned from a long journey through all the different worlds. He is distressed at the state of the world and he wonders why there is so much suffering. In his account of all the terrible suffering that he has witnessed, he describes many hells. The principle hell is *Raurava.* People who tell lies go to this hell.

> *Raurava* is two thousand yojanas [one yojana is equal to eight or nine miles] in measurement. There is a knee-deep pit, difficult to cross. It is leveled up to the ground by a heap of burning coal. And the ground there is well heated by fire. The servants of Yama leave the sinner there in the middle. Burnt by burning fire he runs helter-skelter. At every step his foot is burnt. Day and night he moves here and there lifting and putting his feet.[5]

The text goes on to describe many more hells where people are tortured by insects and wild animals, where people are torn into hundreds of different parts and then reassembled only to be torn apart again, or where people spin on a potter's wheel for thousands of years. People have to endure these hells based directly on what actions they performed in life. Which hell is chosen depends directly on the type of sins committed in life.

The effects of karma are explicit not simply in how one relates to one's own death and rebirth, but also how one relates to the death of others. That is, it is the obligation of family members to care for and interact with the deceased regularly. Failure to perform these interactions can damage not only one's own status, but also the status of one's relatives. Family members must provide for their dead relatives on their travels to heaven or hell; only this link between the world of the living and the dead can ease the suffering after death. With this obligation in mind, let us now turn to some of the ways in which people care for the dead from the moment that physiological death occurs.

FOOD, DEBT, AND SACRIFICE: CARING FOR THE DEAD

Before physiological death occurs, a range of practices takes place. These vary widely according to the family's inclination and ability. They generally include the visiting of relatives, the chanting of religious texts, and travel to sacred places if possible. In some cases families will even move the dying to cities—such as Benares—that are said to help the dead with their postmortem difficulties. The relations that will define how individuals interact with the dead begin the moment that death occurs. Proper performance of the rites that immediately follow death are essential for ensuring ongoing relations with the dead. They also ensure proper transformation of the dead into ancestors and the restabilization of social and familial relations after the deceased is physically gone. The narrative that follows is an in-depth description of the rites performed by the majority of Pahāṛi families in order to establish these relations.

In contrast to the humor and levity that generally characterize Hindu attitudes toward death before the actual death, the behavior that follows it is serious and somber. The moment that death occurs, the family enters a space of extreme pollution and anxiety. Everything they do is filled with meaning and fraught with the potential for failure. For three to sixteen days (in some extreme cases this period can last for a year) they remain in this state, maintaining their ritual duties to the best of their ability. All their ritual actions are highly regulated; contact with people from outside the family is mostly prohibited and normal interactions cease. It is believed that the family is impure at this time, being polluted by the misfortune of death and the impurity of a dead body. Death is the most polluting of human activities. Those who come into contact with it—family members of the deceased, workers at cremation grounds, ascetics who reside near the grounds—are all considered extremely impure. People who have recently lost a family member are generally not allowed in others' houses, even if they are of the same caste. After this period, the humor that was so present before death will slowly creep back into their lives. Of course, how and when this humor returns is highly variable. Though I have often interviewed people who were able to laugh about death only days after the completion of their mourning period, others—such as my best friend—remain in a state of mourning for a prolonged period. In general, it can be said that while most individuals approach their own mortality with a relatively high degree of humor and levity, they navigate the deaths of others with a much graver attitude.

As death approaches, the dying person is generally brought outside the house and laid on the ground. It is considered inauspicious for someone to die on a cot or in a bed because the soul can get caught in the air and may be forced to wander after death. The person is placed on a piece of ground that has been ritually cleaned and prepared with cow dung and banana leaves for the dead ancestor. Catherine Weinberger-Thomas, in her excellent study of widow-burning in India, explains this practice as follows:

> A dying person should be laid on the ground because earth is pure. In order to purify it further, one should carefully apply a coat of cow dung (one of the best filters against pollution) to the soil, and strew it with *kṛṣṇa* grass (this being the procedure for all sacrifices). Dying in one's bed—every Westerner's dream—is the worst of natural deaths for the Hindu because that position, of being neither here nor there, will be reenacted by the dying individual in his next life: he will be born neither in heaven nor on earth, but rather as a spirit doomed to wander in the intermediate region (*antarikṣā*).[6]

The moment after physiological death, water from the sacred Ganges river (*gaṇgājal*) is poured into the mouth of the dead person along with other valuable objects according to the ability of the family. This can be anything from a one-rupee coin to a ball of four, five, or eight metals, or even a ball of gold. Then, refined butter (*desī ghī*) is poured into the mouth of the person, after which the body is washed. In some places, sandalwood paste is then rubbed on the body. Finally, the eyelids are closed and more ghī is rubbed on them.

After the eyes have been closed, all the relatives are notified and they travel to the home of the deceased. They bring gifts to the family and mourn the dead. The body is then put inside a cloth (*chola*) in preparation for its travel to the cremation ground. While cremation is the normal destination of a Hindu dead body, several types of dead bodies are prohibited from being burnt. Although the list of which bodies are not burned varies somewhat, the most common list is as follows: children under five, lepers, snake-bite victims, renunciates, smallpox victims, suicides, and pregnant women. In general, the one thing that links all these individuals together is that—for one reason or another—they are not fit to be offered as a sacrifice. Their bodies are normally thrown into a nearby river.[7] If the body is to be burned, the relatives begin building the bier (*sīḍhī*) on which they will carry it to the cremation ground. Most often the bier is made of bamboo, but the wood can vary greatly depending on what is available. No nails are used in making the bier; instead the wood is tied with a rough rope (*āla dhāgā*). The relatives who have come for this occasion bring shiny new cloth (*kaphan*) that will be placed over the body after it has been positioned on the bier. If possible, the cremation should be done on the same day that the death occurs; however, if it cannot be arranged soon enough due to the timing of the death, the cremation will take place the following day.[8]

Before leaving for the cremation ground, the body is honored (*pūja*). First, the oldest son offers water, incense, and flowers to the body. The oldest son is the principal actor in death rites; he will perform and orchestrate all the final rites. His performance of these rites will both pay his final debt to his parents and assure their safe passage to the realm of the ancestors. This is one of the main reasons why sons are valued so much more than daughters in the Hindu tradition. Although there are other significant reasons, such as the price of a daughter's dowry, the need for at least one son to perform the final rites is an obligation that most contemporary Hindus continue to feel. Debt plays a central role in how Hindus relate to death: not only must a son repay the debt to his ancestors by performing the final rites for his parents, but the body itself is often considered a loan on which payment must be made. "According to brahmanic theory, the body one inhabited in life was in fact a loan from the gods, or, more precisely, from Yama, the Lord of Death. As such, sacrifice was nothing other than a payment on a loan; failure to pay (i.e., offer sacrifices) resulted in repossession (i.e., death). In order that his debtors might keep up on their payments, Yama, Vedic Hinduism's cosmic 'repo man,' threw in a piece of land with the body he loaned: this was the parcel on which the sacrificer installed his household (*gārhapatya*) fire."[9] Thus, all sacrificial activity, not only the final cremation rites, constitutes payment on outstanding debts.

After the oldest son, the other closest members of the family come in succession and offer their final obeisance to the dead relative. When this final pūja is complete, the body is ready to be carried to the cremation ground. In Pahāṛi culture, women are not supposed to go to the cremation ground, though this rule is not strictly enforced. Women are supposed to remain at home and mourn together, while the men go to the cremation ground to perform the cremation. If there is no male relative, the rites have to be completed by a woman and in this case women attend the cremation. Even when there are male relatives to do all the cremation rites, I have seen instances where small groups of women attended the ceremony, though they were generally well separated from the men and somewhat removed from the main ceremonies. At this time, some of the relatives go into the forest to collect wood for the pyre. The wood is supposed to arrive before the body and should be ready to form the pyre when the body arrives. The wood can generally be of any kind, though it should be dry and it is most auspicious (but very costly) if it is sandalwood.

Then the journey to the cremation ground begins. The person (*karmachārī*) performing the final rites (preferably the oldest son) generally leads the group of men. He carries a small earthen pot (*kalas*) filled with smoldering embers that will later be used to light the fire. He holds the pot with a branch from a peach tree or a suitable substitute. Another person has a pot filled with rice, which will be left in two, three, or four places. Generally rice is left at the house where the journey is begun, at a designated rest spot, and at the cremation ground itself. Every family has a designated rest spot. Whenever someone in that family dies, the party of mourners has to stop at this place on their travels to the cremation ground. The giving of rice is understood to be an offering to ghosts and other spirits who live in the area and who are attracted to the dead body. The rice is said to appease their hunger so that they do not create any mischief with the body as it journeys to the cremation ground.

When they arrive, the mourners construct a pyre (*citā*) from the wood that relatives have gathered. To make the pyre, they first lay down the largest blocks of wood and then fill in the spaces with small pieces of dry wood, proceeding layer by layer. After the pyre has been constructed and blessed, the mourners place the body on the pyre with the head facing southward, toward the land of the dead (*yamalok*). Then, the oldest son circles the fire three times with the pyre on his right. He has a pot of water on his shoulder with a small hole in it, where the water is draining out. After three times around the pyre, he throws the pot over his shoulder and goes to the head of the pyre. He then lights the pyre under the head and under the feet.

The pyre is allowed to burn for some time, until all the hairs on the body are burned, and other signs of decay are readily evident. Once the body has been sufficiently burnt the son will take a stick (*daṇḍa*) and perform a final rite called *kapāl kriyā,* literally, "skull work." This rite consists of cracking the skull of the dead relative in order to release both the vital air (*prān*) and the soul (ātman). Indeed, in many folk and textual sources, it is not until this rite is performed that death is actually considered to have occurred. From this time onward during the mourning process, the deceased will be referred to as a *preta,* a disembodied ghost. This rite also marks the beginning of the difficult work of forgetting. The relatives are supposed to leave grief and tears behind, as these only attract the preta back to this world and hinder its progress. For the next year, the preta will wander without a physical body on its passage to the realm of judgment in yamalok.

Many scholars, both ancient and modern, have argued that there is an intimate connection between sacrifice and death, a connection linked through fire (*agni*).[10] Like the ancient Vedic sacrificial rites, which form the loom upon which Hindu traditions were woven,[11] the fire both purifies the ritual offering (in this case a body, but also butter, grass, and many other types of offerings) and forges the connection between the visible world and that of the gods or the dead. The offering of the corpse to the fire, an offering that is understood to be undertaken voluntarily, is thus a final sacrifice that both purifies the body and in turn performs the creative act of regeneration. This regeneration is understood both personally (in terms of the progress of the soul) and by some as cosmological. Hindu religious thought often makes a correspondence between the body of human beings and the cosmos as a whole. Indeed, many of the central creation stories of the Hindu traditions are predicated on the self-sacrifice of a divine being in order to create the universe, which itself takes the form of a body. For example, in the Vedic texts (Ṛgveda), Puruṣa, who is the cosmic being, sacrifices himself so that the universe could be created: "The moon was gendered from his mind, and from his eye the sun had birth; Indra and Agni [important Vedic deities] from his mouth were born and *Vayu* [lord of the winds] from his breath."[12] In this way, the corporeal sacrifice that is made on the funeral pyre re-creates the cosmic sacrifice that produced the universe, a process that provides for the re-creation of the ancestor.

As mentioned in the previous paragraph, the fire also provides purification for one's sins. Weinberger-Thomas argues that in traditional Hindu medical treatises, the word for "sin" (*papman*) "designates fever or, in a broader sense, illness itself."[13] In general, the Hindu medical tradition never treats illnesses as neutral. Illness is a direct result of the ripening of one's karma. Moreover, in many early medical treatises, the expiation of sins is equated with curing. In the case of cremation, fire becomes the final source of healing that purifies the body to be offered as a sacrifice and to be prepared for regeneration.[14]

After the splitting of the skull, many of the mourners offer small bundles of wood (composed of sandal, mango, peach, and *alma* woods) to the fire (*dharm kīlakhri*). This wood is thrown onto the pyre in three successive motions, after which the mourners bow and leave if they wish. At this time, three pieces of bone (*asthu*) are taken from the pyre, at least one of which has to come from the forehead. While many people leave after these rites are completed, the chief mourner and at least a couple of others stay until the pyre is completely burned, a process that can take several hours, after which they bind some ashes and bone together in a cloth. They also go through the ash looking for any rings or precious metals that the relative may have been wearing.[15] The site is then washed with water and they return home, where the cloth with the ash and bones inside is placed in a tree outside the house.

Either the next day or sometime soon thereafter, the cloth is taken to a sacred water spot. For those with the financial means, the asthu is taken to Haridvar, a sacred pilgrimage site in northern India known especially for this purpose.[16] If this is not possible, then the asthu is taken to a river, such as the Satluj, Pabbar, or Beas. The chief mourner and two or three other people also bring seven balls of rice (*piṇḍas*) to this site. These balls of rice represent the body of the ancestor on its journey to the world of the fathers and also provide food for that journey. The mourners offer incense and water to the rice balls and then throw them in the water along with the ashes and bones.

In many ways, the offering of piṇḍas is the most universal of Hindu death rites. It is the fundamental rite that establishes the reciprocal relationship between the living and the dead. These ceremonies have been the subject of numerous studies, significantly the work of Jonathan Parry. His work draws on extensive ethnographic research in the northern Indian city of Benares, a city known preeminently as a powerful place to die. Working with these materials, Parry has shown that the piṇḍa ceremony has specific parallels with birth. Although the number of days and the number of rice balls offered differ in some areas of Himachal Pradesh, the following description provides a general illustration of the process of transforming the preta into a *pitṛ,* an incorporated ancestor able to make the journey to the world of the ancestors. "Each day a piṇḍa—a ball of rice or flour—is offered in the name of the deceased, each of which reconstitutes a specific limb of his body. By the tenth day the body is complete and on the eleventh life is breathed into it and it is fed. On the next day a ritual is performed which enables the deceased to rejoin his ancestors."[17] With this assistance from the living, the ancestor is able to make its difficult journey and to transform the negativity of death into the positivity of (re)birth. Indeed, Parry suggests that this transition of the preta into a pitṛ and the subsequent journey of the dead to the realm of the ancestors both bear a remarkable similarity to beliefs about birth. The ten-day period of building the body is equated with the ten lunar months necessary for gestation. The word piṇḍa itself is the same word that is used for the embryo in the womb and on the ancestor's journey it has to cross the Vaitarani River, a river always represented as flowing with blood, pus, and other unsavory substances. Parry links the forging of this river to the actual emergence of the child out of the womb, which is also represented as "negotiating a river of blood and pollution."[18] Hereby, the sacrificial act that we saw earlier is completed. The death sacrifice has been transformed into an eminently creative act. "Sacrifice is a ritual wrenching out of death. Through it both the sacrificer and the world are reborn."[19] The relations of feeding and caring for the ancestor that are started here in the piṇḍa ceremonies are continued after the closure of the mourning period, a period lasting three to sixteen days. These relations are continued through the mediation of various forms of memorials, to which we will turn in the next section.

The rites described above are drawn from contemporary practice in Himachal Pradesh and are derived from traditional rites that have been practiced across South Asia for hundreds of years. Not surprisingly, things are changing in the contemporary period. While many rites continue to be performed, new challenges require that some practices be adapted. For example, some people can no longer afford the wood to burn the deceased, or the area in which they live has been so ecologically devastated that there are no more trees. In these cases, electric cremation is performed, though many people continue to be petrified by this process. For many of the people I spoke with in Himachal Pradesh, an electric cremation was a horror beyond reckoning. One afternoon a very old woman told me that she would rather have me light her on fire immediately than be cremated inside a machine. Another challenge to the traditional rites comes from those who, like Vijay Thakur, have become skeptical of their efficacy and believe that they are simply a way for ritual priests to make money. These people will often reject the ritual structure described above, but will generally perform something in their place to honor the dead. Most often this is some form of charity work. The money that would have gone to complete the ritual is given to homeless children or lepers. Thus, despite both technical advances and the presence of Western scientific values, most people continue to perform rites that share much in common with those their ancestors performed more than a thousand years ago.

SITES OF COMMUNICATION: MEMORIALS OF THE DEAD

Communication between the living and the dead is most often maintained and transacted through various forms of material culture. Historically in Himachal Pradesh, these material markers have taken three primary forms. The first and most common of these forms is a small stone, sometimes carved, that is placed either in a temple area or in the home. This practice is thought to have been widespread, but few of the ancient stones have survived—though many of the modern and contemporary stones are still in good shape. The second type of material memorial takes the form of inscriptions found on temples, forts, and at watering holes (*bāverī*). These inscriptions were quite common in the western district of Chamba. They generally give the name of the deceased and speak of the good acts that the person performed. Finally, the third common form of material memory is the many water taps that dot the landscape. Along distant mountain paths or the main streets of modernized towns, water taps devoted to deceased relatives provide a cool drink to villagers and tourists alike. These taps bring to light the intimate connection between the dead and the living—water being one of the primary media that can connect the living with the dead—by providing both physical and moral support for the coming generations.

Material memorials have a long history in South Asia. One of Hinduism's early sacred texts, the *Śatapatha Brāhmaṇa*, offers details relating to the construction of a monument over the bones or relics of the deceased.[20] The earliest Tamil works of the Śangam age (third century BCE–third century CE) refer to the erection of a pillar or post in memory of a dead ancestor. There is also considerable evidence of Buddhist monks erecting pillars and mounds in memory of other monks before the beginning of the Common Era. This ancient tradition continues throughout India today, from Himachal Pradesh in the north to areas as distant as south India.[21] Stuart Blackburn describes one particular type found in Tamil Nadu, called *cumai tāṇki* (the load bearer). These memorials are dedicated to women who died in pregnancy or childbirth. Built of three stones—two upright and one across—they are used to hold the loads carried by villagers while they rest. These stone memorials can also turn into small shrines or become the site of larger temples, a process that highlights the connection between the dead and deities, which we will explore in more detail later. Indeed, Blackburn observes, "occasionally, at the base of large temples in Kanya Kumari District, Tamil Nadu, one can find the cumai tāṇki with its three stone slabs still intact."[22]

While these types of markers still continue to be made, the most common type of memorial for the dead in Himachal Pradesh today is the photograph. Photographs of deceased ancestors can be seen in almost every home in the hills as well as in shops and government offices. Photographs of the dead are distinguished from other photographs in a number of ways. The photographs themselves can be family snapshots, studio shots, or even postmortem photographs. Most commonly, they are simply adorned with a garland of flowers, but they can also be hand painted by artists who specialize in "retouching" photographs.[23] They can also be digitally edited. It is this secondary work that is significant. It can run a wide gamut, from basic color correction to the addition of flowers, halos of light, or images of deities, according to the wishes of the family. The type of photograph chosen and the amount of editing is dependent on the economic level of the family. Poor families may have only one or two photographs, while wealthier families can choose from hundreds or spend enormous sums of money restoring old photographs. The demand for these photographs at all levels of society accounts for the large number of photo studios in India. While these studios do not take photos simply for the purpose of worship, many of the photographs originally taken for other reasons end up as ritual photographs. Once transformed into ritual photographs, they are placed in special rooms intended for worship or designed to entertain guests and become the site for daily transactions between the living and the dead. Ritual photographs are used morning and evening in simple rites of remembrance that consist of the offering of incense, light, and/or flowers and a small prayer to the ancestor.

This type of memorial is rapidly transforming how the dead are understood. Here technological transformations have reshaped not only how the dead are interacted with, but also how they are remembered—a process that has enormous repercussions for how both death and personal existence are conceived. Traditionally in Pahāṛi culture, after one or four years the dead merge with other deceased relatives into an anonymous group of remembered ancestors. Interaction with this group of ancestors is a rare event, happening only once every year or two. However, with the visual specificity that photography provides and the material site that is remembered daily, transactions with the dead are becoming more frequent and more individualized.

The close relationship that is established between the living and the dead comes to its most intimate realization through photograph memorials. Many people in Himachal Pradesh now ask these photographs for daily blessings, for blessings on new endeavors, and for help in simple daily tasks. In this way, the deceased are beginning to take on many of the characteristics of deities. Despite people's faith (*viśvās*) in the deities, they are very distant. People have never *seen* them, but people have seen and known their ancestors. This proximity makes them more easily accessible for daily guidance and blessings. The space that was historically reserved for deities or deified dead—an ambiguous group of spirits, both malevolent and benevolent, that interact with the living—is now extended to any deceased ancestor with a photograph.

DEMONOLOGY, DREAMS, THE UNTIMELY DEATH

Death—the most democratic of human experiences—does not always come when it is wanted. To this point we have dealt only with deaths that were relatively expected and that occurred after the person had completed his or her expected lifespan. However, death often occurs suddenly to people whose full lifespan has not been completed. In Hindi there are several terms for this type of death (*alpa mṛtyu* or *achanak mṛtyu*), but each signifies a death that was untimely, that was not expected, and that cut short the "natural" term of life. When a death like this occurs, responses are extremely varied. Sometimes it is treated like a bad twist of fate (kismat) and the traditional death rites are performed. More often, the death is treated specially. People of the family generally travel to the place where the death occurred and perform a fire sacrifice for the peace of the soul, saying prayers and feeding offerings into a fire. At these places of unexpected death, the mourners leave some type of material remains—a small stone, a photograph, a flag, or all of the above. If the body can be found, a traditional cremation ceremony is performed but supplemented with additional rites that vary greatly and depend on the nature of the death. In the mountains, by far the most common type of untimely death is caused by "brain injuries," which generally means that the person involved was driving a motorcycle on the exceptionally dangerous mountain roads without a helmet. In these cases, another rite, called *sūt,* is often performed. In this rite, a rough string is tied from the place where the accident occurred to the place where the body was found. This is done because the spirit (preta) is thought to get stuck wandering in the space above the accident. The string is used to pull the spirit in and to help it begin its path to the world of the ancestors. Once the spirit has been bound, the body is then burned in a sacrificial fire (*havan*) and can proceed along the correct path.

In these types of deaths—because of the nature of the death or the improper performance of the final rites—there is a distinct possibility that the spirit will not be able to make the necessary transition to the world of the ancestors. In that case, it can get stuck between this world and the next, becoming a ghost (*bhūt-pret*). This ghost can show up in a number of ways. It can appear in violent possessions, whereby family members lose control of their bodies and the ghost makes petitions to the family. According to the interviews that I have conducted, however, these unhappy spirits appear most often in dreams. These dreams represent a serious form of communication that often demands action. If, for example, the dead in the dream makes some demands on the living, the demands are almost invariably fulfilled.[24] If an affliction like this occurs, people generally perform a rite of installation for the ancestor, whereby the ancestor is installed in the worship room of the house and is worshipped there as a deity.

In order to prevent this from happening, people in some parts of Himachal consult a death specialist, who is called a *maśānī*. Maśānī are known for their ability to convene with the dead and to intervene between the living and the dead so that proper relations can be forged. This communication between the living and the dead happens in a number of ways, but the following example illustrates the most common way. In the upper Shimla hill states there is a man who is famous for his ability to communicate with spirits of the deceased. This man is said to have never left his village. He lives in a tiny mud hut and appears like any other poor inhabitant of this area. Families who have lost a relative and are unsure of the status of that relative can come to this place. They need only bring a small donation—because the man will not accept large donations—and some dirt from their native village. They sit with the man and he begins to feel the dirt, letting it fall slowly through his hands. He then calls out all the names of the people who have died on that soil. When he arrives at the crucial name (he has not been told this name in advance and generally does not know the family beforehand), he is told to stop and then that spirit takes control of the maśānī's body. His gestures, posture, and voice change radically assuming the character of the deceased. Once present, the dead becomes available for communication. The family asks questions about how the spirit is, what is needed, and so forth. In many of the cases that I have seen or heard of, very little is needed. The living are comforted simply by talking with the dead and generally leave much happier than they arrived. In some cases, however, many things may be required to free the spirit from its unhappy state.

In one extreme case that was related to me, the family had to return to this man three times, offer a cow to be freed, and perform various rituals. Most important, the mother had to forget about her deceased daughter. They had been very close and the ties that bound them were holding the child's spirit to the earthly realm. The case was particularly difficult, because the child had died very young, and it was believed that she died from a curse put on her family by a Tantric sorcerer, which had been solicited by a jealous neighboring family. As if the case were not complicated enough, the daughter also died on a day and at a time when—as a result of the particular constellation of stars and planets—anyone is granted release (mokṣa) from the world of saṃsāra. However, this release could not be granted until the mother released her child from memory. To achieve this, the mother was not permitted to look at the photographs of the daughter. She was kept inside for an entire year and the husband performed more than two hours of daily worship. At the time the story was told to me, the daughter had been totally freed from her bonds and the maśānī related that she would never be reborn, a statement that provided enormous solace to the family—though they were still shaken by the loss of their intelligent and promising daughter.

Cases such as this are extremely common in South Asia. They have been the subject of numerous essays and books. One of the most often quoted of these works is an influential essay by Stuart Blackburn.[25] If the deceased died at an early age through some form of violence, Blackburn shows how such a spirit is transformed into a god.[26] The deified dead are a special class of spirits caught somewhere between this world and the next. Their shrines are found in villages across the subcontinent, in homes and at the heart of some of the large translocal deity cults. Blackburn believes that the deified dead are explained by three interrelated factors. He argues that the creation of these memorial sites and the transformation of the angry, victimized ancestor represents a "(partial) triumph over death" and that this deification becomes a means to make the power of violence available to the living.[27] He believes, moreover, that these deified dead are prohibited from becoming regular ancestors because the violence that contributed to their death "makes them too powerful."[28] In the ongoing and complex relationship between the living and the dead, then, the process of deification in cases of untimely death is a strategy of converting the power that prohibited the deceased from becoming an ancestor into a power that helps both the living and the dead. The dead begin to receive worship, a process that extends the ritual worship received by ancestors. The living are able to transmute the violence into a powerful force that is used to help the family and the local community.

RELATING TO THE DEAD: FAMILIES AND DEATH

As we saw above, the maintenance of the family is dependent upon the proper performance of the sacrificial death rites. On a more practical level, death upsets the basic family order and all of the unwritten norms and habits that are engrained in family life. This upsetting of the social and familial order is a source of great distress. Indeed, when discussing death in Himachal, the only time that people begin to express anxiety is when they worry about a premature death that would leave their family without provision. That is, death is only an issue if one's duties to the family are not complete. In this respect, death is chiefly an ethical issue and not a personal or ontological one. As death approaches, it is understood fundamentally in relation to others, rather than as an individual experience. People worry about death not for their own sake, but for how the death will affect others or how the death of others will affect the family. Indeed, David Knipe has argued that the relation between the living and the dead is one of "social obligation," such that the ancestors "are satisfied."[29] All the somber rites described above can be read as providing this satisfaction both for the ancestors and the living family members.

Death in a family requires reorienting and reconfiguring. As mentioned earlier, the time immediately following death is one of intense pollution and prohibition for the family during which they are not allowed in other people's homes. They do not wash their clothes. They do not eat food with spices and will eat only once a day. Moreover, death is a time when internal family relations are often renegotiated. After death, the ancestor assumes a new position within the family, which alters how other individuals interact with each other. These renegotiations are often fully manifest at a ritual feast called *śuddhi.*

The śuddhi ceremony is one of the most important rituals in the process of mourning. It is the ceremony that closes the time of pollution and inauspiciousness that opened with the death and lasted three to sixteen days. It is cause for celebration because a difficult time has been passed and the deceased is on the way to the abode of the ancestors. At this time, all the relatives and friends are invited to the house of the deceased, where they are lavishly fed. The ritual practitioners who usually perform necessary ritual functions for the family and the local area (Brāhmans) are also invited. Family members offer the Brāhmans gifts, such as clothes, beds, and the deceased person's favorite foods. In the hills, contrary to the practices of the plains, these gifts can include meat and alcohol—both substances that are generally prohibited in the conservative Hindu households. At this ceremony, the humor that characterizes how people approach death in the abstract begins to return. Once again people can laugh and enjoy themselves with their family, providing an effective healing mechanism to help relatives distance themselves from the pain of death and draw closer to the joys of living.

As a time to bring family and close relations together, the śuddhi can be an opportunity for family conflicts to be resolved. Many people in Himachal Pradesh have stories of how their family was reshaped at the śuddhi ceremony or the similar family gatherings held one year and four years after the death. For example, one man from Mandi described how at the śuddhi for his uncle, the underlying tensions between the families linked through his grandfather were overcome. Grudges and disagreements that had lasted for several years were healed. When describing how this reconciliation happened, he emphasized that it was because of the intervention of the deceased, who was able to see more clearly as an ancestor and to guide the family's actions. Such stories of family reconciliation directly linked to the agency of the deceased are common at this time, although Hindus provide various explanations for this healing process. This unifying outcome has been observed by other scholars as well.

As Maurice Bloch asserts, "Death as disruption, rather than being a problem for the social order, as anthropologists have tended to think of it, is in fact an opportunity for dramatically recreating it."[30] Shalini Randeria has graphically shown how the feasts that close the period of morning and pollution after death in Gujarat are used to dramatically reconfigure social relations. For Dalit (low caste) populations, these feasts, in addition to being a time to honor the deceased, are a time for the production of social order, the creation of locality, and the redefinition of the social group.[31] That is, the feasts that follow a death have important social functions that can reaffirm ties to local spaces, to kin members, and caste (*paragṇū*). It is a space where the subcaste can be reunited and reaffirmed through public celebrations, feasts, oration, and gifts even as death physically tears the community apart. "The celebration symbolizes the integration of the paragṇū or the caste—both referred to by the Dalits as '(our) society' [*amāro samāj*]—in the face of disruption and reasserts order in the face of the chaos caused by death."[32] This theme of unifying community through death is present not only in India. It is also seen in the diaspora, to which we now turn.

VARIATION ON A THEME: DYING IN THE DIASPORA

Like many religious populations, Hindus are not located in a singular geographic environment. They are spread across the globe from Malaysia to Milwaukee. In each of these new locations, they alter how they respond to death in accordance with various factors relative to their new environment. As a result, Hindu approaches to death in the diaspora have become even more variegated than the great diversity that already exists in South Asia itself. The intimate relations that we have seen between the living and the dead take on new forms as they interact with and are stressed by different social, cultural, and institutional factors.

Given the scope of this chapter, we will be able to examine only one example of dying in the diaspora: Hindus in England. For the past several hundred years, India has had an ambivalent relationship with England. The colonial experience is still very much a part of the contemporary Indian psyche, both in India and the diaspora. As a result, for many Indians today, England can signify salvation or the root of all contemporary social ills. Many of these tensions and other pragmatic problems are brought to bear on Hindus dying overseas in England. The fieldwork of Shirley Firth in the city of Southampton with Hindu immigrants from Gujarat, Punjab, and east Africa is helpful in this regard.[33] Firth makes several important observations, but I will focus on three items, which I believe are particularly elucidative of changes in the diaspora: the condensation of ritual practices; the barriers to a "good death" in modern, Western hospitals; and the tensions surrounding cultural and religious differences within the Hindu diaspora.

The condensation and simplification of Hindu death practices in England is a trend that is generally applicable to other forms of ritual in the diaspora. In India, and particularly in Himachal Pradesh, the death rites are presided over by several different types of priests who guide the rites and who decide which forms are performed. In England there is a severe shortage of priests not only because it is a diaspora community, but also because few priests are willing to perform these rites due to the ritual pollution that is involved in mediating death. As a result, families are forced either to condense the crucial piṇḍa ceremonies, which traditionally can last for more than sixteen days, into one day when a priest is available, or to rely on knowledgeable friends or family members to perform the ceremonies. This fact has an interesting side effect, which is ritual innovation. Without the traditional priest to control the ceremony, people are allowed the freedom to perform rites that seem appropriate to them and to read materials that were important to the deceased. The rites that take place at the cremation ground are often reduced or dispensed with altogether because cremation most often takes place in a crematorium.

These ritual and technological transformations make the communication between the dead and the living more strained but also open up new possibilities for maintaining traditional practices. The reduction of the piṇḍa ceremonies deprives the dead of a subtle body and sustenance for the journey to the realm of the ancestors. However, many individuals in the community continue to perform traditional rites in their new setting and are successful. They devise ingenious ways to circumvent the difficulties in England, such as bringing priests from India or from other parts of the country, or even substituting rites that are more easily performed to make up for failure to perform a rite. In addition, they employ new methods and media to make the connection with the dead. Just as we saw in Himachal, photographs are also used in England to provide a material site for remembering that can often supplement other rites of communication and transaction.

Another major challenge to traditional Hindu death practices occurs when Hindus die in the modern, Western hospitals of England. While modern medicine has brought innumerable benefits to people, it has also brought enormous difficulties, particularly when it comes to dying. Nowhere are these difficulties more pointed than in communities of diverse cultural and linguistic heritage. The modern hospital does not allow patients to die on the earth as is dictated by most Hindu traditions of dying, nor does it allow the space for many relatives to come and sit with the deceased and sing from religious texts long into the night. Moreover, communication between hospital staff and Hindus is often strained because of the language barrier. This can raise serious problems in the last moments. Often, we in the West hold tightly to technology, hoping for the last-minute miracle cure. However, Hindu traditions dictate a set of practices in the last moments, such as having the name of God on one's lips, hearing sacred scriptures read, being on the floor, and having gaṇgājal and other sacred material poured into one's mouth right after death. When the hospital staff does not communicate that a death is impending, these last rites become impossible. This refusal to acknowledge and accept impending death causes many Hindu families and patients great hardship. What is at stake here is not simply a question of comfort. When family members fail to perform their duty in these last moments, they fail to repay the debt that they owe to their ancestors. So death in modern hospitals can cause problems not only for the dying person, who is unable to die on the earth with the proper sending rituals, but also for the family who bears responsibility for this death.

Finally, dying in the diaspora brings to light latent differences in the community itself. Hindus from all over the world, from different castes, different economic backgrounds, and different sectarian affiliations often find themselves together in a single space. In the diaspora they band together and form communities, building friendships, temples, and economic relationships. The building of these ties requires that differences be overlooked, differences that are often clearly brought to the surface in relation to death. For example, many of the Hindus in Firth's study are Arya Samaj. The Arya Samaj was a nineteenth-century reform movement within Hinduism that sought to return to the "original elements of Hinduism." In concert with this approach, they do not perform the piṇḍa ceremonies and do not worship the dead in any way, as they feel that these practices are not in accordance with the original character of Hinduism. This, however, could not be more different from the practices of Hindus in Himachal Pradesh and throughout South Asia, where rites for the dead are absolutely essential and where ancestor worship is a common and revered practice.[34] In the meeting of these two different Hindu traditions, the intimate relationship between the living and the dead is brought into question. Here a new location and new pressures have brought together communities that would otherwise remain separate in India, creating cultural tensions and reassessments of traditional rites and beliefs. The reassessment of traditional belief, whether caused by internal or external critique, is an ongoing process as Hindus negotiate the space between the traditional worlds they emerge from and the new cultures they live among. Indeed, in many cases, these difficulties are readily overcome by members of different communities. In the same way that death can bring together local caste members in Gujarat, it can also bring together Hindus from all different castes and geographies in the diaspora.

CONCLUSION

We have seen throughout this chapter that Hindu approaches to death and the afterlife are predicated on an intimate set of relationships between the living and the dead. These relationships are mediated by a set of traditional concepts such as fate, karma, saṃsāra, dharma, and debt. Through an intricate set of rituals, familial mediations, psychological strategies, and physical memorials, Hindus cleverly traverse the thorny questions of death and the afterlife. The success of this system for explaining the unexplainable, for making sense of one of the most enigmatic of human experiences, can be seen in the smiles and contagious laughter that always accompany my questions on death and the afterlife. The smiles and easy grace of the many elderly Hindus that I have interviewed in the hills of northern India are testament to a system of beliefs and practices that does not shun the difficulties of human experience—for life in the Himalayas is rarely easy—but that also provides a solid basis for living. By highlighting the often humorous way that Pahāṛi

Hindus negotiate death, I do not want to suggest that they disregard or somehow fail to understand the complexities of personal mortality. Rather, I want to offer what I have experienced in Himachal Pradesh as a successful strategy for dealing with one of life's most difficult questions.

NOTES

1. This man's name has been changed to protect his identity.

2. Lee Siegel, *Laughing Matters: Comic Tradition in India* (Delhi: Motilal Banarsidass, 1987), 401.

3. The term *Pahāṛi* is the appellation used to refer to a broad range of different people who live in the Himalayan region. The word *Pahāṛi* means "mountain" or "hill" in Hindi.

4. Kirin Narayan, in collaboration with Urmila Devi Sood, *Mondays on the Dark Night of the Moon: Himalayan Foothill Folktales* (New Delhi: Oxford University Press, 1997), 154–158.

5. *Garuḍa Purāṇa* 2.3.5–8. *The Garuḍa Purāṇa* (Delhi: Motilal Banarsidass, 1979), 2: 730.

6. Catherine Weinberger-Thomas, *Ashes of Immortality: Widow-Burning in India,* trans. Jeffrey Mehlman and David Gordon White (Delhi: Oxford University Press, 2000), 68.

7. Veena Das, *Structure and Cognition: Aspects of Hindu Caste and Ritual* (Delhi: Oxford University Press, 1977), 123.

8. The timing of this cremation can be a problem in diaspora areas where cremation cannot be arranged on the same day as the death.

9. David G. White, *The Alchemical Body: Siddha Traditions in Medieval India* (Chicago: University of Chicago Press, 1996), 11.

10. The term used for cremation by many of the ritual specialists who carry out these rites is an *antyeṣṭī,* which literally means "last sacrifice."

11. References to this connection are numerous. Veena Das describes it as follows: "Thus the site of cremation is prepared in exactly the same way as in fire-sacrifice, i.e., the prescriptive use of ritually pure wood, the purification of the site, its consecration with holy water, and the establishment of Agni [fire] with the proper use of mantras." Das, *Structure and Cognition,* 122.

12. *ḥgveda* 10.90. *The Hymns of the ḥgveda,* trans. Ralph T.H. Griffith (Delhi: Motilal Banarsidass, 1973).

13. Weinberger-Thomas, *Ashes of Immortality* 45.

14. In this connection, Weinberger-Thomas tells an interesting story of the burning of lepers in the nineteenth century: "In the middle of the nineteenth century, lepers were burned alive in order to afford them access to a higher rebirth (the British abolished this custom). Leprosy was thought to be repulsive less for fear of contamination or for its symptoms than because of the hideous crimes whose delayed manifestation it was taken to be." Ibid., 46.

15. In Benares there is a special caste of people (*doms*) who have this job as their birthright. They are considered the most polluted of all castes, but they have grown quite wealthy collecting precious metal and stones from the ashes of funeral pyres.

16. See Ann Grodzins Gold, *Fruitful Journeys: The Ways of Rajasthani Pilgrims* (Berkeley: University of California Press, 1988). For the intimate relationship between death and water, see Anne Feldhaus, *Water and Womanhood: Religious Meaning of Rivers in Maharastra* (New York: Oxford University Press, 1995).

17. Jonathan P. Parry, "Sacrificial Death and the Necrophagous Ascetic," in *Death and the Regeneration of Life,* ed. Maurice Bloch and Jonathan Parry, 74–110 (Cambridge: Cambridge University Press, 1982), 84. It should be noted that this body of the ancestor is not a physical body. Rather it resembles the subtle body, which is sometimes called a nourishment body. "It is by virtue of this body of sorts that the departed (*preta*) may become an ancestor (*pitṛ*), one who feeds on the rice-balls that constitute the basic ingredient of the post-cremation rituals in the cult of the dead (collectively known as *śrāddha,* derived from *srāddha* 'faith')." Weinberger-Thomas, *Ashes of Immortality,* 79.

18. Parry, "Sacrificial Death," 85.

19. Jonathan P. Parry, *Death in Banaras: The Lewis Henry Morgan Lectures, 1988* (Cambridge: New York: Cambridge University Press, 1994), 5.

20. *Śatapatha Brāhmaṇa* 13.8.2 ff.

21. For a good overview of the regional variation in memorial stones, see Gunther D. Sontheimer, and S. Settar, eds. *Memorial Stones: A Study of Their Origin, Significance and Variety* (Heidelberg: Institute of Indian Art History, Karnatak University, and South Asian Institute, University of Heidelberg, 1982).

22. Stuart H. Blackburn, "Death and Deification: Folk Cults in Hinduism," *History of Religions* 24, no. 3 (1985): 262.

23. See Christopher Pinney, *Camera Indica: The Social Life of Indian Photographs* (Chicago: University of Chicago Press, 1997).

24. For an interesting account of how individuals react to demands that the dead make on the living through dreams, see Weinberger-Thomas on the dreams of women who see the death of their husbands and decide to sacrifice themselves. Weinberger-Thomas, *Ashes of Immortality,* 101–108.

25. Blackburn, "Death and Deification," 255–275.

26. In Himachal Pradesh there are special deities that are known especially for their ability to perform this transformation. Matti Singh, a local deity in the lower Kullu valley, is especially renowned for such a talent, and in the small temple grounds dedicated to this deity are literally hundreds of other deities that were pulled from their state as disembodied *bhūt-pret* to become deified dead.

27. Blackhurn, "Death and Deification," 271.

28. Ibid., 273.

29. David Knipe, "Night of the Growing Dead: A Cult of *Vīrabhadra* in Coastal Andhra," in *Criminal Gods and Demon Devotees: Essays on the Guardians of Popular Hinduism,* ed. Alf Hiltebeitel, 123–157 (Albany: State University of New York Press, 1989).

30. Maurice Bloch, and Jonathan Parry, eds. *Death and the Regeneration of Life* (Cambridge: Cambridge University Press, 1982), 218–219. Quoted in Shalini Randeria, "Mourning, Mortuary Exchange and Memorialization: The Creation of Local Communities among Dalits in Gujarat," in *Ways of Dying: Death and Its Meanings in South Asia,* ed. Elizabeth Schombucher and Claus Peter Zoller (New Delhi: Manohar, 1999), 89.

31. Randeria, "Mourning, Mortuary Exchange and Memorialization," 88. In this area of rural Gujarat, people of the Dalit caste predominantly bury their dead in simple unmarked graves. The practice of burial in Hindu traditions is also present in other castes, including the Naths. See Gold, "Fruitful Journeys," 99–123 for another example of Hindu burials.

32. Randeria, "Mourning, Mortuary Exchange and Memorialization," 90.

33. See Shirley Firth, *Dying, Death and Bereavement in a British Hindu Community* (Leuven: Peeters, 1997).

34. This dispute occurs not only in the diaspora. It also occurred in India (most prominently in the late nineteenth century) and continues there today. For a discussion, see Gyan Prakash, *Another Reason: Science and the Imagination of Modern India* (New Delhi: Oxford University Press, 1999), 86 ff.

Chapter 3

Judaism and Death

Finding Meaning in Ritual

Rebecca Golbert

Aunt Marsha would have thoroughly enjoyed her bat mitzvah-memorial, held on September 13, 2003, at the Beth Shalom Synagogue in San Francisco. It is common to hold a memorial ceremony to mark the close of *shloshim,* the month anniversary of death, but this was much more than a commemoration of my aunt's death; it was a celebration of her life and a continuation of her most passionate goals and values—concerning Judaism, justice, inclusiveness, art, learning, family, and community. Diagnosed with cancer in November 2002, Marsha wanted more than anything to live. In her struggle to tame her body to her extraordinary will, she set herself life-affirming goals—to visit Israel to dance at her nephew Benji's wedding, to see her granddaughter born, and to perform an adult bat mitzvah—an important life-cycle ritual usually conducted upon reaching age thirteen, the age of responsibility in the Jewish tradition, but much less common among women of previous generations. Marsha's bat mitzvah was scheduled for September 13. As my aunt Jane (Benji's mother) described vividly at the memorial, Marsha danced until dawn at Benji's wedding. (In Jane's words, she danced the biblical return of the Israelites to their homeland.) She lived to see her granddaughter, Madison Elizabeth, on several occasions, both at home and later in the hospital. She did not physically make it to her bat mitzvah but succumbed to her illness on August 7. We buried her on August 9, on the eve of the Sabbath.

Marsha's bat mitzvah was held despite her absence, now transformed into a bat mitzvah–memorial or shloshim ceremony. What was most striking about the event was the multiple ways in which Marsha's presence continued to be felt. Rabbi Alan Lew affirmed that we were helping Marsha accomplish her bat mitzvah. Marsha's Torah portion (a designated section of the Torah to be chanted aloud by one or more congregants) was read respectively by her son Paris and daughter Nicole and by Rabbi Lew. The special blessings read before and after the Torah reading were fulfilled by my uncle Toby and my father, two of

> Marsha's brothers. My cousin Chuck and my then fiancé Doug redressed the Torah after the reading. Marsha, living through her family, performed her bat mitzvah splendidly and, in the process, brought us all a little closer to her, to each other, and to Judaism, ensuring the continuity of tradition, family, and community and the continuity of our relationship with Marsha within these realms. In his highly personalized ethnography of Jewish mourning practices, Samuel Heilman writes, "I was struck at how all that we did [as a volunteer in a local *chevra kaddisha,* or Jewish burial society] reflected the continuing community shared by the living with the dead."[1] In reference to his late father, Heilman asserts, "From beyond the grave, he has taught me that death cannot end a relationship."[2]
>
> Rabbi Lew took this notion of a continuing relationship between the living and the dead a step further in his bat mitzvah–memorial sermon, which wove the meaning of the Torah portion Parashat Nitzavim (Deuteromony 29:9–30:20) into a eulogy for Marsha. He suggested that this portion epitomized Marsha's life. The portion began with words calling for an inclusive community—one that would incorporate the young and the old, the elite and the laborers, Jews and also non-Jews. The text went further, he argued, to include within the boundaries of the community even those who were absent, those who had come before but were no longer present, and those who had yet to arrive. In other words, the dead and those yet to be born were also intimately woven into the fabric of the living community. The Torah portion ended with words calling on the people of Israel to choose life over death, to embrace life and live it to its fullest. Rabbi Lew offered this interpretation: there are those who are dead even while they are alive, and there are those who have lived life so fully that it seems they are still alive even after they have died. Marsha exemplified the latter.

This chapter examines Jewish responses to death and mourning from several perspectives, both scholarly and personal. The textual and ritual traditions of Judaism provide a symbolic and historical framework in which to understand the Jewish experience of death. At the same time, the diversity of Judaism across time and space reveals a variety of beliefs and practices surrounding dying, death, burial, and bereavement. Jewish responses to death and mourning reflect a quest for the ultimate meaning of life and death. Like other religions, Judaism in its many forms responds to this vexing question of the meaning of human existence in the face of death by offering a symbolic system of beliefs and rituals to sustain and nurture the ongoing community and to assuage its fears of discontinuity and oblivion. In its exploration of contemporary death rituals, this chapter uncovers tensions within contemporary Judaism between tradition and modernity, continuity and change, consensus and diversity. These tensions echo within the literature on death and Judaism, written from the perspective of rabbis and other Jewish thinkers, and within ethnographic accounts of the Jewish experience of death. Such tensions show themselves most clearly in the juxtaposition of these two contexts, revealing a gap between doctrine and practice, prescribed ritual and ethnographic reality.

It is my goal to place the understanding of Jewish responses to death and mourning within the framework of contemporary Judaism while also probing the limits of that framework and its capacity for change. How do Jewish beliefs and customs surrounding death respond to the challenges posed by medical technology, social and physical mobility, urbanization, secularization, and cultural pluralism? How have sweeping social and political changes impacted Jewish mourning and memorialization practices in different regions of the world? While building on the ethical discussions, philosophical observations, and prescriptive narratives of Jewish thinkers who seek to guide Jews through the "Jewish way" of death and mourning, this chapter relies on ethnographic methods of fieldwork and participant observation, both in the United States and in Ukraine, to expose the greater complexities and contingencies of the Jewish experience of death in real life. In its quest to address the variation of Jewish responses to and meanings of death for those most intimately confronted with its power, this chapter inevitably probes the broader implications of Jewish cultural and religious diversity for the continuity of Judaism and Jewish tradition.

After a brief introduction to Judaism and to the historical development of Jewish death rituals and beliefs, this chapter addresses the ethical dilemmas of death and dying in a Jewish context. Faced with the growing medicalization and professionalization of the process of dying, what constitutes a good Jewish death? The chapter then describes beliefs and practices concerning the preparation for burial, the burial ceremony, and the regulated period of mourning that follows the funeral. The chapter also addresses the impact of the Holocaust on contemporary Jewish responses to death and to life. Finally, the chapter looks at Jewish cemeteries and their role in death education and Jewish historical continuity.

THE PHILOSOPHY OF JUDAISM

Judaism brings together God, the people known as Israel, and Torah within a single symbolic system. As one of the foremost Jewish thinkers of the twentieth century, Abraham Joshua Heschel, asserts, the survival of Judaism and Jews depends on the balancing of these three elements—love of God, love of Israel, and love of Torah.[3] Contemporary rabbis affirm the continuing centrality of God at the heart of Judaism despite modern attempts to rationalize and naturalize the religion to bring it into line with other fashionable doctrines and creeds.[4] David Wolpe writes:

> God is central to Judaism in a way that argument or embarrassment (in this case closely allied) cannot alter. If we are uncomfortable with God, or rejecting, we must at least realize that we reject a central column of Judaism. Belief in God may violate our reason, our sensitivities, even our understanding of justice and goodness; if so, let us at least understand how much of the Jewish tradition is thereby lost.[5]

While this belief in God is fundamental to the meaning of Judaism, the faith of individuals alone cannot sustain Judaism. Judaism has no meaning, no past or future, outside the bounds of community. Thus Heschel probes his own conscience and answers:

> Why is my belonging to the Jewish people the most sacred relation to me, second only to my relation to God?. . . For us Jews there can be no fellowship with God without the fellowship with Israel. Abandoning Israel, we desert God.
>
> Judaism is not only the adherence to particular doctrines and observances but primarily the living in the spiritual order of the Jewish people, the living in the Jews of the past and with the Jews of the present. Judaism is not only a certain quality in the souls of the individuals but primarily the existence of the community of Israel.[6]

The community can survive the life of the individual. The individual, however, cannot survive the life of the community. The historical nature of the Jewish community reinforces the connection between the dead and the living, between the past and the future, thereby preserving the life of the community in the present. In Heschel's words, "[t]he vertical unity of Israel is essential to the horizontal unity of *klal Israel* [all the people of Israel]."[7]

But if Judaism is a monotheistic religion rooted in community, what traditions bind its members together? What ritual and discursive memories are transmitted from generation to generation? What elements of Judaism continue to provide sustenance and meaning to the community despite internal differences of culture, language, and philosophy that reach across time and space? Judaism transforms the everyday life of the community through prayers and rituals, many of which date back over 2,000 years. Such prayers and rituals have been preserved within the written and oral traditions of Judaism, that is, within the five sacred books of the Torah and later in the Talmudic literature of the postbiblical, rabbinic tradition covering the first six centuries of the Common Era.[8] David Ariel writes, "Torah is the foundation of Jewish thought and the source of Jewish behavior."[9] Thus, this third element of the triad of Judaism is also fundamental to the preservation and continuation of Jewish tradition, marking it as a religion that transforms the mundane into the sacred through words and rites of enchantment enacted in every generation.[10]

Jacob Neusner speaks in fact of two Judaisms, the Judaism of the dual Torah (written and oral) and the Judaism of Holocaust and Redemption. He suggests that these two Judaisms coexist side by side in the private and public lives of Jews, be they Reform, Conservative, Orthodox, Reconstructionist, affiliated with a synagogue, or unaffiliated. The Judaism of the dual Torah enchants and transforms through traditional rites and festivals of home and family. The Judaism of Holocaust and Redemption evokes deep emotions on behalf of political issues in the corporate community.[11] This second Judaism speaks to an overriding concern with justice and freedom in the Jewish tradition and to the need to reevaluate the meaning and purpose of Judaism in the wake of the devastation of the Holocaust. Whether or not the private and public lives and passions of Jews—save the most observant Orthodox whose lives revolve fully around the Judaism of the dual Torah[12]—can truly be separated into two Judaisms as Neusner suggests, the implication that a meaningful Judaism in the post-Holocaust era must address suffering and despair in both the private and public worlds of Jews finds strong support in the writings of Heschel and Wolpe. Wolpe confronts the most private level of despair:

> Ultimately, we want to touch what God means in the most pained and private chambers of the human soul. Where anguish is greatest, the religious message is most significant. If God does not speak to suffering, to the shattered hearts of the Psalmist's plea, then He must remain peripheral to our lives. That which does not touch my pain leaves me as I was.[13]

Heschel stresses to the communal level of suffering, the need for Judaism to carry a collective burden rooted in real suffering in its quest for the meaning of Jewish and human existence:

> Judaism is not a chapter in the history of philosophy. It does not lend itself to be a subject of reflection for armchair philosophers. Its understanding cannot be attained in the comfort of playing a chess game of theories. Only ideas that are meaningful to those who are steeped in misery may be accepted as principles by those who dwell in safety. In trying to understand Jewish existence a Jewish philosopher must look for agreement with the men of Sinai as well as with the people of Auschwitz.[14]

The study of Jewish responses to death is rooted in this same tradition. In its examination of Jewish beliefs and customs of burial and mourning, this chapter probes the capacity of Judaism to bring meaningful transformation and continuity to those individuals and communities who suffer the greatest anguish and despair.

THE DIVERSITY OF JUDAISM

Contemporary Judaism is by no means homogeneous in its approach to the world and the place of Jews within it. The different movements of Judaism take (and have taken) very different social, political, and philosophical stances in relation to the larger societies in which they find themselves. So, too, they have responded in diverse ways to the challenges posed by political movements (including Zionism), modern technologies, migration, secularization, social integration, and cultural and religious pluralism. While ultra-Orthodox Judaism has developed an antimodernist strategy of social and physical segregation from the larger society in an effort to preserve a religious lifestyle defined solely by the values and principles of Torah, other movements of Judaism—including modern Orthodox, Conservative, Reform, and Reconstructionist branches—seek to negotiate a range of compromises between the traditions of Judaism and the demands of a modern, secular world. Such compromises find articulation in language, liturgy, dress, ritual practice, food customs, social and gendered behavior, community relations, political outlooks, and religious philosophies. The Conservative movement has consistently sought the middle ground between the social and religious adaptations of the Reform and the literal interpretations of Jewish law and practice of the Orthodox. The debates among the Orthodox and the Reform and Conservative movements of Judaism concern at their heart different approaches to the impact of social change and historical development on Judaism and the degree to which that impact is or should be acknowledged.[15] The smaller branch of Reconstructionism broke off from Conservative Judaism but continues to influence the Reform and Conservative movements with its emphasis on Jewish peoplehood, religious practice, and a this-worldly, naturalist definition of God.[16]

In the United States, the Conservative and Reform movements have the strongest hold on the Jewish population, claiming the loyalties of almost four-fifths of American Jews.[17] Over the past century, these movements have most successfully accommodated the struggle of American Jews to assert dual belonging—to the Jewish world and to the secular world of American and Western society. In Europe and other regions of the world, the majority of Jews, regardless of their level of daily observance, maintain an affiliation with Orthodox Judaism, which continues to dominate through official political and religious avenues. In Israel, Orthodox Judaism maintains its dominance through official state and legal channels. In these societies, the Reform and Conservative movements often play a marginal role in the life of the Jewish community. In some renewed contexts of religious organizational activity, such as in eastern Europe and the former Soviet Union, tensions among the movements of contemporary Judaism may lead to battles for hegemony over the hearts and minds of local Jews.

Because the dominance in different societies of one or another movement of Judaism may at times be as much political as religious, it is difficult to describe all Jews affiliated with Orthodox Judaism as highly observant or religious. So, too, belonging to Reform or Conservative denominations of Judaism does not necessarily make an individual less observant or traditional. The antimodernist ultra-Orthodox lifestyle notwithstanding, the application of rigid categories of Judaism may, at times, prove highly problematic, as may the application of the term *observance* to describe Orthodox Jewry alone. Although faced with certain cultural and religious constraints on Jewish membership and belonging, contemporary Jewry has become quite adept at moving across the ascribed categories of Judaism, selecting among traditional and innovative beliefs and practices and frequently blurring their boundaries.

THE HISTORICAL DEVELOPMENT OF JEWISH DEATH RITUALS AND BELIEFS

Despite their roots in the Torah and the Talmud, Jewish burial and mourning traditions have changed significantly over time. Practices and beliefs that Jews today would call traditional may have had no currency in the Talmudic or post-Talmudic eras, absent from the writings of then contemporary Jewish scholars. Death practices described in the Talmudic literature (first through sixth century CE) may be unrecognizable to Jews observing Jewish law today.[18] While elements of some practices and beliefs have survived the generations, their forms and meanings have experienced numerous transformations. An attempt to reconstruct the historical development of Jewish practices and beliefs surrounding death faces many hurdles, posed by the diversity of Jewish traditions spanning world regions and historical eras but also by the lack of scholarship on the subject. For this reason, only some of the rituals and beliefs described in the following sections have a known history. Beliefs about the afterlife, for example, can be traced to the Talmudic period;[19] the origins of the connection of the *kaddish* (a prayer recited in memory of the dead) to death and mourning, however, leave fewer clues.[20] The Talmudic customs of *shiva* (initial seven-day period of mourning) carry over to the present day, although not all elements required of mourners remain.[21] Significantly, the custom of reburial, documented in the Talmudic literature, has largely been forgotten.[22] The post-Talmudic sources occasionally reveal a divide between the prescriptions of the rabbinic authorities and popular practices—such as washing hands upon returning from the cemetery—which continue to this day.[23] This gap between official doctrine and ethnographic practice will be seen in the pages that follow, although it is not always well-documented in the commentaries of contemporary rabbis.

Though no comprehensive account traces the historical development of Jewish death rituals to the present day, scholarship on the history of Jewish beliefs of the afterlife has a more solid foundation. While the Bible contains few references to the afterlife, leading to various interpretations of the meaning of that silence,[24] later rabbis, beginning from the Second Temple period (fifth century BCE to 70 CE), heatedly debated the question of life after death. Ariel explains: "The Sadducees, the priestly nobility, many of whom were biblical literalists, did not believe in an afterlife. The Pharisees, the predecessors of rabbinic Judaism, who believed in the existence of the separate soul, subscribed to the theory of the afterlife."[25] By the rabbinic era (first through sixth centuries CE), beliefs about life after death had developed to include concepts of reward and punishment in the afterlife for actions in this world. The righteous would be rewarded in the heavenly Garden of Eden; the wicked would be punished in Gehinnom.[26] The rabbis were not of one mind, however, about the nature of Gehinnom. How long did the wicked dwell in purgatory? After one year, were they purged of their wickedness and permitted to join others in the Garden of Eden, as Rabbi Akiva suggested, or were they annihilated forever? Debates about the nature of Gehinnom continued in the Middle Ages. Mystics vividly described its horrors (most likely influenced by non-Jewish medieval texts), while rationalists like the twelfth-century Jewish philosopher Maimonides denied its very existence. For Maimonides, the Garden of Eden and Gehinnom were metaphors rather than places, signifying intellectual communion with God or its absence.[27]

The Jewish mystics of the Middle Ages further developed the concept of the immortality of the soul, suggesting that the connection between the body and the soul ends at death. The body dies but the soul returns to its source—to God. While the body and the soul take separate journeys in the afterlife, this process of separation takes time; the soul may travel back and forth between the grave and the heavens during the shiva period and even during the first year after death. Along with the concept of the immortality of the soul, Jewish mystics debated the concept of transmigration of souls, a version of reincarnation. Was transmigration a form of punishment for past sins or was it an opportunity for repentance, an act of divine mercy saving the soul from Gehinnom and allowing it to contribute a second time to humanity?[28]

The concept of the resurrection of the dead has roots in the Book of Daniel, which prophesied a day of judgment at the end of the messianic era in which the Messiah would redeem the world and the dead would rise up.[29] On that day of judgment, individuals would account for their actions one final time, to be rewarded with eternal life in the time to come (*olam ha-ba*) or condemned to Gehinnom. The messianic age and the time to come that succeeds it, however, remain great unknowns, despite attempts in the rabbinic and later eras to describe these worlds in some detail. Although Maimonides offered the most systematic account of these peaceful and spiritual worlds to come, Ariel suggests that Maimonides most likely did not believe in the bodily resurrection of the dead, describing instead an unattainable ideal belonging eternally to the future.[30]

Jewish conceptions of the afterlife and the role of the body and soul within those conceptions remain sources of debate in the contemporary Jewish world. While Orthodox Jewish thinkers continue to emphasize the resurrection of the body in the messianic age, others, most notably in the Reform movement, reject bodily resurrection in favor of the immortality of the soul.[31] Alan Ponn notes that in this noncreedal religion, Jews are not obliged to believe in any view of the afterlife: "It would not be surprising, therefore, to encounter a few Jews who still believe the early biblical view that there is no afterworld";[32] as noted above, this view is also subject to interpretation. Ponn asserts, however, that the majority of Jews do subscribe to some concept of the afterworld. Ron Wolfson, on the other hand, calls attention to alternative Jewish approaches that emphasize immortality in this world through descendants, through deeds, and through a common destiny with the Jewish people.[33] Memory, continuity, and community are fundamental to these interpretations of an afterlife propagated on earth rather than in heaven.

Just as for Jewish rituals of death and mourning, a textual reading of Jewish beliefs about the afterlife does not necessarily coincide with popular beliefs and practices. Ordinary Jews may indeed be conflicted about the emphasis within contemporary Judaism on this world, the here and now, compared to the continued prevalence of concepts of heaven, hell, immortality, and resurrection in religious liturgy, Jewish teaching, and Jewish (Hasidic) storytelling. The events of the Holocaust have sowed further doubt in both this-worldly and other-worldly approaches to Jewish continuity and immortality.[34] As we shall see, the persistence of conflicting ideas within the main movements of Judaism about what happens to the body and soul in the afterlife shapes popular Jewish understandings of the integrity of the body and what entails a proper burial. So, too, the spectrum of Jewish responses to the afterlife affects how the living continue to relate to the deceased after burial. In this way, beliefs about the afterlife and rites of death and mourning are clearly intertwined.

A GOOD JEWISH DEATH?

Every death poses the threat of individual and collective discontinuity, as the anthropologist Barbara Myerhoff notes in her classic ethnographic account of a marginalized community of elderly Jews who confront death and mortality on a far too frequent basis.[35] Myerhoff describes the "drama of continuity" sparked by the death of one distinguished member in their midst, Jacob. Jacob died during his ninety-fifth birthday party, transforming the celebration of his long life into its commemoration. That Jacob died in his chair after completing his birthday speech reflected his tremendous determination to live and die as he chose, to transcend his own death by seemingly controlling his own destiny. For the members of the community in attendance, Jacob had a good death:

> Said Moshe, "You see, it is the Jewish way to die in your community. In the old days, it was an honor to wash the body of the dead. No one went away and died with strangers in a hospital. The finest people dressed the corpse, and no one left him alone for a minute. So Jacob died like a good Yid [Yiddish vernacular for Jew]. Not everybody is so lucky."
>
> Over and over, people discussed the goodness of Jacob's death and its appropriateness. Many insisted that they had known beforehand he would die that day. "So why else do you think I had my *yarmulkah* with me at a birthday party?" asked Beryl.
>
> . . .
>
> It was a good death, it was agreed. Jacob was a lucky man. "*Zu mir gezugt,* it should happen to me," was heard from the lips of many as they left.[36]

Heilman suggests that the desire for a "good death" in the Jewish tradition includes the desire to die without pain, at the end of a long life, in the company of loved ones, preferably at home and not in the hospital. Still, it includes something more in the spiritual and mystical realm. Just as Myerhoff's community compares Jacob's death to that of Elijah the prophet, who also died in his chair, or to Moses, who also died on his birthday, Heilman states, "Thus, a good Jewish death is one that happened at a spiritually auspicious time."[37] It may be on the eve of the Sabbath, during the High Holidays, or at some other auspicious time that confirms the spiritual goodness of the death. In the case of his own father, Heilman and his family seek comfort in knowing that "He died in his armchair, at home with his wife . . . on the eve of the Sabbath. . . . The anguish of his death would be softened by the serenity of the Sabbath."[38] My uncle Jack found solace in knowing that Aunt Marsha died on the ninth of Av, a symbolic day of fasting that commemorates the destruction of the Second Temple in 70 CE, and all subsequent tragedies of the Jewish people, an auspicious day on which to join one's memory to the memory of the Jewish people.

This powerful desire for a good death, however, is complicated in the contemporary world by the medicalization and the professionalization of death and dying. Rabbis and scholars of Jewish ethics and tradition complain that advances in medical technology pose new challenges for living and dying in a Jewish way. New technologies prolong life and reduce pain, but they also may diminish consciousness and severely strain communication. Although the desire for a good death remains a powerful force, many people actually experience death in the sterile isolation of a hospital room, attached to tubes and wires, unable to communicate with their loved ones in an intelligible way, leaving any form of closure elusive both for the dying and for those close to them.[39] Jack Riemer also traces the impact of what he calls "medical mythology" on the culture of death and dying. Medical mythology refers to the collusion of the medical system in "a conspiracy of silence" that "sets in around the terminally ill patient" and fails to confront the reality of death in an honest, dignified way.[40] By hiding or disguising death, medical mythology removes death from the home, the family, and the community and from its rightful place in the life cycle. At the same time, the professionalization of the burial process has transferred significant responsibilities from the family and the community to strangers in distant funeral homes and cemeteries. The services of the local chevra kaddisha, which previously was responsible for burial preparations in most Jewish communities, are now maintained in only traditional, predominantly Orthodox communities.

Much of the literature on death and Judaism struggles to mediate the impact of modernity on the Jewish way of living and dying and to rehabilitate Jewish traditions in a changing world. These texts offer Jewish responses to end-of-life treatments, autopsies, and the dilemmas of euthanasia and organ donation. They also seek to regain control of the rituals of dying, death, and mourning. While these scholars successfully place the experience of death and dying in a Jewish idiom, their prescriptive writings and "advance directives" cannot possibly capture the heart-wrenching complexity of real-life dilemmas surrounding end-of-life decision making and the burial and mourning process. As a result, mourners are left doubting both the medical system in which they placed their faith and the Jewish tradition in which they seek solace and sanctity for their loved ones. They are left wondering whether their loved ones did indeed experience a good Jewish death.

JEWISH APPROACHES TO END-OF-LIFE DECISION MAKING

Judaism, perhaps more than other religious traditions, emphasizes the preservation of life (*pikuah nefesh*) in this world over the world to come. This deeply ingrained attitude of saving life affects Jewish attitudes toward sedation, medical intervention, forms of active and passive euthanasia, and organ donation. William Kavesh, a geriatric physician and Jewish medical ethicist, asserts that Judaism in all its contemporary forms (Orthodox, Conservative, Reform) condemns active euthanasia and assisted suicide, noting that the ultimate authority for life and death lies with God. However, he suggests that Jewish thinking on other forms of medical intervention and nonintervention is far more nuanced. For example, Jewish thinkers disagree about the relief of pain when sedation may increase the risk of death. Some suggest that Judaism endorses "the preservation of life over the relief of pain"; others assert that "adequate sedation should be given to patients in great pain even if there is a risk of suppressing respiratory drive and shortening life."[41] Even within a single religious movement, Kavesh finds no consensus:

> The Committee on Jewish Law and Standards of the Conservative movement actually has validated two different positions as having legitimacy in these matters. One position asserts that intent to treat is the crucial factor; administration of a high dose of morphine and other pain medications might be required to relieve pain, although this could suppress the respiratory system and simultaneously hasten death. . . . The other position disagrees, stating that the ultimate consequence of death, regardless of intent, overrides the benefits.[42]

If Judaism condemns active euthanasia and assisted suicide and weighs the risks involved in the treatment of suffering and pain, where does it stand on active intervention to preserve and prolong life? Kavesh and Heilman point to highly nuanced discussions in the Talmud and other classic Jewish sources. Early Jewish thinkers sought to allow death (*petira*) to occur "naturally," neither postponed nor brought on prematurely by active intervention. Contemporary Jewish thinkers draw on these early sources to argue that while the death of a person in the dying condition (*goses*) must not be hastened in any way, it need not be delayed by life-prolonging measures such as antibiotics for pneumonia or a feeding tube for one who can no longer eat.[43]

Such guidelines for life-and-death decision making rely on the ability to determine that death is imminent, that a person is goses, in a dying condition. Who is granted the authority to make that determination? Does a family consider it only when the doctors, concluding that the death of a loved one is inevitable, recommend the cessation of life-preserving treatment? Does not the cessation of treatment—and most of all the cessation of hope that accompanies this medical resignation—precipitate death? What constitutes necessary and unnecessary intervention thus often remains unclear. When does the discontinuation of treatment remove an impediment to death? When does it hasten death to occur prematurely? Kavesh notes that debate continues in this area of Jewish thinking among all movements of Judaism. For example:

> There are two positions accepted by the Conservative movement as legitimate options regarding care of the terminally ill. One permits the withdrawal of the terminally ill from respirators as well as antibiotics, artificial nutrition, and hydration. . . . The second permits the withdrawal of machinery but not nutrition and hydration.[44]

Such medically defined approaches largely overlook or at least seriously restrict the autonomy of the patient, or a guardian on the patient's behalf, in determining whether to live or to die. Real-life examples prove much more complicated than the ethical discussions of Jewish thinkers let on. For my aunt Marsha, quality-of-life issues conflicted with her tremendous will to live and pushed her to test the limits of medical technology, including chemotherapy, radiation, and experimental drugs. Even after her doctors had given up on her—hesitant to treat her raging pneumonia strengthened by an embattled immune system, resistant to putting her on a respirator when she could no longer breathe on her own due to a collapsed lung—Marsha was still fighting to survive, adamant that her doctors and family and friends fight with her and for her. Jewish ethicists, I imagine, would clearly have resigned themselves, like her doctors, to the inevitability of death and recommended against the final decision to put Marsha on a respirator. Indeed when our family witnessed Marsha in intensive care, struggling in vain to maintain consciousness and the ability to communicate, dependent on the respirator and a web of tubes for all her bodily functions, ultimately denied her autonomy in the fullest sense of the word, we, too, were left to grapple with enormous ethical dilemmas about the power and limitations of medical technology and the significance of quality-of-life and quality-of-death issues. How did Marsha get to this point? Should treatment have been stopped, and when? When Marsha finally died a few days after being placed on the respirator, none of us was convinced that she had experienced a "good death," despite my uncle Jack's consolation that she had died on the ninth of Av. We nonetheless came to realize that for Marsha, a good death was the result of a good fight, regardless of the mental and physical costs.

PREPARATION OF THE BODY FOR BURIAL

The body in the Jewish tradition must be treated with respect and dignity but also with simplicity. It is viewed as a divine gift,[45] as "the creation and property of God."[46] Jewish customs preceding the funeral reflect this reverence for the body. The preparation of the body for burial—called *tahara*—entails a ritual washing and shrouding of the body. This ritual of purification cleanses the body of the initial impurities of death (the body before tahara is caught in the liminal, impure status of *niftar*).[47] While the local chevra kaddisha may continue to perform this duty in traditional Jewish communities, tahara has become increasingly professionalized, removed from the sphere of the immediate family and community.[48] Relatives and friends did not witness the preparation of Marsha's body for burial. Marsha's best friend Jennifer deeply regretted not having ritually washed her body as a final act of love and friendship.

In addition to washing and shrouding the body before burial, someone is expected to watch over the body until it is laid to rest in the grave. With the removal of the body to a funeral home, however, this obligation has also become increasingly difficult to fulfill. Jewish beliefs in the integrity of the human body and in the protection of the body until burial have historically established a strong tradition of opposition to autopsies and organ donation. Both procedures violate the wholeness of the human body after death, raising questions about proper burial and also about the afterlife—as many Jews believe that the body will eventually be resurrected and must remain intact. The practice of cremation raises these same concerns, its perception as "an unnatural means of treating the human body" heightened by the Holocaust.[49] In reality, Jewish authorities in the Reform, Conservative, and Orthodox traditions have revised their thinking on organ donation and autopsy. In those cases where autopsy or organ donation can be shown to save life (pikuah nefesh), these procedures are deemed consistent with Jewish values of preserving life over death and are indeed mandated.[50] A gap remains, however, between changes in official Jewish thinking on the subject and the continuation of popular Jewish beliefs in the integrity of the body.

Jewish tradition also prescribes simplicity in the preparation of the body for burial. The body is wrapped in a simple white shroud or *kittel* (the white garment worn by traditional Jews on Yom Kippur) and placed in a plain wooden coffin. These traditions, recognizing the inequalities of social status in life, seek to ensure equality in death. They also encourage the natural decomposition of the body and thus typically reject the practice of embalming.[51] Consequently, Jewish burial normally takes place within two days. Jewish traditions notably diverge from other cultural and religious traditions in which the choice of clothing and coffin may reflect the family's final act of respect for the newly deceased (just as elaborate tombstones may signal the prestige of an individual within a community). Thus Marsha's husband Jerry, in a bittersweet moment of comic relief, was wracked with guilt at the funeral home when he was encouraged to choose a simple pine box, despite his inclination (having been raised as a good Catholic boy) to select a more elaborate, expensive coffin as a show of love, devotion, and generosity. I should note that the preservation of Jewish burial traditions in mixed marriages is largely overlooked in the literature on death and Judaism. While I did come across a few authors who sought to address how a Jew should mourn a non-Jewish loved one, no one asked what are the obligations of a non-Jew in mourning for a Jew.

JEWISH BURIAL RITES

Aunt Marsha's funeral contained all the necessary, sacred elements of a Jewish burial, and it transformed all who were present. The traditional Jewish elements of the ceremony carried a symbolic power that tied this Jewish funeral to those that had come before and those that would follow, enfolding my aunt into a historical community rich with cultural meaning and making the moment of her funeral greater and more significant than ourselves. At the same time, many of the sacred rites woven into the ceremony were personally meaningful for those present, even if they had never experienced them before, even if they were not Jewish. Finally, the very presence at the funeral of a large population of family and friends, students and colleagues, from different religious, ethnic, racial, and economic backgrounds, brought many to tears, knowing that the gathering together of a diverse community of people to celebrate the beauty of life and to mourn its passing was what my aunt had indeed lived for. The streaming in of so many people in time for the funeral was made even more significant by the short notice that Jewish funerals permit: Marsha died on Wednesday night and was buried at midday on Friday. My uncle had called many people; many more came by word of mouth.

The ceremony was conducted at the graveside. Rabbi Lew called on everyone present to come closer together to encircle the grave. He began by "rending the garments" of the immediate family, a symbolic act of rending the deceased from her family.[52] For most, this meant cutting a black ribbon worn on the right lapel, representing the traditional "rent garment." Marsha's brother Jack, more observant than the rest of the family, cut the lapel of his own shirt, which he then wore the rest of the week while sitting shiva (the seven days of mourning that follow the funeral). Rabbi Lew led the gathering in the recitation of prayers designated for mourning the dead, psalms 23 and 90, which offer comfort to the mourners, and the beautiful chant *el molei rachamim,* with its haunting melody recalling all those who have come before. Having met with Marsha's family on the eve of the funeral and listened with care to the reflections that flowed from the mouths of the bereaved—stories of Marsha as sister, wife, mother, aunt, teacher, friend, and muse—Rabbi Lew proceeded to give a eulogy that drew strongly on these reminiscences as well as on his own knowledge of Marsha as a longtime congregant and friend (this eulogy developed into his sermon at the bat mitzvah–memorial described above). Marsha's three brothers then gave eulogies of their own, each in his own way paying tribute to Marsha and probing the meaning of her life for the community that survives her. In their own very different styles, my uncles and my father each asked: How can we, personally and collectively, move beyond our aching sorrow and yet continue to remember and draw sustenance from Marsha's life? How can we ensure that she is not forgotten, that all that she stood for is not cast away, that a part of her continues to live on in each one of us?

With the completion of the eulogy, the mourners stepped aside to allow the pallbearers —an honor given to relatives and friends of the deceased—to carry the coffin to the grave. After the coffin was lowered into the grave, Rabbi Lew called family members forward to shovel earth onto the coffin. He welcomed all others who wished to do so to join in this physical and symbolic act of covering the grave. Many scholars note the power of this traditional rite during the Jewish funeral. Cytron explains: "For many, it symbolizes a powerful way of accepting the finality of the death as well as a means by which those in attendance illustrate their concern for the deceased's vulnerability by seeing to a proper burial."[53] Heilman describes his own experience of confronting the finality of death during the act of shoveling earth on his father's grave: "As I held onto my mother and wife, staring through tear-soaked eyes into the abyss of my father's open grave, watching my sons shovel earth into it, I—like so many before me—at last confronted death not as some stranger lurking in the shadows or the object of an anthropologist's curiosity. Death became my father."[54] In her ethnographic account, Myerhoff vividly describes this moment at Jacob's funeral:

> Spontaneously, at the graveside, without benefit of direction from funeral officials, many old men and women came forward to throw a shovelful of earth on the grave, sometimes teetering from the effort. Each one carefully laid down the shovel after finishing, according to custom. Then they backed away, forming two rows, to allow the Angel of Death to pass through. They knew from old usage what was appropriate, what movements and gestures suited the occasion, with a certainty that is rarely seen in their present lives.[55]

At Marsha's funeral, this moment of taking turns to shovel earth on her coffin, as many shovelfuls as each individual had the strength for, brought the ceremony to a climax. Watching my father, my uncles, and my cousins shovel earth into the open grave blurred my vision with tears. When my turn came to peer down into the grave, I staggered, forced against my will to confront the realness of death as I witnessed the body returned to the earth from which it came. As family members completed their turns and sought each other out for comfort in their grief, they looked back to see the line extending beyond the immediate family to include extended relatives, friends, colleagues, and former students. For many, participation in this rite was not "from old usage," and yet the meaning they drew from participating in this act, their faces soaked with tears, was palpable. As they participated in this ritual, they also altered it; many, having brought flowers to the funeral (not traditionally a Jewish death custom), threw them into the grave along with the earth they shoveled.

The ceremony came to a close with the collective recitation of the mourner's kaddish. This prayer, which never mentions death but instead praises and blesses God, is chanted collectively in remembrance of the dead on many significant occasions: at the funeral, in the days and months to come during the period of mourning, in the years that follow during the *yahrzeit* (anniversary) of the dead, and at other select moments of the Jewish calendar when *yizkor* (a traditional service of remembrance) is observed. Anita Diamant writes about the power of the kaddish prayer in terms both of the meaning of its words (it was written in Aramaic, once the vernacular language of the Jews) and the repetition of its sounds:

> The mystery of Kaddish is revealed every time it is spoken aloud with others. The truth is that the sounds of the words are more important than their definitions. The text is secondary to the emotional experience of its recitation. The meaning only comes clear when given communal voice.

> Even so, the words are not insignificant. Kaddish addresses the meaning of life and death, immortality and redemption, the purpose and efficacy of prayer, community, and the ultimate goal of peace. It even speaks—in its silence—about the predominant Jewish view of the afterlife.
>
> . . .
>
> But the bottom line is startlingly clear. In words and through practice, Kaddish insists that the mourner turn away from death and choose life.[56]

Myerhoff too emphasizes the power of the kaddish prayer to bring together a community and ensure its social and spiritual continuity. At the celebration-turned-commemoration of Jacob, the recitation of the kaddish was a spontaneous collective response that became a transformational moment for all present, both generalizing and particularizing the significance of Jacob's death for each individual:

> The Kaddish prayer was probably the most important single ritual that occurred the day of Jacob's death. It was the most frequently and deeply experienced aspect of Jewish custom for the people there, the most ethnically rooted moment, sweeping together all the individuals present, connecting them with earlier parts of self, with Jacob the man, with each other, and with Jews who had lived and died before.[57]

In the religiously diverse community that gathered for Marsha's funeral, the recitation of the kaddish could not have held the same meaning for everyone present. Nonetheless, its collective incantation by those familiar with it (and, I would assert, for those unfamiliar with it) was eerily moving, its sounds choking the participants with tears as they formed them. Like the rite of placing earth on the grave, it confirmed the finality of death and placed the emphasis on remembrance. Unlike the stark ritual of shoveling earth on the coffin, the mourner's prayer reassured us of the continuity of our relationship with the deceased, with each other, and with those who had come before and were yet to come. The kaddish alone, of all the prayers and rituals enacted the day of the burial, would remain a significant part of the mourning process in the aftermath of the funeral.

Although Marsha's funeral had essentially concluded and the cemetery officials sought to "finish the job" of filling the grave with earth, Marsha's son Paris, joined by a handful of other male relatives, resumed the task of shoveling earth onto the coffin, unwilling to relinquish this task to strangers. This need to cover her grave personally reflected a powerful urge to protect my aunt in her vulnerable, defenseless state. Perhaps, for Paris, this was also a physical act of taming death, wrestling it down by hand, and in so doing, affirming that despite the earth that now separated them, his relationship to his mother and his protection of her could not be severed by anyone or anything.

As we prepared to leave the graveside, Rabbi Lew invited family and friends to return to the home of the bereaved for the meal of consolation as well as to visit the home during the week of shiva. How can the bereaved attend to guests in their home on such a day as this? The tradition intends, on the contrary, to bring the community into the home to attend to the bereaved. This process continues throughout the week that the family sits shiva. Relatives and friends prepare the meal of consolation, which often includes eggs, symbolic of the cycle of life and death. For many mourners outside the immediate family, this is the first visit to the home after the death of the loved one. The presence of the deceased remains palpable in the house of mourning. The traditional meal after the funeral is meant to reinforce that life continues after death, that the living must go on living within a community and not in isolation.

THE JEWISH PERIOD OF MOURNING

Recognizing that grief does not diminish in the aftermath of the funeral, Judaism imposes a structure of mourning that marks certain periods of the coming months and years in significant ways. Like other rites of passage, Jewish rituals of mourning occur as a transformative process over time, during which the mourner passes through different stages of grief and healing. Diamant describes this structure of time:

> The blueprint for the mourner's "cathedral" [a reference to Heschel's description of Jewish ritual as "architecture of time"] can be imagined as a series of concentric circles defined by the passage of the first week, the first month, the first year, and the anniversary of a death. The innermost circle is the darkest, but as the weeks pass, mourners move from the dimness of remembering and weeping to the light of rejoicing in the memory of life.[58]

The initial seven-day period of mourning, called shiva, acknowledges that the family of the deceased is not yet ready to reenter society but needs time to act out and talk through feelings of grief and despair. The family must come to terms with the tremendous rupture and loss that death incurs before the healing process can begin. During the week of shiva, relatives and friends visit the mourners, bring food, share their memories and stories of the deceased, and participate in the repetition of the kaddish (for which a *minyan,* or quorum of ten, is needed) at both a morning service and an evening service that are held in the home in place of the synagogue. In remembrance, the family also lights a yahrzeit candle that burns throughout the week. The presence of members of the community within the home acts as a bridge between the isolation of the mourners and the everyday life continuing outside the home, helping to ease the inevitable transition to the resumption of personal, social, and professional responsibilities. However, the seven-day period of shiva is sometimes complicated by contemporary realities that reflect growing secularization and religious pluralism.

How does a Jewish family in mourning contain within its boundaries the needs and actions of its more and less observant members, its Jewish and non-Jewish members? For whom is shiva (like other mourning rituals) enacted? Was it for my aunt Marsha, who would have desired that her family observe her death in a Jewish way? Was it for her brother Jack, whose Orthodox ways commanded that the full seven days of shiva be observed through traditional ritual and the recitation of the kaddish with a proper quorum of ten Jewish men? Was it for her husband Jerry and children Nicole and Paris, who struggled to overcome their tremendous sense of loss but did not necessarily find comfort in all the traditional Jewish customs and restrictions? Whose needs and actions take precedence in the home of mourning?

Tensions over tradition were evident at Marsha's home as family and friends of diverse backgrounds gathered in the days that followed the funeral. Those who came to pay their condolences and offer their support, both during the meal of consolation and during the week of shiva, were not always knowledgeable about Jewish tradition. In one humorous instance, a couple brought a clam dish (shellfish is forbidden by Jewish law) to the meal of consolation, which observant relatives mistakenly partook of. This food was subsequently removed from the table, marked *treif* (ritually unclean), and hidden in the back of the refrigerator, yet some questioned whether it was appropriate to discard food offered out of respect to the mourning family.

Since the funeral took place on the eve of the Sabbath, shiva was initially postponed by the arrival of Shabbat (the Hebrew word for "Sabbath"), which supersedes the rites of mourning. Observant Jews do no form of work on Shabbat—lighting fire, turning on electricity, answering telephones, cooking, exchanging money. This, in and of itself, created a problem for how to feed a house of mourners, among other things. The most interesting dilemma, in my opinion, concerned the yahrzeit candle, which my family initially lit after returning from the funeral. This candle, which was to burn in memory of my aunt throughout the week, blew out on several occasions and required relighting. When my cousin Nicole noticed that the candle needed relighting during the Sabbath, Aunt Jane gently intervened, suggesting that she wait until that evening, when the Sabbath came to a close. For Nicole, however, preserving the burning light of the yahrzeit candle, symbolic of her mother's memory, far outweighed the other ritual obligations entailed by Shabbat or later by shiva.

With the close of Shabbat, the home services entailing the recitation of the kaddish began. Who must and who can participate in the mourners' service? Can non-Jews show their respect for the deceased by reciting the prayer of remembrance? Who leads the service and shapes its degree of inclusiveness? Under Jack's guidance, this service maintained its traditional form as a minyan of Jewish men, although a few non-Jews (no women) did participate. Even among the Jewish men present, a religious schism appeared to divide the members of the minyan, dictating where they stood, how they prayed, and how they were dressed.

Although the kaddish is traditionally recited twice a day for seven days, Jewish scholars note that shiva in the contemporary, secularized world is frequently shortened to two or three days—a phenomenon to which Cytron refers quite cynically as "fast grief."[59] While Jack and Toby continued to sit shiva at Jerry's home in San Francisco until the end of the traditional shiva period, many other relatives returned home earlier to resume their daily lives, my parents and myself included. When I mentioned to Jack later that week that I found it hard to grieve alone away from the family, he replied that we should not have left; the point of shiva was to share our grief and console each other. In this he is undoubtedly correct. Cytron writes, "In many ways, it seems that the ultimate intention of this shiva period is to enable the mourners to engage in the fullest range of grief by bringing the family together so that they may share memories and stories and talk through their normal feelings of loss, anger, or guilt."[60] Our family did spend much of the early shiva period together reminiscing, laughing and crying, looking over old photographs of Marsha at different stages of her life, and struggling to comprehend the reality of her absence from our lives.

BEYOND THE FIRST WEEK

The first thirty days (shloshim) and the first year also mark the journey of the bereaved. These temporal stages of mourning are accompanied by ritual. I described in the beginning pages the memorial ceremony for my aunt that marked the close of the month-long period of shloshim. In essence, shloshim, like the longer twelve-month period of which it is a part, simply acknowledges that the mourners have begun to heal but continue to grieve; the rituals that accompany these periods of mourning little by little strengthen communal bonds and facilitate reentry into society. These communal rituals also provide an external focal point for grief. Marsha's husband Jerry invested his emotional energy into the planning of the bat mitzvah–memorial, her children into studying their sections of the Torah portion and writing brief eulogies. In so doing, even if only for a moment, they translated their sorrow into action, their loss into remembrance, their deep sense of rupture into the affirmation of continuity and community. Similarly, at the end of the first twelve months, the bereaved family customarily gathers at the cemetery to unveil the tombstone and recite the kaddish, bringing to a close the first cycle of mourning.

In the years to come, the yahrzeit, or anniversary of death, continues to be marked with the lighting of the yahrzeit candle (which burns for twenty-four hours), visits to the cemetery, the recitation of kaddish, words of memory, and other acts of remembrance. In addition to the annual yahrzeit, the Jewish calendar provides four specific ritual occasions for communal remembrance in the synagogue, during which the yizkor (remembrance) prayer is recited—Yom Kippur, Passover, Shavuot, and Sukkot. Although the full yizkor service is restricted to these festivals, when mourners attend religious services throughout the first year of mourning or on the anniversary of death, they are obliged to stand and recite kaddish (mourners for this ritual purpose are defined as children, parents, and siblings). While the congregation sustains and supports them, these mourners are singled out from the community. In the past my heart has gone out to those mourners who have stood for this portion of the service, knowing that they are in pain. The fall after Marsha's death during the Rosh Hashanah service, as I watched my father join the ranks of mourners selected to stand and recite kaddish (and as I sat and recited the kaddish quietly myself), I was shaken by the intimacy of this ritual and could scarcely control my tears. I should note that although a traditional community of mourners is expected to come together to pray and recite kaddish twice a day throughout the first year, this level of observance is not practiced by many Jews today. In this context of truncated ritual observance, the High Holy Days (the ten days from Rosh Hashanah to Yom Kippur), among other rarer moments of synagogue attendance throughout the year, offer an even more significant moment for mourners to seek comfort in the context of the religious community and for that community to reach out and console mourners.

The significance of the High Holy Days for mourning goes beyond the role of community and consolation. The High Holy Days emphasize the fragility of life and force us to dwell on our own mortality.[61] During this period as well as during the yahrzeit, Jews are encouraged to visit the cemetery to pay respects to their loved ones.[62] So, too, during this period, survivor communities frequently pilgrimage to mass graves to commemorate the Holocaust. On these days, Jews acknowledge that God has the power to give life and take it away, and they ask themselves whether they are living each moment of life to its fullest. The rabbis challenge congregants to confront the potential of death in each individual and to draw from this potential not despair but the courage to "choose life." On Yom Kippur, rabbis and Jews observing strict tradition wear the kittel, or shroud, just as they will at the moment of death. Judaism thus confronts death not only during the life cycle of the individual but also during the life cycle and yearly cycle of the community. As I prayed in synagogue on Rosh Hashanah and Yom Kippur following Marsha's death, the community role in the mourning process became clearer. Through deliberate rites, the congregation binds the mourner to the ongoing social and ritual life of the community. During the service I attended, those who had lost a loved one in the past year were invited to receive a collective *aliyah* (blessing) by reciting the prayer before and after the reading of the Torah. At the same time, through kaddish and yizkor, the memory of the deceased becomes entwined in a historical community, a community that is "not only horizontal but vertical as well," incorporating within its boundaries those who have become ancestors and those who are yet to come.[63]

HOLOCAUST MEMORIALIZATION

When death occurs on such a great scale as the Holocaust, it inevitably challenges a community's ability to confront it with words or with actions. The Holocaust raises philosophical and theological questions about the meaning of life, the existence of God, the role of an afterlife, the destinies of those who perished in the Holocaust, and the continued relevance of Judaism and its traditions in the face of so much destruction. Does the recitation of kaddish restore Holocaust victims to their rightful place in Jewish history? Does it have the power to console us as collective mourners? Do the traditional burial and mourning rituals described in the above pages continue to carry meaning in the larger context of the Holocaust, for victims who did not receive proper burials, whose very modes of disposal violated Jewish laws of burial, and who have been forgotten in unmarked graves? Are the ritual, discursive, and memorial traditions of Judaism equipped to cope with the "crisis of continuity and the threat of irrevocable and total discontinuity"—of a people and its way of life—in the wake of the Holocaust?[64]

The creation of communal rituals in commemoration of the Holocaust would suggest that many Jewish communities have addressed this crisis of continuity by searching within Judaism for responses to the meaning and mystery of human existence, ultimately reinvigorating and transforming Jewish traditions in the process. Yom HaShoah, or Holocaust Remembrance Day, is the most prominent example, now marked on the ritual Jewish calendar and observed as a national holiday in Israel. But this is not the only form that Holocaust memorialization may take. In locations such as eastern Europe and the former Soviet Union, where the mass graves and killing sites of the Holocaust have irreparably scarred the physical and memorial landscape, local and national Jewish communities have embarked on extensive memorial projects—some beginning in the immediate postwar years, others only in the postcommunist years—unveiling memorials and plaques, gathering annually to visit marked and (as yet) unmarked mass graves, documenting the past in small and large museums. Through the symbolic rituals and "words against death" of Holocaust commemorative ceremonies, death on an incomprehensible scale is confronted and given meaning.[65] These ceremonies incorporate many of the ritual elements of a traditional yahrzeit, including candles, prayers, memories, and often the sacred sites themselves. The "taming" of the Holocaust is a difficult if not impossible feat. And yet, as I observed on numerous occasions in Ukraine, such commemorative performances are used as a ritual tool to transmit a powerful sense of Jewish consciousness to participants (often young people), a consciousness not of despair, but of hope engendered through a shared knowledge of the past and its continued relevance in the present.[66] Holocaust sites have in significant ways replaced synagogues and other communal settings as primary sites of community gathering and cultural practice.[67] It is often here that the social, ritual, and spiritual continuity of the community is ensured.

JEWISH CEMETERIES

Jewish cemeteries provide another more historically continuous forum for death education and the transmission of community consciousness. As sites rich with layers of social history and intergenerational continuities, Jewish cemeteries bind death to the life cycle and to the ongoing social life of the community. This continuous relationship between life and death, between the living and the dead, is reinforced through the rituals of burial and mourning, yahrzeit and yizkor, but also through cultural and religious practices at the cemetery that seek to instill in young Jews (who rarely feel as of yet any direct relationship to the dead) a sense of their own mortality and a sense of belonging to a vertical community inclusive of those who once were and those who will be. I would like to close by way of an ethnographic description of a communal cemetery visit in Ukraine in 1998.

The Cemetery at Svalyava

That the Jewish cemetery is a site invested with social, cultural, and ritual knowledge about the Jewish past was certainly the understanding of Rama Yakhad, the Conservative Jewish summer camp held in the Transcarpathian mountains in southwestern Ukraine. The camp incorporated campers from age eight to seventeen and many young counselors in their early twenties (most campers and counselors came from the surrounding region; some counselors were from Israel and America). On the day of the excursion, we got on buses and drove to a town called Svalyava, known for its old Jewish cemetery. Hearing that we were heading to a cemetery, the young kids complained: "Who wants to go to a cemetery? We want to do something fun." When we arrived, we had to pass through a narrow walled entrance from which the cemetery was not visible. When we stepped out of the passageway, an enormous, sprawling cemetery was revealed, scattered with gravestones of many different ages and sizes. Some of the gravestones dated back three hundred years or more. Further down the cemetery lanes toward the far end, the gravestones were overgrown with weeds, but the cemetery as a whole looked groomed, certainly in comparison with other Jewish cemeteries I had seen on my travels through Ukraine. Later we learned that the local Jewish community, only a handful of families but quite prosperous and well organized, had begun to look after the cemetery, cleaning up the jungle of weeds growing up over the graves and repairing the broken gravestones.

As we explored the cemetery, I came across groups of campers attempting to read the inscriptions. When they realized that most of the inscriptions were in Hebrew, they began to call the Hebrew-speaking counselors to translate. Walking along the lanes, I found clusters of campers and counselors bending before the gravestones, straining to learn about the person buried there. The two rabbis in the group and some counselors training to become rabbis began to explain what inscriptions might indicate about a person and about the values and educational levels of the community. They also pointed out the craftsmanship of the gravestones, the meaning of the different symbols—two hands, two lions, and so forth—and what they might indicate about the social qualities and artisanry skills of the community. Campers and counselors alike were engrossed; many had never imagined how much they could learn about a past community from its cemetery. In fact, we were never given an official historical account of the Svalyava Jewish community. We had only this cemetery and its contents on which to base our imaginings, but that appeared enough for most of the people present. The same children who moments before had complained about the perceived tediousness of a trip to the cemetery were now running from gravestone to gravestone, wide-eyed with fascination, soaking in everything they could about the Jewish history contained within this one site.

This field trip was not only intended as a lesson in the social and cultural history of Jewish cemeteries. Rama Yakhad sought also to transmit to its campers a sense of Jewishness embedded in traditional ritual. Thus, having reunited the campers at one end of the cemetery, one of the rabbis, an American now living in Israel, explained in English the importance of reciting the mourner's kaddish when visiting a cemetery. A young counselor translated his words into Russian. Then he recited the mourner's kaddish. This was followed by another moving prayer in memory of the dead, el molei rachamim, sung by the rabbi from the Jewish Theological Seminary in New York. His voice was beautiful, the melody was solemn, and many were moved to tears. With these memorial prayers, the social distance from the past was suddenly bridged for those present. Rather than standing in a quaint cemetery learning about the distant past of others, we were reminded that we were standing among our own ancestors, whom we had an obligation to remember. A message of Jewish genealogical and cultural continuity was reinforced through ritual.[68]

CONCLUSION

Like responses to death and dying within other religious traditions, contemporary Jewish responses to death and dying reveal a story of cultural change and continuity. While much of the literature on death and Judaism dwells on the discontinuities of Jewish traditions, viewed as a symptom of modernity and its ills, I would argue that Jewish burial and mourning rituals have proved incredibly resilient in the face of dramatic social change. These rituals, even as they have been adapted to the changing demands of a post-Holocaust, increasingly secularized and technological world, continue to provide meaning and hope to those who participate in them. By binding the deceased and the bereaved to a continuous community that reaches far into the past and into the future and embraces within its boundaries those who are present and absent, Jewish mourning rituals affirm the continuing relationship of the dead to the living and yet guide them on separate journeys—assuring the deceased a place in memory and the bereaved a renewed outlook on life.

What has perhaps changed (or is this just our perception?) is the nature of the community that participates today in Jewish mourning rites. As Jewish communities have grown more inclusive through secularization, intermarriage, and widening family and friendship circles, Jewish rituals have sought to appeal to a wider audience, including strangers to the Jewish tradition.[69] This is particularly true of rituals of death, as death affects personally everyone touched by the deceased regardless of cultural or religious background. In this desire to accommodate a greater diversity of people, Jewish rituals of burial and mourning must strive to convey a message of continuity and of community to those with wide-ranging traditions and experiences. The literature on death and Judaism expresses concerns about the continued "authenticity" of Jewish memorial practices even as they are adapted to changing communities with diverse needs. Yet as the ethnographic examples in the preceding pages reveal, the traditional Jewish nature of these practices is in no way under threat by the stretching of community boundaries in the face of death. On the contrary, whether appealing to a diverse group of friends and family seeking solace at a funeral or memorial or to young Jews from diverse (often mixed) backgrounds on their first visit to a Jewish cemetery, the power of authentic ritual—be it the recitation of kaddish or the shoveling of earth onto the grave—lies in its ability to convey tradition as one seamless line of history. This tradition is made personally and collectively meaningful for those present, even if they have never experienced it before, even if they are not Jewish. Jewish mourning practices may inevitably become more educational and more self-conscious as they are introduced to a wider community—whether a community inclusive of non-Jews with no institutional Jewish memory or a community of Jewish youth in Ukraine whose ritual knowledge, suppressed under communism, is experiencing renewal. But is this not the same as for every new generation of children that needs to be introduced to Jewish ways of death? The challenge for Jewish death practices is to remain adaptive to the pressures of social change while preserving a message of cultural and spiritual continuity that all who are in mourning may find meaningful and transformative.

NOTES

1. Samuel Heilman, *When a Jew Dies: The Ethnography of a Bereaved Son* (Berkeley: University of California Press, 2001), 3.

2. Ibid., 11.

3. Abraham Joshua Heschel, *Moral Grandeur and Spiritual Audacity: Essays,* ed. Susannah Heschel (New York: Farrar, Straus and Giroux, 1996), 48, 51.

4. Heschel, *Moral Grandeur and Spiritual Audacity,* 4; David J. Wolpe, *The Healer of Shattered Hearts: A Jewish View of God* (New York: Penguin Books, 1990), 5.

5. Wolpe, *Healer of Shattered Hearts,* 6.

6. Heschel, *Moral Grandeur and Spiritual Audacity,* 7.

7. Ibid., 9.

8. David S. Ariel, *What Do Jews Believe? The Spiritual Foundations of Judaism* (New York: Schocken Books, 1995), 268.

9. Ibid., 156.

10. Jacob Neusner, *The Enchantments of Judaism: Rites of Transformation from Birth Through Death* (New York: Basic Books, 1987), ix.

11. Ibid., x.

12. Ibid., xi–xii.

13. Wolpe, *Healer of Shattered Hearts*, 8.

14. Heschel, *Moral Grandeur and Spiritual Audacity*, 4.

15. Ariel, *What Do Jews Believe?* 155–156; William Kavesh, "Jewish Perspectives on End-of-Life Decision Making," in *Cultural Issues in End-of-Life Decision Making*, ed. Kathryn L. Braun, James H. Pietsch, and Patricia L. Blanchette (Thousand Oaks, CA: Sage Publications, 2000), 184.

16. See Neusner, *Enchantments of Judaism*, x.

17. Steven M. Cohen and Arnold M. Eisen, *The Jew Within: Self, Family, and Community in America* (Bloomington: Indiana University Press, 2000), 147.

18. David Kraemer, *Meanings of Death in Rabbinic Judaism* (London: Routledge, 2000), 133.

19. Neusner, *Enchantments of Judaism*, 153–154; Ariel, *What Do Jews Believe?* 53, 137; Alan L. Ponn, "Judaism," in *How Different Religions View Death and Afterlife*, ed. Christopher Jay Johnson and Marsha G. McGee (Philadelphia: Charles Press, 1998), 147–148.

20. Kraemer, *Meanings of Death in Rabbinic Judaism*, 137.

21. Ibid., 140.

22. Ibid., 141.

23. Ibid., 138.

24. Maurice Lamm, *The Jewish Way in Death and Mourning* (New York: Jonathan David, 1969), 221–222; Ron Wolfson, *A Time to Mourn, a Time to Comfort* (New York: Federation of Jewish Men's Clubs and University of Judaism, 1993), 300.

25. Ariel, *What Do Jews Believe?* 74.

26. Ibid., 74–75.

27. Ibid., 76–77.

28. Ibid., 77–81.

29. Ibid., 218.

30. Ibid., 228–232.

31. Ponn, "Judaism," 148.

32. Ibid., 150.

33. Wolfson, *A Time to Mourn*, 301–302.

34. Ibid.; Simcha Paull Raphael, "Is There Afterlife after Auschwitz? Reflections on Life after Death in the 20th Century," *Judaism: A Quarterly Journal of Jewish Life and Thought* 41, no. 4 (1992): 346–360.

35. Barbara Myerhoff, "A Symbol Perfected in Death: Continuity and Ritual in the Life and Death of an Elderly Jew," in *Life's Career—Aging: Cultural Variations on Growing Old*, ed. Barbara Myerhoff and Andrei Simic (Beverly Hills: Sage Publications, 1978), 164.

36. Ibid., 192.

37. Heilman, *When a Jew Dies*, 19.

38. Ibid., p. 21.

39. Jack Riemer, "Introduction: Modernity and the Jewish Way of Death," in *Jewish Reflections on Death*, ed. Jack Riemer (New York: Schocken Books, 1974), 6–7.

40. Ibid.

41. Kavesh, "Jewish Perspectives on End-of-Life Decision Making," 187–189.

42. Ibid., 189.

43. Ibid., 190–191; Heilman, *When a Jew Dies*, 15.

44. Kavesh, "Jewish Perspectives on End-of-Life Decision Making," 192.

45. Barry D. Cytron, "To Honor the Dead and Comfort the Mourners: Traditions in Judaism," in *Ethnic Variations in Dying, Death, and Grief: Diversity in Universality*, ed. Donald P. Irish, Kathleen F. Lundquist, and Vivian Jenkins Nelsen (Washington, DC: Taylor & Francis, 1993), 116.

46. Elliot N. Dorff, "Choosing Life: Aspects of Judaism Affecting Organ Transplantation," in *Organ Transplantation: Meaning and Realities*, ed. Stuart J. Youngner, Renee C. Fox, and Laurence J. O'Connell (Madison: University of Wisconsin Press, 1996), 171–172.

47. Heilman, *When a Jew Dies*, 25.

48. Cytron, "To Honor the Dead and Comfort the Mourners," 117.

49. Ibid., 118.

50. Ibid., 116–167; Kavesh, "Jewish Perspectives on End-of-Life Decision Making," 194; Dorff, "Choosing Life," 170–171.

51. Cytron, "To Honor the Dead and Comfort the Mourners," 117.

52. Ibid., 119.

53. Ibid., 119.

54. Heilman, *When a Jew Dies*, 3.

55. Myerhoff, "A Symbol Perfected in Death," 193.

56. Anita Diamant, *Saying Kaddish: How to Comfort the Dying, Bury the Dead, and Mourn as a Jew* (New York: Schocken Books, 1998), 14.

57. Myerhoff, "A Symbol Perfected in Death," 201.

58. Diamant, *Saying Kaddish*, 4–5.

59. Cytron, "To Honor the Dead and Comfort the Mourners," 121; see also Arlene Rossen Cardozo, *Jewish Family Celebrations: The Sabbath, Festivals, and Ceremonies* (New York: St. Martin's Press, 1982), 203.

60. Cytron, "To Honor the Dead and Comfort the Mourners," 120.

61. Jack Riemer, "Introduction: Jewish Insights on Death," in *Jewish Insights on Death and Mourning*, ed. Jack Riemer (New York: Schocken Books, 1995), 8.

62. Cytron, "To Honor the Dead and Comfort the Mourners," 121.

63. Riemer, "Introduction: Modernity and the Jewish Way of Death," 12.

64. Myerhoff, "A Symbol Perfected in Death," 164.

65. Douglas J. Davies, *Death, Ritual and Belief: The Rhetoric of Funerary Rites* (London: Continuum, 2002 [1997]), 4.

66. Rebecca Golbert, "Holocaust Commemoration Ceremonies in Contemporary Ukraine: Enacting Identity through Sites of Jewish Memory," in *The Holocaust in Ukraine*, ed. Wendy Lower and Ray Brandon (Washington, DC: U.S. Holocaust Memorial Museum, forthcoming).

67. James E. Young, *The Texture of Memory: Holocaust Memorials and Meaning* (New Haven: Yale University Press, 1993), 170.

68. Barbara Myerhoff, *Number Our Days* (New York: Simon and Schuster, 1980 [1978]), 86.

69. Myerhoff, "A Symbol Perfected in Death."

CHAPTER 4

Buddhisms and Death

ROBERT E. GOSS AND DENNIS KLASS

On the first night of the summer festival in Japan, lanterns guide the spirits of the dead to a three-day reunion with living family members. In ancient India, Buddhist monks taught that only by supporting the *sangha,* the community of monks, could family members assure their dead relatives a favorable rebirth. In contemporary North America, converts to Tibetan Buddhism find the same truth in their grief as they find in their meditation practice. Death is a universal human experience, yet we find wide variations in the ways different intellectual and spiritual traditions understand and manage what psychology calls grief and mourning. For virtually all Buddhist traditions in Asia and more recently in the United States, death is the fundamental transition in human life. Death presents an opportunity and a crisis both for the person approaching death and for the human community dealing with grief and loss. Death presents an opportunity to Buddhists for fundamental change and transition into another rebirth or to escape entirely from the cycle of rebirth.

To understand how Buddhists in contemporary societies respond to death, this chapter will focus on a wide variety of Buddhism traditions or Buddhisms as they have developed in different cultures: ancient India, Thailand, Tibet, Japan, and North America. We will see that for lay people the ideas of merit transfer, Pure Land, and ancestor rituals provide the means by which the living can maintain their bonds with the dead. We will also see that esoteric Buddhism, the monks' path, provided a seemingly different way of coming to terms with grief. Yet in this wide variety of cultures and in both lay and monastic Buddhism, we will see that the teaching on impermanence and the possibilities for escaping the cycles of rebirth are consistent in Buddhisms across cultures.

MINDFULNESS OF IMPERMANENCE

"This only is the Law, that all things are impermanent."[1] The realization that all things are impermanent forms the basis of Buddhism. According to all Buddhist traditions, the sheltered life of Siddartha Gautama (c. 560–480 BCE) was radically shaken by the sight of an ill man, an elderly man, and a dead man. These individuals shocked the future Buddha into an awareness of suffering and death, precipitating his own renunciation of the ordinary world of desire and leading him into a symbolic and social death as a forest-dwelling ascetic or world renouncer. Under the Bodhi tree, the Buddha conquered Mara, the king of death, through mindfulness. According to Buddhist tradition, mindfulness of death leads to the initial stages of meditation, finally leading to transcendental insight or nirvana.

For the Buddha, death was a separation of the life principle or consciousness from the body, and the cycle of rebirths resulted from ignorance and attachment. Suffering became the starting point for the future Buddha as he embarked on his own spiritual journey and practice. The Buddha recontextualized death in terms of his concept of the three marks of existence: impermanence, suffering, and no self. Impermanence deals with change: aging, illness, death, rebirth, and the religious path. For the Buddha and later Buddhists, the greatest change in existence resulted from death. Beginning with a phenomenological analysis of impermanence, the Buddha expounded his Four Noble Truths. First, suffering is an inescapable condition bound up with human existence. Second, suffering results from clinging to permanency and failing to let go of the illusion of a permanent self. Thus the Buddha asserted that there was no permanent or fixed entity called a self. A person, he taught, consists of a bundle of changing mental and physical processes and character patterns developed over time. The no-self teaching was aimed at overcoming attachment to the self. Impermanence was fundamental to the Buddha's analysis of life as suffering and his no-self teaching. Impermanence allowed for breaking the cycle of rebirth. Third, the ending of suffering resulted from the uprooting of clinging. Finally, the eightfold path (right view, right intention, right speech, right action, right livelihood, right effort, right mindfulness, right concentration) allowed the Buddhist disciple to alter the direction of *saṃsāra*, the cycles of birth and death, and break the links of attachment to realize nirvana.

The Buddha conquered death in his realization of enlightenment or nirvana. At death, the enlightened person, whose mind is purified and generates no karma, that is, no actions with future effect, escapes rebirth and enters into final nirvana or a perfectly integrated state of rest. The Buddha refused to intellectually or ontologically define nirvana. He was primarily interested in its realization, not its definition. Nirvana is an alternative to the endless cycle of rebirth, a deathless state, or the final death or liberation. While it is beyond impermanence and suffering, nirvana also includes the detachment that is the heart of the Buddha's no-self teaching. Nirvana is a radically integrative or unitive experience in which the individual, self-centered existence is transcended; it is "free from coming and going, from duration and decay, there is no beginning and establishment, no result and no cause; this indeed is the end of suffering."[2]

Two stories from the life of the Buddha are particularly useful for our study of Buddhist attitudes toward death. The first story is of the death of the Buddha himself. Various versions of the *Mahaparinibbana-sutta* (*MPNS*), a late narrative in the development of the Buddhist movement, chronicle the last days of the Buddha. In this story, Ananda, the cousin and close attendant of the historical Buddha, was aware that his teacher's death was imminent and sobbed bitterly, imploring him not to enter final nirvana. While enlightened monastics do not grieve, Ananda, who had not yet reached enlightenment, grieved openly and was chastised by his teacher.

> Enough, Ananda, do not sorrow, do not lament. Have I not formerly explained that it is the nature of things that we must be divided, separated, and parted from all that is beloved and dear? How could it be, Ananda, that what has been born and come into being, that what is compounded, and subject to decay, should not decay? It is not possible.[3]

The Buddha's death was a great loss to his followers, who, with the exception of the enlightened disciples, were plunged into deep grief. In the *MPNS*, the Buddha hinted on several occasions that a sage had the power to live as long as he desired. The 499 enlightened disciples of the Buddha scolded Ananda, reminding him of his every fault and his failure not to request the Buddha to live longer. Ananda was therefore expelled from their community. As he raced to the garden grove meeting of the sages, he began to swoon and realized the intent of the Buddha. He instantaneously achieved enlightenment. The text makes it quite clear that the Buddha used his own death as his final teaching and to assist Ananda to attain enlightenment. It was through mindfulness of his grief that Ananda realized enlightenment. In the Elders' Verses attributed to Ananda, we read:

> For one whose comrade has passed away, for one whose master is dead and gone, there is no friend like mindfulness concerning the body. The old ones have passed away; I do not get on with new ones. Today I meditate all alone, like a bird gone to its nest.[4]

Mindfulness is the Buddhist method for confronting death and the ensuing grief. Mindfulness enables a person to perceive and pay attention to the arising and passing away of all conditions, emotions, the mind, and the body. The mindful observer can put distance between the self and the impermanence of reality.

The story of the Buddha's death is a model for other deaths. In fact, the death of the teacher is a literary theme within many Buddhist traditions. Buddhists have understood the death of the Buddha as setting an example for his disciples and as a skillful means for inspiring those in training. In Asian Buddhisms and more recent American variations, there are numerous stories of the good deaths of teachers. The teacher becomes the performer in a death drama, and the disciples become the audience in this final legacy of teaching about impermanence and release. Death stories strengthen the practice of disciples by deepening their awareness of impermanence and increasing their mindfulness of life experiences.

The second story we can review is about Kisa Gotami. This story is traditionally used to illustrate the notion of dependent-origination, that whatever is born must die. Often cited as the parable of the mustard seed, it illustrates both a realistic acceptance of death and the Buddha's great compassion for the bereaved. Whether this parable goes back to the historical Buddha is open to debate; nonetheless, it reflects the historical Buddha's teaching on the impermanence of life. In this parable, a woman named Kisa Gotami loses her son in death. Grieving uncontrollably, she carries his body in her arms as she desperately searches for someone to bring him back to life. She comes to the Buddha and asks him to bring her son back. The Buddha instructs her to go into the city and to bring back a mustard seed from a household in which no person has ever died. That mustard seed will provide an antidote to the child's death. After searching from household to household, she discovers that death affects every family. She realizes the truth of impermanence, and that realization transforms her denial of death and inconsolable grief. Taking her son to the cremation ground, she holds his body in her arms, saying, "Dear little son, I thought that you alone had been overtaken by this thing which men call death. But you are not the only one death has overtaken. This is a law common to all mankind."[5] The fires of the cremation ground heighten her realization of the impermanence of life. Gotami becomes a disciple of the Buddha, and at the end of her life, she attains enlightenment.

The story of Kisa Gotami is a parable with multiple levels of meaning. For our discussion, it provides a generalized, cultural model of how Buddhists confront death and grieve. The Buddha used what psychologists call performance-based technique to help the bereaved woman accept the reality of her son's death. He sent Kisa Gotami on a mission to bring a mustard seed from a household that has not experienced death because he knew that this mindfulness of death would lead her to recognize that death is ever present in the human condition. The Buddha understood that mindfulness was the only way for Gotami to overcome and transform her grief. The story of Kisa Gotami illustrates that through awareness, grief becomes a vehicle for awakening insight into the impermanent nature of reality. The death of her son is not merely the ingredient for tragedy but also the condition for further insight. For the Buddhist, grief may be attended to skillfully or unskillfully. Unskillful handling of grief, anger, guilt, sadness, depression, and loneliness leads to destructive clinging. Gotami eventually faces the reality of her son's death skillfully by concluding their relationship, grieving, and finding new meaning in life as a disciple of the Buddha.

As these two stories illustrate so well, Buddhists confront death as a real and inevitable part of life, for it is integral to the path of enlightenment. Though death can be difficult to accept it can also be the occasion for learning impermanence and the inevitability of suffering (*dukkha*). The significance of death in Buddhism reaches far beyond the physical death of the body. In the Pali canon, death (*marana*) is described as "the falling away, the passing away, the separation, the disappearance, the mortality or dying, the action of time, the breaking up of aggregates, the laying down of the body."[6] Death is continually repeated in the dissolution and vanishing of each momentary physical-mental combination; in other words, we are always dying and being reborn. Mindfulness of this constant dying and birthing process is not only a way of preparing for the final death of the body but also a means of reaching enlightenment and the end of rebirth or nirvana.

The Buddha's teachings of impermanence, no-self, and the inevitability of suffering form the core of Buddhist beliefs about death. Also integral to Buddhist approaches to death is belief in karma—the law of cause and effect. Put simply, good actions have good effects and bad actions have bad effects. By doing good deeds, one accumulates merit, which leads to a better rebirth. As was discussed in the chapter on Hinduism, belief in karma is found in the brahmanical teachings of ancient India. Before turning to the ways Buddhism is practiced in various contemporary societies, it is important to understand how karma and the transfer of merit were incorporated into Buddhist death practices in ancient India.

ANCIENT INDIA: MERIT TRANSFER

Buddhist death practices for laypeople arose from a complex cultural interaction with the rites of death performed by Brāhmans. The Buddha and his followers accommodated some existing practices and challenged others. In doing so, they gave new meaning and twists to brahmanical religion. In ancient India, Brāhmans performed ritual sacrifices to help the deceased be either reborn in the realm of the ancestors or reincarnated into a new life. Both conceptions—rebirth in the realm of the ancestors and reincarnation—coexisted in ancient India. The Buddha challenged the ritualism of blood sacrifices described in the Vedas with new rituals of meditative practice and ethical practices for accumulating and transferring merit. The Buddha taught that prayers and rituals for the dead could not alter the karmic fruition of previous deeds. In criticizing the brahmanic practices, he also rejected the underlying caste system.

The early Buddhists appropriated the Brāhman idea that merit leads to a better rebirth, but at the same time they radically altered the concept. The story of King Bimbisara provides a model for Buddhist notions of transference of merit. Bimbisara, whose patronage had assisted the Buddha and his early movement, invited the Buddha and his disciples to a meal in his palace. During the meal, there was a disturbance outside. The Buddha revealed that the noise was Bimbisara's deceased kinsmen, who were now hungry ghosts. The Buddha told the king that food offerings were of no avail to quench the thirst and hunger of the ghosts. However, the Buddha said that the merit that the king gained from feeding the Buddha and his disciples could be transferred to the hungry ghosts to relieve their suffering.[7] In this way, Buddhist notions of merit transfer were fused with ancestor rites practiced in ancient India. In Buddhism, ancestor rites continued to be vehicles for survivors to maintain their familial bonds with the deceased and a cultural means for resolving grief, but they also provided an occasion for the living to perform spiritual works to assist the deceased in their journey toward rebirth. In this way, grief in Buddhism is redirected into compassionate acts for the benefit of the deceased.

In *Tirokudda Sutta,* the Buddha preaches that the greatest gift that the living can impart to deceased kin is their accumulated merit:

> Those who are compassionate towards their deceased relatives give, on occasion, as alms (to holy men) pure, palatable, and suitable solid and liquid food, saying, "May the merit thus acquired be for the comfort and happiness of our deceased relatives." And they (the relatives) who receive the merits of almsgiving wish thus: "May our relatives, from whom we have received this boon, live long." Those who give alms receive the fruits of the deeds . . . in the world of departed spirits there is no sowing or agriculture, nor any cattle keeping. There is no trading, no buying or selling for money. They who are born, there from this

> world live on what is given from this world. . . . Alms should be given in their name by recalling to mind such things as, "(When he was alive) he gave me this wealth, he did this for me, he was my relative, my friend, my companion, etc." There is no use in weeping, feeling sorry, lamenting and bewailing. These things are of no use to the departed spirits.[8]

This story has exercised tremendous influence on the grieving practices of Buddhists. The dead are frequently remembered when any good deed is performed, especially on birth and death anniversaries. Merit transference became one of the major social vehicles for Buddhist grieving, transforming it from the shock of death and the reality of impermanence to consolation. In second-century BCE India, then, Buddhist monks attempted to replace the brahmanic approach to death with their own as Buddhism changed from a reform movement to a religion in its own right. The changes they brought, however, did not last in India because Brahmanism was revised into what we now call Hinduism. Buddhism almost completely disappeared from India, but as it moved into other cultures, it carried with it a new relationship between the living and the dead that had been developed in India.

Early Buddhists transformed the post-Vedic funeral or *shraddha* rites of transitioning the hungry ghost into an ancestor with the notion of transference of merit. When laypeople converted to Buddhism, their family dead, especially those who had been reborn into the realms of suffering, needed help. The monks injected themselves into the continuing bonds between the living and the dead in two ways. First, they taught that the living did not have the power or means (merit) to help the dead. Second, they taught that although laypeople could not help the dead directly, the dead relatives would receive the benefit or merit if the living made gifts to support the monks, thereby transforming the *preta,* a person reborn to the lower realms, into a *deva,* a person reborn into the higher divine realms. Power to help the dead was vested in the sangha, the community of monks, whose purity allowed them to be conduits for the transfer of merit. Buddhists thus set up a social mechanism for the laity to continue a relationship with the deceased. The Buddhist notion of transfer of merit, however, changed the underlying worldview, thereby changing the ways that the living could interact with the dead.

In the new Buddhist system, brahmanic ritual action for the dead was replaced by ethical actions on behalf of the dead. This move to ethics made Buddhism appealing to members of the merchant class, who had a lower standing in the caste system and were reliant upon the ritual expertise of brahman priests to gain merit. The merchants could earn merit by their own effort just as they could earn money in their business relationships. The idea of merit thus legitimated the economic power of the merchant class. Giving gifts activated a complicated mechanism of social exchange. A layperson offered material gifts for the benefit of monks, and in return, the virtuous power of the monk granted a spiritual reward of merit. To the more sophisticated monks, merit was just a term for doing good. Buddhist scholastic philosophers wrestled with the notions of karma and merit transfer as they tried to reconcile lay practices with monastic ideals. The scholastics, who maintained what they saw as orthodox teaching, said no merit was transferred to the deceased. They said that the physical act of giving should be accompanied by a mental intention and a verbal formulation of a resolute wish to use the merit for the path of enlightenment.[9] The hungry ghosts might rejoice in the good deed and their gratitude in turn allowed the dead to improve themselves in the afterlife.

Orthodox doctrine, however, could not overcome the pre-Buddhist idea that the dead could cause harm and injury to the living. Early Buddhist funerary rites, incorporating this idea, were performed to prevent the deceased from harming the living. Monks chanted scriptural verses, or *paritta,* as "safety runes" to secure the efficacious power of the Buddha against spirits and ghosts.[10] While the parittas were used for general protection, they also could be used to ward against hungry ghosts, spirits, and death. This apotropaic form of chanting canonical scriptures for protection gave Buddhist monks social power in those Asian cultures where spirits and magic were deeply ingrained.

The ability to perform rituals to generate merit and transfer such merit to the dead, thus assisting them in attaining a favorable rebirth, remains at the heart of Buddhist death practices in many contemporary societies. In the following sections we will see how these practices are carried out today in Thai, Tibetan, Japanese, and American Buddhisms.

THERAVADA IN THAILAND BUDDHISM: LIFE WITH THE SPIRITS

In Theravada Buddhism in Thailand, monks and laypeople respond to death in different ways. The monks' path, devoted to achieving the end of suffering in deathless nirvana, includes the practice of meditation on death. In the fifth century CE, Buddhaghosa described two meditations on death, an eightfold mindfulness of death and a contemplation on decaying corpses, which continue to be used today.[11] The eightfold mindfulness is a powerful method, guiding the practitioner through successive steps of confronting and understanding the reality of death, leading the practitioner to a realization that the true nature of reality is impermanence. The meditation on corpses familiarizes the monk with the actual fact of death and decay, subverting physical desires and increasing a sense of nonattachment toward the world. These meditation practices have been emphasized in English books on Buddhist death practices, but they are not representative of how the vast majority of Buddhists approach to death.

Thai Buddhism blends within itself popular Hindu, Theravada Buddhist, Chinese Mahayana Buddhist, and animistic traditions. Spirits play an important social role in Thailand. They can function as members of the family. In northern Thailand, the household spirits are viewed as deceased ancestors and given a special place within the household. In central Thailand, the household spirits are given their own houses at the corner of the property. These spirit houses are slightly bigger than a birdhouse and shaped like temples. Family members make daily offerings to appease the spirits. Buddhist monks also use ritual like chanting to ward off the return of a spirit who might cause mischief or harm.

A popular Thai story of Nangnak Prakanong, which was made into the movie *Nangnak* (1999), illustrates the depth to which spirits and ghosts are intertwined with popular Buddhism in Thailand. In the movie, Nangnak, a soldier, goes off to war and is wounded. A high Buddhist abbot nurses him back to health and encourages him to join the *wat* (monastic temple), devoting his life to Buddhist practice. Nangnak refuses because of his attachment to his wife. During the war, his wife dies giving birth to a dead child. He returns to a wife and child who have become ghosts, but Nangnak does not realize that they are dead. The ghost wife harms the villagers and the local wat, and it takes the abbot to save the husband and the villagers by exorcising the ghostly wife and binding her to serve Buddhist *dharma*. In this story, the abbot has an apotropaic function that conquers the ghost and restores religious and social order.

While the cult of the spirits is extremely important in Thai culture, traditional Buddhist practices that can be found in many other cultures are also incorporated into Thai death practices. We can see this blending of practices in this description of a "typical" Thai death. Donald Swearer describes some of the practices for aiding the dying as follows": "Near the moment of death Buddhist mantras may be whispered into the ear of the dying, possibly 'Buddho' or the four syllables the structure of the Abhidamma [a division of Pali scriptures]—*ci, ce, ru,* and *ni* (mind, mental concepts, and nibbana [sanskait, hirrand])—or written on a piece of paper and put into the deceased's mouth."[12] Such actions assist the dying person to achieve a state of devotion and faith to the Buddha with the least amount of emotional distress. After a person has died, the family prepares the corpse by bathing, perfuming, and dressing it in new clothes. The corpse is laid out in the home in a coffin with a one-*baht* coin in the mouth so the deceased can buy passage into the afterlife, and the mouth and eyes are sealed with wax. Stanley Tambiah observed that a two-baht note is frequently placed in the hands of the deceased as well.[13] The deceased's hands are arranged in the traditional Thai greeting of wai folded in reverence and tied with a white thread, three times around. The ankles are also tied with a white thread and often tied to the coffin.[14] A white cloth is hung at the head of the coffin. White signifies death in Thailand, and grieving relatives often wear white clothes while the more Westernized Thais wear black. Family and friends pay their respects to the deceased for the next three days. They may also ask for forgiveness for harm they have done the deceased. Such reparation frees both relatives and the deceased from the lingering negative aspects of their bonds to each other.

On the third day after death, monks from a local wat arrive to chant during the morning. The chants tell the spirit of the deceased the way to heaven. After the first set of chants, the family presents the monks with a meal. The monks' chanting helps the family to cope with the death and helps to transfer good merit to the dead. The laypeople provide the monks with food for a week after the funeral and on the three-month and yearly anniversaries of the death. The merit attained by family members for their generosity to the monks is transferred to the deceased.[15]

When the coffin is taken from the house in procession to the crematorium, the body's feet are kept pointing west. The white cloth is placed as a cover on the coffin. Because the deceased's spirit may take possession of them, the coffin bearers are given candles and flowers to protect themselves. Family members carry pictures of the deceased, wood for the fire, and a jar for the cremated remains. The monks lead the funeral procession to the wat, where, as an indication of the negative, the coffin is carried counterclockwise around the cremation oven. A monk then removes the white cloth. Symbolically, monks are immune to pollution, and the pollution of the corpse, now absorbed into the white cloth, is rendered innocuous. At some funerals, the white cloth is removed and thrown to the coffin bearers three times, or the cloth may be stitched into an outer garment for a monk, following the ancient Buddhist custom of stitching pieces of cloth from corpses at cremation grounds.[16] The most senior monk chants scriptural verses on the inevitability of suffering and death. Then the family presents the monks with food, robes, and other gifts. Two monks pour coconut water on the corpse, followed by family members who also bless the corpse with oblations of coconut water. The corpse is then cremated.

That evening, monks return to the deceased's home to chant once more. Often the monks return for two more evenings to chant scriptures. This is to purify the house from death and to comfort the bereaved family members. A senior monk often gives a sermon on the uselessness of mourning or on impermanence. This funeral aftermath is both a sad and happy occasion. Mourners are sad because of their loss, yet also happy because the deceased person will have no more misery or illness. Such familial celebration of the deceased's escape from all suffering also functions to show the spirit of the deceased that everyone is happy and that the deceased need not worry about those left behind.

In Thailand, then, lay Buddhism is integrated with a strong sense that the spirits, including the spirits of the dead, are active and potentially harmful. The mixture of Buddhism and animism can be seen in funeral rituals that include merit transfer as well as rituals by which Buddhist monks neutralize the destructive power of the spirits and ensure that the dead can journey safely to the other world. Lay Buddhism in Thailand exists alongside the more esoteric Buddhism of the monks in which meditation on death is part of a whole set of practices designed to free the monk from attachment to the world and allow the monk to enter nirvana.

TIBET: JOURNEY THROUGH THE *BARDO*

In October 1950, the Chinese People's Liberation Army invaded Tibet. The next two decades witnessed the tightening of Chinese control over Tibetan culture and religion, the flight of the Dalai Lama and 100,000 Tibetans to India, and the excesses of the Chinese cultural revolution, which destroyed 6,000 monasteries and led to the deaths of 200,000 monastics. Traditional Tibetan religious practices have been curtailed in Tibet under Chinese occupation but remain alive in India and the Himalayan kingdoms of Nepal and Bhutan.

Tibetan or Vajrayana Buddhism has hundreds of texts and images about death. The texts and images cross the boundaries of all Tibetan Buddhist schools and lineages. Among the genres are inspirational accounts of the deaths of great saints and teachers, ritual texts for the dying, instructional manuals for guiding trainees in death meditation, divination materials on the signs of untimely death, and yogic manuals for the transference of consciousness at death.[17]

There are two significant Tibetan literary traditions around death and dying. The first, the *lâm-rim* (gradual stages of the path) tradition, affirms two propositional truths: death is certain and the time of death is uncertain. Thus death requires advance preparations.

The lam-rim tradition proposes a nine-round death meditation in which a person contemplates the three roots, the nine reasonings, and three convictions.[18] The second significant literary tradition is the *bardo.* The best-known text in this tradition is the Great Liberation through Hearing the Bardo (*bar-do'i-thos-sgrol-chen-mo*) or the *Bar-do thodol,* which was misnamed by the American scholar W.Y. Evans-Wentz as *The Tibetan Book of the Dead,* in imitation of *The Egyptian Book of the Dead.* Here we will focus on this second tradition and on this text.

The authorship of the *Bar-do thodol* is attributed to Padmasambhava, who dictated it to his consort Yeshe Tosgyal, who hid the text during the persecution of Buddhism during the ninth century CE. Karma Lingpa discovered the text in the fourteenth century. The text, then, falls into a type of Tibetan revelational literature called "treasure texts" (*gter-ma*).[19] Treasure texts are discovered long after they were written and because of the original authors are given exalted or canonical status. This fourteenth-century bardo text is still used by monks and tantric adepts in refugee communities in India and the Himalayan kingdoms, and it may still be used secretly in Tibet. Though the text is not utilized universally by Tibetan Buddhists, it has been very popular among Western Buddhists, who have adapted it and use it in a variety of settings.

Bardo literally means "in between." It refers to a number of transitional or liminal conditions: (1) between birth and death, (2) meditational states, (3) dream stages, (4) the moment of dying, (5) the interim between death and rebirth, and (6) the process of rebirth. The bardo teachings are relevant to each liminal stage, but they are most pertinent to dying and death. The *Bar-do thodol* describes in detail the experience of a person migrating from death to rebirth and is read to dying and deceased persons to guide them through this journey. When the *Bar-do thodol* is used to guide the dying and the dead, the preliminary prayers orient the dying person to the death process and instill a proper frame of mind to assure either a good rebirth or even liberation. Ideally, the dying person has practiced the bardo teachings during his or her lifetime as a preparation for death. In meditational training, a person learns to perceive the natural state of the subtle mind as pure luminosity.[20] An untrained person, like most lay Tibetans, even when given the bardo instructions after death, has greater difficulty in overcoming egocentric tendencies and perceiving the true nature of the mind. The reading of the *Bar-do thodol* serves not only to help the dying but also to remind the family of the need to do spiritual practices in order to prepare for their own deaths.

Tibetan Buddhists believe that everyone has a subtle mind, which migrates through the bardo experiences. They view death not merely as the maturation of karma, as in earlier Indian Buddhism, but also as the separation of the life principle (*bla*) from the body.[21] It has become common to translate bla as "soul," though "consciousness" might be better used. Tibetan Buddhism incorporated this notion and the practice of the separation of the life principle from the body into the bardo experience. Tibetan Buddhism also adopted the term *lama* for teacher. Literally, lama means "soul-mother," from the indigenous shamanic tradition of Tibet.[22] The lama guides the separation of the life principle through various liminal situations, including accompanying the subtle consciousness of the dead person step by step on the difficult and sometimes perilous path during the forty-nine days between death and rebirth. The journey of the deceased in the bardo is dangerous because it can lead to an unfavorable rebirth in a lower realm of existence.

The *Bar-do thodol* is read aloud by a lama or tantric adept in the presence of the dead body for forty-nine days. When ordinary deceased persons, unskilled in meditational practices, awaken in the bardo of dying, they are confused. They do not know where they are. In a talk on the bardo, Lama Lodo remarked that the deceased realize their altered condition when they walk in sand or in snow and see that they leave no footprints or when they realize they are not casting any shadow even while walking in sunlight.[23] When the signs of death and physical dissolution have set in, the lama who recites the bardo teachings becomes the spiritual guide, instructing the deceased not to cling to life but to recognize the luminous essence that is the mind.

The lama or tantric adept directs the deceased to rely on whatever spiritual practices and imaginative preparations the deceased engaged in while living and to rely on his guidance. The lama begins with a series of prayers and then speaks into the left ear of the departed:

> Hey, noble one! Now you have arrived at what is called "death." You are going from this world to the beyond. You are not alone; it happens to everyone. You must not indulge in attachment and insistence on this life. Though you are attached and you insist, you have no power to stay, you will not avoid wandering in this life cycle. Do not lust! Do not cling! Be mindful of the Three Jewels![24]

Most people continue to grasp a false sense of themselves, since it is difficult to give up attachments to relatives and to stop struggling to hold onto their past lives. It is difficult to leave things unfinished and to let go of all the things cherished in life. According to Tibetan teachers, the departed are often frozen in their attachments and fears, grieving for their former lives and loved ones. Tensions, attachments, and discomfort can generate negative emotions that propel the deceased toward a less than favorable rebirth.

At some point during the first twenty-one days, or if the lama is present at the moment of death, the lama performs the *powa* (*pho-ba*), or transference of consciousness ritual. Offerings of barley and butter are placed on the head of the corpse. The lama instructs the deceased on how to break attachment to the body. The Tibetan Buddhist tradition maintains that the clairvoyant consciousness of the dead person is seven times clearer than in life. Through such clairvoyant powers, the dead person can see into the wisdom mind of an accomplished teacher and so can be introduced to the luminous nature of the mind and be liberated. At the conclusion of the rite, the lama invokes the blessings of the Buddha and awakened ones. He looks for signs or physical indications of the complete transference of consciousness from the corpse.

The family consults an astrologer who correlates the time of birth and death with other astrological factors to determine an auspicious time for disposing of the body. To prepare, monks and/or family members wash the corpse while reciting prayers for the benefit of the deceased. Tibetans practice four ritual methods of disposing of corpses: (1) ground burial, (2) cremation, (3) sky burial, and (4) water burial. Ground burial is rarely practiced except in the case of contagious diseases. In Tibet, cremation is reserved for incarnate lamas or during the winter months, but Tibetan refugees have followed the

Indian custom of cremation. In sky burial, body cutters dismember the corpse and feed parts to vultures. This practice continues in Tibet but is not common among refugees in India. In water burial, the corpse is dismembered and thrown into a river. Cremation and the more rare practice of sky burial are graphic rituals in which the consciousness of the deceased and the family break off attachment to the physical body.

In Tibetan cremation ceremonies, the body is understood as a fire offering along with butter oil, grains, and sugar. Monks offer chants and prayers for the benefit of the deceased. The funeral pyre is visualized as the mandala of Vajrasattva, a Buddha associated with mental purity. Often the lama performs a ritual of cutting (*gcod*), a meditational dismemberment of the body.[25] As the corpse burns as an offering, the relatives and friends are encouraged to envision the body being devoured by the hundred Peaceful and Wrathful Deities, transformed into their wisdom nature. The mourners chant the six-syllable mantra of Vajrasattva: OM VAJRASATTVA HUM or something similar.[26] When the cremation is finished, the ashes of ordinary Tibetans are gathered and left to the natural elements on a mountaintop, while the ashes of accomplished teachers are often mixed with clay to make devotional images that become linking objects or relics to connect the living with the deceased teacher. Afterward, the house of the deceased is fumigated with incense, and local monks are hired to come in to chant the Perfection of Wisdom in 8,000 lines. A lama exorcizes the death demon from the house.[27] The possessions and the clothing of the deceased are frequently donated to the local monastery, the temple, or to charity.

Like suffering, grief is not repressed or denied but accepted and transformed into motivational energy for spiritual practice. Suffering motivated the Buddha to seek liberation; grief energized Kisa Gotami to engage in Buddhist practices that led to her realization of enlightenment. From a Tibetan Buddhist perspective, grief can be an opportunity for an individual to examine his or her own life and find meaning in it. Grief teaches people about compassion and can provide the motivation to engage in spiritual practices. Feelings of grief return periodically to the mourners. Words of condolence and consolation do not resolve the grief from the death of a loved one. Sogyal Rinpoche, a Tibetan teacher in the United States, shares an experience of grief from his youth:

> While everyone else slept, I lay awake and cried the whole night long. I understood that night that death is real and that I too would have to die. As I lay there, thinking about death and about my own death, through all my sadness a profound sense of acceptance began slowly to emerge, and with it a resolve to dedicate my life to spiritual practice.[28]

Tibetans recognize death all around them; the death of those they know and love causes them to search for the meaning of life with a sense of hope. An unceasing ecology of birth and death form the matrix of grieving, but rebirth does not remove the pain of loss. Yet at the same time, Tibetans discourage excessive emotional expression because, they say, it hinders the progress of the deceased. The dying person is most vulnerable at the moment of death, and the intense grief of loved ones may provoke strong feelings of attachment in the deceased. Excessive emotion and grief are thought to confuse the dead and disrupt the migration toward liberation or rebirth.

The strategy of Tibetan Buddhist teachers and adepts is to encourage family members to channel their grieving energies into spiritual practices to benefit the dead. We can think of this strategy as helping the survivors join with the deceased in a new way. The rituals of body disposal radically end the old physical relationship, but in the powa ritual, as in all the rituals of the first forty-nine days, the bond of the living and the dead is renewed and strengthened. Family members communicate with the dead person through food offerings. Each morning and evening, food is set aside in the bowl of the deceased and is used for burnt offerings.

There is a strong belief that underscores the Tibetan Buddhist practice of transferring merit to another. Death provides an occasion where the living can perform spiritual works to assist the deceased in the bardo journey. Lamas instruct families on their need to generate merit for the deceased before the karmic judgment of the Lord of Death. The notion of the family assisting the dead relatives takes on great importance. It helps mourning family members lower the emotional level in their expressions of grief. Relatives and friends can now join in the process of transferring merit to the deceased and provide a devotional mind, full of compassion for the deceased. Assisting the dying in a peaceful death and transferring merit to the deceased become the paramount goal of mourners.

The most efficacious time to perform spiritual practice for the deceased is during the first twenty-one days after death, since in this period the deceased retains the strongest links with the living. Since the consciousness of the deceased at this time is acutely clairvoyant, the survivors have the greatest access to the deceased and thus the strongest opportunity to assist the journey to liberation or a favorable rebirth. By clearing the mind of grief, generating devotion, and visualizing awakened Buddhas and deities, the living actually assist the wandering bardo consciousness to realize its spiritual goal. The bardo connection with the deceased provides an outlet for transforming grief into compassion and provides solace for the living. Family and friends practice powa or the transference of consciousness meditation ritual on any day during the forty-nine-day period but especially on the same day of the week that the person died. In doing these practices, friends and friends are not only helping the dead, but also providing emotional support for each other in their common cause. Such spiritual practices are also meritorious for each individual. Thus, the transmutation of grief into a compassionate letting go of the deceased continues the path of self-discovery of the luminous mind.

Over the years, relatives festively remember the anniversary date of the death of the loved one with food offerings and rituals. Monks or lamas are again hired to chant rituals. The family can now take comfort knowing that its efforts and the lama's efficacious reading of the *Bar-do thodol* have resulted in the favorable rebirth of the deceased. The death anniversary becomes yet another occasion to continue a relationship with the deceased through the transference of merit.

JAPAN: ANCESTOR RITUALS

Similar to what we saw in Thai Buddhism, Buddhism in Japan provides rituals that transform the dead into ancestors so the dead can remain part of the family. These rituals play such an important role in Japanese culture that Buddhism in Japan is often referred to as "Funeral Buddhism." The funeral rituals provide a means by which Japanese people grieve and manage their continuing bonds with the dead. Though the Japanese term for these rituals, *sosen suhai,* is usually translated "ancestor worship," this translation is misleading but no good alternative has emerged. The term divides into parts. *Suhai* means deep, respectful feelings toward another person. "Veneration" might be a good English translation. *Sosen* are the objects of veneration. Some are lineal ancestors, that is, individuals from whom the family is descended. But deceased children, relatives outside the formal hereditary line, and nonrelatives such as a respected teacher or friend may also be included. Where are these spirits?

> The world beyond cannot be described in any but equivocal phrases. Spatially it is both here and there, temporally both then and now. The departed and ancestors always are close by; they can be contacted immediately at the household shelf, the graveyard, or elsewhere. Yet when they return "there" after the midsummer reunion they are seen off as for a great journey. They are perpetually present. Yet they come to and go from periodic household foregatherings.[29]

The ancestors are those who could be reborn. In Japanese Buddhism, the religious elite strive for nirvana in this life. But ordinary people become a buddha only when they die. They are not reborn. They become ancestors who are also revered as buddhas. The largest Buddhist sects are Pure Land, relying on the merit and compassion of Amida Buddha, the Buddha of Infinite Light, to insure the individual's entrance into the Pure Land after death. Having journeyed to the Pure Land, the dead thus remain part of the family as ancestors for three to five decades, which is as long as any living person remembers them.

We might best understand the relationship between the ancestors and buddhas with a traditional Buddhist idea that religious practice can be understood at two levels:

> (1) *laukika* (Chinese: *shi-jian,* Japanese: *seken),* secular or popular religious ideas such as funeral and memorial services, rites of passage, and magical practices like exorcism;
> (2) *lokottara* (Chinese: *chu-shi-jian,* Japanese: *shusseken),* transcendence, that is, the state of enlightenment, which can be sought only in the negation of the ego.

These two levels seem similar to the common idea of a world of suffering and a world of enlightenment. In true enlightenment, however, these two worlds are discovered to be actually the same. That is, the distinction between suffering and enlightenment is a dualism that is resolved as are all dualisms. When we look at the world, however, the distinction is apparent, and it is a useful way to think about the level on which people function. The two levels are descriptive, even though the distinction is not ultimately real. "Since they do function on different levels, it is possible for them to coexist."[30]

A pattern throughout Buddhist history is to take the lower-level magic and expand it in a way that it moves toward the higher level. For example, at the lower level, the idea of merit seems like magic, casting spells, or doing incantations to achieve immortality, and so the elite rejected it for themselves. But rebirth, either in heaven or in higher human status, is a step toward the ultimate goal of enlightenment. Gaining merit at the secular level gets the person to a higher birth and so closer to enlightenment. The secular level is different from, but coordinated with, the transcendental level. When the bodhisattva concept developed, merit could be from the top down—not only the laypeople helping the monks, but the monks out of compassion aiding the people. In Pure Land, Amida's merit is enough for everyone, but in some sense everyone can be bodhisattva, so everyone can perform actions of merit that can be transferred to others.

It seems, then, that the concept of enlightenment and transfer of merit could be seen either as a corruption of the idea that everything has a Buddha nature or as supporting the idea that the Buddha nature is what is always there beneath the concepts we form to deny impermanence. Japanese Buddhists have consistently chosen the second option. When the form is removed by death, Buddha nature-formlessness remains. There is thus no contradiction between the ancestor rituals of Funeral Buddhism in Japan and the larger body of Buddhist teaching and practice.

The veneration of ancestors in Japanese culture is interwoven with veneration of the buddhas and bodhisattvas and the Shinto practice of veneration of the *kami* (gods). Until the Meiji Restoration (1868), there was very little popular distinction between Buddhism and Shinto. In ancestor worship today, there is a consistent flow between these ideas. Some of the dead go on to become kami. To some extent, this is a function of where and by which rituals they are venerated (Buddhist or Shinto). For the shogun or emperor, the easiest way to become kami is to die in war. But for others, the movement is slower and occurs at the end of the funeral rituals:

> The death of a person sets in motion a series of rites and ceremonies that culminates in the observance of a final memorial service, most commonly on the thirty-third or fiftieth anniversary of the death. Between a person's last breath and the final prayers said on his behalf, his spirit is ritually and symbolically purified and elevated; it passes gradually from the stage of immediate association with the corpse, which is thought to be both dangerous and polluting, to the moment when it loses its individual identity and enters the realm of the generalized ancestral spirits, essentially purified.[31]

The first set of rituals transforms the newly dead (*shirei*) to a new buddha (*hotoke*) over forty-nine days. During that time, the relationship between the survivor and the dead person is restructured. A central part of the ritual is to inform the person that he or she is dead. As one Japanese described it, the person is told, "You are dead. You have to go away now. We regret that you have to go away, but you can't stay here any more." If the dead person continues hovering around because of some unfinished business—for example, if the dead person wishes to get married and have children—the survivors kindly tell the dead person: "Well, you can't do that now. It's time for you to go away." If the dead person persists in staying, then a Buddhist priest might be called in to add some authority. People offer condolence to the survivors in the form of an announcement of status: "Now you are experiencing how the end of life is." It is a formalized expression, used only on this occasion. Thus, the issues of denial and acceptance of reality are addressed directly in a ritualized way. The dead are told they are dead now. The living are told they are experiencing death.

Cremating the body and then placing the bones in the grave also provide a strong dose of reality early in the Buddhist funeral rituals. Cremation, which occurs within a day or two after death, is full of Buddhist meaning. Shakyamuni Buddha (the historical Buddha) was cremated, thus creating relics that could offer a concrete, yet disembodied continued presence at the *stupas* created in his honor. For Japanese families, cremation provides a disembodied presence of the ancestors at the grave and on the *butsudan,* the Buddha altar in the home. After the cremation, the family gathers, and the bones are brought out on a tray. Two people pick up the bones with chopsticks and put them into a pot, which is then put in the family tomb. The bones of all family members are placed in the same tomb, so the symbolism of the dead joining the other ancestors of the family is strong.

Japanese culture has many folk beliefs about the newly dead as harmful wandering spirits. Indeed, shirei (newly dead) can be translated as "ghost," in the sense of "spook." Until the dead are safely in the ancestor world, they may cause harm to the living. Part of the reason for the funeral rituals is to make sure the dead do not remain wandering spirits. Dead spirits wander when no ritual is performed for them. As an act of compassion, a person can perform rituals for spirits who have no one to care for them. Many Buddhist temples maintain a place where rituals can be performed in front of gravestones of families with no survivors.

During the forty-nine days after death, a kind of settling of the relationship between the living and the dead takes place. All human relationships entail unresolved conflict and unmet obligations. It is very common for the dead to return in a dream and say, "It's okay. You did your best." In effect, the dead forgive or say the relationship is now even. If it is not in a dream, a survivor may experience the feeling at some point during that forty-nine days that "It's okay. The deceased is happy and has forgiven me." When the survivor lets go of any ambivalence in the relationship, the deceased is free to go on and become an ancestor. If the relationship between the living and the dead is not settled, the dead can become a harmful spirit, even a hungry ghost, but that need not be a permanent condition. The living and the dead are in continual interaction, so reconciliation and the integration of the dead into the community always remain a possibility.

The dead are still part of the family but in a new way. When people are troubled they often feel the presence of their ancestors near them. The dead may come in a dream to comfort and to just be with the living. There is an expression that pictures the ancestors as "standing by the dream pillow." Interactions with the dead, however, are not left only to such spontaneous moments; rather, interaction with the deceased is regularized and ritualized. We will briefly describe one ritual place, the butsudan or household Buddha altar, and one sacred time, the *O bon* festival in which the dead return.

The butsudan is the focal point for ancestor rituals in the home. The altar contains memorial tablets for departed spirits and often also photographs of the deceased. In traditional homes, each morning Buddhist rituals are performed in front of the altar. In the center of the altar is usually a statue or image of a buddha or bodhisattva, usually

Kannon (the bodhisattva of compassion) or Amida, but the main reason for having the butsudan in the home is veneration of the ancestors.

Traditional memorial tablets are upright lacquered wood plaques, four to six inches high. Recently, rather than having tablets, some families keep a book on the altar with the names of all the deceased family members. Written on the tablet or book is a posthumous name. Giving a posthumous name grew from the practice of giving a person a Buddhist name when he or she was initiated into monk's vows. The posthumous name reminds the family that ancestor rituals were integrated into Buddhism by initiating the dead as monks and therefore helping them toward enlightenment. The reverse side of the tablet has the person's name in life and age at death and often includes the relationship of the person to the head of the household.

We can get a better understanding of the meaning of ancestor rituals if we ask what is going on in the lives of people when they are in the presence of their ancestors on the butsudan. Yamamoto and his colleagues give us a sense of the personal quality of those moments.

> If you would for a moment give up your Judeo-Christian beliefs and attitudes about one's destiny after death and pretend to be a Japanese, you might be able to feel how you are in direct daily communication with your ancestors. The family altar would be your "hotline." As such, you could immediately ring the bell, light incense, and talk over the current crisis with one whom you have loved and cherished. When you were happy, you could smile and share your good feelings with him. When you were sad your tears would be in his presence. With all those who share the grief he can be cherished, fed, berated, and idealized, and the relationship would be continuous from the live object to the revered ancestor.[32]

O bon, the major summer festival in Japan, celebrates the temporary return of the dead for a three-day visit with the living. Spirits of people who have died since the last *bon* have a special place in the ceremony. "The periodic merging of the two worlds (living and dead) strengthens the sense of continuity of the house and reassures the dead of the living's continuing concern for their well being. Neither death nor time can weaken or destroy the unity of the members of the house."[33] We can get a sense of the survivors' grief and their continued interaction with the dead by looking at the ritual that ends bon. There is a large gathering and a dance in which the spirits are entertained before their departure. "Many of the songs that accompany the dance are laments, expressing the community's regrets that the visit is drawing to a close." And then the spirits return to their own realm. There are many local variations, but in one of the most easily understood, a candlelight procession moves "toward the river where one by one, representatives of each household place small boats, bearing the candles, into the current. As far as the eye can see the flickering flotilla plies on. When the candle goes out, it is said, the spirit has been released to the other world."[34]

AMERICAN CONVERTS: PSYCHOLOGIZING BUDDHISM

Making friends with death is a very direct way to understanding the First Noble Truth that the Buddha taught: all life is suffering. That truth, some contemporary Americans say, is the beginning of the path to liberation and enlightenment. Buddhism is a large and diverse religious tradition in America. There are many groups of American converts to Buddhism, while hundreds of immigrant communities from various Buddhist cultures are also now firmly established in North America. In this section we will not try to explain how all these communities manage death and grief but will focus on the community of American converts to Tibetan Buddhism that is centered around Naropa, a Buddhist university in Boulder, Colorado. The university developed a master's of arts program in Engaged Buddhism. Students study classical Buddhist philosophy, meditation, ritual, and the practice of Buddhism in socially activists traditions. The program applies Buddhist spiritual practice to the reality of suffering and pain by training students in human service, pastoral care, and social action. One of the tracks of the Engaged Buddhism program prepares students for hospice work. We spent a week in Boulder in 1996 conducting extended interviews with community members. The material in this section comes largely from those interviews.

The Naropa community founded in 1974 and developed through the lineage of its founder and teacher, Chogyam Trungpa. Until his death in 1987, Trungpa contributed significantly to the development of Western Buddhism. He did not require his followers to follow Buddhist tradition as closely as did most other Tibetan lamas. The Naropa community is thus a complex interaction of cultural narratives between Tibetans whose culture underwent a traumatic destruction by the Chinese government and Americans whose own culture seemed inadequate for their spiritual journeys. The community was ripe for new outlets, such as the hospice movement that had recently developed in the United States.

American converts to Tibetan Buddhism at Naropa have found that care of the dying and coming to terms with their own grief are meaningful ways to connect with the Buddhist tradition. Since the beginning of Buddhism, death and grief have proved fertile ground for Buddhism to interface with new cultural settings. And just as happened when Buddhism entered Asian cultures centuries ago, these Americans are integrating Buddhism into their culture while at the same time they are transforming their culture. With his Shambhala tradition, this mixing of cultures was welcomed by Trungpa, who allowed other religious practices and traditions into Buddhist practice. Thus, American converts at Naropa stepped outside their cultural heritage and at the same time brought their cultural heritage into their new Buddhist framework. The individuals in the Naropa community had self-consciously left mainstream American culture to find symbols and myths that were meaningful to them. In their encounter with Buddhism they created something new. Indeed, members of the community see themselves as creating a new worldview from the remains of Tibetan culture and from their own practice that cultivates self-conscious being-in-the-face-of-death.

The practice of hospice and Tibetan rituals have been rather directly combined at Naropa in those deaths that can be anticipated. As the time of death approaches, a community of people gathers. The dying person is surrounded with religious images of Buddhas, bodhisattvas, and teachers, as well as friends and people meditating. This intentional practice is to create a positive religious environment for a good death. While Tibetan

Buddhism is predominantly ritual-centered for the laity, Buddhism at Naropa is principally a meditation movement for the laity—that is, laypeople practice Buddhism in a way that is reserved for monks in traditional Tibetan Buddhism. As we saw above, in Tibet the family spends its time and energy generating merit for the dying and then for the deceased. Merit making, however, means little to the American converts at Naropa. Because their practice is meditation-oriented, Naropa Buddhists have psychologized the assistance of the living for the dying and the deceased. That is, rather than seeking to gain merit, they cultivate a sense of compassion and thus a sense of communion with those who are dying and those who have just died.

The Naropa community understands that during the last days or hours of dying, the person is entering the bardo state in which she or he will need as full clarity as possible in order to find the way to the next incarnation. Just as merit does not translate well into American culture, neither does the concept of rebirth. Still, in the time of dying and during the funeral rituals, theological problems surrounding merit and rebirth recede as the truth of dying and transformation becomes a living reality. One way the living provide support for the dying is by supplying instructions to guide the dying through the bardo, just as lamas do in traditional Tibetan practice. One person reported that she put a photograph of the dying person's teacher in front of him and, on instructions from another teacher, asked people to leave the room for a few moments while she repeated the instructions to the dying that the teacher had given her. After the death, the community continues to practice meditation for several days.

In hospice work, the Naropa Buddhists bring a more secular way of knowing into their practice. Hospice work can be authentic action done within the virtues of goodness, gentleness, fearlessness, letting go, and nonaggression. The people caring for the dying and bereaved retain the personal autonomy that is an important part of American culture, but are still somewhat removed from the mundane, commercial world of everyday contemporary life. This is not an exact imitation of the Buddhism that came from Tibet. It is something new, yet at its core is the truth that Kisa Gotami learned when she brought her dead son's body to the Buddha.

Sitting in the room and meditating while someone is dying and then for several days after the death are the central elements of the Americanized Tibetan ritual. There is a synergy between the dying person and those gathered to meditate. Later the synergy is between the deceased and the survivors. It does not involve the cultural mechanism of transferring merit to the deceased as it does in Asian cultures. Rather, the teaching is, as one person said, "Practice, take care of yourself; practice for the benefit of the other person on their journey." The technique is rather direct. The larger ritual is called Sukhavati. In the meditation practice during Sukhavati on the in-breath the mourners take whatever negativity, whatever pain or confusion the dying person might be experiencing in the bardo state. Then, on the out-breath, the mourners give their wakefulness, healthiness, or whatever the deceased needs in the moment wherever he or she is. The stress is on assisting the dying and then the deceased in the journey to reincarnation or liberation. In Tibet, the doctrine of rebirth and the traditions of family cohesion mean that the powa, or transfer of consciousness ritual, assumes a central place in the death rituals. Because Americans at Naropa have looked to the Tibetan teachers for ritual leadership, powa is part of the Sukhavati, but it does not play the central role. Still, the connection between the deceased and survivors is very strong in the Naropa Sukhavati.

The American Buddhists we interviewed at Naropa grew up in families that were not originally Buddhist, so when it falls to them to care for a parent who is dying, or to find the rituals by which to mourn, they find ways to bring the death into the Buddhist community. One man who cared for his dying father told us that his father said that it was all right "if you want to practice with me and around me and be with my body for three days." The father's worldview was scientific. When he died, the father believed that was the end. But he appreciated that his Buddhist son wanted to follow his own religious practices in mourning for his father. As it happened, it seemed to the son that the father was dead and gone the moment he died. He stayed with the body for two days and then had the body taken to a local crematorium. A few months later, during an extended stay at a retreat center, he gathered a group of friends together. They threw the ashes over a cliff and then incorporated the forty-ninth day Sukhavati into their time at the retreat center.

To understand these new death practices that have developed in the American Buddhist community at Naropa, it is useful to look at them within the context of the modern, Western approach to death, which is described more fully in the second half of this book. Industrialism and, later, consumer capitalism transformed the experience of dying and grief in Western cultures. On the one hand, the great majority of deaths have no public meaning and as the twentieth century wore on, the expected public rituals, namely funerals and burials, were increasingly incongruent with the survivors' inner experiences. Grief and mourning were relegated to the private sphere and therefore removed from commercialism. On the other hand, the time period right before and right after death became the province of the professional. Professionals maintain their control by keeping possession of the body. Most deaths occur in hospitals. The death is legally real only after it has been certified by a medical doctor. Hospitals control access to the dying person with visiting hours and rules about visitors' age and behavior. The funeral industry takes over where the medical industry leaves off. Corpses can be shipped by interstate commerce only if a certified technician has embalmed them. The corpse is prepared and displayed in a factory-made casket in a funeral "home" where the funeral "director" controls access to it. Family and friends may only "view" the corpse after it has been embalmed, dressed, and had makeup applied to make it look peacefully asleep.

Hospice is a development of the latter part of the twentieth century in direct response to these problems with the modern, Western way of dying. In hospice, physicians relinquish control of patient care to family, friends, and hospice staff. Most hospice care is done in the home by family and friends while the hospice team of nurses, aids, social worker, and chaplain provide support and guidance. In relinquishing control of patient care in hospice, the medical industry relinquishes control of the body. The dying person is no longer sequestered from the family and community. Rather, the dying person is returned to the family and community where, it is hoped, the dying and the caregivers can find private meaning that will allow them to construct this chapter of their individual and family narratives in as positive a way as possible. In finding such deep meaning in hospice care, then, the members of the Naropa community are participating in and contributing to a new development in American culture.

The death rituals at Naropa are a radical repudiation of the funeral industry's control of the body. It seemed to us that the way the American Buddhists dealt with the body, and then the disposal of the body, was much like the traditional Tibetan practice, although details have been changed. Survivors spend up to three days with the body, so they experience a strong sense of connection along with the unmistakable realization that the relationship is changing. The Naropa community has almost fully adopted the ways of relating to the corpse that the Tibetans have taught them. They take charge of the body during the dying process and continue after the death happens. They care for the body themselves, they sit with the body as they want, they do rituals that are important to them, and then they dispose of the corpse in a way that seems fitting to them. What they do with the corpse has been adapted to North American circumstances and funeral requirements for public display of corpses, but the funeral rituals have more of the spirit of Tibet than of America. The body is surrounded with plastic and dry ice to prevent decomposition for the three days of rites. The usual means of disposing of the body is cremation. Rites accompany the cremation of the body. Meditation practices and rituals are often performed for the entire forty-nine-day bardo period with a Sukhavati ritual on the last day.

When we look at continuing bonds between the living and the dead at Naropa, it is clear that in coming to the West, Buddhism has come to a culture in which the idea of rebirth does not sit easily. The Buddha taught in a culture that could hardly imagine individuals having only one life. Naropa Buddhists do not explicitly reject rebirth as a religious doctrine, but they do not find the idea particularly useful to them. As they drop the idea of rebirth that is so central to the Asian worldview, the Americans at Naropa establish a very different kind of continuing bond with their dead. In the converts' continuing bonds to the dead, then, is another way in which Buddhism is transformed by the culture into which it has moved.

At Naropa, the esoteric teachings, which had been the province of the monks in Tibet, are for everyone. There is no lay Buddhism that aims at achieving the Pure Land based on the merit of the bodhisattvas or that hopes to achieve a higher rebirth by giving gifts to the monks. At this point, there seems to be no movement to develop rituals by which the dead can become ancestors as they do in Japan. The possible exception is Trungpa, who died in 1987 and remains an ancestor in the form of a root teacher. In their new kind of Buddhism, these American converts take death and grief seriously as a vehicle to truth. They are like Kisa Gotami, who failed to find a household where there was no grief. The Buddha helped her learn that if she attended skillfully to her grief she would become enlightened. In experiencing death and grief, those who attend skillfully know the basic truth of Buddhism that everything is impermanent and so suffering is inevitable. The converts at Naropa have followed two interconnected paths as they have integrated Kisa Gotami's lesson into their Buddhism. They have attended to their own grief, and they have learned to help others die and grieve in hospice.

Naropa Buddhists attend to their own grief, however, in a very different cultural context than do the monks and lay people in Tibet. They have adopted the American psychological culture in which experiencing and exploring feelings and expressing those feelings in intimate interpersonal situations are a way to truth. The truth of the feelings in grief is for many at Naropa the same truth as they find in their meditation. Thus, the traditional insight has been put in a new context. For Tibetans to focus on emotions is thought to be a mistake because the negative emotions of grief hold the dead person back on the journey through the bardo state toward the next rebirth. Tibetans try to manage their grief in positive identification with the deceased in a way that will aid the dead. Among Naropa Buddhists, if any person is giving aid to another, it is much more likely that the dead person is helping the living. In the psychologized American culture, emotions facilitate movement; they do not retard it. The movement that is important to the Naropa Buddhists is the movement of the survivor through grief, not the movement of the dead through the bardo realm. When people experience and articulate how they feel, the world seems clearer to them. The action a person takes based on that clarity is often perceived to be in harmony with the world as it is. The emotions of grief are suffering, dukkha. When individuals experience and articulate grief, they know and can attend to the First Noble Truth: all life is suffering. Rather than something to be avoided, the emotions of grief become the vehicle that puts American converts on the path of enlightenment.

As they join their Buddhist practice to hospice, these American converts bring Kisa Gotami's insight to the newly developed Engaged Buddhism. Chogyam Trungpa not only brought his Tibetan Kagyu lineage to the West, now the largest form of western Tibetan Buddhism outside of Asia, he also gave a new teaching, the Shambala warrior path, in which action in the secular world is also a practice leading to enlightenment. Indeed, perhaps we could say that the Shambala teaching allowed esoteric Buddhism to be transformed into a lay religion for the Americans. Engaged Buddhism bridges the gap between monastic and lay practice. It is not clear how much abstraction lay Tibetans are expected to do. Theirs is a ritual religion in which action is knowing. The monks know by doing too, but in a more consciously constructed way. The role of the teacher is to introduce practices designed to produce particular insights and states of being when the disciple is ready for them. In their engagement with hospice, the American lay Buddhists at Naropa take on the whole task at once as they give themselves fully to the care of the dying and take what insight and growth from it they are ready for at the time, or later as they reflect on the engagement. Engaged Buddhism, then, is very different from either the monastic or lay Buddhism in Tibet. This new Western Buddhism provides a spiritual tradition that appeals to many in the North American cultural mainstream. It is possible, then, that we are now seeing a spiritual and religious development in the meaning ascribed to death and grief in America that may have as much historical importance as when Buddhism entered southern China or Japan.

CONCLUSION

In Buddhism's history, as it has changed and has been changed by the cultures into which it has moved, one of its points of entry has been its teaching about death. We showed in the stories of the Buddha's death and Kisa Gotami's grief that dying and grieving can be an occasion for learning, and even for enlightenment, and we have seen that those stories continue to be a model for Buddhist teachings on dying and grieving in contemporary societies. The ideal way to die or to grieve is a state of calm or with a mind concentrated in devotion to the Buddha and with compassion. Yet those stories allow for wide cultural variation in the practices Buddhists use to assist the dying and to assist each other in their grief.

We have tried to show the wide variety of Buddhisms as they have developed in different cultures from ancient India to contemporary Thailand, Tibet, Japan, and America. We have seen that for laypeople the ideas of merit transfer and Pure Land provide the means by which they can maintain family bonds and yet at the same time be part of Buddhism, where the ultimate goal is nirvana. Though that task is accomplished differently in the different cultures, the teaching on impermanence and the possibilities for escaping the cycles of rebirth are consistent in Buddhisms across cultures.

Compassionate care for the dying and the dead is no less significant for contemporary Buddhists than care for the living. Buddhism has provided the rituals by which individuals and families express their grief and continue their bonds with the dead. These rituals of merit transference have been very effective in assisting Buddhists to live with their grief and face their own deaths. In Japan, where family lineage is important, Buddhism has been fully integrated with ancestor rituals to the extent that those rituals provide the major connection laypeople maintain with Buddhism. In the United States, where merit transference has not taken root, rituals originally designed for merit sharing have become psychological mechanisms for assisting the dying and helping the dead purify their lives for a heavenly realm.

NOTES

1. Edwin A. Burtt, ed., *Teachings of the Compassionate Buddha: Early Discourses, The Dhammapada and Later Writings* (New York: Penguin Books, 1982), 45.
2. Samyuta Nikaya 1:157–159.
3. Rupert Gethin, *The Foundations of Buddhism* (New York: Oxford University Press, 1998), 26.
4. Theragatha, *Elders' Verses* 1:1035–1036
5. Burtt, *Teachings of the Compassionate Buddha*, 45.
6. Majjhima-Nikaya 1.49, Digha-Nikaya 2.305, Samyuta-Nikaya 2.2, quoted in George D. Bond, "Theravada Buddhism's Meditation on Death and The Symbolism of Initiatory Death," *History of Religions* 19, no. 3 (February 1980): 239.
7. George Pieris Malalasekera, "'Transference of Merit' in Ceylonese Buddhism," *Philosophy of East & West* 17 (January 1967): 87.
8. Ibid., 80–81.
9. John S. Strong, *The Legend of King Ashoka: A Study and Translation of the Ashokavadana* (Princeton: Princeton University Press, 1983), 175–186; Melford Elliot Spiro, *Buddhism and Society* (San Francisco: Harper & Row, 1971), 140; Bond, "Theravada Buddhism's Meditation on Death," 237–258.
10. Peter Harvey, "Devotional Practices," in *Buddhism,* ed. Peter Harvey (New York: Continuum, 2001), 136–138; Christopher Lamb, "Rites of Passage," in *Buddhism,* ed. Peter Harvey (New York: Continuum, 2001), 167; Donald K. Swearer, *The Buddhist World of Southeast Asia* (Albany: State University of New York, 1995), 57.

11. Stanley J. Tambiah, *Buddhism and the Spirit Cults in North-East Thailand* (New York: Cambridge University Press, 1970), 180.

12. Swearer, *Buddhist World,* 60–61.

13. Tambiah, *Buddhism and the Spirit Cults in North-East Thailand,* 180.

14. Lamb, "Rites of Passage," 171.

15. Malalasekera, "'Transference of Merit' in Ceylonese Buddhism," 85–90; Lucian M. Hank, "Merit and Power in the Thai Social Order," *American Anthropologist* 64 (1962): 1247–1261; Stanley J. Tambiah, "The Ideology of Merit and the Social Correlates of Buddhism in a Thai Village," in *Dialectic in Practical Religion,* ed. Edmund Ronald Leach (Cambridge: Cambridge University Press, 1968), 41–131.

16. Lamb, "Rites and Passage," 171.

17. Mullen gives a range of the Tibetan literature on death: Glenn Mullen, *Death and Dying in the Tibetan Tradition* (Boston: Arkana, 1986).

18. Glenn Mullen, "Mindfulness of Death," in *Religions of Tibet in Practice,* ed. Donald S. Lopez Jr. (Princeton: Princeton University Press, 1997), 421–441; Glenn Mullen, *Living in the Face of Death* (Ithaca: Snow Lion Publications, 1998).

19. Janet Gyatso, *Apparitions of the Self: The Secret Autobiographies of a Tibetan Visionary* (Princeton: Princeton University Press, 1998), 145–181.

20. Robert A.F. Thurman, *The Tibetan Book of the Dead* (New York: Bantam Books, 1994), 53–81; Sogyal Rinpoche, *The Tibetan Book of Living and Dying* (San Francisco: HarperSanFrancisco, 1994), 56–81.

21. Giuseppe Tucci, *The Religions of Tibet,* trans. Geoffrey Samuel (Berkeley: University of California Press, 1988), 44–45.

22. Turrell V. Wylie, "Etymology of Tibetan Bla-ma," *Central Asiatic Journal* 21 (1977): 146–147.

23. Lama Lodo, speech at a workshop on the *Bar-do,* St. Louis, Missouri, July 2000.

24. Thurman, *Tibetan Book of the Dead,* 131–132. The Three Jewels, which all Buddhists vow to take refuge in, are the Dharma (teaching), the Buddha, and the sangha community.

25. Stan R. Mumford, *Himalayan Dialogue: Tibetan Lamas and Gurung Shamans in Nepal* (Madison: University of Wisconsin Press, 1989), 205–209.

26. Rinpoche, *Tibetan Book of Living and Dying,* 251.

27. Ibid., 386–387.

28. Ibid., 7.

29. David W. Plath, "Where the Family of God Is the Family: The Role of the Dead in Japanese Households," *American Anthropologist* 66, no. 2 (1964): 308.

30. Yasuaki Nara, "May the Deceased Get Enlightenment! An Aspect of the Enculturation of Buddhism in Japan," *Buddhist-Christian Studies* 15 (1995): 19–42.

31. Robert J. Smith, *Ancestor Worship in Contemporary Japan* (Stanford: Stanford University Press, 1974), 69.

32. Joe Yamamoto, Keigo Okonogi, Tetsuya Iwasaki, and Saburo Yoshimura, "Mourning in Japan," *American Journal of Psychiatry* 125 (1969): 1661–1665.

33. Smith, *Ancestor Worship in Contemporary Japan,* 104.

34. Edmund T. Gilday, "Dancing with Spirit(s): Another View of the Other World in Japan," *History of Religions* 32, no. 3 (1993): 273–300.

CHAPTER 5

Roman Catholic, Anglican, and Eastern Orthodox Approaches to Death

LIZETTE LARSON-MILLER

Three years ago I attended the funeral of a fifteen-year-old girl. She was a friend of my oldest daughter, and her tragic and quick death from leukemia shook the community, particularly her extensive network of teenage friends, classmates, and Girl Scouts. She had lived her brief life as a faithful Roman Catholic in a Los Angeles suburb, and the funeral in all three of its stages—wake, funeral Mass, and committal—was faithful to the contemporary Roman Rite with its American adaptations. But no two funerals are exactly alike; each should reflect the particular circumstances of the deceased and of the mourners while, at the same time, expressing the universal and traditional imagery of sorrow, consolation, and hope. This funeral did that, from the chorus of young voices who formed the choir at the funeral liturgy to the Girl Scout honor guard at the cemetery. It was at the cemetery, however, that a remarkable example of the inculturation of love and remembrance occurred. Following the Rite of Committal, as friends and family members gathered around the parents to console them, a group of girls, friends of the dead, gathered around the shiny, expensive, steel-gray coffin. Their mixture of laughter and tears caught my attention and drew me in close enough to see what they were doing. Two of the girls had purchased their dead friend's favorite lipstick, and as it was passed around the group of twenty or so girls, each girl applied it to her own lips and then kissed the coffin. By the time they were done, the coffin had lost its shine. Covered in kisses, the coffin sat there, waiting in typical large-cemetery protocol for a later lowering into the ground. I realized as both a mourner and a scholar of liturgy that these girls had created an authentic ritual from the heart of their culture and had added it to the layers of ritual words and actions that had attempted to make sense of the incomprehensibility of the death of a child.

Everyone has stories of funerals they have attended, some funny, some pathetic, some poignant. These stories are not just ways to begin book chapters, however; they get to the very heart of how we remember and commend our dead. Narrative is a central expression of many of the world's religions, including Christianity, because story is often the vehicle for the communication of fundamental truths in a way that allows interpretation, development, and, above all, the inclusion of individuals and communities into the story. This inclusive nature of narrative is what gives stories a timeless nature and makes them an invitation to imagination and identification by which others are invited to make the story their own. Much of the core of the traditional Christian funeral rites is somehow related to story, the story of the deceased individual, the stories of the mourners, particularly family, and above all, these stories woven into and emerging from the story of the life, death, and resurrection of Christ.

This chapter looks at three broad Christian traditions that represent continuity with early Christian traditions as well as organic development through ongoing inculturation. All three traditions—Roman Catholicism, Anglicanism, and Eastern Orthodoxy—are catholic in that they are universal expressions of Christianity, global communities not bound to a particular nation or ethnicity. (The third, Eastern Orthodox, is simply a way to group diverse individual communions under a single title, recognizing the autonomous nature of these Christian communities around the world). All three are also "tribal,"[1] in that they have been shaped by and continue to shape ritual, and thus self-identification, from local and culturally specific sources. All three self-identify as "the Body of Christ" and avoid the categorization of "denomination,"[2] and all three present themselves as discerning divine authority and guidance through more sources than scripture alone.[3] The point of these selected markers is that there are ecclesiological, theological, and liturgical similarities between these three Christian communions as well as profound differences and disagreements, and these similarities and differences can be seen in their contemporary beliefs and practices relating to death.

ROMAN CATHOLICISM AND DEATH: "LIFE IS CHANGED, NOT ENDED"

An Orientation to Catholic Christian Practices

Roman Catholicism is the largest branch of Christianity in the world, 1,070,315,000 strong.[4] It is "Roman" because the center of the church, both in the person of the pope and in the geographical location of Vatican City, is in Rome. This was the ancient Western patriarchal see, one of four and then five, each with its own patriarch (or the more popular "pope") and each with its own territory. The Roman Catholic Church bases its foundation on the Apostle Peter and represents one of the most centralized institutions in religion. Both in its juridical organization and in its own theology, the universal church represents best the ongoing presence of Christ, out of which flows the local church and local leadership, rather than vice versa, as is the theological preference in many Eastern Orthodox churches.

Because the "catholic" nature of the Roman Catholic Church means that it must speak many languages and cultures in order to communicate its message of salvation, the actions and beliefs surrounding death need to call forth what is consistent with that Gospel message as well as reflect the customs and practices that speak to a particular people. In light of this requirement, there are three categories of practices to which the observer must turn in order to understand the full spectrum of practices surrounding the death of a Christian: official, those from popular religiosity, and normatively secular.

Official Practices

While the definition of *official* has developed and changed over the centuries, this is generally held to be the official funeral rite designated as such by the universally recognized bodies responsible for these. As of 1989, the *Order of Christian Funerals* (OCF) is the official contemporary rite for the United States. Other English-speaking countries have a slightly different version of this rite, and countries speaking other languages have their own vernacular edition, all stemming from the Latin.

Popular Religiosity

Also known as popular devotions, piety, or sacramentals, these are actions and texts that fall outside the official rites, but are still tangentially related, a "set of spiritual attitudes and cultic expressions which are variedly connected with the liturgy."[5] Popular religiosity is often presented as having the following characteristics:

> It is bound up with basic human problems and sentiments; it possesses a spontaneous and creative quality, which sometimes puts it at a distance from the doctrine and discipline of the church; it is traditional in orientation; it is often associated with particular places, cultural expressions, social conditions, and the natural disposition of a particular group; it is suited generally for modest and simple people, though it is not necessarily the correlative of social and cultural privation.[6]

Within the context of funeral practices there are many religious rituals that are not official or approved, but they are often of equal importance to the mourners and represent the meeting place of lived culture and official rite. To mention just a few, the washing of the body, the type and place of vigil (wake, rosary), music choices, the use of candles, incense, holy water, fasting or eating certain foods, wearing certain clothes, and particularly the frequency and activities at the postfuneral commemorations, often done at the graveside, all would be examples of popular religiosity surrounding death. In addition, in all three of the Christian traditions discussed in this chapter, individual clergy members will change some elements to fit the particular circumstances of individual deaths. These public and private adaptations may produce different meanings or theologies as they form a type of bridge between "official" and "popular religiosity," an example of living liturgical theology in action.

Secular Practices

There is a third category of practices surrounding death that practicing Roman Catholics may engage in, specifically those of the larger secular or multifaith community.

Some of these practices are legalities pertaining to a country or municipality: how the body must be treated; where it can be buried or cremated; how the death certificate must be filled out. Some of the practices pertain to the particular community in which the deceased lived: what funeral arrangements are available; what types of financial assistance can be expected; what impact the climate may have on burial. And some of the practices are religiously syncretistic but culturally expected: the particular roles of men and women in countries where Christianity is the minority religion; the choice of foods; the patterning of the funeral liturgies; the use of additional alternative rituals within the official rites; or the assumptions and guidelines of "civil religious institutes," as in military burials.

All three of these categories—official, popular religion, and the larger society—are sources of and influences on the practices surrounding death that Roman Catholics in any country might engage in and through which their Christian faith and their cultural expectations may be expressed.

Historical Development

The historical development of practices surrounding death in Roman Catholicism is simply the early history of Christian rites for the first six hundred years.

The Foundational Early Centuries

> The actions surrounding the death, burial and commemorations of a Christian person in the first six centuries of this era reveal a profound faith in the promise of the resurrection expressed through practices that reflected a continuation of cultural norms. Only secondarily and very gradually do distinctive Christian elements emerge through particular rituals and prayer texts which manifest a growing Christian identity.[7]

In the first three centuries, the primary sources for our knowledge of these rituals are cemetery remains and inscriptions found at Christian graves, along with some written descriptions, especially from martyr accounts.[8] By the fourth century, a growing body of liturgical texts, the "official" category of ritual texts, began to emerge. From both of these early resources we can discern three different moments in a sequence of practices; death rituals, burial rituals, and commemorative practices. Charting these three categories with their constitutive elements would result in the following:

1. Death rituals (practices surrounding the dying and moment of death)
   a. viaticum
   b. the kiss of peace
   c. the preparation of the body
   d. psalm singing
   e. prayers
   f. exposition of the body

2. Burial rituals
   a. processions
   b. burial proper
      i. prayers
      ii. Eucharist
      iii. secular requirements of burial
3. Commemorative practices
   a. meals and prayers

Of the elements from the first category, death rituals, perhaps the most important elements are viaticum, the singing of psalms, and prayers. The Latin word *viaticum* has its origins in pre-Christian associations with provisions for a journey, what is necessary to take with one on the way, but the specific Christian association is focused on the Eucharist for the living instead of the pagan Roman tradition of placing a coin for Charon in the mouth of the dead.[9] The Christian "theology of such an action continued the idea of strength for the journey and for the battle of the soul with adversity, while manifesting the belief in the Eucharist as the 'medicine of immortality,' the deliverance from natural corruption."[10]

The singing of psalms represents a substitution for the cultural mourning music and was presented by Christian writers as a counterpart to the apotropaic music (and noise) of contemporary non-Christian practices.[11] The natural human tendency to mourn must have continued among Christians, however, as the scoldings by Christian leaders were frequent.

Prayer at the death of a Christian has its roots in the very dawning of Christian liturgy. Robert Taft reminds his students that a wake, or vigil for the dead, "is an act of faith in the resurrection of the dead," finding its model in the women who brought the aromatic spices to anoint the body of the Lord after his death, "inaugurating the first watch before the tomb."[12] The classic Christian theological concerns of prayer around death are as follows: praise of God, a commendation of the dead to God, a petition for God not to remember the sins of the deceased, and a petition to console the mourners.

From the second category, burial rituals, a word should be included about processions and the celebration of the Eucharist. Processions were an important part of ancient Mediterranean cultures, and Christians continued to see the movement both as ritual necessity and as symbol of the pilgrimage of the soul from one world to another.

The route of the procession in the first four to five centuries of Christianity was from the home (or place of the preparation of the body) to the cemetery. It is only in the mid- to late fourth century that we begin to see evidence of another station at the church building itself. As some churches developed the special status of martyr churches, burial within the church became increasingly desired and then restricted to the wealthy and/or important members of Christian society, with others buried around the churchyard in developing cemeteries. This "extra" station in the church building proper, however, eventually became a step on the way for all Christians, and the resulting change affected the primary procession. By the seventh and eighth centuries, the procession from the church to the cemetery, even if very short, became the primary focus for ritual enactment and theological interpretation rather than the earlier procession from home to burial.

In a number of geographically diverse churches, a primary ritual focus at the time of burial was the Eucharist. Augustine of Hippo, writing at the end of the fourth century, describes the funeral of his mother, Monica, and how the tradition at Ostia (port of Rome) varied from his own in North Africa.

> When her body was carried away, we went out, and we returned without tears. Not even in those prayers we poured forth to you when the sacrifice of our redemption was offered up in her behalf, with the corpse already placed beside the grave before being lowered into it, as is the custom of that place, not even during those prayers did I shed tears.[13]

This meal of communion represents a Christianizing of long-standing Mediterranean tradition of eating with the dead, at the burial and in annual commemorations to follow.

The final step of the death sequence was commemorative. To be assured of remembrance after death was of great importance to people in late antiquity, Christian and non-Christian alike, and the ritual actions that took place at measured intervals following the death date and annually on the birth date (for non-Christians) and on the death date (for Christians) remembered and honored the deceased. The central action of these commemorations was the meal with the dead at the tomb or at a *memoria* for the dead if the body was not present. This meal, eventually to be known by the name *refrigerium,* was the Christian inheritance of a long-standing Mediterranean tradition. In addition to the meal, the Christian remembrance of the dead included the celebration of Eucharist and prayers for the dead, both of which emerged in the early centuries as two of many ritual expressions and then developed theologically into the primary means of commemoration.

The particular days of commemoration, with some regional variance, followed existing traditions, with preeminence given to the third day following death, which was celebrated universally in both Eastern and Western Christian communities. On the third day, and in local patterns of days following, the meal took place directly on the grave, and the dead person shared in the meal either by a literal pouring of wine into the tomb or by a symbolic toasting of the deceased with wine and shared food. By the fourth and fifth century, the cemetery celebrations with their mixing of the sexes, drinking, and nighttime eating drew the ire of a number of Christian bishops, but the continuing popularity of these commemorations, even after being replaced by anniversary Masses in church buildings, was a witness to their rootedness in culture and in faith.

One important dimension of these annual or timed commemorations of the dead was prayer, and in these early centuries a notable change occurred with lasting ramifications. Almost simultaneously (the end of the fourth century), in Jerusalem and in North Africa, a distinction arose between the deceased for whom prayers are offered and the deceased whose prayers are solicited.[14] This tradition of offering prayers by the living for the dead was instrumental in shaping Catholic funeral rites in the centuries that followed.

Throughout these three stages—death rituals, burial rituals, and commemorative practices—early Christians continued the outward cultural rituals and practices they knew but endowed them with distinctly Christian meanings. Above all, the rejection of futile mourning, the expression of confident hope in the resurrection, and the conviction that communion and love transcended death defined the Christian interpretation of the cultural practices. Thus, for the Christian believer, life changed, but did not end, at death.

Late Medieval Changes

By the eighth and ninth centuries, the Latin-speaking church of the West had deviated far from the pan-Mediterranean unity of the early centuries. The Western church, made up of many cultures and languages, was fast becoming a church of uniformity if not unity, brought about by political and theological necessity. With the ascendancy of Charlemagne to the seat of Holy Roman Emperor in 800, the desire to create a uniform liturgical practice became a useful political tool to unite disparate tribes and peoples into a centralized kingdom. Ironically, much of the development of the Roman rite in the ninth century is not Roman, or at least has only some Roman elements. The rites that were shaped and continued somewhat intact into the twentieth century were already multicultural, the result of Greek, Oriental, Gallican, Spanish, North African, and other influences as much as elements indigenous to the city of Rome. This is particularly apparent in the rites that had to be augmented or created from scratch as they did not exist in the papal rituals sent by Pope Hadrian to Charlemagne's court between 784 and 791.

Of the many rituals missing from the sacramentary, the funeral rite was one of the most urgent, and it was pieced together by the editor, Benedict of Aniane, who drew heavily on his own background as a Benedictine monk and a Christian from southern France.[15] The harsh life of rural Christians living in Europe certainly contributed to less confidence and hope in the face of death, but the cultural shift was not alone in creating a shift in the theology of death. The increase in commemorative liturgies and the "increasing importance of prayer directed toward the good of souls after death"[16] spiraled to create a decrease in confidence and an increase in fear that the prayers (let alone baptism) would not be enough to save the deceased. When placed in the context of a monastic Christian culture of frequent and intense prayer, the result was a sharpening of the division between those of the dead for whom Christians prayed and those whose prayers were solicited. This general (and gradual) shift from hope to fear was buoyed by the particular prayer language that Benedict of Aniane chose to use.

> By introducing terms with legal connotations (*reatus, delinquere*), Benedict brought a new element of personal guilt and responsibility into the penitential quality of the prayers for the dead. This suggestion of guilt contrasts sharply with the traditional language, in which sin is represented as the result of earthly fragility and the snares of the devil. . . . Sin is the result not of corporeal fragility in the face of the devil's wiles but of conscious choice and responsible action. Thus one has a greater need to rely on the absolute mercy of God, all the more awesome given the obstinate and freely chosen sinfulness of his children.[17]

The direct results of Benedict of Aniane's deliberate textual changes may have been minimal, but when combined with many other changes in the official liturgy of the church, the ritual experience of medieval Catholics gradually resulted in a changing theology, which in turn further influenced changes in ritual practice.

First, with regard to death rituals, the most profound change was the disillusion of viaticum as *the* last rite. For complex reasons, it had become intertwined with the changes in the rites of reconciliation, increasingly a sacrament for the end of life, and in the evolution of the anointing of the sick to the anointing of the dying.[18] Partially due to Peter the Lombard's system of seven sacraments,[19] extreme unction replaced viaticum as the pivotal rite. This last anointing was part of a new sequence of last rites: confession and absolution, viaticum, and extreme unction, earnestly desired of every dying Christian as an outward ritualization of having performed well the *ars moriendi.* By the fifteenth century, Peter the Lombard's numbering and definition became canonical, but long before that, they had become popularly understood as the correct way to view the sacraments along with the understanding of the last rites as necessary for a good death.

Parallel to these official rites of dying, a flourishing of popular religiosity surrounding death arose in the eleventh through the fifteenth centuries. The text-focused practices of the earlier church (such the recitation of the Passion accounts while dying) were often retained, but more common were their visual counterparts, holding up a crucifix to the eyes of the dying person, the use of holy water and candles, the catching of the last breath, and the last words. Outside of the bedchamber of the dying Christian, visual, theatrical, musical, and ritual reminders of death abounded in the forms of crucifixes, stained glass art, dances of death, popular music, and, for the literate wealthy, illuminated manuscripts of the Book of Hours.[20] All of these were reminders not just of one's own death, but that death was a constant part of life. The modern Western industrialized "denial of death" and its concomitant masking of all *momento mori* would not be recognized in the late medieval world of Christianity.[21]

The burial rites were another place of great change in the category of official rites. The ancient two-station burial movement (home to cemetery) had already evolved into a three-station burial movement (home to church to tomb). It is that second step, the station in the church building, that now takes priority. The early medieval emphasis on praying for the dead, combined with the Carolingian emphasis (through Benedict of Aniane and others) on personal guilt and culpability for sin, led the Latin-speaking West to focus on the Mass as the supreme prayer expression for the dead. This was a gradual development; not all Christian centers even included the celebration of the Eucharist as part of the burial rites at all. But by the Middle Ages, the Mass had evolved to a specially composed liturgy for the dead known as the Requiem Mass: "The inclusion of the eucharist reflects the evolving situation in which the celebration of Mass came to be considered the prayer *par excellence* to effect the forgiveness of sins and was therefore to be offered on behalf of the deceased *as part of the liturgy of burial.*"[22] The ritual element that best reflected the changed theology and ritual of the new liturgy was the addition of a short service, known as the absolution, added to the end of the Mass before removing the body to the place of burial. Structurally it was a series of prayers and responses like those that accompanied the procession of the body to the cemetery in earlier centuries, but this was a service of absolution, which asked again for the forgiveness of sins and for mercy for the deceased. It represents like no other ritual element the profound change from the confident hope in the resurrection of the early church to the fear of the late medieval church.

> Deliver me, Lord, from everlasting death in that awful day, when the heavens and the earth shall be moved, when you will come to judge the world by fire. Dread and trembling have laid hold upon me, and I fear exceedingly because of the judgment and the wrath to come. O that day, that day of wrath, of sore distress and of all wretchedness, that great and exceeding bitter day, when you will come to judge the world by fire.[23]

Theologically this ritual development grew in tandem with a changed theology of the afterlife, from the early church view of life after death as the *refrigerium interim,* the antechamber of heaven,[24] to its firm replacement in the thirteenth century by an understanding of purgatory, more akin to the antechamber of hell.[25]

The changes at the burial itself were less profound, but the continuity with the escalation of fear and sense of unworthiness affected the growing emphasis on blessing the grave and the addition of a final prayer of absolution, as well as a number of ecclesial and civil restrictions on who could be buried in the cemeteries of the church (only the baptized and those in good standing, i.e., not the excommunicated). This restriction, of course, excluded the many infants who died unbaptized, giving rise to the poignant tradition of burying them in secret around the church building, where the rainwater, understood as a popular substitute for the waters of baptism,[26] would run off the roof of the church onto their graves.

Tridentine Practices

The official liturgy partially described above continued with few changes through the medium of the Franciscan Breviary of 1260, in which some of the monastic complexity was simplified for ease of travel, to the sixteenth-century Council of Trent. The official text of the council was the 1614 *Rituale Romanum,* promulgated at a time when the Counter-Reformation against Protestant reformers demanded uniformity even in highly inculturated practices such as those surrounding death. This first "universal" funeral rite was an attempt to strike a balance between "confident hope and realistic prayer for forgiveness," but it had to do so through some of the most extraordinary changes in Western history while remaining a fixed rite. Certainly the experience of the ritual in 1614 was very different from the experience of the same ritual in 1962.[27]

As in earlier eras, the official liturgy reflected only part of the story. The popular devotions of Christians in many different parts of the world played a major role in Christian death practices, spanning many audible and visible reminders of death (tolling bells, inscriptions on graves, mourning clothes, cultural times of mourning, the traditions of home wakes, and particular pieces of music) as well as crossing into societal or civic practices. The two overarching concerns—the reminder that the death of a loved one provided to the living to prepare for their own death, and the sense of urgency to do something for the deceased—were reflected in the official liturgy and in the popular religiosity of the time. The most characteristic element of the time was the Mass offered for the dead.

> This is not to say that . . . faith did not exist. Faith was indeed alive, but it concentrated its attention on the lot of the deceased in purgatory, mirrored in the funeral rites, and expressed its vitality more in popular devotions than in the liturgy. Novenas and pious practices such as visits to the Blessed Sacrament and the rosary, as well as an emphasis on indulgences gained "for the poor souls" meant more to the faithful than the funeral liturgy. In this context, even the Mass was "applied" for the release of souls from purgatory. By this point in ritual history, "saying Mass" had come, by way of later medieval piety, to mean performing the ritual of the order of Mass correctly so that the fruits of Calvary could be applied to the living and the dead. In the same way, funeral liturgy, including the funeral Mass, came to be performed for the repose of the soul of the deceased.[28]

The remoteness of the unchanging official, universal liturgy was often an impetus for Catholics in cultures far removed from Western Europe to create and maintain popular devotions that "spoke the language" of their participants. Many of these local traditions addressed the hopes and fears regarding death far better than the official liturgy. This was the ritual situation in 1962 when Vatican Council II was called, resulting in the *ordo exsequiarum* of 1969 and its subsequent changes and translations.

Contemporary Roman Catholic Death Practices

The official contemporary funeral rites were presented above in the preliminary orientation section. In the United States, the OCF has been an accepted part of the landscape for close to fifteen years. One of its great strengths is the outward ritualizing of an interior process of narrative and grief. In its three steps (hence the use of the word *order*), the vigil or wake allows ritual space for the telling of the story of the deceased and for expressions of grief and lament. The funeral liturgy proper, normatively a Eucharist, incorporates the story of the deceased into the story of the death and resurrection of Christ. In the liturgy, the medieval service of absolution is replaced by a service of commendation, which in its central prayer summarizes much of the early church theology while rejecting the emphasis on unworthiness of the late medieval church.

> Into your hands, Father of mercies, we commend our brother/sister N. In the sure and certain hope that, together with all who have died in Christ, he/she will rise with him on the last day. Merciful Lord, turn toward us and listen to our prayers: open the gates of paradise to your servant and help us who remain to comfort one another with assurances of faith, until we all meet in Christ and are with you and with our brother/sister for ever.[29]

The honoring of the body with incense at the commendation rejects the late medieval emphasis on purification and instead stresses the theology of the incarnation and the belief that the human body functions as a temple of the Holy Spirit.

The third ritual step, the Rite of Committal, continues the comforting of the mourners and the honoring of the deceased while intentionally countering the cultural "denial of death." The insidious cultural traits of North America that contribute to this denial, particularly the ideal of rugged individualism,[30] are seen as antithetical to funeral liturgies striving for integrity.

> The denial of death, or more broadly, the denial of mortality and ageing for many Americans, is really a terror of death so extreme that Ernest Becker defines "real heroism" as "first and foremost a reflex of the terror of death. We admire most the courage to face death." But for the many who do not wish to be heroes, facing a Christian funeral liturgy, in the vernacular with understandably clear statements about physical death, gestures towards the corpse, and a giving up of control to God, is to face head on the terror of death. Even many church-going Christians think their faith is on firm ground until faced with this ultimate challenge, and must then decide if Christianity is indeed an "immunity bath" from fear of death and death itself.[31]

The Rite of Committal strives against this denial of death in several ways, most notably in the leave-taking gestures at the grave itself. There is a clear preference to lower the coffin into the ground in the presence of family and friends. "The OCF views the *actual committal of the remains* as the real climax of the rite. . . . Now these remains are committed to their final resting place. This act of 'letting go' is perhaps the most difficult for family and close friends."[32] Popular religion and pressures of the larger culture, however, contributed to another practice that makes the psychological and ritual finality even more difficult to manage. The rise of cremation as the preferred method of committing the remains of the dead presents a challenge to the 1989 rite. Cremation for Roman Catholics has been permitted since 1963, but the official stance is still for burial, as stated in the theological introduction to the rite: "For the final disposition of the body, it is ancient Christian custom to bury or entomb the bodies of the dead; cremation is permitted, unless it is evident that cremation was chosen for anti-Christian motives."[33] In spite of this official position, many Catholic Christians in North America and Western Europe opt for cremation. The elements of the ritual that focused on the body (reception, final commendation) remain problematic with regard to cremated remains, and this cultural phenomenon will undoubtedly change the rite in future publications.

On other issues the 1989 OCF challenges and changes long-standing theological assumptions. Two additions are noteworthy. First is the augmentation of the funeral rite for children, which did not exist as a full rite until after the reforms of Vatican II. The expansion includes, for the first time, the official blessing of funeral rites for an unbaptized child. In a prayer for those who mourn:

> God of all consolation, searcher of mind and heart, the faith of these parents (N. and N.) is known to you. Comfort them with the knowledge that the child for whom they grieve is entrusted now to your loving care.[34]

The second is the inclusion of prayers for those who died at their own hand, both prayers for the dead and prayers for those who mourn suicide victims.

> God, lover of souls, you hold dear what you have made and spare all things, for they are yours. Look gently on your servant N., and by the blood of the cross forgive his/her sins and failings. Remember the faith of those who mourn and satisfy their longing for that day when all will be made new again in Christ, our risen Lord.[35]

Thus the official rite itself has both absorbed cultural influences and prophetically challenged centuries of theological assumptions.

While the official rites are fundamentally the same throughout the world, there are cultural differences, particularly in adaptations to the rite and through nonliturgical practices of popular religiosity, where the genius of particular cultures has shaped and added to the practices surrounding death. Nowhere are these inculturations more necessary than in non-Mediterranean, non-European, non–North American contexts, where Christianity meets cultures with radically different worldviews. For a religion in which inculturation is a fundamental act (God become human), the ability to express faith in Jesus Christ through customs and rituals meaningful to communities is essential. "The Incarnation of the Word . . . is not only the theological foundation and the 'raison d'être' of adaptation but also the prototype and paradigm of the same."[36] True inculturation changes two cultures, the culture of the universal liturgy and the local culture in which it is incarnated. Two examples from different continents may suffice as an introduction.

African cultures are diverse in their cultural expressions and in their degree of adaptation in the liturgy, but a common thread in many countries is the respect for ancestors and rituals that reiterate the ongoing communion and mutual responsibility of the living for the dead and the dead for the living.

> In African Christianity—at least in principle—there is no conflict between invoking ancestors and respecting the ontological uniqueness of God because ancestors are never considered the ultimate recourse. That role remains with God. If the role of the ancestors were ever considered to be absolute, then invoking them could be the sin of idolatry. . . . The ancestors are allies of God. They are always at God's side doing the divine will. Because of their dedication to the will of God, they find a place alongside belief in the gospel, which is God's word expressing God's will.[37]

This ongoing relationship with ancestors is expressed in two ways particularly related to death practices. The first is prayer in which God is recognized and named as the great ancestor—"O Father, Great Ancestor, we lack adequate words to thank you"[38]—and in litanies of saints expanded to include more immediate ancestors. François Lumbala explains the ritual relationship between ancestors and saints in the litany in the following way:

> The preoccupation is on the communion in life between parents and children, which must be in place prior to any important action. The saints are added after the ancestors to underscore the act that those who are beyond "the clan" form part of the union of members as well, thanks to the new source of communion, that is, the blood of Christ. But this new source for the communion in life between members does not sublimate the original resource, that of ancestral mediation.[39]

Second, this mediation of Christ and the ancestors is most clearly expressed in the meal of integration, the Eucharist, and some adaptations, such as those in the Congo, in which the ancestors, represented by a white vase (the color of ancestors and death), are symbolically given a host during the communion rite of the Eucharist. The priest "takes the host, dips it in the wine, and moves toward the vase," saying:

> You, our ancestors, Jesus, who we call the Christ, has come among us with a new pledge. His offering exceeds everything that we have thus far offered to God, all that we have offered you. We participate in his sacrifice to flourish and be saved. Be with us. We join with you so that you also may attain the fullness of life in the new heaven.[40]

In this ritual and in others, the unity of the living and the dead is particularly expressed for a number of African Christians.

From Latin America, a number of indigenous cultures with high regard for remembering the dead met colonial Catholicism's view on commemoration and enriched the practice immensely. This syncretistic pattern in which a European faith was "naturalized" resulted in a type of "living Christian creed," not so much recited as lived out in a yearly pattern of fasting and feasting.[41] In Mexico, this syncretism created the days of the dead (*Dias de los Muertos*) out of the meeting between an eighth-century European establishment of "All Souls Day" and indigenous traditions. Unlike the early church tradition of observing the death date of the family member every year, the primary remembrance here is November 2 (or over a span of days for different categories of the dead). It is primarily a family day commemorated in two locations—first in the home, where it "is a time of family reunion not only for the living but also the dead who, for a few brief hours each year, return to be with their relatives in this world,"[42] and then at the grave in the cemetery, which each region decorates in particular ways. The offering (*ofrenda*) is set up at the grave and at the home, with food, flowers, candles, and artwork often centered on skeletons representing the dead engaged in the activities of the living.

> Clothing and personal goods, either favourite possessions of the deceased when alive, or new items, specially made or purchased for the occasion, are added to some offerings. These will be placed to the side of the table. . . . As with the food offering, these items will eventually be used by the living. . . . When the souls have had their fill, it will be the turn of the living members of the family to take their share of the ofrenda. Some part of the offering will also be distributed among relatives, godparents, friends and neighbours and some part will be taken to the cemetery to be placed upon the graves of the deceased. The community-wide sharing of the offerings is an important social occasion during which relationships of all kinds are reaffirmed.[43]

Hence, the dead, at the invitation of the living, have closed the gap between the living and the dead and renewed the bonds among the living. In many ways, these practices hark back to the late medieval period of church history in which death was not so much the enemy but a part of life, and the celebrations were both family reunions and a commentary on "the vanities of life."[44]

These examples are only two of many around the world where the Roman Catholic Church, with its universal liturgy, still feeds and encourages cultural differences that give expression to cultural and Christian beliefs about death. In its threefold ritual intent—to praise God, to commend the dead to God, and to console the mourners—and in many languages and cultural practices, the Roman Catholic liturgy still "confidently proclaims that God has created each person for eternal life and that Jesus, the Son of God, by his death and resurrection, has broken the chains of sin and death that bound humanity."[45]

THE ANGLICAN COMMUNION AND DEATH: "IN SURE AND CERTAIN HOPE"

An Orientation to Anglican Practices

"Anglicanism is a mystery." That was the perfect response from a colleague to my question of how to succinctly describe the riddle that is the Anglican Communion. Anglicanism is neither Catholic nor Protestant, both Catholic and reformed, the via media, the harmony of balance between scripture, tradition and reason, the Church of England in different clothes, a global religion in which the "average Anglican is a forty-year-old African woman,"[46] all of these, none of these.

What began as a political reform movement in Roman Catholic England at the declaration of ecclesiastical independence by Henry VIII in 1534 also became an opportunity for the increased reception of continental Reformation ideas and indigenous vernacular writings regarding the state of the church. Despite the views of the contemporary Parliament, which "declared that ecclesiastical independence did not imply any intention 'to decline or vary from . . . Christ's Church' concerning 'the Catholic faith of Christendom,'"[47] the break from Rome plunged the official Christian Church of England into centuries of a tug of war between radical Protestants, "Puritans," opposed to anything ritually or theologically resembling Rome, and "Catholics" who saw the Church of England as the legitimate continuation of the sixth-century see of Canterbury.[48] At the heart of that struggle was (and still is) the corporate manner of prayer. How the liturgy is done, how the sacraments are celebrated, how the rite represents and creates unity in a Christian community that has neither pope nor magisterium, are all of crucial importance. As Anglicanism became more than the Church of England throughout the sixteenth and seventeenth centuries in particular, carried by "explorers, traders, and colonists" throughout the world,[49] the liturgy and the episcopacy (actually all three orders of ministry: bishop, priest, deacon) became the distinctive hallmarks of this church.

The contemporary structure is synodical, similar to Eastern Orthodox churches, with independent churches represented at gatherings of the episcopacy known as the Lambeth Conferences. In addition, there are several layers to the "Instruments of Unity," whose bonds are strengthening, rather than weakening, through concerted efforts in recent years. The Archbishop of Canterbury himself, the now-annual meetings of primates and archbishops, and the Anglican Consultative Council all function as ways to link the "Churches of the Anglican Communion . . . by affection and common loyalty."[50]

This excursus on ecclesial structural is by way of explaining that the Anglican Communion has no universal binding authority in liturgical matters other than the national or locally structured hierarchical churches. Therefore, to speak of "official" liturgies of burial is to recognize the great similarities in the member churches of the Anglican Communion but to also acknowledge that there is not an "Anglican burial rite" that fits all sizes. *The Book of Common Prayer* (BCP) is what binds the churches into a form of unity, but each church has its own version of the BCP, and increasingly the common root (often considered the 1662 *Book of Common Prayer* of the Church of England) is enriched and diversified by both local culture and ecumenical discussions.

To take two examples of "official" texts of death practices: In the United States, the 1979 *Book of Common Prayer,* with its two rites for "the Burial of the Dead," remains the official text. It also now contains a supplement in *Enriching Our Worship 2* for the "Burial of a Child," and *Enriching Our Worship 3* (forthcoming) will augment the burial services for adults. These together constitute official and/or authorized texts in the United States. In the Church of England, the 1662 prayer book still contains the official burial liturgy. It has also been supplemented with an authorized, but not required, series of rites under the title "Funeral," included in *Common Worship: Pastoral Services,* published in 2000.[51]

These are official rites, but as with the Roman Catholic rites above, there are also practices of popular religiosity and civic religion that factor into the overall experience of death for modern Anglicans.

Historical Development

Just as with the difficulty of succinctly defining *Anglicanism,* choosing a starting point for the historical development of Anglican burial rites is also a controversial issue. Many Anglicans would begin with the first century of the common era, tracing the theology from the Gospels and the practices as described above in the Roman Catholic section. Others would begin in the mid-sixteenth century, when Thomas Cranmer and others adapted and translated the medieval rites of funerals for their English constituency. However, because so many of the contemporary official rites are products of the late twentieth-century ecumenical liturgical movement, with its emphasis on the practices of the early church, the former seems far more accurate and authentic. In that case, much of the historical development has already been traced above, and this section will be concerned with a few aspects peculiar to the history of English popular religion and the Anglican prayer book traditions over the last 450 years.

Characteristics of English Burial History

Archaeological evidence in southern England reveals the active presence of Christians by the early fourth century,[52] confirming the longevity of Christianity in the area. Key to English Christian history, however, is the establishment of the see of Canterbury through the sending of St. Augustine by Pope Gregory I and the contemporary northern missions of St. Aidan and other Irish missionaries.[53] These two differing approaches shaped English Christianity until the Norman invasion, with the Roman Christian approach gradually taking precedence over Celtic influence. One of the primary vehicles of the triumph of Roman Christianity was Benedictine monasticism, a movement that shaped the church, liturgy, and particularly the practices surrounding death, until the Reformation.[54] It is in the emphasis on the office for the dead, in imitation of the monastic vigil and office, where the "monasticizing" of Christian liturgy in these centuries in best seen, conforming the prayer patterns of laypeople to those of the monastery.

In addition to the monastic overlay to death practices, there were several practices in England that were either unique or emphasized to a greater degree than the medieval practices listed under Roman Catholicism in general and that continued to influence (either negatively or positively) Anglican practices after the Reformation.

First is a situation reflective of a political emphasis in England after the Norman Conquest (and particularly after the promulgation of the Magna Carta in 1215) that saw a relatively strong sense of the right of the individual. As death approached, this appreciation for the individual person gave rise to an emphasis on hearing the last requests of the dying person: "The dying person was responsible for leaving both the material and spiritual estates in good order by the writing of a will. . . . The will and testament allowed the deceased to gain spiritual benefits for the soul and control the distribution of funds to family and friends."[55] While last requests and verbal wills were acceptable (and probably for the lower economic classes, the only option), the rise of executors and written wills in the fourteenth century leaves an interesting record of material and spiritual concerns.

Another area of emphasis in England was ritually centered on the procession from the home to burial, which was an outward expression or opportunity for a web of social obligations and opportunities. As the body was moved from the home, it was preceded by bells rung to announce the procession and the identity of the deceased (one's social status was apparent in the number of bells and strokes), to call for prayers for the deceased, and to "frighten off devils."[56] Religious guilds, not unique to England but important in the social fabric, added elements to the procession and helped pay for the funeral, mourn the dead, care for the family, and pray for the soul of the deceased.[57] The procession (and the previous preparation of the body) were also considered the proper time for alms, particularly in the form of clothes given for the poor (who were then often invited to participate in the procession) and of food to be served at a meal following the burial, to which some poor people were invited. "The poor were an important part of the funeral, as it was thought their lowly and humble status meant that their prayers for the departed were especially beneficial."[58]

With the emphasis on the preparation for dying and on the procession, the actual burial was not augmented or extended in any particular way in the early medieval period, but it gradually took on more significance as the Reformation swept through England. In the early centuries of English Christianity, the burial of a Christian was distinguished from that of the pagans by the lack of inclusion of things in the grave, resulting in simple burial finds. Christians were buried with their feet to the East (to be ready to stand at the second coming) and one to a grave, even for most infants. In later centuries, clergy were buried with their vestments and with the ritual materials handed them in their ordination, and eventually this practice was extended to the nobility, who were buried with the signs of their office and status.

With the advent of the Reformation, how one was buried became an outward symbol of whether one was truly Protestant (the simplest being Puritan burial of the body with no prayers) or truly Catholic (with commendations and prayers for the soul). Ironically, the less emphasis there was on the soul's future in Protestant circles, the more concern there was about the burial place, particularly in the form of ostentatious tombs, at least for the wealthy and elite. They were elaborated with carved effigies, images of the deceased, and/or secular imagery, and the burial became more a matter of "social status rather than religious desire to help the soul."[59] Perhaps a more positive spin on the elaborate graves might be to see them as fulfilling a prophetic role. As post-Reformation piety diminished the stress on praying for the dead, the sometimes gruesome carved figures on graves functioned as reminders to the living to put their lives in order, a sort of evangelism from the dead.

The final emphasis that is discernible in English burial practice is how the commemorative practices for the dead shift before, during, and after the Reformation. The English countryside was laced with burial chapels and chantries based on the Benedictine monastic character of the church and the popular piety of Christians in general, built and endowed to maintain the practice of commemorating and praying for the dead. But this system of buildings, prayers, endowments, and beliefs collapsed with the dissolution of the monasteries under Henry VIII and the Protestant questioning of the fate of the soul after death. If purgatory was the immediate repose of the soul, and the soul moved through its own remorse and through the prayers of the living, then the systematic theology regarding the dead could remain intact. But the combination of theological challenge and political greed affected burial practice like no other event could have.

> In 1531 the reformer John Frith wrote *A Disputacion of Purgatorye.* Frith rejected the idea that prayers for the dead could have any beneficial effect. The only way to purge sin was by the blood of Christ, who stood between God and mankind. It was Christ, and Christ alone, who could save: priests, prayers, alms or the other traditional methods were of no consequence to the soul's salvation.[60]

In many areas traditional burial practices and beliefs continued, in spite of the wholesale destruction of churches and open attacks on suspect theology, but in city parishes particularly the changes in belief regarding the location and status of the soul destroyed more than the buildings in which those prayers were housed. The mutual need and complex relationship between the living and the dead was strained and broken, and a more social idea of memorial by the living for the dead began to take its place.

The Burial Practices of the Books of Common Prayer and Popular Religiosity

The gradual simplification of the funeral, at least in the official rites of the Anglican prayer books, resulted in a focus on the office of the dead and the prayers at the actual burial. Because of the narrow scope of the official rites, the whole service came to be known as "the Order for the Burial of the Dead," rather than as the Requiem Mass or the funeral. The office, basically a short, noneucharistic prayer service of prayers, psalms, and scripture, normatively took place in the church. At the conclusion of the office, the service moved to the grave, where prayers accompanied the lowering of the body and the throwing of earth onto the body or coffin in its resting place. The commendation of the dead to God, so central to the funeral rites for centuries, was replaced by a committal to the ground (although restored to the ministration to the dying in the 1662 BCP):

> Forasmuch as it hath pleased Almighty God of his great mercy to take unto himself the soul of our dear *brother* here departed, we therefore commit *his* body to the ground; earth to earth, ashes to ashes, dust to dust; in sure and certain hope of the Resurrection to eternal life, through our Lord Jesus Christ; who shall change our vile body, that it may be like unto his glorious body, according to the mighty working, whereby he is able to subdue all things to himself.[61]

The graveside service concludes with the Lord's Prayer and a prayer for the mourners, not so much for consolation but to be raised "from the death of sin unto the life of righteousness."

This simple service, fixed in the 1662 prayer book and then spread to the prayer books of Anglican churches outside of England, reveals only the official rite. In many places there were still requiem masses, elaborate processions, home services at the preparation of the body, and various cultural additions, depending on where the Anglican church found itself.

One element of popular religiosity that found root in the Church of England earlier than in the Roman Catholic Church was cremation, legally dating from the turn of the twentieth century.[62] Since then, the rate of cremation has risen to include nearly three-fourths of all Britons and 70 percent of Christians in Britain.[63] In spite of the popularity of cremation, however, there is little in the way of a parallel theology. The language and imagery of Anglican funeral rites is still primarily focused on burial and the body, a focus emphasized by a twentieth-century restoration of the centrality of the image of the human body as the temple of the Holy Spirit. But, as the practice of cremation grows in other countries with sizable Anglican populations (as it has in Japan particularly), there is a need to bring the popular practice and the official rites more into alignment. In all of these geographical locations, the relationship between the church, the officiating clergy at a funeral, and the crematorium itself is yet to be worked out. J. Douglas Davies has raised a concern that the move to cremation may result in more "secular funerals," partially because the location and method of cremation has the potential to underemphasize Christian theological issues.[64]

Another element that falls under the heading of inculturation or popular religiosity is the rise of the memorial service as opposed to a funeral. Memorial services were ordinarily done at a temporal remove from death and without any body or physical reminder of the deceased present. Reaching back to roots in the Reformation, with the stripping down of the official ritual and the rise of social funerals, and escalating through the public process at memorials for major public figures, the memorial service emerged from being an occasional service done when the body was lost at sea or the family scattered to a more socially acceptable service for "Christianity lite." In other words, the memorial service has the potential to be used as an alternative service, not out of necessity, but on occasions when all overt reminders of death, such as a body, and the accompanying need to reflect on Christian faith in life after death are avoided as too much harsh reality.

Anglican funerals, on the other hand, are clearly and unapologetically Christian, with belief in the Resurrection central to the ritual actions and prayers. They engage people emotionally, mentally, spiritually, and physically in a process that is necessary to healthy acceptance and living. All good liturgies contain fundamental tensions that are necessary to allow participants access into the symbolic world expressive of faith and perceived truth, as well as to ritually enable people to move from one place to another. Funeral liturgies in particular are both comforting and prophetic, proclaiming both death and resurrection, this life and future life, mortality and immortality. These tensions and others like them are outwardly represented in symbolic things and actions which give the liturgy its liminal power, because symbols "work" only in juxtaposition with other symbols, contexts, or experiences. Traditionally funerals embody these tensions, saying many different things simultaneously out of necessity. Memorial services may do this also, but they often are ritual attempts to remove all tension, all fear, all questioning, and all confrontation with death, which strips them of the ability to engage people in the threefold work of praising God, commending the dead to God, and consoling the mourners.

Developments like these, as well as the simplification of the official rites in the prayer books, have met a serious challenge in the contemporary funeral rites of various Anglican communities. These new rites—the products of scholarship on early church practices, anthropological and sociological studies on the processes of grief and rites of passage, and ecumenical sharing—have produced official death practices that share much with what we know of the first millennium of Christian practice.

Contemporary Anglican Death Practices

Unlike the Roman Catholic official rites, which begin with a universal rite and then become incarnate through various adaptations, the rites of Anglican funerals are produced locally (understood to be a country or linguistic grouping of dioceses) and united by a generalized sense of historical tradition, scriptural interpretation, and prayer book *ordo.* In addition to the official rites, there are reflections of popular piety and culture in all the actual practices surrounding death, as well as civic obligations and incorporations. Below are two examples of Anglican rites, from the United States and from New Zealand.

The Episcopal Church of the United States: Death Rituals

The expansion of official funeral liturgy in the 1979 BCP reveals the ecumenical and early church scholarship mentioned above. Although awkwardly presented, the BCP includes the elements of a full order of rituals accompanying the seriously sick, the dying, and the dead. Under "Ministration to the Sick," the communion to the sick from the reserved sacrament is found restored, which continues the ancient tradition of viaticum. A unique element is the assurance by the priest to the sick and dying that if they are unable to "eat and drink the Bread and Wine . . . [they will still enjoy] all the benefits of Communion . . . even though the Sacrament is not received with the mouth."[65] In the subsequent ritual section, entitled "Ministration at the Time of Death," the Reformation image of "this miserable . . . world"[66] is dropped and several ritual texts restored from early Church sources. There is also the bare outline of a vigil, which, like the Roman Catholic restored vigil, focuses on comfort for the mourners and prayer for the deceased.

The funeral liturgy (still called "The Burial of the Dead") is presented in a single ritual structure with two linguistic forms. The body, covered by the white pall as a reminder of baptism and preceded by the Paschal Candle, is carried in the funeral procession into the church. The pall and the candle are both outward signs of a renewed theology of Easter hope: "The liturgy for the dead is an Easter liturgy. It finds all its meaning in the resurrection. Because Jesus was raised from the dead, we too, shall be raised."[67] The funeral liturgy is structured as a Eucharist, which restores the ancient Christian idea of the relationship between the living and the dead in a communion of saints. A grassroots revolt following the "tepid, abrupt quality of the ending of the 1928 burial rite"[68] resulted in the adaptation of the commendation of the dying to construct an ending commendation, very much along the lines of the commendation in the contemporary Roman Catholic funeral service. The liturgical texts were taken from the Eastern Orthodox tradition, which has been the source for many of the liturgical texts for the Anglican Eucharist over the past 450 years. The commendation, however, is also an honoring of the human body and its theological meaning as the temple of the Holy Spirit. This is the rationale for officially proposing that if there is no body there is no commendation (and the ritual action of walking counterclockwise around the body while incensing or sprinkling with holy water is eliminated also).

The final station or step of the funeral liturgy is the committal at the place of burial. This retains many of the textual elements of the earlier Anglican burial services, including the Sarum prayer of committal "while earth is cast upon the coffin." The 1979 text adapts to nonburial (including the possibility of cremation) here by substituting "we commit *his* body to the ground" with "to the deep" or "to the elements" or "to its resting place."

In addition to this official text of 1979, there are more recent texts which reflect the interplay between culture and liturgy in the United States. The first to note is from the 1994 *Book of Occasional Services* (BOS), which contains a "Burial of One Who Does Not Profess the Christian Faith." The funeral service in older common prayer books was clearly for those who died as baptized members in good standing, and the 1979 BCP interprets that as "baptized Christians are properly buried from the church." The BOS ritual addresses the death of a nonbeliever without compromising the faith statements of the normative burial rite. The service of scripture readings and prayer focuses on the wisdom and mercy of God, whose ways are unknown to human beings. It is particularly the prayers for those who mourn that address the grief in a different way, neither pretending that the deceased was a believer nor assuming that the mourners are not believers.

> O God of grace and glory, we remember before you this day our *sister N.* We thank you for giving *her* to us, *her* family and friends, to know and to love as a companion on our earthly pilgrimage. In your boundless compassion, console us who mourn. Give us quiet confidence that we may continue our course in faith.[69]

Another example of ritual adapting to cultural reality is found in the 2000 publication *Enriching Our Worship 2.* In the ministry to the dying contained therein, there is a new ritual (with two optional rites) that addresses the reality of dying in an American hospital in the twenty-first century: "A Form of Prayer When Life-Sustaining Treatment Is Withheld or Discontinued." Intended for either the move from aggressive medical care to palliative care or the actual removal of extraordinary methods of treatment, the ritual presents prayers in language that addresses the mixture of emotions and spiritual doubt that families face at this time. It also contains an act of commitment to the individual who is dying.

> May Christ comfort you as you follow him on the path now set before you. With God's help, I will journey beside you. With God's help, I will watch and wait with you, and with God's help, I will witness the love of Christ by my presence and prayers with you. Before God and your loved ones, I commit myself to you in the Name of Christ.[70]

These are only two of many ongoing adaptations and evolutions occurring in official death rituals today. The next generation of adaptations may draw on different cultural experiences and concerns of piety in a rapidly evolving church in the United States.

The Anglican Church in New Zealand

The Anglican Church in New Zealand produced a new prayer book that was copyrighted in 1989. In the extensive section titled "Funeral Liturgies and Services in the Time of Death," the similarities to other new funeral rites within the Anglican communion are readily apparent, both in structure and in their return to the Easter theology of the early church. Two rituals stand out, however, as representing well the interplay of Anglican liturgical theology and Maori and other island cultures. The first is the ritual titled "Prayers in a House after Death":

> Returning to a house after the death of a family member can be a painful experience for a family. Friends may support them by accompanying them and sharing in a meal. In this service the Church marks the family's return home. It reflects the continuing care for their well-being as they take up their life again. In *Te Takahi Whare* and the meal, the house is re-hallowed for the now smaller family. This is marked by a formal entry into the house.[71]

The bilingual rite begins outside the house and moves through the house, functioning partially as an exorcistic rite ("We sprinkle this place to wash away the effects of all evil, whether of people, or of spiritual powers"), partially as consolation for the mourners, and partially as a blessing for the dwelling and all that live in it. The eating of a meal at the home draws together the Christian imagery of the communion of saints and the necessary human (and indigenous) traditions of funeral meals.

The second ritual is the "Unveiling of a Memorial":

> For many people the final resting place focuses a family's grieving, and their memory of the one who has died. The memorial stone placed there may be their only tangible link with that person. *Te Hura Kohatu* marks the placing of the stone, and brings the family together again to renew their bond once more. It is a symbol of a new beginning. It normally takes place about a year after the death.[72]

As an adaptation of the ancient Christian tradition of commemorating the death of a loved one on the anniversary of the death date, this ritual uses prayer language based on Psalm 139 ("If I climb up to heaven, you are there. If I make my bed in the grave you are there also"), which reminds the mourners that even a year after death, the dead person is still known and loved by God. The dedication of the memorial (usually stone) and the subsequent meal provide a way to begin a new relationship with the deceased as well as a place for ongoing rituals of mourning.

These two examples represent the ongoing evolution of the Anglican burial rites and practices as they put down deeper roots in cultures very different from that of England while still exhibiting a theological faithfulness to the confident hope in the resurrection. "As for me, I know that my Redeemer lives and that at the last he will stand upon the earth. After my awaking, he will raise me up; and in my body I shall see God" (Job 19:25–27).

EASTERN ORTHODOX CHRISTIANITY: "GIVE REST, O LORD, WITH YOUR SAINTS"

An Orientation to Eastern Christian Practices

The Christian churches of the East, so called because of their origins in the eastern part of the Mediterranean and because of their linguistic origins (Greek and Syriac), represent an unbroken continuity with some of the oldest Christian practices. Many of the Eastern Christian churches are also the contemporary heirs of the earliest Christian communities, grouped around the ancient Christian sees of Jerusalem, Alexandria, and Antioch, with Constantinople joining them in the fourth century. These four centers, like Rome for the West, were the primary sources for the development of ecclesiology and liturgy, giving rise to the great liturgical families of the East with all their diversity of practice, culture, and language. From these sees, or in conversation with them, other early church centers were formed farther from Mediterranean origins. The term *Orthodox* (literally "right praise" in Greek) is used by those churches "faithful to the Christological teaching of Chalcedon . . . under the liturgical influence of the see of Constantinople"[73] and by non-Chalcedonian churches (Oriental Orthodox), such as the Coptic and Armenian churches.

The Armenian Church

The Armenian Church is one of the oldest "national" churches, having officially accepted Christianity in the early fourth century, a conversion attributed to St. Gregory the Illuminator. The work of St. Gregory and other Syriac and Greek-speaking missionaries was aided by the invention of the Armenian alphabet and translations of the Bible and patristic writings by the monk Mesrob (360–440). Armenian Christians have long lived as a religious minority since Persian dominance in the fifth century, emerging only in the late twentieth century from Communist rule. During that long tenure, the liturgy of the church has reflected the multiple cultures that conquered the land and influenced Armenian theological discourse. At the same time, the Armenians tenaciously hung onto their Christian belief and their own unique liturgical contributions. Today the Armenian Church, free from anti-Christian rule, is overseen by the catholicos, or patriarch, of Echmiadzin in Armenia, with two lesser patriarchs in Jerusalem and Constantinople. The majority of Armenian Christians live outside of Armenia, the product of a diaspora often forced through centuries of persecution.

The funeral liturgy[74] of the Armenian Church reflects the early influence of Eastern Syrian liturgy, as well as the Antiochene Western Syrian pattern and Latin church influences from the time of the crusaders on. As with other Eastern churches, there are different funerals for the different ranks of Christians (priests, monks, and laity), similar to each other but each with unique texts and ritual actions. In each funeral rite, the texts and rituals are fixed, so the official death practices are done as presented in the ordo, while the popular religious practices (and the different civil practices) vary from area to area and even family to family. The Armenian funeral for laypeople (male and female) is unique in that its basic shape and elements are traceable back to the ninth century.[75] Like many Eastern rites, these funeral rituals represent not so much a liturgical revolution, as in the West, with radically different theology and rituals usurping the place of the older ones, but rather an accretion, with the oldest rituals remaining and new (or duplicate) rituals added over the centuries.

The basic shape of the death rituals is similar to what has already been seen above; what is probably unique is the uniformity of theology throughout. The funeral is a sequence of stations and rituals, spread over several locations and even days. The first station is in the home (understood to be wherever the person has just died). Participation in the psalms, hymns, intercessory prayers, and scripture readings is shared between the family, the deacon, and the priest, representing the various orders and hence the totality of the church as it gathers to pray. Included here is one of the "oldest and at the same time, best known, prayers of Eastern Christendom,"[76] the archetype of which is already seen in fourth-century Coptic texts. This prayer, "God of all spirits and of every flesh," which will be repeated at the graveside service, is a text that links the Armenian tradition with most of the other Eastern funeral liturgies. The second step is the procession to the church, where the hymns, psalms, scripture readings, and prayers are traditionally done at the door (usually before the door or before the inner door in the narthex, or vestibule, of the church building). The placement of the coffin at the door traditionally signified the lower status of laypeople, but it is, however, now common to carry the coffin at least into the nave of the building, lessening the spatial difference between the ranks of church members.[77] The church door, or the area of entrance, has historically and symbolically been important in most Christian liturgies, representing, as it does, liminal space. For funerals, the beginning of the liturgy at the door represents the liminality of the soul between heaven and earth, more than a devaluation of the deceased's lay status. The next procession to the cemetery is accompanied by a hymn, and at the arrival of the procession to the gravesite another set of psalms, readings, and prayers is done, with a hymn ending the procession part. The burial service proper reflects a multiplication of rites, with three different burial rites merged into a single sequence consisting of sets of psalms and prayers accompanying the priest's actions. These actions include the mourners taking a handful of dirt and making the sign of the cross; throwing the dirt into the grave; lowering the coffin into the grave; the actual burial (completely filling in the grave with dirt); a final set of prayers; a blessing; and a dismissal of the people to go in peace. The final station of this sequence is back at the house, where the "popular religious" practice of the funeral meal is preceded by the official house ritual of psalms and prayers, again led by the priest. There is an additional step in the ritual of a visit to the grave on the following (or other) day for another noneucharistic rite of prayers, hymns, readings, and psalms.[78]

Throughout this fixed, official order of death rituals, there is an underlying theology of trust and hope, expressed through praise of God and intercessions. "A characteristic motif in the delivery of the prayer texts is the petition for the raising up [of the deceased] and the rest of the souls of the dead 'in the bosom of the Patriarchs Abraham, Isaac and Jacob.'"[79] In addition, the psalms as prayed are to be understood as spoken in the voice of the deceased, which contributes to a theological stance from the ninth century to the present devoid of the Western urgency of praying for the deceased to avoid the terrors of judgment. In these Armenian interpretations of funeral texts notable theological differences between the medieval West and the medieval East become apparent, especially with regard to the emphasis on praying for the dead to relieve them from suffering. The lasting inheritance of these differences is still apparent in the language and actions of the funeral rites.

It should be noted that the Armenian Church at present, like most Eastern churches, does not allow cremation. Burial in the ground (with the recognition that that is not possible in all situations) is the normative pattern, ritually and theologically.

The Greek Orthodox Church

The so-called Byzantine churches or Byzantine rite churches within Eastern Orthodoxy can be defined as "a group of churches that today are spread throughout the world. They accept the first seven ecumenical councils and celebrate a common form of liturgy."[80] These are Christian communities who chose to agree with the teaching of the council of Chalcedon in 451, and the various centers of their collegial grouping were the ancient sees of the East (Constantinople, Alexandria, Antioch, and Jerusalem). Eventually Constantinople came to be seen as the center of Byzantine Christianity, and the patriarch of Constantinople (Istanbul) has a primacy "of honor" over the other patriarchs and hence is known as the Ecumenical Patriarch.[81] While Greek was (and in many places still is) the primary liturgical language, Orthodox churches in the Slavic areas use old versions of various Slavic languages, and other national churches use a combination of Greek and vernacular.

Turning to one of the Byzantine rites as an example, the Greek Orthodox Church in America represents the common inheritance of the official funeral rites of Eastern Orthodoxy. There are three funeral services, the first being a general service for all adults, another for those who die during "Renewal Week" or Easter Week, and a third service for infants.

The general funeral service for adults has multiple stations or steps, as seen in other traditions. The first station is in the home (or wherever the person has died or is laid out). The clergy go to that place, "put on their vestments, take up the censer, and begin" a service that contains many ancient Christian liturgical texts and chants and focuses on commending the dead to God.[82] When ready, the body is taken to the church in procession (and all the deceased, regardless of rank, are placed on the *solea*—the raised platform in the center front of the church). This second station in the church, the "Funeral Service" proper, begins with a number of liturgical and biblical texts, representing the "accretion" rule of much Eastern liturgy, and continues through scripture readings and the fundamental prayer text "God of all spirits and flesh . . . ," which is read at the coffin. The deceased is blessed by each priest present, and if there is a bishop presiding, he pronounces "Prayers of Absolution," which have obvious affinities with Western traditions of the Middle Ages. The service concludes with the "Last Kiss" or "Farewell," during which all present are invited to give a farewell kiss to the deceased (who is in an open coffin during this liturgy, unlike most of the traditional Western liturgies). The procession to the place of burial follows and a brief station at the graveside is sung, including the sign of the cross first with oil (a remnant of the anointing of the body of the deceased) and a second time using earth with the traditional language, "You are dust, and to dust you will return."[83]

As in the Armenian Church, the rituals and practices of popular religion and civil observations vary from culture to culture and country to country. In many places an extended and obvious period of mourning is still very acceptable, and the meal (funeral lunch) carries ritual weight, as do its extensions in the various commemorations at the grave at measured intervals following death. And finally, as in most Eastern Christian traditions, cremation is not allowed: the theological focus on the importance of the body, on the incarnation, and on the model of Jesus's own burial has shaped a funeral rite that emphasizes the reality of physical death, the reality of spiritual life for the soul, and the eventual resurrection of the dead as whole beings.

CONCLUSION

Like most of the world's major religions, Christianity is rich in diversity of thought and practice. The three Christian communions described above represent only some of the practices that have both handed down the traditions of centuries and adapted them to meet new cultures and ideas. At the heart of the practices surrounding the death of a Christian is the story that for Christian believers makes sense of the mystery that follows life as we know it, the story of the life and death and resurrection of Christ as known through the life and death of the individual Christian commended, honored, mourned, and remembered before God. Like all stories, the funeral is a story told and acted that mediates between what is common to all human death and to all Christians and what is unique about this individual, known and mourned by those left behind, and known and named by God as loved and redeemed. The story, in word and action, reaffirms that "love is strong as death" (Song of Songs 8:6) and that both the communion of persons experienced here on earth and the individual life continue, in ways yet to be imagined.

NOTES

1. Victor Turner, "Ritual, Tribal and Catholic," *Worship* 50 (1976): 504–526, and Catherine Bell, "Ritual Tensions: Tribal and Catholic," *Studia Liturgica* 32 (2002): 15–28.

2. Although the term *denomination* is useful in delineating particular ecclesial groupings, especially in their legal and institutional structures, an important theological point underlies the rejection of the "denomination" label in order not to break the unity of the Body of Christ in the creedal "one, holy, catholic and apostolic church." See Claude E. Payne and Hamilton Beazley, *Reclaiming the Great Commission* (San Francisco: Jossey-Bass, 2000), xi, for an explanation of the denominational label.

3. Usually considered *tradition* (especially using the language of "Church Fathers" for Eastern Orthodox, and adding to that "Doctors of the Church" for Roman Catholicism), *reason,* especially with the Anglican Communion, *historical creeds* for all, *episcopacy* or *apostolic tradition* for all. These are not replacements for the authority of scripture, which still stands as "the norm for which there is no other norm" in all the traditions, but scripture alone is not proposed as the sole authority. All three communions would agree with the ongoing revelation of God through the Holy Spirit as an authority to be acknowledged also.

4. *2005 Catholic Almanac* (Huntington, IN: Our Sunday Visitor, 2005), 333.

5. Domenico Sartore, "Le manifestazioni della religiosità popolare," *Anamnesis* 7 (1989): 232.

6. Ibid.

7. Lizette Larson-Miller, "To Imitate Their Perfection: A Comparison of the Relationship of Christology and Martyrial Liturgy in Sixth Century Gaul and Syria" (PhD diss., *Graduate Theological Union,* 1992) 7.

8. The "very special dead" of the Church, the martyrs, were commemorated in rituals that emerged from private funeral practices into public ecclesial events. See Peter Brown, *The Cult of Saints: Its Rise and Function in Latin Christianity* (Chicago: University of Chicago Press, 1981).

9. See Gregory Grabka, "Christian Viaticum: A Study of Its Cultural Background" *Traditio* 9 (1953): 1–43. The Roman legend of afterlife in the Elysian field and paying the goatman, Charon, to cross the river Styx, had great influence on popular customs surrounding viaticum.

10. Larson-Miller, "To Imitate Their Perfection," 10.

11. Johannes Quasten, *Music and Worship in Pagan and Christian Antiquity* (Washington, DC: Pastoral Press, 1983), 158.

12. Robert Taft, *The Liturgy of the Hours in East and West* (Collegeville, MN: Liturgical Press, 1986), 166.

13. Saint Augustine, *Confessions* 9.1250, trans. R.S. Pine-Coffin (London: Penguin Books, 1961), 201.

14. Edward Yarnold, *Cyril of Jerusalem, Mystagogical Catechesis* 5.8–9 (London: Routledge, 2000), 183–184, the discussion regarding John Chrysostom in Gabriele Winkler, "Die Interzessionen der Chrysostomusanaphora in ihrer geschichtlichen Entwicklung" (Part I). *Orientalia Christiana periodica* (OCP) 36 (1970): 306; and Augustine of Hippo, *De cura pro mortuis,* "The Care to be Taken for the Dead," PL40.596 and *The Fathers of the Church,* vol. 27 (New York: Fathers of the Church, 1955).

15. Frederick S. Paxton, *Christianizing Death: The Creation of a Ritual Process in Early Medieval Europe* (Ithaca, NY: Cornell University Press, 1990), 132–133.

16. Ibid., 143.

17. Ibid., 141–142.

18. The historical evolution of these two rites, essential for understanding how viaticum was "bumped," is too extensive to trace in this brief chapter. The reader is referred to Paxton, *Christianizing Death;* David Coffey, *The Sacrament of Reconciliation* (Collegeville, MN: Liturgical Press, 2001); and Lizette Larson-Miller, *Anointing of the Sick* (Collegeville, MN: Liturgical Press, 2005).

19. The appeal of Peter the Lombard's numbering of seven had much to do with numerology, not simply sacramental theology. But in addition, his succinct definition of a sacrament made a clear differentiation between sacraments and sacramentals: "Something is properly called a sacrament because it is a sign of God's grace, and is such an image of invisible grace that it bears its likeness and exists as its cause." *Sentences* 4,1, 2. Cited in Joseph Martos, *Doors to the Sacred: A Historical Introduction to the Sacraments in the Catholic Church,* rev. ed. (Tarrytown, NY: Triumph Books, 1991), 50.

20. See James M. Clark, *The Dance of Death in the Middle Ages and Renaissance* (Glasgow: Jackson, 1950); Danièle Alexandre-Bidon, *La Mort au Moyen Age: XIIIe-XVI3 siècle* (Paris: Hachette Littératures, 1998); Philippe Ariès, *The Hour of Our Death,* trans. Helen Weaver (New York: Knopf, 1981); Patrick J. Geary, *Living with the Dead in the Middle Ages* (Ithaca, NY: Cornell University Press, 1994); and Paul Binski, *Medieval Death: Ritual and Representation* (Ithaca, NY: Cornell University Press, 1996).

21. The early morality plays, such as the famous *Everyman,* which focused on a "summons of death," captured much of the extraliturgical popular theology that put death firmly in the midst of everyone's life. See O.B. Hardison, *Christian Rite and Christian Drama in the Middle Ages* (Baltimore: Johns Hopkins Press, 1965), 289.

22. Richard Rutherford and Tony Barr, *The Death of a Christian: The Order of Christian Funerals,* rev. ed. (Collegeville, MN: Pueblo, 1990), 58.

23. Contemporary English translation from the *Saint Andrew Bible Missal* (Bruges: Biblica, 1962), 1152. Cited in Rutherford and Barr, *Death of a Christian,* 62–63.

24. "The destination of the soul after death and while waiting for the parousia was often perceived as an intermediate and provisionary state in the theology of the early church. One of the clearest examples of this thought comes from the North African church, where Tertullian begins the discussion on the *refrigerium interim,* a rest for the soul until the second coming of Christ and subsequent judgment (Tertullian, *De anima,* 53, 54, 55)." Larson-Miller, "To Imitate Their Perfection," 57.

25. See Jacques le Goff, *The Birth of Purgatory,* trans. Arthur Goldhammer (Chicago: University of Chicago Press, 1981).

26. Rutherford and Barr, *Death of a Christian,* 92–93.

27. Ibid., 96.

28. Ibid., 95.

29. Prayer of Commendation, 175A, *Order of Christian Funerals* (Chicago: Liturgical Training Publications [LTP], 1989) 90.

30. See M. Francis Mannion, "Liturgy and the Present Crisis of Culture," *Worship* 62 (1988): 98–123, for an explication of the three cultural norms that he presents as antithetical to Christian liturgy (the subjectification of reality, the intimization of society, and the politicization of culture).

31. Lizette Larson-Miller, "In Sure and Certain Hope," *The Way* 33 (1993): 278. Cited within the article are Ernest Becker, *The Denial of Death* (New York: Free Press, 1973), 11; and G. Stanley Hall, "Thanatophobia and Immortality," *American Journal of Psychology* 26 (1915): 562.

32. William Cieslak, *Console One Another: Commentary on The Order of Christian Funerals* (Washington, DC: Pastoral Press, 1990), 147–149.

33. *Order of Christian Funerals,* General Introduction, #19.

34. *Order of Christian Funerals,* Prayers and Texts in Particular Circumstances, "Prayers for Mourners," #14.

35. Ibid., "Prayers for the Dead," #44.

36. Theodore Pereira, *Towards an Indian Christian Funeral Rite* (Bangalore: Asian Trading Corp., 1980), 171.

37. François Kabasele Lumbala, *Celebrating Jesus Christ in Africa: Liturgy and Inculturation* (Maryknoll, NY: Orbis Books, 1998), 44–45.

38. Ibid., 36. Lumbala quotes from a Kikuyu eucharistic prayer.

39. Ibid., 42.

40. Ibid., 49.

41. Virgilio P. Elizondo, "Living Faith: Resistance and Survival," *Mestizo Worship: A Pastoral Approach to Liturgical Ministry,* ed. Virgilio P. Elizondo and Timothy M. Matovina (Collegeville, MN: Liturgical Press, 1998), 5.

42. Elizabeth Carmichael and Chloë Sayer, *The Skeleton at the Feast: The Day of the Dead in Mexico* (Austin: University of Texas Press, 2001), 14.

43. Ibid., 21.

44. Ibid., 11.

45. *Order of Christian Funerals,* General Introduction, #1.

46. This description of the "average" Anglican in the world is from the 1998 Lambeth Conference, "Called to Be a Faithful Church in a Plural World," www.anglicancmmunion.org/lambeth/3/report7.html#1.

47. *The Study of Anglicanism,* ed. Stephen Sykes and John Booty (London: SPCK, 1988), 7.

48. Ibid., xiii.

49. Ibid., 21.

50. From the official Web site of the Anglican Communion, www.anglicancommunion.org/unity.html.

51. (London: Church House Publishing, 2000), 214–401.

52. Kenneth Hylson-Smith, *Christianity in England from Roman Times to the Reformation.* Vol. 1, *From Roman Times to 1066* (London: SCM Press, 1999) 39–48.

53. Ibid., 137–138.

54. Ibid., 195.

55. Christopher Daniell, *Death and Burial in Medieval England, 1066–1550* (London: Routledge, 1997), 32.

56. Ibid., 52.

57. Ibid., 45.

58. Ibid., 84.

59. Ibid., 200.

60. Ibid., 196–197.

61. Prayer at the throwing of earth, from the 1662 *Book of Common Prayer* of the Church of England.

62. J. Douglas Davies, *Cremation Today and Tomorrow* (Bramcote, Nottingham: Grove Books, 1990), 8.

63. Ibid., 6.

64. Ibid., particularly 12–24.

65. BCP 1979, 457.

66. Marion Hatchett, *Commentary on the American Prayer Book* (San Francisco: HarperSanFrancisco, 1995), 474.

67. BCP 1979, 507.

68. See Gregory M. Howe, "Death: Appearance and Reality: A Consideration of the Burial Rites of the 1979 BCP," *A Prayer Book for the 21st Century,* ed. Ruth A. Meyers (New York: Church Hymnal Corp, 1996), 136.

69. *The Book of Occasional Services 1994* (New York: Church Hymnal Corporation, 1995), 176.

70. *Enriching Our Worship 2* (New York: Church Publishing, 2000), 122–123.

71. Introduction to the *Te Takahi Whare* in *A New Zealand Prayer Book* (San Francisco: HarperSanFrancisco, 1997), 871.

72. Ibid., 881.

73. Manel Nin, "History of the Eastern Liturgies," *Handbook for Liturgical Studies: Introduction to the Liturgy,* ed. Anscar J. Chupungco (Collegeville: Pueblo-Liturgical Press, 1997), 127.

74. The Western use of the term *liturgy* as a descriptor of all official ritual events (sacramental and not) is not a correct use for Eastern Christians. "Liturgy" or, better, "Divine Liturgy" refers only to the Eucharist in most Eastern churches. For the sake of continuity and comprehension, it will be used here in the Western sense, recognizing that most Eastern funeral rites do not include the Eucharist.

75. Andrea B. Schmidt, *Kanon der Entschlafenen: Das Begräbnis rituale der Armenier, der altarmenisch Bestattungsritus für die Laien* (Wiesbanden: Harrassowitz Verlag, 1994).

76. Ibid., 110.

77. Schmidt, *Kanon der Entschlafenen,* 101.

78. Ibid., particularly 150–152.

79. Ibid., 116.

80. Nin, "History of the Eastern Liturgies," p. 127.

81. Ibid.

82. *An Orthodox Prayer Book,* trans. John von Holzhausen and Michael Gelsinger (Brookline, MA: Holy Cross Orthodox Press, 1977), 97.

83. Ibid., 118.

CHAPTER 6

Protestant Approaches to Death

Overcoming Death's Sting

GLENN LUCKE AND RICHARD B. GILBERT WITH RONALD K. BARRETT

On February 22, 2001, twenty-five hundred invited guests gathered at Calvary Chapel in Charlotte, North Carolina, for the memorial service of Dale Earnhardt. No photographs or memorabilia of the famed NASCAR racer's career decorated the sanctuary, but a floral arrangement near the pulpit formed the number three, Earnhardt's stock car number.[1] The funeral was a time of ritual remembering that resulted from the shared input of family, the minister, and the funeral director. The service was solemn and brief, twenty-two minutes in all, and according to the Calvary Chapel pastor, it was a simple Lutheran service focused on "gospel hope" and "the resurrection."[2] Two ministers, one from Motor Racing Outreach, a parachurch ministry, eulogized Earnhardt, and longtime friend Randy Owens, of the country music group Alabama, sang a song titled "Angels Among Us."

The actions surrounding the death of Dale Earnhardt illustrate the significant role of the funeral home in contemporary American deaths, a role unheard of in Protestant funerary practices stretching back to the Reformation. The singing of a contemporary country song reveals the influence of individualism and, in some minds at least, is evidence of secularization. Yet the service, according to the officiating pastor, reflected traditional Lutheran practices and expressed beliefs true to the Protestant orthodoxy that Martin Luther articulated in the sixteenth century. Thus, we begin with the Earnhardt memorial service because it provides a snapshot of Protestant beliefs and practices in the new millennium, representing a mix of the traditional and new. This chapter examines recent developments in Protestant response to death in the United States. The authors approach the subject matter from two quite different directions, one a sociologist and the other a thanatologist and chaplain. It is our hope that together these viewpoints yield a comprehensive picture of how contemporary Protestants respond to death. To further broaden our understanding of the diversity among Protestant Christians, we have included a section on the unique role of death rituals in the African American Protestant community, written by Ronald Barrett, a specialist in this field of study.

Studying the diverse beliefs and practices related to death in cultures around the globe and throughout history yields insightful comparisons and contrasts, and American Protestant forms are no exception. These forms invite comparison in their own right, but their importance is heightened when considered in light of the globalizing influence of American Protestantism. The dramatic surge in globalizing multinational corporations and international nongovernment organizations, the equally dramatic expansion of media technology, and the increased mobility through transportation technology has resulted in the dissemination of American Protestant cultural forms throughout the world. Between the missionary initiatives of churches and parachurch organizations and the "carrier" function of individuals in multinational organizations, the American Protestant version of Christianity—especially the charismatic forms—has gained millions of new adherents throughout the world.[3] While Protestant death practices vary greatly around the world, the strong influence of American Protestantism on the growing global rise of Protestantism makes the study of American Protestant death practices relevant.

From a sociological perspective, the work of Peter Berger provides a very useful starting point for understanding Protestant death practices.[4] Berger writes that a primary task of religion is to organize the chaotic swirl of information in life and to construct a meaningful cosmos. He draws on the Greek term *nomos*, meaning "order," to suggest that a society is an order or structure that arranges the information and activity of daily life into manageable, coherent categories. A nomos also describes and prescribes the appropriate or normal relations between these categories. In this way, the overwhelming information that floods an individual and the many decisions regarding this information that must be made daily are made more meaningful through constructed categories of ordering. Across history and cultures, the nomos has most often been in the form of a religious system that provides a sacred, cosmic frame of reference. Berger calls religion the "sacred canopy" because it provides human beings with a transcendentally based system of meaning and moral order, which shields them from the anxieties of meaninglessness and chaos.

*Dis*order (a state Berger calls *anomie*) is characterized as the "oldest antagonist of the sacred."[5] There is no more disordering and destabilizing event in the life of an individual or collective society than death. "Death radically challenges all socially objectivated definitions of reality—of the world, of others, and of self."[6] Thus, religion, if it serves its purpose, must find ways to account for the terror of death and to organize the anomic aspects of death into a meaningful worldview. However, as Berger says, humans forget. It is not possible for religion to account for death and organize anomie into the larger worldview in a single religious moment. For the terrors of death to be kept at bay and for a semblance of constructed order to be maintained, humans must be reminded of religion's ability to order. As Berger writes, "Religious ritual has been a crucial instrument of this process of 'reminding.'" Ritual alone, however, is insufficient: "Both religious acts and religious legitimations, ritual and mythology, *dromena* and *legoumena,* together serve to 'recall' the traditional meanings embodied in the culture and its major institutions."[7]

For Protestant Christians, death is a time to remember both the unique individual who has died and how this life is given its ultimate meaning through the life, death, and resurrection of Jesus Christ. Though Protestant Christianity is marked by its splintering into numerous denominations, the centrality of Christ is common to all, as are the common symbols of the Bible, prayer, liturgy, church community, and clergy. All these symbols are drawn upon in the Protestant response to dying, death, and bereavement and the response of the church as an institution, formally and informally, to all three. These expressions and connection points are common, and, like the cross that is central to the Protestant faith as it is to all of Christianity, it is important to bear in mind that all of them are filters and filtered. Each point is influenced and, perhaps, at times confused or corrupted by the baggage of denominationalism. Within each denomination there is diversity, often contentiously expressed and contentiously received. To these denominations come the individual flavorings of each member, guided by her or his own expectations, needs, demands, and spiritual definitions. This chapter describes elements that one can *generally* assume are present in each Protestant denomination, but we have also been alert for, and open to, denominational meanderings, both official and unofficial, as well as personal meanderings of the committed Protestant. Of course, there are many loosely committed Protestants and uncommitted Protestants. For some people, and for diverse reasons, the Protestant church is a place they visit only on Christmas and Easter and perhaps for special events in the life of the family. Others, often encrusted by bitterness over some loss or wound, have no aspirations for church participation other than "It's there when I need to be buried." In this chapter we focus on those who are committed to an expression of Protestantism to which they turn when forced to grapple with their own death or that of a loved one.

The first section provides a brief overview of the emergence of Protestantism *ab ovo* from the Reformation and how sociologists map the current array of Protestant denominations in the United States. Here we also discuss the central symbols that Protestants turn to when they put their faith into practice. The second section shows specifically the development of Protestant approaches to death, beginning with pre-Reformation forms, continuing to the rupture of Reformation reactions against Catholic death practices and beliefs, and then focusing on American expressions. The third section describes the "typical" Protestant funeral rites and then examines them from a pastoral perspective, that is, how Protestants turn to their faith, prayer, liturgy, church community, and clergy in response to death. Also included in this section is an essay by Ronald Barrett on the unique responses to death among African American Protestants, which reflect their experiences of oppression and community strength. Finally, the fourth section utilizes interviews with clergy and funeral directors to examine how cultural trends toward pluralism, individualism, and secularization are impacting contemporary funeral practices among U.S. Protestants.

ORIGIN AND DEVELOPMENT OF PROTESTANT CHRISTIANITY

Along with Roman Catholicism and Orthodoxy, Protestantism constitutes a major segment of worldwide Christianity. Like all Christians, Protestants believe that the Bible, which consists of what they call the Old Testament (the Hebrew Bible) and the New Testament, is the revealed teachings of God. They believe that God is a Trinity, a being who is three-in-one: God the Father, God the Son, and God the Spirit. God the Son incarnated as a human 2,000 years ago and is known as Jesus Christ (*Christ* means "anointed one"). The New Testament depicts Jesus teaching the need for love, mercy, holiness, forgiveness, and salvation through belief in him. Christians believe that Jesus was crucified by authorities threatened by his teaching, and that he rose from the dead or was resurrected three days after his death, and that he ascended into heaven. Christians also contend that, while Jesus reigns in heaven, he will come a second time to earth to consummate his reign here as well.

The particular version of Christianity that is the focus of this chapter, Protestantism, originated in sixteenth-century Europe as a reformist reaction to perceived abuses in the dominant Roman Catholic church. The origins of Protestantism can be traced to a theological revolt against the Roman church begun by Martin Luther. While Luther was not the first reformer—William Tyndale and Jan Hus anticipated Luther's views and in some instances were Luther's sources—he was the first to gain widespread popular support for church reform. Like his predecessors, Luther was outraged by a number of practices encouraged by the Roman Catholic church. As we shall see in the next section, Roman Catholic death practices and beliefs related to the afterlife figured centrally in Luther's critique. Luther went public with his criticisms on October 31, 1517, when he tacked his Ninety-Five Theses to the door of the Wittenberg church.

Central among Luther's criticisms was concern over the appropriate role of the church in salvation. In the Gospel of St. Matthew, Jesus says to Peter, "And I tell you that you are Peter, and on this rock I will build my church, and the gates of Hades will not overcome it. I will give you the keys of the kingdom of heaven; whatever you bind on earth will be bound in heaven, and whatever you loose on earth will be loosed in heaven."[8] The Roman Catholic church understood Jesus's words to mean that Peter was the head of the church, with power to allow and prohibit human entrance into the kingdom of heaven, and that each priest who succeeded Peter as the pope was also the head of the church with the same power over people's salvation. The Protestant reformers rejected the role of the priest as mediator between humans and God and insisted that salvation was not earned through the Roman Catholic church, but was found through individual faith guided by study of the scriptures. Though he had not intended to start a new church, but merely to protest (thus the word *Protestant*) certain Roman Catholic practices, the debate Luther launched led to the unintended consequence of the schism between Protestants and Roman Catholics. Protestant forms of Christianity subsequently spread through parts of Europe and later became the primary religious tradition in the northern hemisphere of the New World.

Contemporary Protestantism in the United States

Identifying and mapping the numerous Protestant groupings in the United States can be a daunting task. Denominational divisions are based on teachings or interpretations of doctrine, as well as ethnicity, country of origin, language, liturgical styles, and attitudes toward women in ministry and homosexuality. The *Handbook of Denominations in the United States* is a good basic guide for studying the histories and uniqueness of the various denominations in America.[9] From the Table of Contents we learn that there are five divisions under Anglican/Episcopal, twenty-three divisions under Baptist, seven under Brethren, ten under Church of God, and eleven under Lutheran. To simplify the situation, sociologists have typically grouped Protestant denominations into two groups: the more theologically liberal mainline Protestants and the more theologically conservative Protestants. This division between mainline and conservative Protestants is, of course, an oversimplification of the myriad expressions of the Protestant faith, but such characterizations do help us see with broad strokes the increasingly important division between liberal and conservative views occurring not only between denominations but also within them.[10]

The major denominations within mainline American Protestantism are the Episcopal Church (U.S.) reporting 2,320,221 members (2002), the Presbyterian Church (USA) reporting 2,451,969 members (2002), the Evangelical Lutheran Church in America (ELCA) reporting 5,038,006 members in 2004, and the United Methodist Church (UMC) reporting 8.3 million members in 2003.[11] Sociologists call these churches "mainline" because they historically inhabited a central place in American cultural life and enjoyed prestige, intellectual credibility, institutional infrastructure, and wealth. Mainline denominations underwent significant social change in the last century and recast many of their beliefs and practices in ways that conservative Protestants cannot accept as orthodox. The fact that mainline denominations have experienced numerical stagnation or decline while the rest of the United States is growing, both in terms of overall population and in religious interest, suggests that mainline Protestantism is not thriving.[12]

Conservative Protestants include what today are called evangelicals, fundamentalists, and Pentecostals, though the boundaries among these three groups are far from rigid. The growing division between mainline and conservative Protestants can be traced to the end of the nineteenth century, when mainline churches were adapting more liberal stances on matters of faith. The term *fundamentalism* comes from a series of essays called *The Fundamentals,* published from 1910 to 1915, which criticized the growing liberalism among mainline Protestants and identified five nonnegotiable beliefs of orthodox Christianity: the authority of the Bible; the deity of Jesus, including his virgin birth; the substitutionary atonement of Jesus on the cross; the bodily resurrection of Jesus; and his second coming. By the 1930s the conservative Protestantism, called fundamentalism, increasingly was stigmatized for its anti-intellectualism and uncompromising stances on matters of orthodoxy, and a split developed within the group as some members wanted to have a greater engagement with culture. Calling themselves "neoevangelicals," they renounced the separatism that had come to characterize fundamentalism in favor of an "engaged orthodoxy" stance toward culture.[13] In the contemporary United States, mainline Protestant denominations are increasingly becoming marginalized both in terms of numbers and public influence, as the ranks of evangelical churches swell along with their public presence in the political realm. While

Pentecostal and fundamentalist Christians are not as visible in the public sphere, their churches are also thriving. To give some perspective on the changing landscape of American Protestantism, it is useful to note that the conservative Southern Baptist Convention alone, with 16 million members, is larger than all the so-called mainline denominations put together.

Protestant Faith in Practice

Mapping the denominational groupings of Protestants reveals how varied this religious tradition has become, but it tells us little about what they all hold in common. It is important to establish the common symbols or points of spiritual connection that, in varying degrees, are significant to all Protestants today. The word *symbol* does not negate or mythologize their efficacy. What it means is that you can enter any Protestant church and expect these expressions to be present in some form: the centrality of Jesus Christ as the path of salvation and eternal life, the Bible, liturgical rituals, hymnody, prayer, and the division of roles between the laity and minister. If we are to understand how Protestants face death today, we need to consider the importance of these symbols.

The earliest creedal statement in the Christian church was "Jesus is Lord" (Romans 10:9). For Protestants, Jesus is the Savior, the one who opens the door to eternal life. According to the New Testament, Jesus told his followers, "I am the resurrection and the life" (John 11:25–26). In the face of death, Protestants seek Christ's consolation and assurance through the Bible, the living community of believers, and their shared worship. The dying approaching eternal life and the grievers who mourn them expect Jesus's presence, whether they reach out through doubts, anger, despair, praise, or hope. Religious education provides opportunities for children and adults to explore the teachings about eternal life and what grief is. These lessons, often learned in childhood, become the foundations of faith in times of trial, though it can be a difficult struggle to bring the simple truths learned as a child to bear meaningfully on adult experiences.

The Bible, also known to Christians as the Word of God, is central to preaching, teaching, pastoral care, bereavement care, and all that is the church. Christians find hope, compassion, and direction in the Bible. For some, even to hold the Bible gives a sense of the presence of God. The psalms, the comforting words in Isaiah, Jesus's statements of hope, the empowering words of St. Paul, and the visions of the heavenly life in The Revelation of St. John—all of them direct people in their journey through grief. Grievers may or may not say, "Show it to me in the Bible," but that is what they are asking. It is in the Bible that Christians find the God that they seek in their grief.

The earlier chapter on Catholicism explores the sacraments as experienced in the more liturgical Christian churches, but Protestants also have sacraments or special rituals that bring them God's love and forgiveness. Though not all denominations refer to them as sacraments, the two most important rituals are baptism (the rite of initiation that welcomes Christians as Children of God) and Holy Communion, the Lord's Supper or the communion meal. Many funeral liturgies refer to the baptismal rites and some liturgies include Holy Communion, a feast that, for many denominations, connects adherents with those who have gone before them and is a "foretaste of the things to come." Music, singing, or other corporate acclamation is a central part of Protestant rituals. Music serves to edify congregants and lead their praises. Many churches invest significant time, labor, and funds in organs, bands or other instrumentalists, choirs, and music. At times like funerals, hymns and other music are a great source of comfort and faith for the bereaved. Many people, when meeting to prepare the funeral, will discuss favorite hymns, anthems, or other musical selections that speak of the deceased's beliefs and story and provide comfort in a particular way.

Prayer is vital to a Protestant's active relationship with God. Many bereaved relate their inability to pray in these difficult times: "I prayed and prayed and God didn't answer my prayers." This level of honesty cuts to the heart of prayer, for prayer is about relationship with God (even when that relationship feels strained beyond recognition). Through prayer, formal or occasional, traditional or otherwise, Protestants are drawn closer to the God who listens to them and speaks to them.

Protestants view the role of the clergy in different ways, including levels of authority, church structure (polity), garb (vestments), and expectations. What is essential is the role of the laity. Particularly in recent decades, there has been a renewed interest in empowering the laity to take ownership of their church and to be Christlike just as clergy are called to be Christlike. "This is my church," we were reminded by one parishioner in a recent parish squabble. It was a reminder that the laity also has a stake in the care of the bereaved, whether through organized bereavement programs or the simple act of listening.

THE PROTESTANT WAY OF DEATH

Understanding contemporary Protestant funeral practices demands a look back to their cultural past. In pre-Reformation Europe, death was a common, public, and thus ubiquitous reality. Full participation by the family, friends, and church was required to prepare for the disposition of the corpse and to console the survivors. Roman Catholicism at this time stressed the importance of repentance prior to death and taught the existence of a three-tiered afterworld consisting of heaven, hell, and purgatory. Upon death there was an immediate judgment that determined the soul's destination. It was believed that, though sins could be forgiven in life upon absolution by a priest, the soul must still undergo a temporal punishment before entering heaven. Purgatory was understood as a state of purification and preparation for entrance into heaven, but the time spent there could be shortened through prayers and penance undertaken by the living on behalf of the dead. This was possible because the faithfully departed became part of the communion of saints and could share in the grace or surplus merit generated by the good deeds of the saints. It was believed that with the second coming of Christ, the dead would be resurrected as the body reunited with the soul. A final judgment would then occur that would determine who would live eternally with Christ and who would be eternally damned. Because of the belief in the eventual resurrection of the body, burial was the accepted practice of disposition, and the body was treated with great respect throughout the funeral proceedings.

At the start of the Crusades, popes began to offer indulgences for services or sacrifices made by the living for the dead. Christians believed that indulgences could reduce the temporal punishment of the dead in purgatory, speeding their entrance into heaven, and that popes had the power to draw on the surplus merit of the communion of saints and transfer that merit to those in purgatory. In their desire to lessen the suffering of the dead, Christians would engage in service for the church, like fighting in the Crusades, and purchase indulgences if they could afford them. This often took the form of gifts of money or goods to a monastery in exchange for the promise that masses would be said for the dead. Over the centuries, the church came to abuse indulgences by using them to raise funds. For example, in the sixteenth century Pope Leo X sold indulgences in order to finance the ongoing work on St. Peter's Basilica in Rome. The abuse of indulgences was one of the many signs of corruption in the church against which Martin Luther railed. While he and other reformers accepted the Roman Catholic teachings on judgment and resurrection of the body as biblically sound, Protestant teachings on salvation entailed significant theological and ecclesial changes that continue today to differentiate Roman Catholic and Protestant approaches to death.

Reforming Death

The founders of the Protestant Reformation, Martin Luther and John Calvin, rejected the idea of purgatory and taught that upon death the soul immediately entered heaven or hell. Luther explained that, while there is temporal death in which the body and soul are separated, eternal death "is the death of sin and the death of death, by which the soul is released and separated from sin and the body is separated from corruption and through grace and glory is joined to the living God."[14] There is also a second kind of eternal death: "It is the death of the damned, where sin and the sinner are not the ones to die, while man is saved, but man dies, while sin lives on and continues forever."[15] For the Protestants, then, the possibilities for afterlife were limited to heaven or hell. Luther instructed his followers not to sorrow over the dead like others who have no hope, but to comfort each other with God's Word and a certain hope of life and the resurrection of the dead.[16]

Luther's instructions for funerals reflect these new beliefs about the soul's destination as well as his rejection of Roman Catholic practices. Luther writes, "We have removed from our churches and completely abolished the popish abominations, such as vigils, masses for the dead, processions, purgatory, and all other hocus-pocus on behalf of the dead."[17] No longer were the churches to be places of wailing and mourning, but rather resting places for those who were peacefully "asleep," awaiting the second coming of Christ. The proper, decorous way to conduct funerals was praise and celebration of the resurrection of the dead, thereby showing Christian disdain for and defiance of death. Luther's opposition to the ritualism of Roman Catholicism and his emphasis on the soul's glad reunion with God in heaven provide a point of agreement with his contemporary, John Calvin. However, Calvin and his theological heirs introduced their own innovations in Protestant belief and practice related to death.

Even more than Luther, John Calvin rejected the ceremonialism of the Roman Catholic rituals and stressed what Max Weber later termed "this-worldly asceticism."[18] The same simplicity with which a believer was to live was to be maintained in dying and the disposition of the dead. In addition to his insistence on asceticism, Calvin's emphasis on the solitary sinner facing God at the final judgment furthered the shift toward individualism that had begun many centuries earlier. While Luther did not reject entirely the possibility that the dead could be aided by the prayers of the living, Calvin forbade the practice as idolatrous and futile. As his teachings took hold among Protestants, contact between the living and the dead, which was dependent on the idea of purgatory and the obligation of the living to aid the dead, ceased.

Reforming Heaven

The Protestant reformers emphasized the God-centeredness of earthly life and eternal life. Their exalted view of the greatness of God entailed a humble view of humanity. While humans were of great worth as images of God, Luther and Calvin held that, as creatures who were weak, frail, and prone to mistakes, humans were in a considerably lower position than God. Death offered the soul liberation from the frail body inclined to sin, but even in heaven humans were at a lower order of perfection than God. Luther and Calvin depicted blissful communion with God. Yet the bliss was not that of intimate peers, but rather of subjects of God in harmonious, righteous relationship.[19]

The intensity of the Protestant Reformation subsided over time and the charismatic leadership of Luther and Calvin became institutionalized in their churches and cultural life. Protestant beliefs about heaven evolved. Some, like Puritan Richard Baxter, emphasized the spiritual aspect of heaven even more, to the exclusion of material aspects of life. Others went in the opposite direction, emphasizing the material dimension of heavenly life on the new earth that would come. Still later, the Romantic period in the arts influenced ideas about heaven, and greater sensuality between men and women in heaven gained credence for some. While not all Protestants accepted the idea of celestial sex in the glorified state, many came to believe in a "modern" heaven that included work, responsibility, and, most of all, reunion with friends and relatives. The early Protestant idea of heaven as an unending celebration of God in worship receded over the centuries as a more human-centered conception of the afterlife took hold. This conception continues to be strongly held among contemporary Protestants.[20]

Early American Protestant Funerals

The first settlers in what would become known as North America were Puritans, a variety of Protestants, whose approach to death clearly demonstrates the influence of Calvin:

> Thy body, when the soule is gone, will an horrour to all that behold it; a most loathsome and abhorred spectacle. Those that loved it most, cannot now finde in their hearts to looke

> on't, by reason of the griefly deformedness which death wil put upn it. Down it must into a pit of carion and confusion, covered with wormes, not able to wag so much as a little finger, to remove the vermine that feed and gnaw upon its flesh; and so moulder away into rottennesse and dust. . . . When the soule departs this life, it carries nothing away with it, but grace, God's favour and a good conscience.[21]

Because of both their ascetic impulse and their belief that the living could do nothing to aid the dead, Puritans had very simple, unceremonial death practices. "The body was washed, wrapped in a plain white cloth, and placed in a simple wooden coffin."[22] A eulogy would be said, but Puritans did not express grief, which was thought incompatible with certainty in the resurrection. As survival in the "howling wilderness" of this new land became more assured, and as prosperity grew, the Puritan's suppression of aesthetic features in death rituals became more difficult to sustain. As historian David Moller recounts, Puritans began to hold funeral sermons in place of eulogies, to wear symbols of grief, to write verses on coffins, and to give out elaborate funeral rings.[23] By the time of George Washington's death, Protestants were even interested in viewing and honoring his body—a practice Calvin would have considered idolatrous and much too Catholic.[24]

Even though Protestants believed that immediately after death the soul left the body, they came to place a great value on the body and how it was treated postmortem. As scientific advances required the use of more cadavers—that is, corpses that had no inherent value—Protestants became even more insistent that the dead be treated with great respect and given a proper Christian burial.[25] Despite the strong influence of the Puritan founders on American culture, in the development of American death practices the Puritan approach to death, with its emphasis on asceticism and judgment, gave way to a worldview that privileged "romantic, sentimental cultural tendencies geared toward soothing the emotions of the survivors."[26] The practice of embalming, viewing, and burial that became the norm by the beginning of the twentieth century reflected new American values much more so than Protestant ones. Throughout the twentieth century the social forces of bureaucratization and medicalization continued to undermine the role of the church community and the clergy in caring for the dead, though some would argue that the clergy are also to blame for their loss of authority in matters of death.[27] Dying and care of the dead became the purview of medical and funeral experts, and the religious response to death was limited to the funeral service itself and bereavement support.

CONTEMPORARY PROTESTANT RESPONSES TO DEATH

Protestants are accustomed to turning to their religion for support. Some turn inward for private prayer, but many turn to their faith community and pastor especially. The prayers and casseroles offered by the church members, the counseling of the pastor, and the church liturgy, especially the funeral service, are all part of the pastoral response of the faith community to the grievers. Rather than separate the funeral from this wider context, it is important to understand its place within the context of the relationship of the grievers to the church community, the pastor, and their faith. Even before a death occurs, the pastor may be helping the family prepare for it through reflection on their faith. Certainly after the death, the pastor is usually the first person the family turns to for guidance in coping and in planning a funeral that will bring together all the resources of their faith tradition and faith community.

Funeral Rites

There is considerable diversity within the sphere of Protestant funerals, reflecting not only the great diversity of denominational traditions, but also ethnic, class, and regional differences. Despite these variations among the Protestant traditions, Protestant funerals share not only the central symbols discussed above but also American cultural practices such as the reliance on the funeral home and the preference for embalming and burial. This intertwining of religious traditions and cultural traditions makes it difficult to identify what is really Protestant about the contemporary Protestant funeral. To make matters even more complicated, there is a diversity of viewpoints within each person and family as well as each congregation, community, and denomination. Through the various agendas and expectations, even circumstances surrounding the death and the relationship of the grievers to the deceased, the Protestant funeral is still about Jesus, the Bible, the liturgical traditions, prayer, and the faith community. Certainly American death practices have been shaped by many cultural forces beyond religion, but funerals of those who claim to be Protestant Christians continue to reflect explicitly and implicitly the beliefs and liturgical traditions that began with the Reformation.

A helpful starting place is the liturgical orders that have historically provided a kind of road map for how Protestants should turn to faith in response to death. While these orders are used by mainline Protestants, the less liturgically formal Protestants, such as evangelicals and Pentecostals, may also utilize aspects of these orders. The funeral liturgy in its fullest form takes place a few days after the death. It includes a wake or visitation that can last one or two days, a funeral rite in the church or funeral home chapel, and the rite of committal and separation that occurs at the cemetery when the body is lowered into the ground. The three-stage funeral is now frequently compressed into evening visitation before an evening funeral service, with private cremation or burial to follow. Wake services are still held, but frequently have become social events for reunions (among family members living great distances from each other) and storytelling rather than formal prayers and readings. Common too are memorial services, frequently many days after the burial or cremation. These evolutions in funeral practices often move ahead faster than the church's ability to respond to them.[28]

The central funeral rite—what most Americans think of as *the* funeral—remains closely tied to the liturgical orders for mainline Protestants. As an example of a "typical" mainline Protestant funeral service, we include the outline titled "The Funeral: A Service of Witness to the Resurrection" from the *Book of Common Worship* used by the Presbyterian Church (USA):

Sentences of Scripture (from nineteen suggested scriptures listed)
Psalm or Hymn
Prayer
Confession and Pardon [optional]
Readings from Scripture
Sermon
Affirmation of Faith
Prayers of Thanksgiving, Supplication and Intercession
Lord's Prayer
Commendation
Blessings
Procession (Psalm, Hymn or Biblical Song)

Some Protestants, such as Episcopalians (and other Anglicans) and many Lutherans, may also include Holy Communion in the funeral service. To facilitate participation and understanding of the liturgy, some denominations put the liturgy into booklet form to give to families or include it in the church hymnal. While conservative churches that are traditionalist or liturgical in worship style use many or all of the same elements as a mainline Protestant funeral, many other conservative churches emphasize contemporary, nonliturgical worship forms. Because they do not follow a liturgical order, it is much more difficult to generalize about these types of funerals. However, even without a prescribed outline, a nonliturgical worship service would still be structured by the pastor around the basic elements of prayer, scripture, sermon, music, and the theme of salvation through Christ.[29]

It is important to note that the above liturgy does not include a eulogy, something most Americans take for granted as central to the funeral. Traditionally, funeral sermons focused on salvation, and eulogies were an added-on element that many denominations discouraged or forbade. Today eulogies are quite common at Protestant funerals and are often intertwined with the sermon or what some would call the minister's remarks. Most funeral sermons focus on three themes or agendas: something about the deceased, something about grief, and something about God. They are an occasion for expressing gratitude to God for the life of the deceased, but they are also an opportunity for expositing scripture and reminding the grievers of the Easter story of resurrection. Some funerals include a separate eulogy in the form of family remarks or visually through a slide show. Besides accommodating the many viewpoints of the family and friends and the complexity of their relationships with the deceased, the minister must find a balance between stories about the deceased and the spiritual insights sought by the grievers. How much attention is given to each of these elements, the personal and the theological, is an ongoing tension in Protestant funerals.

In addition to the sermon, the central Protestant belief in salvation is particularly expressed through the music and readings. The music played during the funeral service may be traditional hymns or popular Christian songs, but the theme is typically confidence in the reward of heaven. As the Presbyterian *Book of Common Worship* suggests, the hymn sung after the Affirmation of Faith should be a "hymn of confident faith." The scripture passages used in the funeral service also express this confidence in God's blessing on his faithful as a consolation to the mourners. The scriptures most frequently used by Protestants in funeral services are Psalm 23 and the Apostle Paul's 1 Corinthians 15:

> *Psalm 23*
> The LORD is my shepherd, I shall not want. He makes me lie down in green pastures; he leads me beside still waters; he restores my soul. He leads me in right paths for his name's sake. Even though I walk through the darkest valley, I fear no evil; for you are with me; your rod and your staff—they comfort me. You prepare a table before me in the presence of my enemies; you anoint my head with oil; my cup overflows. Surely goodness and mercy shall follow me all the days of my life, and I shall dwell in the house of the LORD my whole life long [New Revised Standard, favored by mainline Protestants].
>
> *1 Corinthians 15:50–57*
> I declare to you, brothers, that flesh and blood cannot inherit the kingdom of God, nor does the perishable inherit the imperishable. Listen, I tell you a mystery: We will not all sleep, but we will all be changed—in a flash, in the twinkling of an eye, at the last trumpet. For the trumpet will sound, the dead will be raised imperishable, and we will be changed. For the perishable must clothe itself with the imperishable, and the mortal with immortality. When the perishable has been clothed with the imperishable, and the mortal with immortality, then the saying that is written will come true: "Death has been swallowed up in victory." "Where, O death, is your victory? Where, O death, is your sting?" The sting of death is sin, and the power of sin is the law. But thanks be to God! He gives us the victory through our Lord Jesus Christ [New International Version, favored by evangelicals].

In general, the Protestant funeral has evolved from a very melancholy occasion, characterized by black vestments and somber music, to a service focusing on a celebration of the resurrection. Many denominations, including United Church of Christ, Presbyterian, and United Methodist, have developed new hymnals with hymns that better reflect the hope of the gospel. Flowers are common, though some services do not include flowers during Lent, and it is not uncommon now for the funeral notice to read "In lieu of flowers . . . , " directing mourners to use those funds to support a designated charity. Vestments, if worn, are now usually white, in keeping with the theme of resurrection and Eastertide. The Easter emphasis is not a rejection of the tumultuous circumstances and the roller-coaster ride of feelings, but affirms them within the Easter victory that says that Jesus's triumph over sin and death will help his followers through the deepest and darkest despair. Taken as a whole, the scriptures, prayers, and sermon or eulogies of the Protestant funeral constitute the comforting "words against death" that are essential to Christian ritual.[30] These words against death are an important reminder to mourners that the sacred canopy, as Peter Berger calls it, carries on, that death's sting has been overcome through Christ's death, and that life together continues meaningfully for the survivors.

The Funeral in the Context of Pastoral Care

The minister undertakes many responsibilities that accompany the funeral. There are legal standards, professional obligations, community mores, and also the expectations of the faith community. Even within the faith community there are multiple layers: the minister's grief and sense of duty, feelings about the deceased and the family, sense of place within the context of the gathered community, and the ritual expectations within the denomination and congregation. The minister has only a brief window in which to balance the needs of family and community, as well as the religious expressions of the denomination, the expectations placed on the minister (particularly challenging when the minister is a stranger to the grievers), and also the minister's own beliefs, professional context, and grief needs. The funeral is essential ritual and meaning, but often a blur to family members, who want to remember every word said but are often too grieved to fully participate in the liturgy. It is important that the minister keep the funeral within the larger context of bereavement care and the much longer need for aftercare felt by the bereaved. In leading the funeral, the minister is both offering the teachings and care of a particular set of beliefs and also endeavoring to build relationships among this community that will remain a resource for the long period of grief ahead.

It is important to understand the enormous emotional investment that surrounds the planning of rituals. Wesley Carr writes extensively on these "occasional services," or what he calls "brief encounters," and the tribulation that can accompany even the planning of these services: "The occasional offices will be problematic moments of ministry. They challenge not only theology and professionalism but also the understanding of the gospel and human sensitivity."[31] Many ministers come to the funeral with their own expectations, whether they be their understanding of their role, the proscriptions imposed by the congregation, or the traditions of a denomination. The mourners arrive with their own needs. Carr explains: "Bereaved people are disoriented. The minister is invited to stand for them on a boundary where they feel at present unable to stand and to manage a process on their behalf."[32] Under these stressful conditions, there is much room for tension, debate, and disappointment, especially when the minister does not know the mourners well.

Expectations for the funeral on the part of the bereaved and the clergy and the faith community vary greatly. Some clergy understand that, especially in a funeral home and when the resources of liturgical space and music are lacking, a funeral will be brief. Twenty minutes is a long time for tired, overwhelmed families, especially after lengthy periods of visitation, lack of sleep, travel, and so on. Other ministers plan to preach for thirty minutes, "preaching the deceased into heaven." One tension that commonly arises is the extent to which the family can personalize the funeral service. The rituals, whatever they may be, may well (strictly speaking) "belong" to the congregation or denomination and the minister may claim the responsibility of "watch keeper" or guardian of those sacred rituals and expressions. In the planning of the funeral, however, the ritual ultimately "belongs" to the grievers. Quoting the reflections of another minister, Carr writes:

> I came to see that what we are asked to perform is *their* ritual, and if we are prepared to do that as one of the still surviving rituals of our society, then we can claim the right to say "can we tell you what *we* see in this?" and to explain the deeper Christian understanding of this ritual . . . the Church is entitled to its "space," but it is not the business of expanding its space at the expense of the world.[33]

Particularly in the case of nominally affiliated Protestants, these tensions between the family and the clergy can force the funeral director into the role of pastoral caregiver and liturgical expert. When it comes time to plan a funeral, many people pick and choose various traditions and "services" from their Protestant tradition but feel reluctant to seek them out in the church. The funeral home often becomes the conduit through which these accommodations and traditions come in an old way, but a new place, to serve the needs of the bereaved. Today's instant satisfaction society demands free access to, and freer choices from, the previously guarded treasures and traditions of the congregation to accommodate today's fashion and today's timetables.

By looking at the funeral within the context of pastoral care, we gain a richer sense of how many Protestants turn to their faith, clergy, and church in the face of death. Some religious traditions have extended mourning rituals beyond the funeral. While there are no formalized mourning rituals in Protestantism, support for the bereaved continues through the pastor and faith community. Many Americans first go to a minister or religious leader for support in times of grief. With the blossoming of support groups, twelve-step programs, psychotherapy options, and bereavement programs, that practice declined in the late 1980s and early 1990s but has again become common as funding for these alternative sources of support has been cut. Today, with 48 million Americans without health insurance, many do not have access to mental health and related programs, and much public and private funding for mental health programs has been cut. By need or by default, Protestants again are turning to their pastors for care and support, and clergy suggest that their counseling load is increasing at a rapid pace.[34]

The laity of the church is also part of the pastoral response to the mourners. Daniel Grossoehme explains this wider sense of pastoral care: "Pastoral care is the formation of relationships with persons of all ages that communicate (both with and without words) and bask in knowing one's self to be a child of God, so that all persons are enabled to live through their life experiences and to understand them in terms of their faith."[35] Though clergy may be the ones to provide formal counseling to the bereaved, lay members of the church are increasingly recognized as playing a vital role during the grieving period, which lasts long after the funeral. Their support may come in the form of meals, cards, prayer petitions, friendship, running errands, or more formally through church-run grief support groups. Through formal pastoral counseling or a Christian support group or the informal support of church members, Protestants find an array of resources that, in addition to the liturgy and prayer of the church, assist them in accepting the reality of death.[36]

The Last Mile of the Way for African Americans and Blacks
by Ronald K. Barrett

The rich diversity within the African American experience cautions us against the temptation to think and speak stereotypically. To do so might suggest that all African Americans are alike. Differences in cultural background, socioeconomics, and religious (or spiritual) orientation among African Americans are important to acknowledge. For example, it has been observed that African Americans differ in their degree of identification with their African ancestry or Africentric values system, which influences end-of-life choices, attitudes toward death, and death rituals. Some African Americans visibly reflect this identification via their self-expressions of dress and personal presentation, hairstyles and grooming, home decor, and other lifestyle choices. It might be fair to characterize African Americans who are Africentric as conservative and traditional in their attitudes, beliefs, and values regarding end-of-life choices, death, and funeral rites. Similarly, in thinking about culture and subculture, it is important to note the distinctions made here between "Blacks" and "African Americans." For the purpose of our discussion here, the term *Black* will refer to persons of African descent, while the term *African American* will refer to that subgroup of Blacks whose sociocultural origin is restricted to the geography of the North American experience. While there is also significant variability in socioeconomics status, most African Americans in the United States can be characterized as clustering around the poverty line—many below and many just above it. It can be said that poor African Americans tend to be conservative in their attitudes toward death and dying and tend to be keepers of tradition (i.e., inclined to do things the old-fashioned way). The religious or spiritual orientation of African Americans will often dictate many end-of-life choices and attitudes and values regarding death and death rituals. A close examination of the diversity of the religious and spiritual orientation of African Americans reveals a wide range of religious traditions, including Islam and Afro-Caribbean religions, but by far the largest religious affiliation falls under the umbrella of Protestant Christianity. Historically, Baptist and Methodist churches were most successful at attracting African Americans, but since the end of the nineteenth century Pentecostal churches have also formed an important base of Black Christianity.[37]

Many of the attitudes, beliefs, and values of African Americans regarding death and dying are believed to have a sociocultural origin in West African religion and philosophy.[38] Contemporary African American funeral customs and practices represent a fusion of both the traditional West African and Western cultural practices. A number of core values have been identified as characteristic of most African Americans' and Blacks' attitudes regarding dying, death, and funeral rites. For example, the sociocultural values of spirituality, death acceptance, a cyclical view of life and death, high investment in and priority of funerals, high social significance of funeral rites, and a preference for ground burials as a form of final disposition are common among most African Americans, Blacks, and people of West African descent.[39]

Spirituality is a primary core value for most Blacks (including African Americans) regarding death and dying.[40] Consistent with this value is a belief in the afterlife, which is common among most Blacks. Examples of this fundamental belief are seen in Black folklore, music, gospels, visual art, novels, and, most recently, rap music and videos. Most Blacks believe that individuals are born on this physical plane and after completing their work here "pass" or "transition" on to the spiritual plane, or the afterlife, to join the community of ancestors. The common reference to funerals as "homegoing celebrations" is a reflection of this belief that there is an afterlife—especially for those who have lived honorably and are believers. This term is particularly common among Black Pentecostals, whereas most Black Protestants (e.g., Baptists, Methodists, Adventists) more commonly refer to the final rites as "funerals." For an individual who has lived an unselfish life of service and been true to the teaching of their faith, the promise of life everlasting and a heavenly afterlife is a traditional belief and expectation. Black Pentecostals refer to this promise as a person being "saved, sanctified, and having the gift of salvation." Contrastingly, individuals who live a life of selfish indulgence and who are unfaithful to the dictates of their faith will experience an unpleasant afterlife filled with hellish toil and strife. Consistent with this belief for many African Americans and Blacks is the belief that the quality of one's life and the spirituality of the individual will also determine the nature and extent of suffering in dying and death. For example, a righteous and spiritual person who has lived a good life and demonstrated kindness and compassion toward others is believed to be likely to die a peaceful, painless death, free of suffering, while unrighteous and less spiritual people might be expected to suffer a more painful death. These spiritual beliefs regarding one's life, death, and afterlife are commonly shared among African American and Blacks. The ancestors and deceased loved ones reside in the community among us and are often acknowledged and paid homage in various religious and traditional ceremonies to honor and reinforce the beliefs and values of maintaining connections between the two communities.

Spirituality provides meaningful insight into a number of cultural beliefs about visitations during and after death. For example, many Blacks report experiencing the visitation and appearance of close deceased loved ones at a deathbed to assist the dying with their transition and passing into the spirit world. Depictions of such imagery are seen in Black spirituals, gospels, and contemporary rap music and videos.

> Precious Lord, take my hand, Lead me on, let me stand, I am tired, I am weak, I am worn; Through the storm, through the night, Lead me on to the light: Take my hand, precious Lord, Lead me home.[41]

Similar imagery is found in other favorite songs, such as "Amazing Grace" and "The Lord's Prayer," performed at many Black funerals.

It is worthy of note that many Black Pentecostals subscribe to a spiritual view and theology that often is in stark denial of the normal experience of grief that accompanies loss via the death of a loved one. For example, many clergy preach or imply that the experience of grief in response to the loss of a loved one is a sign of spiritual weakness or surrender. Instead, true believers should celebrate the loss with joy and happiness in the face of their grief.

> Soon and very soon, we are going to see the King. No more crying there. No more dying there. We are going to see the King.[42]

This contemporary inspirational funeral favorite, characteristically included as a part of many Black homegoing services, suggests that mourners should not be sad or grieve but celebrate with joy the passing of a loved one. Consistent with this spiritual view and teaching is the denial of the attendant emotions of depression, fear, and grief as signs of spiritual weakness that should be avoided or at least not publicly acknowledged at all costs.

It is also a traditional belief that surviving family members may experience visitations of deceased loved ones via dreams, visions, or sensory experiences of the presence of the deceased loved one's spirit. These experiences of visitation during the dying process and after the death of a loved one are fairly commonly reported by Blacks.

As an extension of the value of spirituality, most African Americans and Blacks share a reverence for life and tend to insist on aggressive life-sustaining efforts even when such efforts might appear futile. Culturally, as a group, African Americans and Blacks tend not to complete Advance Directives as compared to Whites. These tendencies seem deeply rooted in the cultural values and spirituality of Africans, African Americans, and Blacks. I have argued elsewhere that the sociocultural experiences of Blacks being denied institutionalized care, cultural alienation, and resulting cultural mistrust may explain the tendency of many Blacks to insist on life-sustaining efforts even in the face of futility.[43]

The communal value and the social significance of gathering at the time of death and final transition are quite characteristic and traditional for many Blacks and African Americans. Most Blacks traditionally believe in the importance and value of the presence of loved ones during this essential passage. Similarly, after the death of a loved one there is a social obligation to attend and participate in the final rites. Funerals and funeral rites are important occasions to renew relational ties and mend social networks as well as pay one's respects to the dead. While many gestures of condolences are important, for many African Americans one of the highest compliments that one can give a survivor is to attend and pay one's respects at the funeral ritual.[44] While friends and loved ones are often given special acknowledgment for their personal sacrifices in attending and participating in a loved one's funeral, the family's expectations of clergy during funeral rites are rather exacting and demanding, since for many African Americans death is a defining moment in the life of a loved one.[45]

Funerals are primary rituals for most Blacks and African Americans. Blacks tend to invest considerable personal energy and resources in the execution of funerals as an esteemed ritual of great importance.[46] African American funeral rites are often characterized as lengthy, delayed, and costly or ostentatious. Consistent with West African cultural traditions, funerals are given great care and planning as they represent an important transition in one's life.[47] In many ways the funeral is a final statement about the role, status, and value of the individual to the family and community. Most African Americans take seriously the task of articulating and declaring that statement. The funeral rites include many symbolic events that reflect cultural beliefs about the afterlife and spirituality. For example, the traditional practice of passing babies over the casket of a loved one is believed to honor and bond the spirit of the deceased with the infant to assure the baby's safety and protection from malevolent spirits in the spirit world. However, this is rarely practiced in contemporary funeral rites. Likewise, the common practice of pouring libations is a ritual of honoring the memory of those loved ones who have moved on to the spirit world but who remain ever-present in the family's thinking as if a part of the family and the community.

In summary, many of the attitudes, beliefs, and values commonly seen among Blacks and African Americans represent a cultural fusion of West African and Western sociocultural influences. While many commonly shared values and practices are seen among Blacks and African Americans, the diversity and variability regarding many crucial concerns can arise from cultural (and subcultural), socioeconomic, and religious (or spiritual) differences. It is also important to note that many of the commonly shared values and practices seen among most Blacks, including African Americans, can be traced back to African cultural influences. Many of the shared life experiences of Blacks and African Americans (e.g., racial discrimination, cultural alienation, cultural mistrust, and so forth) are believed to influence their attitudes, beliefs, and values about dying, especially a reverence for life and the value of life-sustaining efforts rather than other health directives. Blacks and African Americans share many values regarding funeral rites. Most Black Protestants make significant investments in funerals as high spiritual rituals. Funerals for most Blacks are regarded as a significant statement in the life of an individual, and the expectations for others to acknowledge, gather, and participate are quite significant as well.

The Social Context

While the contemporary Protestant funeral is clearly a religious one, it exists within the context of social forces that strongly impact how Protestants respond to death. As we already saw, the trends toward medicalization and bureaucratization that began more than one hundred years ago have radically changed both how Americans die and how they care for the dead. By the mid-twentieth century the vast majority of Protestants were turning to the expertise of medical doctors and funeral directors in these matters, relegating the expertise of the church to the sphere of the funeral and bereavement support. More recently, social forces such as pluralism, individualism, and secularism have had a strong impact on Protestant funerals. In this section we turn to the social context to understand the pressures that are altering long-standing Protestant funeral practices. Much of this analysis is based on in-depth interviews Glenn Lucke held with both mainline and conservative Protestant pastors in mid-Atlantic, Midwestern, and southwestern states in the winter and spring of 2002. These structured interviews, along with sociological literature, are used to explore the story of what has remained status quo and what has changed in Protestant responses to death.

Pluralism

Pluralism occurs when two or more worldviews gain adherents in a particular environment. Sociologists of religion have mixed views on how pluralism is affecting religious life in the United States. Peter Berger articulates one school of thought, that pluralism has negative consequences for religious belief. In his 1967 book, *The Sacred Canopy,*

Berger argues that by presenting alternative worldviews pluralism undermines the taken-for-granted nature of the believer's faith.[48] Against Berger, Christian Smith's more recent research demonstrates that strong religious commitments can flourish in a pluralistic society.[49] However, as Wade Clark Roof has demonstrated, pluralism has led to a new kind of religious style: "What often follows is pastiche, collage, religious pluralism *within* the individual, bricolage, mixing of codes, religion à la carte."[50] By whatever name, this new religious style amounts to sampling a little bit of this religion and a little bit of that religion. While this does constitute vibrant religious activity, it also causes declining respect for religious authority.[51] Clergy have experienced varying degrees of loss in their power to compel belief and action as individuals become their own religious authority.

How does pluralism impact Protestant funeral practices? Pluralism—that is, the experience of other faith traditions—has inclined some Protestants to a more inclusive or universal perspective on salvation. Studies have shown a decline in Protestants holding to traditional orthodox beliefs about the uniqueness of Jesus and the necessity of believing in Jesus for salvation.[52] A declining belief in hell among mainline Protestants means that the two-sphere afterlife of the Protestant reformers has become a de facto single sphere of heaven. These changes in belief indicate that while Protestantism continues, what this faith means to individuals is undergoing significant changes.[53]

The pastors interviewed for this project had varying opinions on the significance of pluralism to their funeral work. None of them could think of instances in which the funeral ritual had been altered to merge two or more faiths, but "spirituality" was increasingly a challenge to the traditional Protestant service. In the words of a mainline pastor, "It is less a scenario of secularization in terms of withdrawal from church and religion, but more so in terms of the increase in spirituality that doesn't translate into anything I would recognize as Christian." In line with this new religious style, one mainline pastor has amended the funeral liturgy of his confessional church, deleting statements that could be taken as promoting the uniqueness of Christianity, even to the point of terminating the reading of John 14:6 before the final clause "no one comes to the Father but by me."

Individualism

Cultural observers frequently remark on the prevalence of individualism in American culture, sometimes with cautions about the diminishment of civil society and the future of democracy.[54] Perhaps the most widely read treatment of this social change came two decades ago with the publication of Robert Bellah's *Habits of the Heart*, which documents the growing impact of individualism.[55] According to Bellah's analysis, many Americans act out expressive individualism as a valued norm of life. In the context of the great bureaucratization of contemporary life, Americans desire to find ways to express their uniqueness. Folkways, norms, and traditions become less valuable and decline in their ability to compel belief and action in this context of expressive individualism. Since tradition has so long regulated Protestant beliefs and practices related to death and dying, investigating the effect of individualism on these beliefs merits attention.

In the qualitative interviews, pastors were asked to describe their perceptions of individualism with respect to death beliefs and practices. The main impact of individualism on Protestant funerals concerns how personalized versus how theological in focus the funeral should be. One southern evangelical pastor valued what he called "personalizing" the funeral and memorial services. Coming from a self-consciously nonliturgical approach to Christianity, he saw the service's celebration of the individual's life as serving a double purpose: to console the bereaved and proclaim the gospel to those in attendance who were not believers. This pastor felt a responsibility to relieve sorrow by highlighting special traits of the deceased, especially kindness and goodness, in one or two humorous stories to accompany the sad necessity of saying goodbye. In his view, personalized services are a worthy goal, in keeping with his church's approach to becoming a Christian, worshipping as a Christian, and living as a Christian.

On the other side of the fence, a mainline pastor was somewhat dispirited by the upsurge in individual expression and the theological shallowness that it reflected. He said:

> I have people now who think a funeral is a show-and-tell of a person's life. You load up the communion table with pictures of a person. You include their favorite songs in the service, even if they're country western songs. There's pressure to let all the family members who want to say something tell a funny story or pine philosophically, because that's what they think it's for. These things are fine, but not in a worship service.

This pastor, a Presbyterian, drew attention to the fact that in the Presbyterian church's *Book of Common Worship,* the funeral service, titled, "A Witness to the Resurrection," was a worship service with God as its focus and humans as secondary beneficiaries. This perspective is at odds with the personalized funeral, which is designed primarily for those in attendance. And yet another pastor noted that an additional effect of personalization was the increase in attendance at funerals. Some pastors made an important connection between personalization and secularization. The focus on the deceased means redirecting attention away from the traditional focus on Christ and salvation. As one mainline pastor explained, "It's whatever people want the funeral to be. A generation ago the funeral was somber, looking forward to the life to come. The funeral entailed sadness, but also forward-looking hope. Now they want to downplay the theology and the religious themes in favor of happy memories." The challenge facing pastors is to find some way to balance the mourners' need for personalization with their need for spiritual guidance in the face of grief.

Secularization

A few decades ago sociologists were talking a great deal about secularization and the supposed death of religion. The linear secularization model, positing an overall decline of religion in society, has not fared well in the last two decades as more and more data show surviving and even thriving religious communities in the United States and the developing world. As we saw in the earlier discussion of the mainline and conservative Protestant groupings, some denominations have declined while others have thrived. Overall, Protestantism remains a vital religious tradition in the United States in both numbers and strength of conviction. The data suggest that secularization, if defined as an absence of religious belief and practice, is not eroding Protestant beliefs and practices.

A more plausible way to understand secularization is as the withdrawal of religion from the public sphere and declining religious authority in institutions.[56] Some evidence suggests that secularization has led to declining religious, or at least ecclesial, authority over the institution of death. As we already saw, beginning in the late nineteenth century, funeral homes increasingly took responsibility for the care of the dead. Though not all clergy view the current prevalence of the funeral home industry warmly, the funeral industry has played a significant role in serving the family of the deceased. With a drop in religious participation in mainline Protestant institutions since the 1960s, it is likely that fewer Americans have a close relationship with a minister. This may account for funeral directors assuming an increased role in attending to the many needs of the family.

The pastors interviewed maintained an ambivalent stance toward the funeral home industry, specifying their own polite relationships with local funeral homes but also reacting negatively to what they perceive as the preponderant role funeral directors have in the services and disposition of the body. One evangelical pastor had very strong views on the relationship between clergy and funeral director:

> The industry defines reality for the death ritual. Loved ones are distressed and don't want to be thinking about the theological implications. The funeral home director calls me and asks, "Can you do a funeral at such and such time?" Which basically means, "Would you like to buy a worship service?" The director is the de facto clergy person, and in some cases he serves *as* the clergy person at the funeral.

However, other clergy enjoy collaborative, harmonious relationships with funeral homes and value the service that the directors provide.

When the funeral home industry spends great amounts of resources in its marketing efforts, it is seeking to influence "customers." Since the funeral industry is the dominant force in disposing of the dead and making arrangements, average Americans rely on the professionals to shape much of what happens after a death. The clergy, family, and death industry professionals each play a role, but the funeral home directors and the families have the most influence in constructing the meaning around death.

CONCLUSION

The death of a loved one or friend brings people to the ultimate realities of life and death, the meaning of life, and that which is eternal for them. The grief that accompanies being bereaved, and the struggles to mourn or express complicated feelings, become the challenges that both bind people together and set them apart. While the turmoil of the contemporary American culture offers many options when it comes to funerals, including the choice to do nothing, essential to all expressions are the need to grieve and the search for meaning (spirituality), hope, and comfort. For Protestants, generally, and particularly so in the case of Black Protestants, this search emerges in the contexts of pastoral care, congregational support, and ritual (liturgy). The particulars vary from denomination to denomination, congregation to congregation, minister to minister, and griever to griever, but all Protestant traditions stress the promise of Jesus as the Savior and Lord, the assurance of eternal life, and the presence of an active Shepherd in the mourner's sorrow.

Contemporary Protestant funeral practices exhibit much that is traditional and much that is new. On the one hand, Protestant beliefs about the meaning of death and salvation are largely intact and bear strong similarity to those of the Reformation. At the same time, funeral practices have changed drastically. The funeral home industry has assumed responsibility for the disposition of the dead and the transition from deathbed to grave. The ascetic practices of Calvin and his Puritan heirs have given way to more expressive, decorative funerals. Dale Earnhardt's funeral is a good example of the mixing of old and new. His traditional Lutheran funeral included singing of a contemporary country song, "Angels Among Us," and flowers arranged as the number of Earnhardt's race car. These unusual elements are part of the growing personalizing trend in American funerals that is impacting funerals of all religious traditions. Personalization in Protestant memorial rites provides one type of comfort in its celebration of the memory of the deceased, though this is a historic change from the kind of comfort that was formerly sought in the emphasis on remembering Christ's conquest of death.

Even in the contemporary context of pluralism, individualism, and secularism, the central symbols of the Protestant faith—Christ, the Bible, ritual, hymnody, prayer, pastor, and community—continue to be the scaffold that Protestants turn to when responding to the death of a loved one. It is in the funeral ritual, words familiar and unfamiliar, traditions old and traditions just starting, perhaps in a funeral home and maybe in a sanctuary, ideally with a minister known to the people, but sometimes with a complete stranger, that strength can be found for the grievers. This strength comes from the gathering of the faith community to remember the sacred canopy that holds their world together: the Christian story of resurrection that insists that death is not the last word.

NOTES

1. Mike Harris, "Earnhardt Remembered with Solemn Service," *Milwaukee Journal Sentinel,* February 22, 2001, www.jsonline.com/sports/race/feb01/funeral23022201.asp1.

2. Edward J. Defort, "The Death and Memorialization of Dale Earnhardt," *American Funeral Director,* February 2003. For more on Lutheran funeral practices, see *The Book of Lutheran Worship.*

3. David B. Barrett, George M. Kurian, and Todd M. Johnson, *World Christian Encyclopedia: A Comparative Study of Churches and Religions in the Modern World,* 2nd ed., vol. 1 (Oxford: Oxford University Press, 2001).

4. Peter Berger, *The Sacred Canopy* (New York: Anchor Books, 1967).

5. Ibid., 39.

6. Ibid., 43.

7. Ibid., 40.

8. Matthew 16:18–19, New International Version.

9. Frank Mead (revised by Samuel Hill), *Handbook of Denominations in the United States* (Nashville: Abingdon, 1995).

10. Robert Wuthnow, *The Restructuring of American Religion: Society and Faith since World War II* (Princeton, NJ: Princeton University Press, 1988).

11. Membership figures are from the denominations' respective Web sites. Episcopal Church in the U.S., www.episcopalchurch.org/documents/EPISCOPAL_FAST_FACTS.pdf; Presbyterian Church (USA), www.pcusa.org/research/compstats/2002Table3rev.pdf; Evangelical Lutheran Church in America, www.elca.org/co/quick.html; United Methodist Church, www.umc.org/umns/backgrounders.asp?ptid=&story={C2AEDCE9-9E2D-4CC9–8058-D675CC63D3D8}&mid=905.

12. Robert Wuthnow, ed., *The Quiet Hand of Mainline Protestantism* (Berkeley: University of California Press, 2002); Christian Smith, *American Evangelicalism: Embattled and Thriving* (Chicago: University of Chicago Press, 1998).

13. Smith, *American Evangelicalism*, Chapter One.

14. Martin Luther, "Lectures on Romans," chapter 6 [Romans 15:33]. *Luther's Works*, ed. Hilton Oswald, vol. 25 (St. Louis Concordia, 1972), 308.

15. Luther, "Lectures on Romans."

16. Luther, "Preface to Burial Hymns," *Luther's Works*, ed. Ulrich S. Leupold, vol. 53 (Philadelphia: Fortress Press, 1965), 325.

17. Luther, "Preface to Burial Hymns."

18. Max Weber, *From Max Weber*, ed. H.H. Gerth and C. Wright Mills (New York: Oxford University Press, 1946).

19. Colleen McDannell and Bernhard Lang, *Heaven: A History* (New Haven: Yale University Press, 1988), 148–150.

20. Ibid.

21. Robert Bolton, *Mr. Boltons Last and Learned Worke of the Foure Last Things* (London, 1635), 82–83, quoted in David E. Stannard, *The Puritan Way of Death* (Oxford: Oxford University Press, 1977), 100.

22. David Wendell Moller, *Confronting Death* (New York: Oxford University Press, 1996), 14.

23. Ibid., 14.

24. Gary Laderman, *The Sacred Remains* (New Haven: Yale University Press, 1996), 15–16.

25. Ibid., 27–29.

26. Ibid., 55.

27. For more on these social forces, see Moller, *Confronting Death.*

28. Some denominations have developed special liturgies for miscarriages, stillbirths, SIDS deaths, and pregnancy loss. See, for example: Richard Deadman, Jeremy Fletcher, Janet Henderson, and Stephen Oliver, eds., *Pastoral Prayers: A Resource for Pastoral Occasions* (London: Mowbray, 1996). For more on the function of the funeral, see Lynne Ann DeSpelder and Albert Strickland, *Last Dance: Encountering Death and Dying*, 6th ed. (Boston: McGraw-Hill, 2002).

29. For more detailed descriptions of funeral practices in many American denominations, see Stuart Matlins and Arthur Magida, eds., *How to Be a Perfect Stranger: The Essential Religious Etiquette Handbook* (Woodstock, VT: Skylight Paths, 2003).

30. Douglas J. Davies, *Death, Ritual and Belief* (London: Continuum, 2002).

31. Wesley Carr, *Brief Encounters: Pastoral Ministry through Baptisms, Weddings and Funerals* (London: SPCK, 1994), 15.

32. Ibid., 118.

33. Ibid., 15.

34. For more on pastoral care, see Wesley Carr, *Handbook of Pastoral Studies* (London: SPCK, 1997), and Ian Ainsworth-Smith and Peter Speck, *Letting Go: Caring for the Dying and Bereaved* (London: SPCK, 1999).

35. Daniel Grossoehme, *The Pastoral Care of Children* (New York: Haworth, 1999), 5.

36. For more on pastoral care, see Jeffry Zurheide, *When Faith Is Tested: Pastoral Responses to Suffering and Tragic Death* (Minneapolis, MN: Fortress, 1997).

37. For a more detailed discussion of the diversity among African Americans and related end-of-life choices, see Ronald K. Barrett, "Contemporary African-American Funeral Rites and Traditions," in *The Path Ahead: Readings in Death and Dying*, ed. Lynne DeSpelder and Albert Strickland (Mountain View, CA: Mayfield, 1995), 80–92.

38. See Ronald K. Barrett, "Psychocultural Influences on African American Attitudes Towards Death, Dying, and Funeral Rites" in *Personal Care in an Impersonal World*, ed. John Morgan (Amityville, NY: Baywood, 1993), 213–230; Barrett, "Contemporary African-American Funeral Rites"; Hosea Perry, "Mourning and Funeral Customs of African Americans," in *Ethnic Variations in Dying, Death and Grief*, ed. Donald Irsh, Kathleen Lundquist, and Vivian Nelsen (Washington, DC: Taylor and Francis, 1993), 51–65; and Elaine Nichols, *The Last Mile of the Way: African American Homegoing Traditions 1890–Present* (Columbia, SC: Dependable, 1989).

39. See Barrett, "Psychocultural Influences."

40. Martha A. Sullivan, "May the Circle Be Unbroken: The African American Experiences of Death, Dying and Spirituality" in *A Cross-Cultural Look at Death, Dying and Religion*, ed. Joan Parry and Angela Ryan (Chicago: Nelson Hall, 1995), 160–171.

41. Thomas A. Dorsey, "Precious Lord, Take My Hand" (Unichappell Music, 1938).

42. Andrea Crouch, "Soon and Very Soon" (Hope, 1996).

43. Ronald K. Barrett, "Advance Directives, DNRs, and End-of-Life Care for African Americans," in OMEGA (forthcoming).

44. Barrett, "Contemporary African-American Funeral Rites."

45. Ronald K. Barrett, "Sociocultural Considerations for Working with Blacks Experiencing Loss and Grief," in *Living With Grief: How We Are—How We Grieve*, ed. Kenneth Doka (Washington, DC: Taylor & Francis, 1998), 83–96.

46. Malidome P. Some, *Ritual: Power, Healing and Community* (New York: Penguin Arkana, 1997).

47. Ronald K. Barrett, "Black Funeral Rites: A Cultural Fusion of West African and Western Cultural Influences" (Open Community Colloquium presentation sponsored by the Department of Psychology at the University of Ghana–Legon at the ISSER Institute in Legon, April 5, 2001).

48. Berger, *Sacred Canopy*, 127ff.

49. Smith, *American Evangelicalism*, 117–119.

50. Wade Clark Roof, *Spiritual Marketplace: Baby Boomers and the Remaking of American Religion* (Princeton, NJ: Princeton University Press, 1999), 73.

51. Mark Chaves, "Secularization as Declining Religious Authority," *Social Forces* 72 (March 1994): 749–774.

52. See Theodore Caplow, *All Faithful People* (Minneapolis: University of Minnesota Press, 1983).

53. I am indebted to sociologist James Davison Hunter at the University of Virginia for this insight.

54. The literature on trust, civil society, and social capital is large and the technical terms used in rather elastic ways. Two of the more well-received works are Adam Seligman, *The Problem of Trust* (Princeton, NJ: Princeton University Press, 2000), and Robert Putnam, *Bowling Alone* (Touchstone Books, 2001).

55. Robert Bellah et al., *Habits of the Heart* (Berkeley: University of California Press, 1985).

56. Chaves, "Secularization as Declining Religious Authority."

CHAPTER 7

Muslim Ways of Death

Between the Prescribed and the Performed

JUAN EDUARDO CAMPO

And when the Compassionate
executed His command—
and what's been decreed
must surely come to pass—
She left her life
in prime of youth, a martyr,
not one to dispute
with death.
Remaining calm,
She bore witness thrice
and died,
and returned to Him.
But she did not die
until she saw her place
in the higher world—
then her soul ascended.[1]

These verses are from an elegy penned by a Muslim scholar in fourteenth-century Cairo in memory of his beloved daughter, who had died at the age of twenty-seven after suffering a long illness. Nudar was the dearest of Abu Hayyan's children, a bright woman groomed by him to become an esteemed scholar of hadith, the extensive assemblage of narrative traditions about the activities and pronouncements of Muhammad (570?–632), regarded as the foremost "prophet" in Islam, and his early followers. Indeed, Abu Hayyan not only wrote at least nine elegies in her memory, but he was so shaken by her loss that he requested and received special permission from the Muslim ruler of Egypt to bury her in his home so that death would not be allowed to separate them. In her passing, he also encountered his own mortality, which gave rise to the hope that he would meet her again in eternity.

A year is enough,
then go in peace;
one who mourns an entire year
is freed.
No. I'll weep for you
till we join together,
my eyes beholding your face,
a shining moon,
While I enjoy the beauty
of your words,
always a delight
to the ear, the eye, the heart.[2]

In this one man's words of love, pain, and hope in the face of death, we also meet with death both as a phenomenon believed to have been prescribed by God and as one prescribed by community authorities through the canons of Islamic doctrine and practice. Abu Hayyan's verses invoke Muslim belief in divine predetermination of the human life span ("when the Compassionate executed His command . . ."), relations between body and soul, death as a return to God, the deceased person's preview of her fate in the afterlife, and the expectation of a joyous reunion with loved ones there. His poem also draws our attention to at least three of the many communally sanctioned practices connected with death: deathbed recitation of the testimony of faith (*shahada*), mourning observances, and memorialization. Indeed, the elegies he wrote for his daughter are a monument built in verse—they preserve memories of her life, personhood, and close relationship to her father from oblivion, transmitting them to posterity. Death loses some of its sting thereby. Even the anecdote about Nudar's burial in her father's home is instructive, because it recognizes interment as the prescribed method in Islam for disposing of a corpse, and it alludes to underlying parallels expressed in Islamic eschatology between the domestic spaces of this world and those of the hereafter.

But Abu Hayyan's grief for his daughter also teaches us that the event of death expresses incongruities between what *ought* to be done and believed and the actual actions, thoughts, and beliefs that occur in life when people are confronted with death's affective, accidental, and often tragic realities. Formal or prescribed funeral practices and beliefs, as Jonathan Z. Smith has stated about ritual in general, involve "creation of a controlled environment where the variables (i.e., the accidents) of ordinary life may be displaced precisely because they are felt to be so overwhelmingly present and powerful."[3] They are, therefore, "*a means of performing* [and thinking about] *the way things ought to be in conscious tension to the way things are in such a way that this ritualized perfection is recollected in the ordinary, uncontrolled, course of things.*"[4] The power that prescribed beliefs and practices may have over memory and experience is not always total, however. Indeed, the very incongruity that characterizes human encounters with mortality can evoke responses that test, transgress, ignore, and negotiate with prescribed religious norms. These responses emerge from specific contexts—local cultural beliefs and attitudes, conjoined with efforts on the part of the bereaved to cope with the experience of pain, loss, anger, guilt, and the transience of human existence. In the case of Abu Hayyan's grief, we find a man who comes from the very ranks of the Muslim scholarly elite (the ulema) testing the limits of Islamic understandings of martyrdom so as to include his daughter in the ranks of martyrs; we find Islamic bereavement rules being transgressed in the attention he draws to a female member of his household, in his desire to mourn for her beyond the customary one-year limit, and in the excess reflected in the nine elegies he wrote for her. Also, we find him negotiating with political authorities over Islamic burial practices so that Nudar can be interred in his home instead of the graveyard. In a more subtle way, Abu Hayyan's verses contest the bleak formality of juristic and doctrinal discourses about death by invoking themes that also recur in erotic poetry and Islamic mystical discourse: themes of intense suffering, separation and death, otherworld visions, and dreams of ecstatic reunion with the beloved.

To understand Islamic beliefs and practices relating to death, therefore, it is necessary to recognize both what is prescribed and what is performed.[5] The prescribed consists of formalized rules governing belief and practice constructed, maintained, and implemented by religious authorities, particularly the ulema. These rules give form to the ruptures and incongruities occurring in life and death; they can also be coercive. Moreover, in Islamic thought, the prescribed gains power by being embedded in divine will and prophetic example, which lends doctrine and practice an eternal authority that they would otherwise lack. The performed dimension of religion, on the other hand, tends to be suppler, giving people the freedom not only to express religious and cultural norms, but also to appropriate, contest, adapt, and change them.[6] Though the example of Abu Hayyan has been drawn from a context that is distant from us in both space and time, it nonetheless reveals the ways the event of death invokes and occasions the interplay of the prescribed, formal requirements of the religion with the specificities and arbitrariness of history, culture, imagination, and experience. Abu Hayyan's poignant responses to his daughter's passing were neither completely scripted by official Islamic beliefs and funerary practices, nor completely improvised; they emerged in a conjunctive discursive space—a space infused with incongruity. In the ensuing pages, we shall see that this conjunction attests to a creative dynamic that is evidenced in Muslim beliefs and practices relating to death today, as well as in history—in the Middle East and beyond. This dynamic has been shaped and sustained both by negotiated interactions and confrontations of Muslim peoples and institutions with each other in different milieus, *and* by encounters, exchanges, and clashes between Muslims and non-Muslims and, in modernity, between Muslims and Western secularism.

WHAT IS ISLAM? WHO ARE THE MUSLIMS?

These are questions that have been addressed for centuries by Muslims; they have also been posed by non-Muslims—never more so than at the onset of the twenty-first century. Insiders (Muslims) offer a variety of responses, depending on their standing within the different communities to which they belong and the specific historical and cultural situations and memories of these communities. Likewise, outsiders (non-Muslims) have also approached these questions in a variety of ways that have been shaped by their historical and cultural circumstances and their encounters with Islam and its followers.

A good way to begin to answer these queries is with the proposition that Islam is above all what Muslims make of it, as members of different ethnic and social groups and as individuals with diverse religious sensibilities. In this regard, many look to the Qur'an, the Islamic holy book, which they believe to be a miraculous revelation from God (Allah) intended to show humanity the way to salvation. This revelation, according to Muslim doctrine, was transmitted in Arabic by Muhammad, a native of western Arabia, who received it intermittently over a twenty-three-year period, ending with his death in 632. According to the Qur'an:

> Upholding equity, God, his angels, and those with knowledge have witnessed that there is no god but he, the mighty and wise. Indeed, religion (*din*) in God's eyes is submission (*islam*). Those who received the book disagreed among themselves out of jealousy only after knowledge had come to them. Whoever disbelieves in God's signs, [let him know that] God is swift in reckoning.[7] (Q 3:18–19)

This statement links islam to recognition of one god and contrasts it to disbelief (*kufr*), which will result in divine retribution. Reception of the book, moreover, entailed both gaining knowledge of God and division among his creatures. Muslims, like angels, and in contrast to disbelievers, are "those who submit" to God's will. A more explicit definition of Islam, which is especially instructive, is provided in the hadith, sacred narratives that contain accounts about what Muhammad and his companions said and did. When the angel Gabriel, disguised as a human being, reportedly interrogated Muhammad about Islam, he responded, "Islam is that you witness that there is no god but God and that Muhammad is God's messenger; that you perform prayer; give alms; fast [the month of] Ramadan; and perform the hajj to the house [of God in Mecca] if you are able to do so."[8] In this statement, Islam is defined in terms of its "five pillars," thus underscoring the foundational importance of ritual practice in the religion. Even the first pillar, the shahada ("witnessing") is performative, because it entails vocalizing the two key tenets of Islamic doctrine. Recitation of the shahada in Arabic occurs throughout an observant Muslim's lifetime and takes special importance in prayer and at the moment of death, when it should be the last words uttered by the dying person or pronounced on his or her behalf by those in attendance. The other four pillars are formally classed in *fiqh* (Islamic jurisprudence) as forms of worship required of all Muslims for divine reward in this life and in the hereafter.

The same hadith narrative also takes up the issue of belief when Gabriel, acknowledging that Muhammad has correctly defined *islam,* continues his interrogation by asking Muhammad to define *iman* ("believing"). Muhammad answers that iman entails believing in God, his angels, his books, his messengers, and the Last Day, as well as predetermination. Again, Gabriel affirms the truth of the response. Death and the afterlife are thus overtly recognized as integral to the Muslim belief system, insofar as people are held accountable for their actions and beliefs in an ultimate sense. Just as the details of the ritual requirements were discussed and debated by Muslim jurists through the centuries, as reflected in the fiqh literature, so were the key tenets of belief debated in Muslim theology. Nevertheless, as the hadith of Gabriel implies, practice and faith are interdependent dimensions of Islamic religion; one does not make sense without the other. The hadith of Gabriel adds a third element to this religion—*ihsan,* which instructs Muslims to be mindful of God's watchfulness and thus do what is good and beautiful. Through ihsan, practice and belief acquire a spiritual aesthetic.

The first generations of Muslim authorities formally organized the Qur'an and hadith; then, after the eighth century, religious experts (ulema) constructed detailed canons of practice and belief that invoked these sacred texts for rulers and commoners alike. With the establishment of the scriptural canon, the ulema sought to inculcate Islam among themselves and the wider community through discursive practices that Muslims learned to incorporate in their daily lives at home, at the mosque, at the marketplace, at war, at sea, and on the road. Study and recitation of the Qur'an was subjected to formal rules, as were prayer, almsgiving, fasting, pilgrimage, and many other practices—including funeral rites. This system of conduct was idealized as the Shari`a and deployed in fiqh, which, as formulated by the Sunni jurist Muhammad al-Shafi`i (d. 822), was based on four "roots": Qur'an, Sunna (customary practice based upon the hadith), *ijma`* (consensus), and *ijtihad* (individual reasoning) or *qiyas* (analogical reasoning). Although several different schools of legal tradition emerged during the ninth century, each aspired to achieve a totalistic sovereignty over human action that spanned the spheres of formal worship, government, family law, crime, commerce, diet, dress, and even hospitality. The ulema maintained that to follow divine law—the Shari`a as implemented through their fiqh traditions—was to incur God's blessing in this world and in the hereafter. To violate it incurred his displeasure and punishment. Funerary practices, which are located at a particularly important juncture in Muslim systems of belief and action, also fall within the purview of religious law. They entail directly or indirectly the five pillars and many aspects of law that pertain to society and cultural life. Moreover, they provide occasions for the expression and embodiment of key Islamic doctrines pertaining to relationships between supramundane beings and humanity, between this world and eternity, and between Muslims and non-Muslims.

If Islam is largely what Muslims make of it, who are the Muslims? Of course there are different ways of answering this question—perhaps the simplest being that Muslims are those who submit to God (*muslimin*), particularly in conformity with the Qur'anic message and the Sunna, or example of the Prophet and his companions. Collectively, Muslims understand themselves to be united into a single ideal community of believers—the *umma.* According to the Qur'an, when Abraham and his son Ishmael completed building God's "house" (i.e., the Ka`ba in Mecca), they prayed, "Our lord, make us submitters [*muslims*] unto you, and make of our offspring a submitting community (*umma muslima*) unto you" (Q 2:128). Muslim concepts concerning the umma have tended to be universalistic, though they have also included specific notions of territory and political sovereignty, particularly in connection with the legalistic concept of the *dar al-islam* "house of Islam." Historically, Muhammad founded the first viable Muslim community in Medina (a city in western Arabia located about 260 miles north of Mecca) after he emigrated from Mecca with a small group of mostly Arab followers in 622. Indeed, this emigration, or Hijra, was such a momentous event in Islamic sacred history that it is used to designate the year one on the Muslim lunar calendar. While the earlier Meccan phase of Islamic history is known for its association with Qur'anic images of the end times, resurrection, paradise, and hellfire, the Medinan phase is regarded as the golden age of Qur'anic legislation when Muhammad was prophet, judge, and ruler for the newly founded community. Ritual activity helped solidify its bonds and set it apart from pagans, Jews, and Arab Christians. Although the Ka'ba inside Mecca's Sacred Mosque served as the focal point for prayer and pilgrimage, Muhammad's house-mosque was the center of community and religious activity in Medina, and after his burial there in 632 it became regarded as a shrine, eventually becoming the second most sacred center in the Muslim world. One widely circulated hadith even claimed that the space delimited by his house and his pulpit was one of the gardens of paradise.[9]

In addition to seeing themselves as a united community founded in fulfillment of a prophetic mission, Muslims also identify with specific strands of Islamic tradition: the Sunni, Shi`i, and Sufi expressions of Islam. Sunni Muslims are in the majority and today constitute some 85 percent of the Muslim population. Their name stems from a phrase meaning "people of the customary practice (of Muhammad and the first Muslims) and the community of believers." Their Qur'an commentaries, hadith collections, legal schools, and theological discourses are the ones most widely circulated and respected, and it is from their ranks that most Muslim rulers and dynasties have arisen.

The minority tradition in Islam is that of the Shi`a, who today constitute up to 15 percent of all Muslims. Known as the faction (*shi`a*) of `Ali, they are found in many parts of the world, but they constitute majorities in the modern countries of Iran (90 percent of its population), Iraq (62 percent), and Bahrain (70 percent).[10] They maintain that the most legitimate religious authorities and leaders are select members of Muhammad's family, known as the imams, beginning with `Ali (d. 661), who was Muhammad's cousin and son-in-law. Since the seventh century, the Shi`a have contested what has come to be known as the Sunni position on authority, which favored the caliphs—leaders chosen initially by community consultation according to their reputation and worldly experience. Most Shi`a believe the imams to be divinely appointed and inspired, free of sin and error, and the source of religious guidance and insight. The largest branch of the Shi`a, the Imami or Twelver Shi`a, maintains that all but one of their twelve imams suffered martyrdom on behalf of their faith and their followers and that the twelfth, after his disappearance in 872, will arise at an appointed time as a messiah figure to inaugurate a reign of universal justice prior to the Last Judgment. The sayings of the imams constitute the core of Shi`i hadith, and their tombs in Iraq and Iran have become sacred centers where pilgrims congregate to gain their blessings and intercession.

Sufism (*tasawwuf*) is an umbrella designation for the mystical expressions of Islam, wherein experiential knowledge of God is a primary goal. Since the eleventh century, most Sufi adepts have been organized into groups of masters and disciples known as "paths" (*turuq*) that follow specific doctrines and ritual practices. Sufis draw heavily upon the Qur'an and Sunna for inspiration and guidance, and have traced the lineages of their doctrines and practices back to Muhammad and the first generation of Muslims. Despite some manifestations of antinomianism, most Sufis regard following the Shari`a as foundational for making the journey to greater spiritual awareness, and their ranks are filled with members from across the spectrum of the Muslim community, Sunnis and Shi`a alike. By participating in Sufi orders, initiates seek experiential knowledge and even self-annihilation and intimate unity with God, especially through ascetic practices, rhythmic chanting, music, and poetry—in sharp contrast to the systems of rational knowledge that were embodied in the scholarly discourses of the Sunni and Shi`i ulema. Sufis often speak of their love for God and experiencing the death of their worldly selves in order to enjoy communion with him before dying in the flesh; that is, they seek to attain death before dying. This idea is captured in verses attributed to a seventeenth-century Punjabi Sufi master:

> *The sea of love has risen to the heavens, where will the ship drop anchor?*
> *The boat of intellect and rationality should be sunk on its very first trip.*
> *Whirlpools and tidal waves assail him when he enters the state of unity.*
> *That death which people fear, Bahu, the lover dies it so that he might live.*[11]

Some Sufis taught that when a saintly wayfarer dies it is as if he were suddenly awakened from a dream to find "that the beloved for whom he had searched throughout his life, he sees lying beside him in his own bed."[12]

Guidance along the mystical path was in the hands of Sufi shaykhs and *pirs,* with whom disciples formed intimate bonds of respect and veneration both in life and in death. Indeed, the shrines that Sufi brotherhoods and their patrons erected to house the relics of their very special dead are among the most ubiquitous features in sacred landscapes of Islam, from Africa to Asia, and from Europe to America. People gain merit by going on pilgrimage to these sites to participate in Sufi rites and festivals, petitioning the saints to resolve problems and cure illnesses. They believe that even in death the spirit of the saint serves as a miracle worker and living mediator between heaven and earth, between the visible and invisible worlds.

In addition to defining themselves as members of an Islamic umma, and as Sunnis, Shi`ia, and Sufis, Muslims also claim a variety of ethnic and national identities. The first generations of Muslims were predominantly Arab, and today Arabs still constitute the largest Muslim ethnic group. Persians, Turks, and Berbers became Islamized by the eleventh century, and together with the Arabs they defined much of the culture and history of classical Islamic civilization. Today only one in four Muslims is an Arab, and when all Middle Eastern ethnic groups are combined they amount to less than half of the current estimated world Muslim population of 1.2 billion. Indeed, there are more than sixty different ethnic groups that include 1 million or more Muslims today, and the largest numbers live *east* of the Middle East. As for their national identities, the largest Muslim populations are citizens of Indonesia (206 million), Pakistan (150 million), India (120 million), and Bangladesh (114 million).[13] Sizable Muslim populations also live in African and Central Asian countries. Many Muslims have also immigrated to Europe and the Americas since the end of World War II, though they have not always been accepted as citizens there.

Muslim ways of death have emerged, become organized, and developed in multiple contexts, defined only in part by the formally instituted and prescribed ritual codes and doctrines introduced above. Islamization—that is, the spread of Islam into new cultures—itself has entailed a complex array of encounters, exchanges, and adaptations over fourteen hundred years of history, involving Muslims and non-Muslims, men and women, townspeople, peasants, and pastoralists, as well as different written and oral cultures of knowledge and practice. Muslim ways of death have not emerged spontaneously, but in relation to other ways of death, and since this has been a historical and cultural phenomenon, they have undergone change and variation in time and space. It would be as erroneous to think that there was only a single Islamic set of beliefs and practices pertaining to death as it would be to imagine that Muslims all belong to one ethnic group or hold fast to a single viewpoint with respect to, for example, God, non-Muslims, or the status of women. Even though the umma remains to this day an ideal of Muslim unity, it is juxtaposed to different Islamic religious traditions, ethnicities, nationalities, and sensibilities. Despite much of the politicized rhetoric and "scholarship" that has pervaded public discourse since the events of September 11, 2001, particularly in the United States, neither Islam nor Muslims can be totalized. Nor can Islamic understandings of death and the afterlife, subjects that have become very much a part of the contemporary public discourse about Islam, be totalized.

VISIONS OF DEATH AND THE AFTERLIFE

Muslim accounts of death and the afterlife first formed through the interactions of Arabs and other Near Eastern peoples in the sixth and seventh centuries. They still shape the imaginations and lives of Muslims around the world today, and they continue to undergo change. In the 1970s, shortly before Ayatollah Khomeini's Islamic revolution, anthropologist Reinhold Loeffler studied religion in an Iranian village and found there a rich variety of ideas about God, the world, and human existence. One of the people interviewed was an elderly hunter who recounted a near death experience he had had during an illness. The hunter described being transported from this world and shown the secrets of the Last Day and of paradise and hell. He was subjected to punishment for his sins "equal to ten thousand years of torment in this life."[14] He also saw others being punished and was instructed to return to earth and tell people what he had seen. In contrast to this near death account is that of an Egyptian Muslim immigrant in Los Angeles, California, which was related, after some prodding, to a friend in 2003.[15] In his narrative, the visionary testified to his "death" on the operating table, an out-of-body journey into a bright light, followed by an encounter with God and Muhammad. He told not only of being overcome by feelings of blissful warmth, but also of being instructed to return to the world and promote the cause of peace.

The Iranian hunter's account echoes the story of Muhammad's Night Journey and Ascension and bears many of the characteristics of premodern near death narratives—

journey to the otherworld, visions of heaven and hell, confrontation with one's deeds, conversion of the visionary into a messenger, and return to life.[16] Muhammad's otherworld journey, an elaborate narrative based on some short statements in the Qur'an, has been recounted in different versions and in many languages since the eighth century, and it has inspired common people, Sufi visionaries, and scholarly elites in many Muslim cultures. It is still celebrated as a holiday on the Muslim calendar.[17] The Muslim immigrant's narrative, in contrast, has been shaped by modern near death experiences in North America, though it bears traces of more ancient traditions. The clinical setting, emphasis on a journey into light, blissful encounter with divine beings, absence of pain and suffering, and commissioning of the visionary with a message of peace are all trademark elements of near death accounts circulated in Western print and electronic media.[18]

These two accounts of death and the afterlife were recounted in the recent past, and they only hint at the significant amount of discussion about these subjects occurring among Muslims today. In addition to what they may hear in a mosque, sermons about death, resurrection, and the afterlife are broadcast in the electronic media and recorded on cassette tapes, which are sold and distributed to Muslims around the world. Publishers issue new print editions of medieval books on death and eschatology, as well as inexpensive booklets by today's popular *shaykhs*, sometimes featuring frightening illustrations of torture in the afterlife on their covers. Articles on Islamic eschatology also appear in magazines and newspapers. Many of these discourses are concerned with inculcating Islamic ethical virtues and rules of behavior at a time when Muslim societies are experiencing profound change and displacement due to colonialism, nationalism, globalization and economic dependence, warfare, industrialization and radical shifts in the work force, and the prominence of scientific materialism and secular systems of knowledge. Radical Islamists have used otherworld discourses to coerce and mobilize people into following their plans of action, from prayer and veiling to participation in violence against enemies at home and abroad. On the other hand, since the early twentieth century, modernists—including respected shaykhs of Al-Azhar University (one of the most esteemed centers of Sunni learning)—have combined traditional Islamic afterlife beliefs with modern scientific concepts and Western spiritualist doctrines to argue for continued existence of the spirit in an intermediate state after death (*barzakh*). In that secret world it is believed that the living and the dead communicate and that spirits experience bliss or suffering based on their deeds in their former worldly existence.[19]

What are the core Islamic doctrines about death and the afterlife? The Qur'an declares, "Wherever you are, death will overtake you—even in lofty towers" (Q 4:78). Thus it is widely held among Muslims that death (*mawt*) is the fate prescribed by God for all living things. For human beings the event itself marks a transition or journey of the soul from worldly existence in the body to bodily resurrection and immortal life in either paradise or hell.[20] God determines the life span, so when a person reaches the end of the appointed term, it is said that God has "brought it to a close."[21] Faced with its inevitability, humans are to accept death and to live their lives in anticipation of having to account to God for their actions in the afterlife. According to the Qur'an, where death and the afterlife are dominant themes, God is the giver of both life and death, and to him will his creatures return after being resurrected (e.g., Q 6:36, 9:116, 10:56). More than once, the Qur'an states, "To God is your return, all of you, and he will inform you about what you did" (Q 5:105, 6:60, 31:15, etc.). It even speaks of human existence as being defined by two deaths and two births: nonexistence and entry into worldly life, then death and resurrection in the hereafter (Q 2:28, 22:66). In Islamic tradition, death is usually personified by `Izra'il, the death angel who is dispatched by God at the appointed time to extract human souls from their bodies. He can appear in a terrifying form to wrongdoers and in a beautiful form to comfort the good in their last moments.[22]

The return to God leads to the final reckoning and immortality for the blessed in paradise and for the damned in hell. In the Muslim *imaginaire* eternity in either realm is more anthropocentric than theocentric—a differentiation first proposed by Colleen McDanell and Bernhard Lang in their account of the development of Western visions of heaven.[23] Muslims regard paradise as a real place where humans experience contact with supramundane beings, as well as pleasurable bodily existence. This understanding of paradise was canonized in the Qur'an and elaborated further in the hadith, theological discourse, and eschatological literature. In contrast to the Bible, extensive passages of the Qur'an deal with the subjects of resurrection and the afterlife, beginning with chapters traditionally consigned by scholars to the Meccan phase of Muhammad's career (ca. 615–622). In Qur'anic eschatology, paradise is a domesticated, arboreal garden where the air is perfumed and rivers of milk, honey, and wine flow (Q 47:15). It is populated by elegantly dressed believers who dwell in luxurious heavenly mansions (Q 9:72, 15:47, 36:55–58, 88:10–16). They are rejoined with righteous family members, they consort with angels (Q 13:23–24), and handsome youths and beautiful large-eyed houris[24] serve them unlimited quantities of food and drink (Q 43:71, 52:19–24, 76:15–22). The Qur'an also intimates that the blessed will enjoy the vision of God there (Q 10:26, 39:75, 75:22–23), an idea that was later subject to much theological debate. As Islamic cosmological ideas developed, paradise was reconceived as a spatial hierarchy for the different ranks of the blessed, consisting of eight different gates and a number of gardens and abodes surmounted by the divine throne.

According to medieval Islamic descriptions of the afterlife, paradise was also a place where the blessed could enjoy unbounded sexual potency. In his descriptions of the hereafter, the medieval theologian and mystic Abu Hamid al-Ghazali (d. 1111) invoked a noncanonical tradition that described the luxurious homes promised to the righteous in the gardens of Eden and what awaits them therein:

> They are palaces of pearls, in each of which are seventy ruby mansions, in each of which are seventy emerald rooms, in each of which are seventy beds, on each of which are seventy mattresses of every hue, on each of which is a wife who is one of the large-eyed houris. And in every room there are seventy tables, on each of which are seventy varieties of food. In every house are seventy servant-girls. *Every morning the believer will be given strength enough to enjoy all of this.*[25] (Italics added)

In his renowned treatise on love, the gifted Andalusian scholar Ibn Hazm (d. 1064) composed a poem in which he imagined encountering his virtuous deeds in paradise in the form of a lovely young woman whom he once loved dearly.

> *She was a pearl most pure and white,*
> *By God fashioned out of light;*
> *Her beauty was a wondrous thing*
> *Beyond all human reckoning.*
> *If on the Day of Judgment, when*
> *The trumpets sound for sinful men,*
> *I find, before the Throne of Grace,*
> *My deeds as lovely as her face;*
> *Of all the creatures God made*
> *I shall most fully be repaid,*
> *A double Eden to reside,*
> *And dark-eyed virgins at my side.*[26]

A Pakistani manual on death and the afterlife published in 1972 provides us with an idea of how anthropocentric medieval conceptions of paradise continue to inform the modern Islamic *imaginaire:*

> This paradise is situated on the seventh heaven near Sidrat al-Muntaha (a jujube tree in the heavens) under the throne of God. There is no trace of death, sickness, pain, old age, weakness, indigence or neediness in this place. Therein youthfulness will prevail along with beauty, grace, and a robust health, with neither sorrow nor fear. Anyone entering this place after the Day of Judgment will remain there forever. Pride, mutual disputes and mischiefs [sic] will be totally absent, nor will anyone feel jealous of, and sorry for, the other. In short everyone in paradise will be happy and contented in his own way. . . . Despite consumption of eatables by the dwellers of paradise, they will not feel the need for rectinal [*sic*] or urinal excretion. Whatever is eaten will be digested through the process of perspiration, cleansing and refreshing the person thereby. The women here will be eternal virgins free from the pollutions of menstruation and childbirths.[27]

Hell is the complementary opposite of paradise in Islamic eschatology—a blazing abode where God punishes unbelievers and wrongdoers with excruciating bodily torments. The Qur'an portrays it as an evil "home" or "dwelling" where wrongdoers don garments of fire, drink boiling water, eat the fruit of an infernal tree, and are dragged about by iron hooks (Q 37:62–68, 22:19–21) at the hands of angels and demons. Subsequently these fearsome visions were elaborated with more gruesome detail in the hadith, theological tracts, and eschatological texts. For example, al-Ghazali wrote that in hell the damned "are thrust down upon their faces, chained and fettered, with hellfire above them, hellfire beneath them, hellfire on their right and hellfire on their left so that they drown in a sea of fire."[28] Hell was also conceived as a hierarchy of seven levels, each assigned a different name derived from the Qur'an (for example, "abyss," "blaze," and "furnace"), to which different classes of the damned will be consigned in the afterlife. Theologians debated whether the damned would suffer there for eternity, but many invoked the Qur'an

(Q 11:107, 78:23) in favor of the opinion that its torments were purgatorial and that eventually many would be admitted to paradise.

Additionally, Muslims know hell as Jahannam, which the Qur'an depicts as an evil dwelling or refuge with seven gates (counterparts for the seven heavens) awaiting unbelievers, hypocrites, and other sorts of offenders (see Q 4:140; 15:43–44). It is inhabited by jinns and satans, as well as humans (Q 11:119; 19:68), including both polytheists and "people of the book," a reference to Jews, Christians, and followers of the Persian religion known as Zoroastrianism (Q 98:6). Indeed, according to one verse, all peoples will go to Jahannam, but God will save the pious and abandon wrongdoers there (Q 19:72). The hadith describe it as a pit of fire seventy times hotter than earthly fire, guarded by the angel Malik, into which plunge the damned attempting to cross a narrow test bridge that traverses it. Among the many kinds of sinners punished there are the Jahannamites—Muslims who have committed major transgressions, but who will eventually win entry to paradise. Medieval commentators supplied it with geographic features such as mountains, valleys, rivers, and seas, as well as houses, prisons, bridges, wells, and ovens.[29] They also provided it with venomous scorpions and snakes that torment its inhabitants. Jahannam and hell remain popular topics in Muslim religious discourse today.

As the topographies of the afterlife were being mapped during the medieval era, eschatological literature was further enhanced by narratives about the exemplary deaths of prophets, saints, and martyrs. Among the prophets, Muhammad's last moments received the most attention, first in the hadith and then in the early biographical literature.[30] Al-Ghazali later assembled a number of these accounts in his famous book, *The Revival of the Religious Sciences,* and wrote, "In his death lies a most perfect lesson, and in him the Muslims have an excellent example."[31] The deaths of the imams, particularly Husayn, are of vital importance in Twelver Shi`i doctrines about redemptive suffering and death; poetic laments about their martyrdom are a core feature of the `Ashura rituals the Shi`a conduct annually during the month of Muharram.[32] For Sufis, accounts of the pain and death suffered by spiritual seekers provide tropes for discussing the experience of separation from God the Beloved, as well as ecstatic annihilation of the self in him. Indeed, popular saints' festivals in Muslim cultures, including that of Muhammad, celebrate the death anniversary of the saint as the occasion of his or her (re)birth (*mawlid*) or spiritual marriage (*`urs*) to God.[33] These observances began in the twelfth century and continue to be widely performed, much to the consternation of reformers and Islamists, who consider them sinful innovations, and secular rationalists, who consider them expressions of popular superstition.

Belief in the continued life of the soul between physical death and the final resurrection is widespread in Muslim cultures. The living believe that they can engage in intercourse with the dead through dreams that occur during sleep, which is said to resemble death. Dead prophets and saints reveal secrets about the afterlife in dreams,[34] and visits to their shrines are predicated on the belief that their spirits are alive and capable of responding to the supplications of pilgrims. The notion of the barzakh, the intermediate afterlife realm, constitutes a space wherein these exchanges can occur, providing the living with a device whereby they can maintain an ongoing attachment to loved ones, perform propitiations on their behalf, or even seek their assistance. The location of this realm is disputed.[35] Many of the Shi`a claim that the souls of the righteous are gathered in the Valley of Peace Cemetery in the holy city of Najaf in Iraq, while the souls of the damned are consigned to a valley in Yemen that has all the characteristics of hell.[36] Other Muslims have speculated that the barzakh is in paradise, in heaven, near God's throne, or at the well of Zamzam in Mecca.

Perhaps the most significant intermediate realm in the Muslim imaginaire is the grave itself, where the soul of the deceased is thought to remain close to the physical body, but not so attached to it as to prevent it from going forth to visit the living or to roam the worlds of the hereafter. According to medieval eschatological texts, souls are rejoined with their bodies in the tomb to undergo a preliminary judgment in the form of a confrontation with their deeds or a purgatorial punishment for infidelity and wrongdoing. The most widely known form of this graveyard scenario, called "the punishment of the tomb," involves an inquisition by Munkar and Nakir, two terrifying angels who visit the deceased on the night after burial.[37] According to one such narrative:

> Munkar and Nakir enter the grave of the deceased and they make him sit upright. If he is a believer, they ask, "Who is your lord?" "Allah," he says. They ask, "Who is your prophet?" "Muhammad," he answers. They ask, "Who is your *imam*?" "The Qur'an," he says. So then they widen the grave for him. But if he is a disbeliever, they ask, "Who is your lord?" "I don't know," he says. They ask, "Who is your prophet?" "I don't know," he answers. They ask, "Who is your imam?" "I don't know," he says. So then they beat him brutally with an iron rod until the grave is consumed by fire and it presses tight against him and his ribs are crushed.[38]

The idea of a postmortem trial in the grave, which was not formally incorporated into Islamic doctrine until the ninth century, drew upon age-old indigenous Near Eastern beliefs in the continuation of the soul's life after death, the desire for retribution for wrongdoing (by others) and reward for virtue, and an inclination to fill the existential void between death and the anticipated final resurrection with an intermediate afterlife scenario. Medieval Muslim jurists could not just leave the preresurrection fate of the soul completely up to the popular imagination, so they devised visions consisting of graphic depictions of corporeal pleasure and pain that would foster conformity with core Islamic beliefs and values. In doing so, they antedated the emergence of the idea of purgatory in medieval European Christendom. Although their scenario has been disputed by rationalists and some Shi`a, it nevertheless continues to hold a place among contemporary Muslims of various orientations.[39]

RITUALIZED BODIES

Human mortality gives rise to a wide range of thoughts and beliefs about life after life, but it also poses more basic questions about what to do with both the corporeal and social bodies. What practices and institutions are mobilized in the removal of the corpse from the world of the living and in confronting the incongruities and breaches in social relations that have been brought about by death? In Islamic contexts, the responses to this question are addressed formally by religious law and by social custom, with ample latitude yielded to contingencies and circumstances. Muslim funerary and bereavement practices take shape in the space between what is prescribed and what is performed, where the performed might also contradict or resist the prescribed.

Some years ago I was awakened suddenly before dawn by a woman's agonized screams echoing through the halls of my apartment building in downtown Cairo. She had run out to the building's stairway crying out for her husband, a young father who had just succumbed to cancer at home. Neighbors rushed from their apartments to calm and console her in her profound grief. They also pleaded with her to stop her crying, since such emotional displays only brought further pain to the soul of her spouse and signaled an unwillingness to submit to God's will. Female neighbors led her back inside her home, where her soul-rending cries turned to occasional moans and muffled weeping. Meanwhile, male relatives and neighbors gathered in the entrance of the apartment of the deceased's sister, which was across the hallway. Within a matter of hours, a sizable group of mourners had arrived—women staying with the bereaved widow, men sitting in the crowded entryway of the neighboring apartment, smoking and drinking unsweetened Turkish coffee. A washer was summoned to perform the ritual bathing and dressing of the corpse for burial. By midday, a bier was brought and placed on the landing outside the deceased's apartment. Male relatives then carried the enshrouded corpse out and laid it onto the bier. Four pallbearers carried the bier on their shoulders to a nearby mosque for funeral prayers, accompanied by a group of male friends and relatives. All the women stayed behind with the widow. By midafternoon, less than twelve hours after death, the corpse had been interred in its final resting place in a medieval cemetery on the eastern outskirts of Cairo. Only later the next day was it deemed appropriate for the widow and her female friends and relatives to visit the grave.

The event of my neighbor's death, which tragically left a young family fatherless, was quickly contained within a familiar framework of Islamic funerary procedures and mourning etiquette. Even the passionate grieving of his widow was soon subjected to the dual pressures of formal religious tradition and social custom.[40]

As performances that ritualize the body, Muslim funerary practices delineate the relations and boundary lines between not only the living and the dead, but also between belief and practice, body and soul, individual and society, religious elites and commoners, virtue and sin, pure and impure, male and female, Muslim and non-Muslim. Like other ritual practices, funerals also articulate temporal and spatial relations—they link the passing of an individual life with the sacred times of the past and the eschatological times of the future; they link the home of the dead with the cemetery, the House of God in Mecca (the Ka`ba), shrines of holy men and women, and the mansions of the blessed in the hereafter. For centuries, even in the most chaotic of circumstances—in times of pestilence and war, in times of family tragedy and profound communal crisis—the canon of Islamic funerary practices has provided a structure of order and meaning for the bereaved. It has also inspired elaborate ritual improvisations and provoked rituals of resistance, such as those that occurred during the Iranian revolution of 1978, and in occupied

Palestine and Iraq today. In addition to reaffirming community solidarity, as anthropologists have pointed out, the ritual canon may also accentuate social divisions and even provoke violence within and between communities.

Prescribed Funeral Rites

The dominant written code of rules for Muslim funerary practices is set forth in fiqh literature—that is, in Islamic legal texts written by religious specialists and jurists (the *ulema* and *faqih*s) living and circulating in a variety of cultural milieus. This literature seeks to prescribe what constitutes correct behavior for Muslims, in contrast to practices that are not in conformity with either the will of God as expressed in the Qur'an or the example of Muhammad and his companions, which is articulated in the vast hadith corpus. Correct practices are required, desirable, or simply permitted, while erroneous ones are either forbidden outright or classed as reprehensible. That there was a need for such texts indicates that, contrary to the wishes of many religious scholars, Muslims have actively drawn upon indigenous traditions and customs or devised new ones.

The Islamic legal canon prescribes four Muslim funerary practices—ritual bathing of the corpse (*ghusl*), shrouding (*takfin*), funeral prayer (*salat al-janaza*), and burial (*dafn*). For a more comprehensive overview we turn to a modern Egyptian compendium of Sunni legal opinion, `Abd al-Rahman al-Jaziri's *Book of Fiqh According to the Four Sunni Schools of Law*.[41] This book provides a summary of rulings pertaining to the main areas of Islamic jurisprudence, both with regard to worship (prayer, almsgiving, fasting, hajj, etc.) and the conduct of worldly affairs (marriage, divorce, inheritance, etc.), as espoused by the Maliki, Hanafi, Shafi`i, and Hanbali legal traditions of Sunni Islam. Like most legal literature, it discusses death and burial procedures at the end of the chapter on ritual prayer (salat) in a section about funerals. The topics are arranged as follows:[42]

1. Caring for the dying person
2. Preparing and washing the corpse
3. Shrouding
4. Funeral prayers
5. Martyrs
6. Funeral processions
7. Lamentations
8. Burial
9. Funerary buildings
10. Improper conduct at the grave
11. Transporting the corpse
12. Multiple burials
13. Mourning and visiting the grave

A detailed discussion of these canonically prescribed practices for ritualizing the body of the deceased, and all the variations allowed by the different legal schools, must be deferred to another occasion, but it is appropriate here to present some of the salient features. The paradigmatic corporeal subject in funerary ritualization is that of the adult male Muslim who dies among good friends and family. In his dying moments (1), his face should be turned toward Mecca, and he should be prompted to pronounce the shahada, or it should be pronounced for him, while those in attendance perform supplications on his behalf. People in conditions of ritual impurity, including menstruating women and women who have recently given birth, should be removed from his presence at this time. Immediately after death has been ascertained (2), the mouth is bound shut, clothing is removed, the body is covered with a sheet of cloth, and the death is publicized. Every effort should be made to prepare the body quickly for burial. A complete ritual bath (ghusl) is required, with the exception of miscarriages, martyrs of war, and corpses that are not in suitable condition for bathing (for example, badly burned bodies).[43] The corpse should be placed on an elevated surface and washed by a knowledgeable person of the same sex as the deceased, but a spouse or close relative of the opposite sex can also do it. A woman may wash the body of a young boy, and a man may wash that of a young girl. When possible the water should be clean, cool, and perfumed with camphor or other aromatics. A partial ablution (*wudu'*), as if preparing for prayer, should also be done. When the corpse has been purified, it is then completely wrapped in a ritually pure white shroud consisting of one or more pieces of cloth (3). Ordinary clothing is permitted, so long as it is in conformity with the legal dress code and is not too ostentatious or costly. Thus, a turban may be placed on the head of a man and a veil (*khimar*) on a woman.

Once the body has been purified, funeral prayers (4) must be performed. These are done in the presence of the corpse; they cannot be performed when there is no body, or from afar. Like daily prayers, they require intentionality, repeated pronouncements of the formula of sacralization known as the *takbir* ("*Allahu akbar!*"), performances of the ritual prayer postures, and closing blessings. Supplications are also recited on behalf of the deceased, asking God to magnify his good deeds and to disregard his wrongdoing. Martyrs (5), who may require exceptional funerary procedures, are discussed next in the compendium, but we will devote more attention to them further on. The corpse should be carried in procession (6) to the cemetery on a bier that is shouldered by four men, who proceed at a quick but dignified pace. It is a customary practice (*sunna*) for men to accompany the bier on foot, but it is wrongful (*makruh*) or even forbidden (*haram*) for women to join the procession out of fear that they might cause a public disturbance (*fitna*). Participants in the procession should remain quiet—even religious texts are to be recited in silence. Moreover, there is to be no audible weeping or lamentation, blackening the face, slapping cheeks, tearing clothes, or engaging in other such practices deemed by jurists to be wrongful (7).

The corpse should be buried in the ground deep enough to prevent its being ravaged by animals or emitting noxious odors (8). It should be turned on its right side, facing Mecca, and the head and feet supported by earth or a brick; a coffin should not be used unless circumstances require it. Once the body has been placed in the grave, participants in the funeral should each throw three handfuls of dirt into it. The burial site may be capped with a small mound or leveled with the surface of the earth. Jurists strongly disapprove of decorating the gravesite or erecting a building (a room, dome, religious school, mosque, or enclosure wall) over it (9), but they generally permit an object of stone or wood to be used as a marker. Most rule that epitaphs are reprehensible (makruh) or even forbidden (haram), even when verses from the Qur'an are used. Sitting, sleeping, or walking on graves when it is avoidable is reprehensible in the eyes of most jurists, and urinating or defecating on them is forbidden (10). Transporting a corpse to another site for burial (11), is allowed as long as there is a good reason to do so, the body has not already been buried, and it does not yet reek of death. Shafi`i jurists allow for this especially when someone dies near a holy site, such as Mecca, Medina, or a cemetery containing the graves of saints. Multiple burials in a common grave (12) are also permitted, with those of higher status (older males) placed toward Mecca in front of the others, each body separated from the next by a layer of dirt.

Mourning practices vary greatly among Muslim cultures, but the fiqh also seeks to regulate these (13). Grieving is allowed for three days after death—any longer is reprehensible, unless either the corpse or the mourner is not available. All kindred are expected to mourn, whether the deceased is male or female, young or old, except if the deceased is a young woman or infant, in which case only close relatives should mourn. Neighbors and friends should prepare food for the bereaved family and encourage them to eat despite their grief. A number of grieving rites are explicitly condemned: multiple mourning observances for the same person, slaughtering an animal at home when the corpse is removed or at the cemetery, preparing and serving food to condolers as if it were a festive occasion, visits to the cemetery by women who may cause trouble (fitna) or engage in immoral activity, and circumambulating or kissing the tomb (a practice typically performed at shrines). As a general rule, visiting cemeteries must be done in conformity with religious law, with little room allowed for deviation.

Sacred Speech

Muslim jurists also prescribe what ought to be said during the performance of death, burial, and mourning rituals. Ritualization, as with other Islamic religious practices, involves the use of formal Arabic religious language, regardless of the deceased's mother tongue. In addition to reciting the shahada and the invocations that constitute the formal funeral prayers, specific chapters and verses from the Qur'an are recommended, such as the opening chapter (the "Fatiha"), which speaks of judgment day and asks for God's guidance on the path to salvation, and chapter 36 *Ya Sin,* known as "the heart of the Qur'an," which is considered to be especially efficacious for alleviating the death agony and obtaining God's forgiveness.[44] Family members or friends may perform the Qur'an recitations, but professional reciters are also available, who may be asked to chant the Qur'an in its entirety. Today, portable audiocassette systems may be employed instead of the live readers. Often participants in funeral and bereavement activities are themselves called upon to recite specific texts of scripture. For example, when the body has been interred, all in attendance are urged to throw three handfuls of earth upon the grave and repeat these verses: "From it [earth] we created you, then we put you back into it, and from it we will bring you forth once again" (Q 20:55).[45] In addition, special prayers and supplications—many drawn from hadith collections—are recommended for the different phases of death and mourning outlined above.[46] Among the most important words prescribed for funerals are those of the *talqin,* which prepares the deceased for interrogation at the hands of the angels Munkar and Nakir in the grave:

> O so and so (name the deceased), son/daughter of so and so (name the parent of the deceased), remember the covenant with which you have left this world: the *shahada* that there is no god but God and that Muhammad is God's prophet. [Remember] that paradise is real; that the fire is real; that the resurrection is real; that the hour of judgment shall surely come; and that God will resurrect the dead from the grave. [Remember also] that you accepted God as your lord, Islam as your religion, Muhammad as your prophet, the Qur'an as your imam, the Ka`ba as your prayer direction, and the believers as your brethren.[47]

Although the content of the talqin has varied among different Muslim communities at different times in its history, it nonetheless reflects the linkage of core Islamic doctrines with the event of human mortality. It is a form of orientation for the deceased and funeral participants, analogous to how the corpse is physically oriented toward Mecca in burial. As is the case with other forms of authoritative Islamic discourse used in such contexts, the talqin is part of a complex of ritualizing practices that embeds the death of an individual within a larger frame of meaning and gives the bereaved a sense that they are coming to the aid of the deceased in the passage to the otherworld, as well as accruing benefit for themselves in this world.

Ritual Performances

Al-Jaziri's compendium of Islamic law discloses points of consensus as well as difference among the ulema charged with teaching and implementing the Shari`a as embodied by the four Sunni legal traditions. Admittedly, the differences among them may seem insignificant, but they teach us that what is prescribed is not immune from the effects of history, culture, and human imagination. Even greater ranges of variation and difference occur on the level of actual performance when the specific identities of the deceased, the participants, and the wider audience are at play, as are the dynamics of their interrelationships with each other and with the holders of authority. This raises questions pertaining to the performative situation as it shapes Muslim practices of death, bereavement, and memorialization, and the degree to which any given performance conforms to the script set forth by the religious elites. If the performance in whole or in part were to deviate from what the authorities have determined to be the divinely sanctioned norms, then they may well classify it as *bid`a*—an innovation. Innovations may be good or bad, or finer differentiations may be drawn between those that are classified as prohibited, disapproved, permitted, and recommended. Indeed, fiqh manuals and compendiums such as al-Jaziri's go to some lengths to classify innovations, as well as set forth what Muslims *ought* to do in accordance with the Qur'an and the Sunna. The author of one modern manual on Muslim funerary rules fears that fellow Muslims are neglecting or changing the prescribed practices and are devising their own instead, or they "blindly accept and follow the mutilated teachings of other faiths and thus fall into absurd customes [*sic*]."[40] Among the popular funerary observances that have attracted the most attention from the ulema are those involving uses of the Qur'an, women's mourning customs, and the building and visitation of shrines and monumental tombs.[49]

While jurists endorsed Qur'an recitations at funeral and mourning rites, they decried doing so in settings where the sacred sound or the written Qur'an might be profaned.[50] In actuality, according to Edward Lane, there were elaborate Qur'an recitations in public arenas, supplemented by performance of lamentations and songs in praise of Muhammad at funerals in nineteenth-century Cairo. Lane also mentioned displays of the bound Qur'an in the funeral procession and the inscription of Qur'anic verses on gravestones, a widespread practice that jurists frowned upon.[51] According to epigraphic field surveys in medieval cemeteries in the Middle East, the verses favored for headstones were concerned with God's unity and permanence, intercession, the afterlife, and the inevitability of death.[52] In Iran and India, the burial shroud itself may be embellished with Qur'anic and other religious declarations.[53] In deference to the sacredness of the Qur'an, however, the gravestone or coffin may lack scriptural quotations, but refer to a chapter by its name only, asking the reader to recite the "Fatiha" on behalf of the soul of the deceased person.

In many Muslim societies, women gather together in mutual support when death strikes, engaging in an array of bereavement practices that can include wailing, breast-beating, singing lamentation songs, tearing garments, slapping and scratching the face, breaking bangles, and leaving their hair disheveled. Some may besmear themselves with mud. They are also involved in preparing quantities of food and drink, especially for members of the bereaved family. In northern India, grieving Muslim women conduct a household rite called *fatiha,* after the first chapter of the Qur'an. It involves creating a ritual space in the home where food offerings are placed and Qur'an recitations are performed to transfer merit to the deceased and to living family members.[54] A more widespread practice is visiting cemeteries on major holidays and death anniversaries (for example, the third-, seventh- and fortieth-day anniversaries, as well as the one-year anniversary), when both women and men place flowers on the graves of loved ones and distribute food and sweets to the poor on their behalf.[55] All of these practices have been condemned by jurists in whole or in part as innovations that violate Islamic norms or had the potential to do so.[56] In recent times, such distinctive traditional local funeral practices appear to be waning—middle-class women living in cities and abroad attempt to exhibit more controlled forms of behavior. In conformity with what is prescribed by religious authorities and influential family members, especially those attracted to revivalist Islamic currents, they moderate their weeping, avoid ostentatious social displays and entertainments, and dress in somber colors during the mourning period. Some women who have migrated to non-Muslim societies in Europe and North America find that when confronted by the cultural suppression of death in the West, in the absence of the traditional practices and support networks of their homeland, they must seek out grief counseling from Western-trained therapists and non-Muslim religious organizations.

As noted by al-Jaziri, religious authorities have also opposed ornamenting the grave and erecting monumental structures over it. Strict obedience to this ban is evident in Saudi Arabia and among bedouin peoples, where the dead are often interred in simple, unembellished graves. However, the same does not hold true for many other Muslim cultures, where cemeteries display works of mortuary ornamentation and construction that we may regard as forms of religious performance. Indeed, many of the most spectacular examples of Islamic architectural expression were created to commemorate prophets, rulers, and saints, such as Muhammad's mosque-tomb in Medina, the shrines of `Ali and Husayn in Najaf and Karbala, the numerous mosques dedicated to members of Muhammad's family in Cairo, and the tombs of Mamluk, Mongol, Persian, and Turkish elites in Egypt, Turkey, Iran, and Central Asia.[57] Medieval texts cataloged and extolled the holiness of the tombs and mausoleums found throughout Muslim lands, leading one Western scholar to observe, "Every major city of Islam claims the honor of possessing the tombs of [saints and righteous men], irrespective of the fact that several cities may boast of the burial place of the same individual."[58] Thus both Cairo and Karbala have shrines for Husayn, and Cairo and Damascus have shrines for his sister Zaynab. Among the most renowned examples of mortuary architecture are the mausoleums of the Mughal rulers of India. The Taj Mahal in Agra, wherein the tombs of Shah Jahan (1592–1666) and his wife Mumtaz (d. 1631) lie, is popularly interpreted as a monument to one man's immortal love for his spouse. Scholarly reassessments, however, have found that it was originally designed to reflect Qur'anic images of resurrection, the gardens of paradise, and God's throne in heaven.[59] The tradition of building funerary monuments continues in modern nation states, producing the tombs of famous national figures like Muhammad `AliJinnah (d. 1948) in Karachi, Pakistan; Sukarno (d. 1970) in Indonesia; Anwar Sadat (d. 1981) in Cairo; and, most recently, Ayatollah Khomeini (d. 1989) in Tehran. Muslim nations, like many modern non-Muslim countries, have also erected monuments to commemorate soldiers who have died in battle.

Shrines, tombs, and funerary mosques have attracted countless pilgrims through the centuries from across a broad spectrum of the Muslim community—Sunnis, Shi`a and Sufis alike. People journey to them to seek the intercession and blessing of the saints whose remains and relics they contain. Muhammad himself is reported to have said, "Whoever visits my tomb deserves my intercession."[60] Such "visits" (*ziyarat*) usually coincide with calendrical saints' festivals, so pilgrims have opportunities to congregate, share stories and food, and enjoy entertainments, in addition to more structured forms of religious activity. Moreover, many pilgrims and devotees prefer to be buried in the vicinity of the holy dead. This is especially so among the Shi`a, who transport corpses to the shrines of their imams in Iraq and Iran when political conditions permit.[61] Despite their popularity, pilgrimage rites and beliefs in saintly blessing and intercession have been condemned by the more puritanically minded, especially by the followers of the teachings of Muhammad ibn `Abd al-Wahhab (1703–1792), whose radical reformist ideas shaped the ideology of the Kingdom of Saudi Arabia. The Saudi-Wahhabi conquest of the Arabian Peninsula resulted in the destruction of many shrines and tombs, including those of the Shi`a in Iraq in 1801.[62]

Violent and Anomalous Deaths

Prescribed doctrines and practices in effect seek to rectify two kinds of incongruity that arise in relation to Muslim ways of death—the existential occurrence of death itself and the variety of sociocultural beliefs and practices that surround it, which can often occur as a result of Muslim interactions and exchanges with non-Muslims. Concomitantly, the social milieu and the anomalous circumstances of the death may demonstrate the limited reach of the ulema, the preeminence of local beliefs and practices, or the need to improvise and adapt.

In December 2003, when an earthquake in Bam, Iran, took the lives of tens of thousands people, there was no time or capacity for performing burial rites or even identifying the bodies. To avoid an epidemic, emergency relief workers collected corpses from ruined buildings, hastily slipped them into body bags, and deposited them in the city's cemetery in mass graves that had been excavated by bulldozers. Most survivors and relatives living abroad had to mourn in the absence of the bodies of deceased loved ones, proceeding *as if* they had been properly buried.

In neighboring Iraq, years of bloodshed under the rule of Saddam Husayn and now the occupation of U.S. troops have strained the ability of mourners to perform proper funerary rites. Shi`i Arabs and Sunni Kurds have been engaged since spring 2003 in the gruesome task of searching newly discovered mass graves for remains of relatives who died at the hands of Saddam Husayn's tyrannical government so that they can be buried properly. International press accounts indicate that when corpses are exhumed, they are given funerary ablutions with sand (permitted when water is unavailable) and wrapped in simple shrouds. Iraqi exhumation teams attach bags containing belongings found with the body to help provide identification. Nonetheless, the bereaved have complained about denial of access to the mass gravesites, the handling of the remains, and delays in being able to claim them for final reburial.[63] As bloodshed continues to beset the country in the aftermath of the U.S. invasion and occupation, the number of severely traumatized corpses that need to be prepared for burial each day is overwhelming professional body washers in the holy city of Najaf. Following the Shari`a, they segregate the bodies according to sex so that male washers care for men and female washers care for women. Sometimes assisted by family members, they dress the wounds and cleanse the deceased using water scented with camphor, then wrap the body in a shroud. Contrary to prescribed Muslim practice under more peaceful conditions, burial is often delayed when civilians are killed in a bombing because families must first search for the body, file the official papers, and transport the body to Najaf from outlying areas. Even under conditions of war, people still attempt to follow local burial customs, such as singing lamentations and wrapping the body in shrouds stenciled with Qur'anic verses.[64]

Acknowledging the occurrence of such large-scale death and destruction, the Indian author of a recent handbook on Muslim funerary and inheritance practice observes:

> It is the nemesis of our deeds that life in our so-called civilized societies of the modern world has become some sort of shooting range where disorders breed and accidents happen

> in breathless frequency. The media is loaded with tales of terror and hundreds die unnaturally as a matter of routine, which, of course, includes a large number of Muslims as well. . . . There are occasions when the death of Muslims presents very complex and involved situations, so much so that arranging for timely bathing, shrouding and *salat al-janaza* [prayer for the deceased] becomes an embarrassing problem. In the event that there is no knowledgeable person around to guide into the correct Islamic method of burial in a given situation, the confusion is worse confounded.[65]

The handbook's author provides guidelines grounded in Islamic law for anomalous funerary situations, such as miscarriages, stillbirths, drowning victims, a rotten corpse or skeleton, burned remains and charred bodies, motor vehicle accident victims, lack of a body, people lost at sea, mixed Muslim and non-Muslim bodies, burial of a pregnant non-Muslim wife of a Muslim, unknown corpses, cases where a body is buried without following ritual requirements, suicides, burial of body parts, treatment of parts separated from a living body, burial of corpses that have become exposed, and burial of criminals.[66] This list reflects the impact that core Islamic beliefs in bodily resurrection and final judgment can have on funerary practices and reveals the totalizing impulse in Islamic law, which seeks to govern every conceivable situation, even when this requires some imaginative stretches of reason. The event of death causes people, both religious elites and commoners, to mobilize multiple practices that transform the corpse (if only parts of it) into a ritualized body and memorialize the deceased, even in the most extraordinary circumstances. Such practices seek to remedy the accidental, incongruous, and horrific aspects of death, as well as affirm life and its meanings. They may also provide symbolic occasions for social and political action.

On August 29, 2003, Ayatollah Muhammad Baqir al-Hakim, the highly esteemed Shi`i leader of the Supreme Council for Islamic Revolution in Iraq, who had just returned to his native country after more than two decades of exile in Iran, was blown to pieces by a car bomb after Friday prayer at the mosque of Imam Ali in Najaf, along with a number of his aides and bystanders. According to press accounts, the force of the blast was so tremendous that there was little left of him for burial, except a watch, a pen, shreds of his black turban, and a wedding ring. Under these conditions, and in the wake of years of suffering under an oppressive regime, three wars, and a foreign invasion, the Iraqi Shi`a rallied to ceremonially bury and mourn the loss of one of their most popular leaders. The ayatollah's remains were first transported ceremonially from Najaf north to the holy Kadhimayn shrine near Baghdad, where they were placed in a coffin, then carried back southward in a three-day funeral procession that passed through the holy city of Karbala, then Kufa, and back to his final resting place in Najaf, some 115 miles from Baghdad. Hundreds of thousands of mourners joined in the funeral, chanting "There is no god but God," "God is greater!" and other religious phrases; some beat their chests and flagellated themselves with chains, reenacting Shi`i Muharram rituals customarily performed in commemoration of the martyrdom of Imam Husayn. Mourners carried banners that referred to al-Hakim as a martyr, and others displayed pictures of him joined with pious portraits of Imam Husayn. At Karbala, one cleric proclaimed, "They cut off your head just as they cut off the head of Imam Husayn. The martyr has come to the Lord of Martyrs!" The crowds also chanted political statements: "We will humiliate Saddam. We will humiliate Bush." After funerary orations, and amid much public weeping, al-Hakim's remains were buried, together with those of fifteen of his bodyguards, in the cemetery of Najaf's Revolution Square, where martyrs killed in the 1920 Shi`i revolt against the British occupation also are interred. Thus, Iraq's Shi`a incorporated al-Hakim into the community of martyrs.[67]

The ritualization of al-Hakim's body, or what stood for his body, continued with a U.S. Department of Defense interfaith ceremony held in Arlington, Virginia, later in September 2003, where Deputy Secretary of Defense Paul Wolfowitz quoted verses from the Qur'an in Arabic and included himself among those who mourned the ayatollah's untimely death:

> And if anyone needed proof about the commitment of the Iraqi people—in particular the commitment of the Shi`a of Iraq—to a peaceful and democratic Iraq, they had that proof when tens of thousands, probably hundreds of thousands, of people came out in peace to greet the funeral procession of Muhammad Baqir Al-Hakim's funeral procession. Like them, we say today, "Peace on Hakim's soul," that we should "think not of those who are killed in the way of God as dead. Nay they are alive with their Lord and they have provision."[68] (Q 3:169)

The Qur'an verse quoted here by Wolfowitz is one frequently invoked by Muslims in connection with the afterlife fate of martyrs. The Ayatollah's stature and the circumstances of his death thus necessitated a round of ad hoc performances that uniquely joined prescribed Muslim burial practices with theatrical Iraqi Shi`i mourning rituals, Iraqi civil religion, and U.S. Department of Defense memorial protocol. An additional level of meaning that the Ayatollah's funeral may have held for many of Iraq's Shi`a is that it also served as the vicarious funeral for the thousands who perished in war and at the hands of Saddam Husagn's regime, but whose bodies had never been recovered.

Systematic analysis of actual funeral, bereavement, and memorial performances is beyond the scope of this study. There are numerous descriptions of death rituals in ethnographic literature,[69] but there is a need for more systematic comparative research that combines fieldwork on ritual performances in Muslim societies with critical readings of Islamic literature to trace the genealogies of the authoritative discourses that seek to regulate them. Reading fiqh literature "against the grain" would be an especially fruitful undertaking, for in their criticisms and condemnations of Muslim practices, piety-minded ulema actually portray for us what Muslims living in different countries actually do in the event of death, rather than just what jurists think they *ought* to do.[70]

God's Martyrs

Any discussion of Muslim ways of death must include consideration of martyrdom. As we have seen from the foregoing discussion, the victims of Saddam Husayn's tyranny and of the Bam earthquake, as well as the Ayatollah al-Hakim, have all been called martyrs by family, associates, religious authorities, the regional press, and assorted government officials. Muslims also use *martyr* as a designation for those who die on pilgrimage, for women who die in labor, for those like Abu Hayyan's daughter who have succumbed to disease, and for soldiers who die in battle. There are even hadith that promise a martyr's rewards in the afterlife to those who recite designated chapters of the Qur'an.[71] Martyrdom constitutes a foundational component of Shi`i doctrine, especially with regard to the redemptive suffering of the imams, and it holds an important place in Sunni and Sufi discourses. The special rewards promised for martyrs in the afterlife include exemption from the trial of the grave and immediate access to paradise, as opposed to delay until the Day of Judgment. Muslim radicals use martyrdom as a powerful rhetorical device to legitimate and incite attacks against civilian and political targets in their own countries, Israel, Europe, and the United States. The instructions found among the belongings of Muhammad `Atta and other 9/11 attackers constitute a script calling for bodily ablutions, Qur'an recitations, pronouncement of the shahada, and supplications—all with the aim of achieving martyrdom.[72] The document even quotes the same Qur'an verse—the one most frequently cited in relation to martyrs—that Paul Wolfowitz read at the memorial for Ayatollah al-Hakim in September 2003: "Think not of those who are killed in the way of God as dead. Nay they are alive with their Lord and they have provision" (Q 3:169). Martyr and martyrdom therefore have enjoyed wide application among Muslims for centuries, with significant differences and disagreements about their meaning. Concomitantly, their use by Muslims has provoked anger, fear, and misunderstanding among non-Muslims, though non-Muslims themselves have not been averse to drawing upon the rhetoric of martyrdom when it serves their interests.

The Arabic term for "martyr" is *shahid* "witness"; "martyrdom" in Arabic is shahada, the same designation used for the first pillar of Islam—witnessing or testifying "There is no god but God, and Muhammad is his messenger."[73] In its root meaning, shahid is equivalent to the English word martyr, which developed from a Greek word for "witness." Indeed, early Islamic notions of martyrdom appear to have their beginnings in the widespread cult of the martyrs that shaped the early Christian tradition, when Christians who suffered death at the hands of Roman persecutors earned saintly status.[74] Al-Jaziri summarizes the key elements of Sunni law pertaining to martyrs among rules pertaining to funeral prayers and processions, which occur in the section on prayer in his compendium.[75] He uses a threefold classification of martyrs, which determines the burial rites that ought to be performed: (1) martyrs of this world and the hereafter, (2) martyrs of the hereafter, and (3) martyrs of this world. The first grouping consists primarily of those killed swiftly in battle against unbelievers; as long as they are rational and free of major impurity, they are exempted from the prescribed ritual ablutions, shrouding, and funeral prayers. This "battlefield martyrdom" represents what is probably the earliest stage in the development of Islamic understandings of the topic, dating back to the foundational years of the Muslim community under Muhammad's leadership in Medina (between 622 and 632), first while it was under attack by its Meccan opponents, then later during its armed expansionist phase.[76] It is therefore intimately connected with Islamic concepts of the "struggle" (jihad) against unbelievers. The second division applies to those who die in battle, but do not meet one or more of the stipulated criteria. It can also include those who have died under varying circumstances: by fire, drowning, disease, scorpion sting, fulfilling a religious duty, giving birth, or while living away from home. This group can even include "a pious lover who conceals his love and dies lovesick."[77] Though such people will be rewarded in the hereafter, they are subject to the same mortuary rites as ordinary Muslims—ablutions, shrouding, and funeral prayers. The "martyrs of this world," a less widely recognized grouping, applies to insincere Muslims ("hypocrites") who may die in battle along with other Muslims or who die primarily in a quest for worldly gain and are not assured a reward in the hereafter.

With the anger and anxiety that Islamic martyrdom ideology and practice have sparked recently in the West, as well as among Muslims themselves, much attention has been given to the claim that Muslim martyrs are promised seventy-two celestial virgins (or wives) in paradise and that this belief causes young men to actively seek martyrdom by strapping explosives around their bodies and launching suicide attacks against unsuspecting civilians, soldiers, or government authorities. Explanations based on this belief fail to take into account that in the traditional Muslim imaginaire the reward of celestial mates is promised to all the righteous in paradise, not only to martyrs, and that the designation "martyr" can apply to a wide array of deceased Muslims, as we have seen.[78] Moreover, this explanation neglects to account for the more immediate causes of religious violence in the modern world, the specificities of the performative contexts within which such violence occurs, and the wider ideological and historical milieu. Though the linkage of jihad with martyrdom was established early in the history of the Muslim community, its use as a tactic by radical organizations against civilian targets is of recent origin, closely linked to the reinterpretation of armed jihad as a revolutionary struggle directed internally against ruling elites or externally against colonial powers, occupation forces, and civilians. This change in thought occurred during the nineteenth century, when colonizing Europeans held sway directly or indirectly over most Muslim homelands, and it now constitutes a core belief among radical Islamist groups in Egypt (the Jihad Organization), Palestine (Islamic Jihad and Hamas), and Lebanon (Hizballah), as well as the transnational organization of al-Qa`ida. Since spring 2003, it has also proved to be a significant factor among various Iraqi groups fighting against the occupation of their country by the United States.

CONCLUSION

My dear beloved husband:
O dearest of those I have loved and most precious of what I have lost!
Once there was joy when I saw you, now I become tearful when I remember you.
With every beat of my heart I lament for you,
And if it were in my power I would ransom myself for you.
You sacrificed so much for me, and withstood so much to make me happy.
Your memory will stay with me until I meet you again.
—Your sad wife Nadia[79]

These verses, published during the 1980s in the obituary pages of the leading Egyptian newspaper, *Al-Ahram,* reflect both continuity and discontinuity with those that Abu Hayyan composed in memory of his daughter six centuries earlier in Cairo.[80] Both Nadia and Abu Hayyan express their grief over the loss of a loved one in poetic language and assuage their pain with the expectation of meeting the deceased in the afterlife. However, Abu Hayyan's elegies, excerpts of which are given at the beginning of this study, were a product of a sophisticated scribal culture and circulated mainly among scholarly elites in a medieval society. They make explicit references to authoritative Islamic beliefs about God and the afterlife, but they also reflect a capacity to reshape and contest them. By way of contrast, Nadia's elegy reveals the perspective of the wife of a modern doctor—a member of the new technological elite that has emerged in twentieth-century Egypt. The social status of both Nadia and her husband is indicated by the medium of print publication, and also by the notice accompanying it, which states that the observance of the fortieth-day anniversary of the doctor's passing was to be held in the `Umar Makram Mosque, a modern mosque in downtown Cairo favored by the privileged. More importantly, Nadia's elegy makes no mention of key Islamic doctrines concerning God and the hereafter, other than a vague hope for a happy reunion in the future. This notice exemplifies the interweaving of traditional funerary performance and modern secular understandings about the afterlife. It also reflects the emergence of women's voices in the public sphere, thus challenging the prescriptions of traditionally-minded jurists who recommend their silence, especially in connection with death and grieving.

In the modern period the conjunctions and divergencies of prescribed Islamic funerary rites and beliefs with those that are actually practiced continue to occur. Unlike the past, however, new print and electronic media technologies have allowed Muslims to instantly consult with religious experts over great distances about burial practices, and to obtain information for themselves about death and the afterlife from books and magazines, radio and television, and now the Internet. Yes, the new media may have given the prescriptions of even the most conservative ulema a wider reach than in Abu Hayyan's time, but they also enabled Nadia and fellow Muslims to become more cognizant of a variety of alternative views and to give voice to their own feelings and opinions to an unprecedented extent. Muslims in different historical and cultural contexts have struggled to deal with death's incongruities in a variety of ways, and they continue to do so in their native lands and in newly adopted homes in Europe and the Americas. Fruitful textual study, fieldwork, and comparative research, which can now be further enriched by access to information transmitted via the electronic media and the Web, awaits to be done on this vital topic that we have only begun to explore.[81]

NOTES

I have avoided the use of diacritics in transliterating Arabic words, except for the letters *`ayn* (`) and medial and final hamza (written with an apostrophe, as in the word *Qur'an*). Conventional spellings are used wherever possible. The Qur'an translations, unless otherwise indicated, are my own, based on the Egyptian Standard Edition of the Arabic text (1924).

I wish to thank my gifted and patient undergraduate research assistants Maria Reifel Saltzberg and Sarah Rathburn for helping with gathering the resources used for this study. It is dedicated to the civilian victims of armed violence in Iraq, Palestine, and Afghanistan, and to the memory of Jesús E. Campo-Varona, my uncle, who passed away while I was writing it.

1. Translated from Abu Hayyan's *Diwan* by Th. Emil Homerin, "A Bird Ascends the Night: Elegy and Immortality in Islam," *Journal of the American Academy of Religion* 58 (1991): 272.

2. Ibid., 264.

3. Jonathan Z. Smith, "The Bare Facts of Ritual," in *Imagining Religion: From Jerusalem to Jonestown* (Chicago: University of Chicago Press, 1982), 63.

4. Ibid.

5. I have adapted the notions of the prescribed and the performed from Isabelle Nabokov, who uses them in a study of Hindu rituals processes in South India. Here, I apply them more generally to religious belief as well as ritual. See Isabelle Nabokov, *Religion against Itself: An Ethnography of Tamil Rituals* (Oxford: Oxford University Press, 2000), 12–13. In addition to the work of Jonathan Z. Smith (cited above), I have benefited from Catherine Bell's *Ritual Theory, Ritual Practice* (New York: Oxford University Press, 1992) and *Ritual: Perspectives and Dimensions* (New York: Oxford University Press, 1997). In the Islamic milieu, see Leila Abu-Lughod, "Islam and the Gendered Discourses of Death," *International Journal of Middle East Studies* 25 (1993): 187–205. Abu-Lughod shows the benefits of examining the multiple discourses and practices a society may invoke in the event of death, but I disagree with her contention that Muslim funerary practices "are similar across societies" and that religious discourse is primarily defined by elites, in contrast to localized social and cultural practices.

6. On ritual performance, see Bell, *Ritual Theory,* 37–46, and *Ritual: Perspectives and Dimensions*, 72–76. I do not restrict performance to ritual, theater, and festival. Rather, I understand it more broadly to encompass a range of situations in which the content of a cultural "text," in the form of verbal discourse or ritual activity, is shaped by a dynamic interaction between a performing subject and an audience.

7. The Arabic *din,* rendered here as "religion," also means "judgment."

8. Muslim ibn al Hajjaj, *Sahih,* Kitab al-iman, 8 vols. in 2 (Cairo: Kitab al-Tahrir, 1963), 1:28–29; al-Bukhari, *Sahih,* Kitab al-iman, 9 vols. in 3 (Cairo: Dar Matubi` al-sha`b, [1957–1960]), 1:19–20. This hadith was also one of those included in Muhyi al-Din Yahya b. Sharaf al-Nawawi's (d. 1277) classic collection of forty exemplary hadith, which, if memorized, promised blessings in the world to come; see *Al-Arba`un al-nawawiyya* (Cairo: Al-Matbaa `al-Salafiyya, 1979), 10–11, 18–19. See further the discussion in William Chittick and Sachiko Murata, *The Vision of Islam* (New York: Paragon House, 1994), xxv–xxxix.

9. For more on the holy places in Mecca and Medina as domestic spaces, see Juan E. Campo, *The Other Sides of Paradise: Explorations into the Religious Meanings of Domestic Space in Islam* (Columbia: University of South Carolina Press, 1991). The hadith about the paradisal quality of Muhammad's home are quoted in al-Bukhari, Muslim, and other authoritative collections; see ibid., 205, n. 32 for full citations.

10. William Spencer, *Global Studies: The Middle East,* 9th ed. (Guilford, CT: McGraw-Hill/Dushkin, 2003), 46, 60, 74.

11. Sultan Bahu, *Death Before Dying: The Sufi Poems of Sultan Bahu,* trans. Jamal J. Elias (Berkeley: University of California Press, 1998), 95.

12. Nizam al-Din Awliya, *Morals for the Heart,* trans. Bruce B. Lawrence (New York: Paulist Press, 1992), 134. Nizam al-Din (d. 1325), one of the leading saints of the Chishti Sufi order in India, supported this opinion with a tradition attributed to Muhammad: "People are asleep, but when they die they awake."

13. Richard V. Weekes, ed., *Muslim Peoples: A World Ethnographic Survey,* 2d ed. (Westport, CT: Greenwood, 1984); Central Intelligence Agency, *World Fact Book,* 2003, www.cia.gov/cia/publications/factbook/index.html.

14. Reinhold Loeffler, *Islam in Practice: Religious Beliefs in a Persian Village* (Albany: State University of New York Press, 1988), 151.

15. Personal communication to the author in May 2003.

16. See Carol Zaleski, *Otherworld Journeys: Accounts of Near-Death Experience in Medieval and Modern Times* (New York: Oxford University Press, 1987).

17. For informative treatments of Muhammad's *isra'* (Night Journey) and *mi`raj* (Ascension), see Anne Marie Schimmel, *And Muhammad Is His Messenger: The Veneration of the Prophet in Islamic Piety* (Chapel Hill: University of North Carolina Press, 1985 ), chap. 9; and *Encyclopaedia of Islam,* WebCD ed. (Leiden: Brill Academic, 2003), s.v. *Mi`radj.* For translations of some of its many versions, see Arthur Jeffreys, ed., *A Reader on Islam* (The Hague: Mouton, 1962), 621–639; Andrew Rippin and Jan Knappert, eds. and trans., *Textual Sources for the Study of Islam* (Totowa, NJ: Barnes and Noble, 1987), 68–73; and John Alden Williams, *The Word of Islam* (Austin: University of Texas Press, 1994), 43–46.

18. See Zaleski, *Otherworld Journeys,* chaps. 6–8; and Lee W. Bailey and Jenny Yates, eds., *The Near Death Experinence: A Reader* (New York: Routledge, 1996).

19. Jane I. Smith, and Yvonne Haddad, *The Islamic Understanding of Death and Resurrection* (Albany: State University of New York Press, 1981), 104–126.

20. The Arabic term for "paradise" in the Qur'an is *janna,* which literally means "garden." The Qur'an also uses the Persian term *firdaws,* which denotes an enclosed garden and is the word from which the English word *paradise* is derived. The most frequently used Arabic terms for "hell" in the Qur'an are *nar* "fire" and *jahannam,* which comes from the Hebrew term *Gehenna,* a word that occurs in both the Hebrew Bible and the New Testament.

21. *Encyclopaedia of Islam,* s.v. *Mawt* by M. Abdesselem.

22. The death angel is mentioned once in the Qur'an (32:11), but there are many narratives about him and his dialogues and encounters with prophets, saints, and ordinary people trying to escape his grasp in later hadith and eschatological texts. Much of this literature has been inspired by rabbinic traditions. See Abu Hamid Muhammad al-Ghazali, *The Remembrance of Death and the Afterlife,* Kitab dhikr al-mawt wa-ma ba`dahu, Book 40 of *The Revival of Religious Sciences,* trans. T.J. Winter (Cambridge: Islamic Texts Society, 1995), 43–45, 50–55; also *Encyclopaedia of Islam,* s.v. *`Izra'il* by A.J. Wensinck.

23. Colleen McDannell and Bernhard Lang, *Heaven: A History* (New Haven: Yale University Press, 1988).

24. According to the Qur'an, the houris are the virgin "companions" and "purified wives" of righteous men in Paradise (Q 52:20, 56:35–38, 2:25); see *Encyclopaedia of Islam,* s.v. *Hur* by A.J. Wensinck and Charles Pellat.

25. Al-Ghazali, *Remembrance of Death and the Afterlife,* 238. The hadith is also cited in the collections of Ibn al-Mubarak (eighth century), al-Tabarani (d. 971), and Bayhaqi (d. 1066); ibid., 272.

26. Abu Muhammad `Ali ibn Hazm, *The Ring of the Dove: A Treatise on the Art and Practice of Arab Love,* trans. A.J. Arberry (London: Luzac, 1953), 237.

27. Trustees of the Peermahomed Ebrahim Trust, *Death and Death Ceremonies* (Karachi: Peermahomed Ebrahim Trust, 1972), 76. I have made minor stylistic emendations in this quotation for the purpose of standardization.

28. Al-Ghazali, *Remembrance of Death and the Afterlife,* 221.

29. See Abu `bd Allah Muhammad al-Qurtubi, *Al-Tadhkira fi ahwal al-mawta wa-umur al-akhira* (Beirut: Dar al-Kutub al-`Ilmiyya, 1987), 444–468. Al-Qurtubi's lengthy account of Islamic afterlife beliefs was written in the thirteenth century CE and is still widely available in Arabic printings.

30. See, Muslim ibn al-Hajjaj, *Sahih Muslim,* Kitab al-salat; Muhammad bin Ishaq, *al-Sira al-Nabawiyya,* 2nd ed., 4 vols. (Cairo: Mustafa al-Baqi al-Halabi wa-Awladuhu, 1955), 4:649–671; and Abu 'Abd Allah Muhammad bin Sa`d, *al-Tabaqat al-kubra,* 9 vols. (Beirut: Dar Sadir, [1957–1960]), 2:250–316.

31. Al-Ghazali, *Remembrance of Death and the Afterlife,* 74.

32. *Encyclopaedia of Islam,* s.v. *Marthiya;* Vernon James Schubel, *Religious Performance in Contemporary Islam: Shi`i Devotional Rituals in South Asia* (Columbia: University of South Carolina Press, 1993); Yitzhaq Nakash, *The Shi`is of Iraq* (Princeton: Princeton University Press, 1994), ch. 5.

33. See *Encyclopaedia of Islam,* s.v. *Mawlid;* Schimmel, *And Muhammad Is His Messenger,* chap. 8. The *`urs* is more likely to be found in eastern Islamic lands, but it is also celebrated in immigrant communities in the west; Pnina Werbner, *Pilgrims of Love: The Anthropology of a Global Sufi Cult* (Bloomington: Indiana University Press, 2003), 242–258.

34. See al-Ghazali, *Rememberance of Death and the Afterlife,* 156–69.

35. See Smith and Haddad, *Islamic Understanding of Death and Resurrection,* 50–59.

36. Peermahomed Ebrahim Trust, *Death and Death Ceremonies,* 21–22; Loeffler, *Islam in Practice,* 24.

37. For modern treatments of this subject, see *Encyclopaedia of Islam,* s.v. *Munkar wa-Nakir,* by A.J. Wensinck, and *`Adhab al-Qabr,* by A.J. Wensinck and A.S. Tritton; and Smith and Haddad, *The Islamic Understanding of Death and Resurrection,* 41–49.

38. Jalal al-Din al-Suyuti, *Sharh al-sudur bi-sharh hal al-mawta wa'l-qubur* (Beirut: Mu'assasat al-Ayman, 1986), 160. *Imam* is usually a designation for an exemplary religious figure or prayer leader. In the passage quoted, it is used instead as an appelliation for the Qur'an—an exemplary religious text rather than a human being. Al-Suyuti, an Egyptian, lived during the fifteenth century. There are many variants of this punishment scenario; see, for example, that of al-Samarqandi (d. 983) in Jeffreys, *Reader on Islam,* 209–210; al-Ghazali, *Remembrance of Death and the Afterlife,* 135–147; and al-Qurtubi, *Tadhkira,* 123–129.

39. See Ahmed Saeed Dehlvi, *What Happens after Death,* trans. Rahm Ali al-Hashmi (Delhi: Dini Book Depot, 1974), 229–242. On Shi`i beliefs in the trial of the grave, see Henri Massé, *Persian Beliefs and Customs* (New Haven: Human Relations Area Files, 1954), 100–101; Loeffler, *Islam in Practice,* 24, 105, 149.

40. That is to say, social custom for the urban middle class in modern Egypt. In premodern Egypt, and today in rural areas and among the bedouin, open weeping by women is customary, and there are also women who hire themselves out to perform ritual lamentations. See Edward W. Lane, *An Account of the Manners and Customs of the Modern Egyptians* (New York: Dover, 1973 [1860]), 516–528; Muhammad Galal, "Essai d'observations sur les rites funéraires en Egypte actuelle releveés dans certaines regions compagnardes," *Revue des études islamiques* 11 (1937): 131–299; `Abd al-Halim Hifni, *Al-Marathi al-sha`biyya Al-`adid* (Cairo: Al-Hay'a al-Misriyya al-Amm li'l-Kitab, 1982), 11–14; Haddad and Smith, *Islamic Understanding of Death and Resurrection,* 59–60; Abu-Lughod, "Islam and the Gendered Discourses of Death," 193–96.

41. `Abd al-Rahman al-Jaziri, *Kitab al-fiqh `ala all-madhahib al-arba`a,* 4 vols. (Beirut: Dar al-Kutub al-`Ilmiyya, 1990 [1928]), 1:455–491.

42. A similar organization of funeral topics can be found in hadith collections and eschatological literature. See, for example, Muslim, *Sahih Muslim,* Kitab al-jana'iz; al-Qurtubi, *Tadhkira;* and al-Suyuti, *Sharh al-sudur.* Some fiqh handbooks add rules concerning the waiting period widows should observe before remarriage and inheritance. For Shi`i funeral rites, see Peermahomed Ebrahim Trust, *Death and Death Ceremonies,* 95–140.

43. *Ghusl* is also required of the living after sexual activity, menstruation, or childbirth so that they can perform prayer, enter a mosque, or hold the Qur'an.

44. See al-Jaziri, *Kitab al-fiqh,* 1:455, 486, 490.

45. Ibid., 486. The pronoun *we* in this verse stands for God, not the human speaker. The verse refers to the creation of the first human being out of earth and the promise of resurrection.

46. See, for example, the supplications provided by the thirteenth-century Sunni jurist Muhyi al-Din al-Nawawi in *Al-Adhkar al-muntakhab min kalam sayyid al-abrar* (Beirut: Dar al-Kitab al-`Arabi, 1984), 122–153. Prayers are also published in contemporary death manuals, such as Peermahomed Ebrahim Trust, *Death and Death Ceremonies,* a Shi`i work published in Pakistan.

47. Al-Jaziri, *Kitab al-fiqh,* 1:455; cf. the Shi`i *talqin* in Peermahumed Ebrahim Trust, *Death and Death Ceremonies,* 137–140, where belief in the twelve imams is of great importance. There are other variants for the *talqin* as well; see, e.g., al-Qurtubi, *Tadhkira,* 34–37; and al-Suyuti, *Sharh al-sudur,* 144–145.

48. Muhammad `Abd al-Hayy `Arifi, *Ahkam-i mayyit;* English translation: *Death and Inheritance: The Islamic Way: A Handbook of Rules Pertaining to the Deceased,* trans, Muhammad Shameem (New Delhi: Kitab Bhavan, 1995), 220.

49. For a more detailed list, see the "innovations" condemned in `Arifi, *Death and Inheritance,* chap. 8.

50. See the fiqh manual by the fourteenth-century Maliki jurist in Cairo, Ibn al-Hajj, *Madkhal al-shar' al-sharif,* 4 vols. (Beirut: Dar al-Hadith, 1981), 3:249.

51. Lane, *Manners and Customs of the Modern Egyptians,* chap. 28; cf. al-Jaziri, *Kitab al-fiqh,* 1:486.

52. For example, see Khaled Moaz and Solange Ory, *Inscriptions arabes de Damas: Les Stèles funéraires,* 1. *Cimetière d'al-Bab al-Saghir* (Damascus: Institut français de Damas, 1977); and Nuha Khoury, "The *Mihrab* Image: Commemorative Themes in Medieval Islamic Architecture," *Muqarnas* 9 (1992): 11–28.

53. Jafar Sharif, *Islam in India or the* Qanun-i-Islam*: Customs of the Musalmans of India* (Delhi: Low Price Publications, 1997 [1832]), 94; Massé, *Persian Beliefs and Customs,* 83.

54. Barbara D. Metcalf, *Perfecting Women: Maulana Ashraf `Ali Thanawi's* Bihishti Zewar (Berkeley: University of California Press, 1992), 145–150.

55. See Sharif, *Islam in India,* chap. 9; Metcalf, *Perfecting Women,* 151–155; Lane, *Manners and Customs of the Modern Egyptians,* chap. 28; Massé, *Persian Beliefs and Customs,* chap. 3; Hifni, *Al-Marathi al-sha`biyya,* 11–14.

56. See Huda Lutfi, "Manners and Customs of Fourteenth-Century Cairene Women: Female Anarchy versus Male Shar`i Order in Muslim Prescriptive Treatises," in *Women in Middle Eastern History: Shifting Boundaries in Sex and Gender,* ed. Nikki R. Keddie and Beth Baron (New Haven: Yale University Press, 1991), chap. 6. For northern India, see Metcalf, *Perfecting Women,* 145–155.

57. See the relevant chapters and bibliographies in Richard Ettinghausen and Oleg Grabar, *The Art and Architecture of Islam 650–1250* (New York: Viking Penguin, 1987); and Sheila S. Blair and Jonathan M. Bloom, *The Art and Architecture of Islam 1250–1800* (New Haven: Yale University Press, 1994).

58. *Encyclopaedia of Islam,* s.v. *Makbara* by S. Ory et al.

59. See Wayne E. Begley, "The Myth of the Taj Mahal and a New Theory of Its Symbolic Meaning," *Art Bulletin* 56 (1979): 7–37; Pratapaditya Pal, Janice Leoshko et al., *Romance of the Taj Mahal* (Los Angeles: Thames and Hudson, 1989).

60. Campo, *Other Sides of Paradise,* 176; see also *Encyclopaedia of Islam,* s.v. *Shafa`a* by A.J. Wensinck and D. Gimaret; and ibid., s.v. *Ziyara* by W. Ende, J.W. Meri, Houari Touati, Abdulaziz Sachedina et al.

61. See Nakash, *The Shi`is of Iraq,* chaps. 6–7; and Massé, *Persian Beliefs and Customs,* 89. For details on rules and procedures for transporting the dead from Pakistan for reburial in Shi`i holy places in Iraq and Iran, see Peermahomed Ebrahim Trust, *Death and Death Ceremonies,* appendix A.

62. See Madawi Rashid, *A History of Saudi Arabia* (New York: Cambridge University Press, 2002), chap. 1.

63. *Houston Chronicle,* "Iraqis Uncover Mass Graves of Civilians," May 4, 2003 (Associated Press), www.chron.com/cs/CDA/printstory.mpl/special/iraq/1895862.

64. *New York Times,* "Cleansing Iraqi Bomb Victims Takes Its Own Toll," March 4, 2004, www.nytimes.com/2004/03/04/international/middleeast/04WASH.html. The lyrics of the lamentations are not quoted in the article, but as a mother assists in washing the body of her daughter, who was killed in the bombing of a Shi`i shrine, she is reported to have said, "I was waiting for you to wash me, and look what happened. Who will wash me now?" For Egyptian lamentations, see, however, Galal, "Rites funéraires," and Hifni, *Al-Marathi al-sha`biyya.*

65. `Arifi, *Death and Inheritance,* 117–118.

66. Ibid., 118–32.

67. Information about al-Hakim's funeral was obtained from an Associated Press report, dated September 2, 2003; *New York Times,* September 1, 2003; and *Washington Post,* September 3, 2003.

68. United States Department of Defense, "Memorial Service for Ayatollah Muhammed Baqir al-Hakim," www.defenselink.mil/speeches/2003/sp20030927-depsecdef0484.html, March 1, 2004.

69. See John R. Bowen, "Death and the History of Islam in Highland Aceh," *Indonesia* 38 (1984): 21–38; Monique Renaerts, *La Mort, rites et valeurs dans l'Islam Maghrébin* (Brussels: ULB, Institut de sociologie, Centre de sociologie de l'Islam, 1986); Unni Wikan, "Bereavement and Loss in Two Muslim Communities: Egypt and Bali Compared," *Social Science and Medicine* 27 (1988): 451–460; and Abu Lughod, "Islam and the Gendered Discourses of Death."

70. For an excellent example of this method of reading fiqh texts, see Lutfi, "Manners and Customs of Fourteenth-Century Cairene Women," chap. 6. For northern India, see Metcalf, *Perfecting Women,* 145–55.

71. Cited in Jalal al-Din al-Suyuti, *Al-Itqan fi `ulum al-Qur'an,* 2 vols. in 1 (Beirut: Dar al-Ma`rifa, n.d.), 2:192–198.

72. The instructions are widely available on the Web in translations of varying quality; see *Guardian Unlimited,* "Last Words of a Terrorist," September 30, 2001, http://observer.guardian.co.uk/international/story/0,6903,560773,00.html.

73. Note that Abu Hayyan plays upon both meanings of the term in his elegy for Nudar: "She left her life a martyr. . . . She bore witness thrice and died."

74. See G.W. Bowersock, Peter Brown, and Oleg Grabar, eds., *Late Antiquity: A Guide to the Postclassical World* (Cambridge: Belknap Press of the Harvard University Press, 1999), 567–568; James A. Bill and John Alden Williams, *Roman Catholics and Shi`i Muslims: Prayer, Passion and Politics* (Chapel Hill: University of North Carolina Press, 2002), chap. 4.

75. Al-Jaziri, *Kitab al-fiqh,* 1:479–481. See also `Arifi, *Death and Inheritance,* 114–116; and *Encyclopaedia of Islam,* s.v. *Shahid* by E. Kohlberg.

76. *Encylopedia of Islam and the Muslim World* (New York: Macmillan Reference, 2003), s.v. *Martyrdom* by Daniel W. Brown.

77. Members of this group are called "martyrs of love" (*shuhada' al-hubb*); see *Encyclopaedia of Islam,* s.v. *Shahid* by E. Kohlberg; and `Arifi, *Death and Inheritance,* 116. For listings of martyrs according to the hadith, see al-Qurtubi, *Tadhkira,* 180–182.

78. Contrary to assertions made in some quarters in the West, the Qur'an makes no mention of the reward of seventy-two virgins for martyrs. It is mentioned in later noncanonical hadith collections, which do not carry as much authority as hadith in the canonical collections. Moreover, the significance of this hadith is further diluted by hadith that claim that *all* righteous males will have seventy-two spouses in heaven. Righteous women are also promised spouses in paradise. See al-Qurtubi, *Tadhkira,* 260–264; and Smith and Haddad, *Islamic Understanding of Death and Resurrection,* 158–168.

79. *Al-Ahram,* Cairo, November 25, 1983. This elegy was published in the announcement for the observance of a fortieth-day postmortem anniversary, the *arba`in.*

80. For a comparative study of Muslim and Coptic obituaries published in Egypt during the 1980s, see K. Wagtendonk, "Mercy to the Deceased, Patience and Consolation to the Family: Death Announcements in *Al-Ahram,*" in *Funerary Symbols and Religion,* ed. Jacques H. Kamstra, Hendrikus Milde, and K. Wagtendonk (Kampen, Netherlands: J.H. Kok, 1988), 138–153.

81. An important book that points to some new areas of research in this regard is Jonathan E. Brockopp, ed., *Islamic Ethics of Life: Abortion, War, and Euthanasia* (Columbia: University of South Carolina Press, 2003).

CHAPTER 8

Sikhism and Death

KRISTINA MYRVOLD

It is a Sunday afternoon in May 2003, in the suburbs of the Swedish town of Gothenburg. About forty Sikh women and men have gathered on the second floor of a former plastics factory, recently rebuilt into a Sikh temple. All sit on the floor facing the Sikh scripture, Guru Granth, royally installed on a throne under a canopy at the end of the hall. Incense scents the air. A framed color photo of a man and a woman rests on the floor in front of the scripture. The woman in the picture died three weeks ago and her body was cremated in India. She was the respected mother of a Sikh immigrant now living in Sweden. The community members have been summoned to perform a last prayer for the peace of her soul. After an hour of reciting compositions from the scripture and expounding the texts, all rise to stand with folded hands, facing the scripture, pleading that her soul will get a place in the court of God.

When the ceremony comes to an end, the scripture is reverentially wrapped in cotton cloths on the throne. In a small procession it is carried on the head of a participant to a bedroom with a four-poster bed and placed under a satin blanket for rest. Everyone goes to the first floor, where the mourning family provides a communal meal in memory of the departed soul. Though some members did not personally know the deceased, her death and the ceremony can be a lesson for all the living. Surjit Singh, the chairman of the temple, explains:

> Today we learned that we all will die one day, but we should live in the present and do good actions. The soul will travel back to God where it comes from. It is a difficult way, to be accepted by God, but when we reach there it is pure bliss. It is a fulfillment of the self and no more wandering in births. Therefore we can learn from the lesson today, learn from real life and perform good actions.

This chapter will treat dying and death in the Sikh tradition and describe how Sikhs in contemporary communities respond to death. After a short introduction to the Sikh religion, the chapter describes the ideological foundation for beliefs and practices surrounding death and traces the formalization of funeral rites in Sikh history. The textual sources from the early period of the Sikh tradition up to the present are mainly normative and the material is too voluminous to analyze in detail here, but I will focus on some general trends and highlight a few significant sources in the process. The chapter then offers a descriptive account of how contemporary Sikhs living in two quite different settings—Varanasi (Bernares) in northern India and Sweden—have come to conceptualize death and practice funeral ceremonies in relation to local customs and regulations. Whereas Varanasi (or Benares) is a stronghold of Hindu culture, Sweden is a more secularized Western society with Christian undertones. Since most Sikhs reside in the state of Punjab in the northwestern part of India, it may seem more natural to have studied Sikh death practices in the Punjab region. My reasons for choosing Varanasi and Sweden are that I have conducted fieldwork in these areas and, in relation to Punjab, they may represent an Indian and a Western diaspora where the communities encounter divergent challenges in the interplay of tradition and modernization.[1] Within the broader Sikh community, the impact of migration during the twentieth century has accentuated issues related to change and modification of the religious tradition in a modern world. As this chapter will show, essential elements of Sikh death ceremonies have a history and linger as a conservative force in the face of contemporary social changes, just as modernization and the diasporic situation force and lead to modification of other elements. In a diaspora, this dual process of keeping and modifying a tradition in relation to a majority society opens up a space of cultural interchange where the tradition may even adopt foreign practices, but create and endue them with new meanings. Given geographic limitations, in the following I will use the Varanasi community as a model of Sikh death ceremonies in one diasporic context and continue by expounding some central features of the challenges faced by Sikhs in the Swedish society.

THE SIKH RELIGION

Sikhism is one of the youngest world religions today, tracing its roots back to Nanak (1469–1539) in the late fifteenth century. Nanak was born to a Hindu family in northwestern India. In his late twenties Nanak had a religious experience, which led him to set aside his domestic life and travel extensively for the next two decades. In the 1520s he settled in Punjab, where he established a community and obtained the title of guru. His followers became known as the Sikhs, meaning "disciples."

Nanak's teaching was centered on the concept of one God who created and rules the whole universe by his divine order (*hukam*). By developing a relationship with God based on love and fear, humans can surmount self-centeredness (*haumai*) and attachments to the world (*maya*). Gradually this process will lead to liberation (*mukti*), the release from the cycle of reincarnation and union with God. For Nanak, humans should not pursue liberation by renunciation from the social world, but by cultivating divine qualities while living a domestic life and actively working for the betterment of society. Equality, hard work, sharing, and service to humanity are key ethical tenets interwoven in his doctrine.

Nanak composed devotional hymns in the script *gurmukhi,* which later came to form the nucleus of the Sikh scripture, and at the time of his death he established a succession of human gurus by appointing his follower Angad. The two centuries following Nanak's mission form a significant period in Sikh history as the community evolved in response to political and social circumstances. With the growth of the Sikh community, its relation with the ruling Mughal administration became marked with tension in the seventeenth century, culminating in the execution of the fifth guru Arjun (1563–1606) in Lahore and the ninth guru Tegh Bahadur (1621–1675) in Delhi. These twin martyrdoms of the gurus had a profound effect on the community by legitimating mortal sacrifice as a way of protecting justice and fending off oppression. After Arjun's martyrdom, his successor guru Hargobind (1595–1644) militarized the community and adopted two swords symbolizing both the temporal (*mir*) and the spiritual (*pir*) authority of the guru. A central event in Sikh history occurred in 1699 when the tenth guru Gobind Singh (1666–1708) declared the Sikhs as *khalsa,* "the pure" military community committed to defending justice. Sikhs were now required to undergo the ceremony of "nectar of the double-edged sword" (*khande di pahul*), in which they recited hymns of the gurus into water while stirring with a double-edged sword. The first five Sikhs who took the nectar were called "the five beloved" (*panj pyare*) and changed their original names to Singh—"lion." The initiated, both men and women, follow a code of conduct: they abstain from tobacco, refrain from cutting their hair (*kesh*), use a comb (*kangha*), and keep a uniform with a dagger (*kirpan*), steel bracelet (*kara*), and a pair of breeches (*kachha*).

By the declaration of khalsa, Gobind Singh initiated the process of dissolving his office of personal guru, shifting the authority to the Sikh community and the scripture.[2] In 1604 guru Arjun compiled the compositions of the first five Sikh gurus, Hindu and Muslim sages, and during the 1680s guru Tegh Bahadur hymns were added to what became Adi Granth, literally "the original book." By the time of Gobind Singh, the scripture had gained considerable status in the community and at his deathbed he declared it the eternal Guru. Thus, in Sikh theology, the revealed divine Word is the *Guru.* It was through the agency of ten holy persons, reverentially called gurus, that the Word of God became accessible to humans. Because the Sikh scripture inherited this authority and mediates the divine Word, it is called Guru Granth, the "*Guru* book."

Today there are about 23 millions Sikhs in the world. While most live in India, some can be found on almost every continent. During the British rule of Punjab (1849–1947), the "homeland" of the Sikhs, they were recognized for their martial skill and recruited into the imperial army, which also initiated resettlements to parts of the British empire. Today migration is a part of the Sikh heritage, and whether Sikhs live in Asia, North America, Europe, or Africa, Guru Granth is the focal point of their religious life. They read, recite, sing, and base their beliefs and values on the scripture. Almost every ceremony includes text recitations and is performed in the presence of Guru Granth. A Sikh temple, *gurudwara* or the "guru's door," is by definition the place where Guru Granth resides. By dignified acts cloaked in royal symbolism, Sikhs have created a diurnal rhythm for the scripture; in the early morning they install the scripture on a throne and in the night put it to rest in a special bedroom. Many Sikhs visit the gurudwara daily as if they are seeking audience with an eternal guru. Guru Granth also remains the primary source for the gurus' views on death during the early period of the Sikh tradition.

DEATH IN NANAK'S THEOLOGY

In Nanak's language death is often referred to as time (*kal*), as opposed to the eternal (*akal*), which connotes both an attribute of God and the state beyond both time and mortality. Utilizing themes from Hindu mythology, Nanak recurrently personifies death metaphorically as Yama, the lord or Messenger of Death, with his domain in the south or *Yumpur,* the city of death. Holding a club (*danda*), Yama seizes people by their hair, nooses them, beats them terribly, and at the time of death smashes their head with his club.[3]

For Nanak, however, death is a creation of God, as are all things in the universe. Before the beginning of time, only the command or order (hukam) of God existed: "there was no hell or heaven, nor birth or death, nor coming and going in reincarnation."[4] In Sikh cosmogony, everything springs forth from the hukam, and, following this order, mortality is imbedded in the creation of all living things. Human beings are bound to the cycle of reincarnation, but they are given the opportunity to achieve mukti—liberation. In Nanak's teaching, liberation does not lie beyond death but may be achieved while retaining a bodily and worldly existence. A person who has attained a liberated state is often referred to as gurmukh, a person who is oriented toward the Guru, in contrast to the manmukh, the self-willed person who is deluded by worldly attachments.[5] To become a gurmukh, a person has to conquer the fear of death while one is alive. For Nanak, the revealed and divine Word is the Guru that burns self-centeredness, which keeps humans alienated from God and attached to the material world. It is only through the Guru that humans may break free from transmigration by singing, meditating, and reflecting on the divine.[6] The state of a gurmukh is not achieved through seclusion from society, but, quite the contrary, by cultivating divine qualities and attuning to the divine order while living an active social life for others. To surmount death in life is thus to sublimate the self to the divine and stay detached from the world but actively work in it. As Nanak says, the one who dies in the divine Word is blessed and lives in peace.[7] Death serves the gurmukh whereas those without the Guru are haunted by the Messenger of Death and doomed to reincarnation.[8]

The significance of martyrdom in the Sikh tradition must be understood in light of Nanak's theology of liberation.[9] A martyr is a gurmukh who fearlessly sacrifices his or her life to uphold divine ideals in the world, and as Louis E. Fenech writes, "Where in other religious traditions martyrdom is an act which redeems . . . in Sikhism only the redeemed are capable of martyrdom."[10] Martyrdom is the greatest selfless service (*seva*) of the liberated.

For a gurmukh, physical death means the release from the cycle of reincarnation, the final separation from the world and union with the divine, so it is not an occasion for grief. In Guru Granth there are five elegies by Nanak and in one of them, "Song of Mourning,"[11] he explains that although all relatives of a deceased person cry out in mourning, death should be seen as a natural thing. Everyone has to pass through it, and weeping for worldly things is in vain as it makes people forget God.

The gurus often use the words *svarg* or *baikunth* (heaven) and *narg* (hell) in their religious discourse. Within their cosmological framework these are not states or regions beyond this world but rather refer to conditions in the mundane world. Humans are subject to heaven and hell as they are reincarnated.[12] In a verse of Nanak's composition *Japji,* recited every morning by most Sikhs, Nanak asks: what is that place like through which God takes care of everything? Nanak depicts the divine threshold where everyone and everything is singing the praises of God. Because the ideal of gurmukh requires working in the present to transform this world to an epitome of divine qualities, concern for what happens after death remains a peripheral motive in the gurus' teaching.

FROM METAPHORS TO RITUAL ACTS

Nanak originated from a Hindu family. It is therefore not surprising that he often employs Hindu rites as metaphors in his religious language. These linguistic images refer to God or serve as analogies to express key devotional elements of his teaching. A composition in which Nanak treats a Hindu funeral ceremony exemplifies this usage:

> The one Name is my lamp. I have put the oil of suffering into it. Its flame has dried up this oil and I have escaped my meeting with the Messenger of Death. O people, do not make fun of me. Thousands of wooden logs, piled up together, need only a tiny flame to burn. The Lord is my festive dish of rice balls and leafy plates, the True Name of the Creator is my funeral ceremony. Here and hereafter in the past and in the future, this is my support. The Lord's praise is my river Ganges and my city of Benares, my soul takes its sacred cleansing bath there. That becomes my true cleansing bath if night and day I enshrine love for you. The rice balls are offered to the gods and the dead ancestors but it is the Brahmins who eat them. Oh Nanak, the rice balls of the Lord are a gift, which is never exhausted.[13]

The offering of rice balls, leaf plates, and the feeding of Brāhmins mentioned in this hymn are essential parts of Hindu death practices, performed after cremation to assist the soul's travel to the abode of the ancestors. The lamp is lit to show the way for the soul's journey. In Nanak's paraphrase these elements are transformed to metaphors that move the reader to a new semantic context—devotion and the state of a gurmukh. His composition also embeds a strong criticism of the original context of these metaphors. The Hindu practice of ancestor worship hardly receives his approval.[14] This does not necessarily mean that Nanak rejects all ritual practices as such, but rather he criticizes the reliance on ritualism as a way to liberation and tries to make people aware of their personal way of life on a much broader basis. Often he emphasizes the danger of rituals performed without true understanding of life and with pride, fear, and selfishness, which lead humans away from God. Rituals are not the sole means of liberation and without an understanding of the divine they become worthless.[15] On the other hand, he acknowledges that rituals can be effective tools to cultivate a religious life and a close relationship with God. In the early Sikh community at Kartarpur (Punjab), founded by Nanak, it seems clear that ritual acts such as daily reciting of the guru's compositions were an integral part of the Sikh religious life.[16] As the Sikh tradition evolved, rituals acts such as singing and reading texts became interlinked with the occasion of death.

The tradition of reading one hymn at the time of death seems to have been established at an early stage. Bhai Gurdas (1551–1636), the Sikh scribe, explains that gurmukhs do not weep on the occasion of death, but recite *Sohila* in the company of holy persons.[17] *Sohila* or *Kirtan Sohila,*[18] "the song of praise," was later prescribed as the Sikh bedtime hymn, but since death, elimination of fear, and liberation are central themes in the text, it also became associated with death as the end of life.

The first guru was aware of funeral practices in different religious communities of his time. Nanak mentions five different ways of taking care of dead bodies: cremation, burial, leaving the body to be eaten by dogs, and throwing the body into water or a well.[19] Similarly guru Arjun notes three ways a body can be consumed—thrown in water, given to dogs, or cremated to ashes.[20] From their compositions it may be inferred that cremation was pursued as the most appropriate way of taking care of dead bodies. Nanak explains that Agni, the god of fire, burns the trap of death and that the body, made of blood and semen and under the power of the breath, shall be consigned to fire in the end.[21]

A more illuminating passage in Guru Granth on how Sikhs should act at the time of death is "The Call of Death,"[22] a work ascribed to Baba Sundar, the great-grandson of the third guru Amardas (1479–1574). When God is calling him to merge with the divine, Amardas summons his followers and family to appoint Ramdas as his successor. After ordering that no one should weep after his departure, he tells them to call in sages to talk about God (*hari katha*), read the story of God, and hear the name of God, but not to bother performing Hindu rites such as lighting lamps or offering rice balls and leaves. In Sikh historiography, Amardas often represents the guru who designed Sikh ceremonies for birth, marriage, and death. Baba Sundar's work remains the most explicit reference in Guru Granth of a guru instructing his followers about the procedures to be followed after his death and today the text is often recited in funeral ceremonies.

According to Baba Sundar, Amardas instructs his followers to bring his bones to *harisar*—the "pool of God." With the later gurus, the custom of immersing the "flowers," the remaining bones of a cremated body, became associated with the village Kiratpur, by the river Sutlej in Punjab. Guru Hargobind (1595–1644) built this village on the plains bordering the Shivalik hills, and at the time of his death his body was cremated and the bones consigned to the Sutlej. It is likely that the remains of the next two gurus, Har Rai and Har Krishan, were similarly immersed at Kiratpur. Today people bring the bones of deceased family members to Kiratpur, where a gurudwara was constructed in the 1970s.

WRITING FUNERAL RITES

The declaration of khalsa by Gobind Singh in 1699 was a defining moment in the Sikh tradition: authority was transferred from this guru to the Sikh community. Members were required to go through a ceremony, be armed, and follow a more explicit code of conduct. Gurinder Singh Mann observes that this new situation, when the authority no longer resided with one person who could answer queries from the community, created a need for written manuals that delineated the Sikh code of conduct.[23]

Written manuals of the Sikh code of conduct, the *rahitnamas,* are a tradition traceable to the eighteenth century. These texts are valuable sources for our understanding of the formalization of death practices in the Sikh tradition. The process of compiling these manuals is an example of what Catherine Bell calls "textualization of ritual," in which existing practices are selected and fixed in written ritual manuals.[24] The process of textualization encourages the rise of more standardized rituals, in which "orthodox" rituals are differentiated from local practices and codified. The manual gives certain practices authority and is foundational for "ritual institution."[25] The rahitnamas were written by different authors who deal with numerous aspects of Sikh life so they are not ritual manuals exclusively, though rites and liturgy take up a great deal of space. Their existence reflects an endeavor to define Sikh beliefs and practices in normative writing, and in this effort Guru Granth is given a prominent position. The rahitnamas literature crystallizes the practice of using Guru Granth in different ritual contexts, including at the time of death. It would not be too far-reaching to state that the process of textualizing rituals (rahitnamas) had the effect of formalizing the ritual use of the Guru Granth in Sikh funerals.

A more comprehensive manual from the beginning of the eighteenth century that should be mentioned is *Chaupa Singh Rahit-Nama,*[26] attributed to a Brahmin Sikh with the same name. According to this text, Sikhs should not, in contrast to Hindu death practices, lament in public or shave the hair of the deceased. From Chaupa Singh we learn that Guru Granth should be recited prominently in the center of all Sikh rituals. He offers a detailed description of how to prepare, read, and take care of the volumes in daily life and prescribes complete readings of the scripture. According to Chupa Singh, devotional singing (*kirtan*) should be performed when a Sikh relative has passed away. After the corpse has been washed, sacred food (*prashad*) should be distributed to as many people as the family can afford to feed. The manual does not mention cremation, but it instructs the readers to perform obsequies according to their own wishes and deposit the bones in the "pool of God" (harisar)—in other words, in the Ganga or any other river. By the eighteenth century there is a clear description of the basic elements of a Sikh funeral rite: Sikhs should perform devotional singing, wash the body, offer the sacred food, and immerse the bones in a river.

This rahitnama also provides interesting instructions for the handling of Sikh postcremation ceremonies: devotional singing as well as expounding of the scripture (*katha*) should continue for as many days as the family can afford. Within eleven, thirteen, fifteen, or seventeen days the auspicious conclusion (*bhog*) of a complete reading of Guru Granth should be arranged, Sikhs should be fed, and the Sikh prayer (Ardas) should be recited. Here is probably one of the earliest sources available to scholars stipulating a complete reading of Guru Granth after a cremation. Still, the manual leaves other ceremonies open to individual choice by telling the reader to perform offerings and rites according to existing customs. On the anniversary of a death, Sikhs should perform an ancestor ceremony and, as the manual notes, offerings should be given to Sikhs and food served at the place of religious congregations or to poor Sikhs.

THE PRESENT NORMATIVE RITUAL

During the colonial period in the late nineteenth century, a movement called Singh Sabha emerged in the Punjab. In view of uprising reform movements in the Indian colonial context, scholars have often labeled the Singh Sabha as the Sikh reform movement, while others do not attribute it with a reformative force but see it as a confirmative effort to refine the Sikh doctrine and religious materials that were already at hand. Regardless of these different scholarly approaches, the Singh Sabha had a considerable influence by standardizing and codifying Sikh standards and rituals for a community that, due to new means of communication and migration, was no longer restricted to the Punjab region. The *Sikh Rahit Maryada,* completed in 1950, is the present *rahit,* or the code of conduct that Sikhs should observe. Preceded by several endeavours to define Sikh rituals, as discussed above, it can be seen as a prolonged result of the efforts by the Singh Sabha movement. It is a manual that deals with the personal and communal aspects of Sikh religious life. Besides prescribing practices and explaining how to perform rituals, the manual also lists a set of forbidden customs.[27] The outline of the Sikh funeral it advocates should be briefly sketched, since the manual today exerts a global influence on Sikh ceremonies:

After death
- Read Guru Granth and repeat the name of God (*vahiguru*)
- Bathe and dress the body in clean garments with the five Sikh symbols and place it on a bier
- Perform the Sikh prayer Ardas before the hearse is taken to the cremation ground

Cremation
- Perform the Sikh prayer Ardas before the son, relative, or friend offers the fire
- The congregation should sing and listen to devotional music
- Perform the hymn "Kirtan Sohila"
- Perform the Sikh prayer Ardas

After cremation
- Read Guru Granth
- Arrange devotional singing every night after the cremation
- End the funeral rituals after the tenth day

The manual presents the basic ritual structure of a Sikh funeral. As it prescribes, a Sikh funeral should be centered on the performing of the Ardas and singing and reading of texts from the scripture; "Kirtan Sohila" has been stipulated as a funeral hymn. Today this normative ritual structure can be found in funerals performed by Sikhs in the Punjab and beyond.

As we turn now to examine the death practices of contemporary Sikh communities in Varanasi and Sweden, we shall see that the *Sikh Rahit Maryada* manual has succeeded in standardizing the centrality of textual recitations at funerals. In the following description the general attitudes, beliefs, and the broad structure of practices are valid for the mainstream community and the Punjab region, while the local context and the urban setting color other features. In Varanasi, for example, the presence of Hindu funeral priests and the ritual uses of mantra and Ganga water can be seen as contextual influences, just as the presence of funeral directors and the use of coffins have forced ritual modifications in Sweden. Sikhs in these settings have from their interpretative framework created new meanings and explanations for these contextual adaptations and alterations.

SIKH DEATH IN VARANASI

According to *Kashi khanda,* a section of the Hindu *Skanda purana,* the whole universe was created in Varanasi, the city of the god Shiva, and it is popularly believed that everyone who dies in the city will gain liberation. The significance and the various social and religious aspects of death and dying in Varanasi, according to its dominating Hindu paradigm, have been thoroughly documented by scholars.[28] Today Varanasi presents a multifarious brocade of cultures and religions blended in the townscape, and Sikhs have attached their own meaning to the place as well. The community traces the history back to the beginning of the sixteenth century when guru Nanak visited the city and supposedly debated with the learned Hindu Brahmins. Later, in the seventeenth century, guru Tegh Bahadur resided there for more than seven months. The gurus' visits sanctified the city and today two major gurudwaras (Nichibagh Gurudwara and Gurubagh Gurudwara) under the control of an independent local committee mark the places where the gurus stayed. Most Sikh families in the city, the majority in business and Khatri by caste, originated from west Punjab and settled in Varanasi after the partition in 1947.

In Varanasi, death is always present at two major cremation grounds on the riverbank of the Ganga—Harishchandra ghat and Manikarnika ghat. Most Sikhs cremate at the latter, which holds a special platform called Punjabi or Khatri chabutra, reserved only for dead bodies of Punjabi or Sindhi origin or of the Khatri caste. Sikhs often tell how the place of Khatri chabutra was purchased in the nineteenth century by the Maharaja of Punjab, Ranjit Singh. On a visit to Varanasi he found that Hindu funeral priests refused Sikhs cremations at Manikarnika, and he purchased a place for them by laying out a grid of gold coins, later replaced by a platform.[29] The story illustrates the challenge Sikhs face in being represented within a ritual space many find subject to Hindu domination.

The two gurudwaras in Varanasi offer the service of arranging cremations for Punjabi and Sindhi families at Manikarnika ghat. In practice this implies access to the platform, fixed prices for wood, and the religious service of the Sikh granthi, the professional reader and custodian of Guru Granth in the gurudwara. One important result of the Sikh reform movement in the twentieth century was the increasingly significant ritual role for the granthi office, which took over duties traditionally incumbent on Hindu priests.[30] Today most death rituals are performed in private homes and gurudwaras, and the cremation ground is the only space where Sikhs interact and depend on Hindu priests for ritual procedures. For at least three decades the granthi has been an integral part of Sikh cremations in Varanasi, and the community members consider his presence at the ghat momentous. Within the ritual structure of a regular Hindu cremation, he performs a reading of the Sikh prayer Ardas beside the Hindu funeral priests who direct mourners and recite their verses in Sanskrit. To keep this arrangement and avoid territorial disputes at the cremation ground, the gurudwaras have reached agreements with some of the local Hindu funeral priests who are especially summoned for Sikh cremations.

Written Fate and Reading Karma

Because Sikhism, like all religions, is continuously adapting to changing social conditions, the local beliefs and conceptions of death are multiple and varied within this community. Transmitted through a range of media, normative standards are often blended with cultural and popular beliefs, colored by individual experiences and motives. Surmounting life and death through a final liberation seems to be an idea more palpable in normative teachings of traditions than in lived religion. The Sikhs in Varanasi are well aware of the popular belief that dying there leads to immediate liberation, but they do not pay much attention to it. It is a Hindu and not a Sikh belief. Many Sikhs believe that mukti, liberation from the cycle of reincarnation, is a remote possibility granted only to a few in the present dark and degenerating age (*kali yug*) when upholding moral and religious action is getting more challenging. Many define liberation instead as a human birth in which a close relation with the guru is achievable, while others do not even conceptualize mukti at all. To live without desires, including the desire for a favorable reincarnation, is also considered a sign of humbleness in compliance with the divine order and will.

Sikhs believe that two interwoven forces condition life and death: the laws of karma and human fate predestined by God. The soul (*atma*) travels through millions of births before it is born as a human and given free will to improve the future by good action. The purpose is not so much to "burn" karma and thereby end the cycle of reincarnation but to accumulate good karma for a fair reincarnation. Devotion to God is the primary means of accumulating good karma. A thirty-eight-year old woman in Varanasi explained it in the following way:

> It is in the human birth you can recite the name of God and not in other births. The person who performs good actions—recites the name of God, like *Sukhmani Sahib,* and goes to *gurudwara*—will get rid of sins and improve possibilities for the future. The person who does not do this will go back through 8.4 millions births.

Equally significant and intertwined is the notion that human fate follows a divine order. Several hymns in Guru Granth recurrently refer to the fate written on the forehead of humans when they enter the world.[31] In Varanasi many speak of this fate in terms of a divine "writing" (*likhna*) in the court or at the place of God. Everything in a human life is noted in this divine writing, and only God determines this fate. Whereas humans should engage the divine words manifested in Guru Granth through their recitations, God is writing their fate in the divine abode. For example, the word *bhog,* which means a pleasurable ending, is used to designate both death and the reading of the conclusion of Guru Granth.[32] The symbolic relationship between the Guru, the divine words in the text, and the human life often convenes in local usage and beliefs. Human life becomes a text ordained and written by God.

Sikhs depart from the Hindu belief that the soul travels to divisions of hells or heavens before it is sent back to a new reincarnation. Sikhs believe that heaven and hell are both in this world, where everyone reaps the fruits of karma. In this view, what will happen *between* death and reincarnation is often more significant than what will happen *after* death. Sikhs believe that when the soul leaves the body it travels to the court of God, where the divine accountants implement a balancing of books. Chitra Gupt, the minister or scribe of Yama, keeps the records and will weigh the good and bad karma. It is important to note that figures from Hindu mythology, such as the god Yama, are often reflected in popular Sikh beliefs about the interlude between death and reincarnation. A sixty-year-old man explains the accounting before God as follows:

> When a person reaches the court of God his accounts will be checked. What he has done, how many times he has recited the name of God, will be seen, no other things. According to that he will get another body, another birth.

When Chitra Gupt has completed his work, God pronounces a judgment, which relegates the soul to a new reincarnation.

Religious and Secular Medicine

The Indian culture presents a rich heritage of medical and healing practices, integrated in the religious traditions and traceable to Vedic times. Today the use of Western-style medicine, commonly labeled "English medicine," has overshadowed the classical art of ayurvedic medicine, even though it is still employed as an alternative treatment. Sikhs have a very receptive attitude toward the use of modern medicine. They encourage medical care by establishing hospitals and care centers and are prominent among medical practitioners. This respect for the healing arts is embedded in Sikh doctrine and tradition. There are several accounts of the human gurus helping their contemporaries with medicine, and the beloved legend about the humble Bhai Kanhaiya offering water and medicine to both Sikh soldiers and their enemies in battle continues to inspire and serve as a model for many Sikhs.

The Sikh community in Varanasi runs Guru Nanak Hospital within the precinct of the gurudwara, where free ambulance service and medical treatment are available day and night. This social service is an integral part of the Sikh concept of *seva,* selfless service. Giving medicine and helping the dying is not just a social activity but a religious action, which is institutionalized through the gurudwaras. At festivals commemorating the Sikh martyrs many communities set up temporary blood donor camps, where visitors donate blood, just as the martyrs sacrificed theirs in the greatest service. Most families also approve of surgery and autopsy, with the exception of operations requiring hair removal. When facing surgery, Sikhs who have undergone the khalsa initiation (khande di pahul) are often firmly resolved to keep their hair despite the consequences.

The use of modern medicine has not replaced religious action within the Sikh community as it has in many parts of the Western world. Instead, secular and religious remedies are intertwined and complement each other. In one case, for instance, when a child was born in poor health, the family let the doctors treat the child in a hospital, while a relative went to the gurudwara and arranged an *Ardas* for the child's protection. When the father of the household underwent a surgical operation in the hospital, the same family arranged a complete reading of Guru Granth in the gurudwara, as well as recitation of 65,000 mantras in a Shiva temple for seven days. For Sikhs, oral accounts of how people have been cured of fatal diseases by recitations, prayers, regular temple visits, and other religious practices, are evidence of the curative power of having a close relationship with the Guru, especially in cases where surgical or medical treatments have either failed or have been refused. These incidents are looked upon not as miracles but as proof of the divine power exerted on humans through the gurudwara and the religious texts. Paradoxically, most Sikhs believe that life and death are in the hands of God and not even the most devoted human efforts can postpone the time of death decided by God and one's own karma. Performing religious rituals in life-threatening situations serves more to relieve suffering and elicit divine protection and kindness than to change the fate that has been ordained.

Sikhs have developed numerous methods of reciting texts during times of illness and have attached different meanings to the recitations, depending on the content and the sentiment they may evoke. For instance, in Gobind Singh's composition *Chaupai* the guru is invoking God for protection, and many Sikhs recite the hymn five times to become courageous and fearless. A reading of guru Arjun's beloved work *Sukhmani* is believed to bring peace to the human mind and heart, and its twenty-four stanzas purify the breath for the entire day. When a relative becomes seriously ill, many Sikhs make a promise to recite this text either five or twenty-one times daily for forty days so the sufferer will recover. There are two popular collections of hymns from Guru Granth that are used especially in times of serious crisis. *Dukhbhanjani,* "the destroyer of suffering," contains thirty-four stanzas and is read daily for forty days to prevent suffering and to cure the sick. While reciting the text, many Sikhs keep a pot of water beside them. It is believed that as the text is recited the water converts to nectar, which can later be sprinkled onto the sufferer. Similarly, all 108 stanzas of a collection called *Sankat Mochan,* "the savior from troubles," are recited usually for forty days. Many Sikhs choose a special hymn from the scripture, which they keep with them through life and recite whenever they experience troubles or sadness. In serious cases, families may arrange a continuous, complete forty-eight-hour reading of Guru Granth, *akhand path,* in the gurudwara in order to offer the ill or dying person divine support. Besides these specific recitations, it is common to perform or arrange a reading of Ardas in the gurudwara, to present offerings in the temple, and to do social work for the community.

Death and Dying

At a deathbed family members usually read *Sukhmani* or *Japji* to protect the dying person from suffering and whisper the divine name in his or her ear. As is the Hindu custom, the dying should also be given Ganga water in the mouth to assure a good death. However, most Sikhs bring this water from a well in one of the gurudwaras where it is said the river Ganga is flowing under the building. According to local lore, when guru Tegh Bahadur visited Varanasi in 1666 he made the river spring forth on this very spot. The guru did not go for a holy dip in mother Ganga, as was the Hindu custom. Instead, the river came to him on his command and for that reason Ganga water from this well is believed to be immortal nectar (*amrit*).

Many Sikhs in Varanasi reject the idea that there are auspicious times and places to die, a view they find support for in the gurus' teachings and often use as a reply to the strong Hindu culture they are living in. Whatever humans receive in life, even their own dying and death, is submitted to the decision of God. As a fifty-year-old woman put it:

> A human has to suffer according to what God has written and she has to suffer here. Dying is real suffering, when the soul goes out that is really a hard time. . . . In this area a woman died. Two days before [she died] she did the reading of *Sukhmani Sahib.* She was well, got some trouble in the night and died in the morning. Everyone was saying that she had done really good karma and got a good death.

In general, dying at an old age without too much suffering is recognized as a good death, in contrast to death caused by violence, aggression, or against the will of the dying person. Homicide and accidents belong to this latter category. Set under strict taboo, suicide is often explained away as either a homicide or an accident. The deaths of martyrs and soldiers are exempted from this taboo, because although they die voluntarily, they sacrifice their lives for a cause.

Sikhs accept a medical-legal definition of death—when the brain and heart cease to function—which in religious terms connotes the time when the soul leaves the body. Today it is mandatory to get a death certificate issued by a doctor or the local council. This will be handed over to the office of Municipal Corporation at the cremation ground where the permission to cremate is granted. But even though a person is declared dead, many still believe that the soul is conscious in the world until the fire consumes the head. A sixty-year old woman explained:

> When a person dies, after death he can see and listen to what is happening around him, but he cannot speak. He can see that people are crying beside his dead body. When they bring him to the cremation place, when they offer the fire, he is seeing even that! In *gurbani* [compositions of the gurus] there is a stanza saying: when Yama's staff hits you then you won't remember. It takes time to get this head burnt and after that you do not remember a thing. He does not know the worldly things after that.

According to this perception, the person is dead when the soul leaves it, but the soul is still present until the body is fully destroyed in the fire. Rituals for preparing the dead for cremation and the cremation itself are therefore especially important for the soul's proper departure from the body.

Preparing the Dead

The immediate responses to death in Varanasi are various, depending on many factors such as the circumstances of a death; local family traditions, origin; the status, gender, and age of the deceased; and which family members are left behind. Nonetheless, there are several actions most Sikh families perform between the time of death and the time that the body leaves the house for cremation: immediately after death they arrange readings of *gurbani* hymns from Guru Granth, give the body a bath, dress it, and pay the last respects to the deceased at the house.

Sikhs do not require any set duration for mourning and discourage public expressions of grief. Business owners usually close their shops for at least four days after a death in the family and many keep a period of mourning until they have completed a reading of the scripture. The immediate family is responsible for the practical arrangements, and they invite relatives from outside the city to attend. While waiting for their arrival, the family may cover the body with ice, light incense, and recite *Sukhmani* or *Japji,* play recordings of these hymns and Sikh devotional music, or invite people from the gurudwara for readings. In Varanasi Sikh women have arranged several clubs for weekly recitations of *Sukhmani* in their neighborhood or the gurudwaras, and these groups are often summoned to the house of the deceased for readings in the presence of the dead. The recitation provides peace for the departing soul and pacifies the emotions of those who remain.

When all relatives have gathered, the family gives the deceased a last ritual bath (*antim iznan*). While some simply bathe the dead body in water, others use curd from the market for this ceremony. As Sewa Singh Kalsi notes, this last bath signifies a transformation of the body to a more pure state.[33] Many in this community would agree, that although in general Sikhs have a very ambivalent attitude toward death pollution, ritual impurity occurs when the living come into contact with a dead body. Purification rituals are often explained by Sikhs within a conceptual framework of death pollution, but many reject the belief that the dead are polluted and view this ritual simply as an act of reverence for the deceased.

After the ritual bath, the chief symbol for the Sikhs, the hair (kesh), is covered with a cloth and in the case of a man a new turban may be tied on his head. If the deceased has undergone the ceremony khande di pahul and is a khalsa Sikh who keeps the five symbols, he or she should be adorned with the comb (kangha), the steel bracelet (kara), breeches (kachha) and the dagger (kirpan). For Sikhs the color white signifies purity and widowhood. The dead is dressed in a white suit, just as mourners wear clothes, shawls, and turbans of light colors. The son or some other family member shrouds the corpse in a white cotton sheet and ties the body to a bier made of a wooden board with bamboo poles for carrying it.

When the body is set on the bier, all family and community members are invited for the last offering (*antim bhet*), to pay respect by folding hands, touching the feet of the dead, offering money and flowers, and placing white woolen shawls over the shroud. The latter is a typical Punjabi custom, and frequently a pile of shawls will cover the bier before it reaches the cremation ground. Wool is considered both a pure and a costly fabric, and this combination makes it an ideal offering to a respected community member. During this ceremony the granthi from the gurudwara is invited to perform an Ardas in the family house before the bier leaves in a mourning procession.

The Last Journey

The death procession carrying the bier from the house of the deceased to the cremation ground is called the last journey (*antim yatra*). In Varanasi all relatives and friends of the family, both men and women, may participate. Before proceeding to Manikarnika ghat, the mourning party brings the deceased to the gurudwara for an obligatory last visit. Most often these processions pass by the Nichibagh gurudwara near the Ganga River, which holds the well of Ganga water. Today mourners usually transport the biers on cars or trailers to the gurudwara and carry them by hand only for the last part of the procession.

The dead body is brought into the courtyard of the gurudwara but should not enter the inner sanctum where Guru Granth is installed. It is placed outside, aligned toward the place of the scripture. The granthi brings Ganga water from the well inside the gurudwara, opens the shroud, and pours the water into the mouth of the dead. He covers the complete body with a saffron-colored robe of honor (saropa), a cotton cloth about six and a half feet in length, and completes the visit by reciting Ardas at the feet of the body. The mourning procession then continues directly to Manikarnika ghat for cremation. Incense is usually lit and placed at the feet of the bier, while the participants cry out *Satnam Waheguru*—"the true name, oh Guru"—all the way through the narrow lanes leading down to the river.

There are many explanations of the rituals in this brief ceremony in the gurudwara. The granthi strongly emphasizes that he is only acting as a representative for the guru's house (*gurughar*). Giving a robe of honor illustrates how Sikhs often translate themes from Guru Granth into actual practice. In several hymns Nanak tells how the Sikhs are embellished with robes of honor in the divine court; as he puts it in one hymn, "Drinking the nectar they are contented and go to the Court of the Lord in robes of honor."[34] In Varanasi drinking the nectar is not a metaphor, but a ritual act. Some think the stop at the gurudwara offers the soul, which is still present after death, a chance to pay a final visit at the guru's house and to make a last act of contrition. As one woman explained, "The body is placed in the hall outside the gurudwara to let it [the soul] say it is sorry for its sins." During this time both the soul and the guru are preparing for the end of the soul's worldly journey. For those mourners who do not continue to the cremation ground because modern transportation has replaced the need to carry the bier, the stop at the gurudwara has become the last opportunity to pay reverence to the departed before cremation.

The Fire Ritual

The cremation ceremony, which is called the last ritual (*antim samskar*) or the fire ritual (*agni samskar*), consists of four central acts: breaking of the pot (*dhamalak bhanana*), offering the fire (*agni bhaint*), reading Ardas, and reciting the hymn "Kirtan Sohila."

When the mourning procession has reached the cremation site, the chief mourner, usually the eldest son of the deceased, is given an earthen pot filled with Ganga water. He pours the water over the dead body from head to feet before breaking the pot into pieces by throwing it on the ground. Kalsi explains that the smashing of the pot symbolizes the liberation of the soul from the body.[35] In Varanasi, however, no such meaning is attached to it, and many Sikhs regard it simply as a custom belonging to the original Hindi ceremony from which the Sikh cremation evolved, which they are instructed to perform.

When the pyre is ready, the body is moved from the bier. If a number of woolen shawls have been offered, all except for a few are removed and donated to the Dom, the caste of funeral attendants who watch over the pyre. The corpse, wrapped in a shroud, is lifted up by hand and placed on the wooden pyre with the feet in a southerly direction toward the Ganga. The chief mourner opens the upper part of the shroud to anoint the eyes and mouth of the deceased with clarified butter (*ghee*). The rest of the body is then smeared with ghee and pieces of sandalwood and resin are spread over it before the chief mourner re-covers it with the robe of honor.

When the funeral pyre is fully prepared, everyone gathers around it in a circle. The granthi steps out of his sandals to stand barefoot on the ground, turns toward the pyre, and recites the Sikh Ardas. Many Sikhs regard this as the most crucial part of the cremation ceremony. As one Sikh put it: "The [Hindu] funeral priest who was there, he performs whatever the custom is over there, that is not really important for us, only the *Ardas* is." The mourners join the reading by standing with folded hands, and some follow the granthi's example and take off their shoes. After its completion, all cry out the Sikh ovation (*Jo bole so nihal sat sri akal*) and bow toward the pyre or touch the ground with their hands. The Hindu funeral priest hands over a sheave of burning grass to the chief mourner, who circles the pyre three times clockwise holding the burning grass in his right hand, while the Hindu priest recites mantras in Sanskrit. The wood is lit on fire at the head and feet of the corpse. When the pyre is in flames, the gathering is dissolved and only some of the mourners and the Dom will watch over the pyre until it has burned down to ashes.

As soon as the funeral party breaks up the granthi performs the recitation of the hymn "Kirtan Sohila." After washing his hands, feet, and mouth, he finds a quiet spot at the cremation ground where he recites the text from memory. The mourners do not always participate in this reading, but fully entrust the granthi with the duty. In any case, the reading is considered to be paramount for a cremation. Sikhs recite "Kirtan Sohila" daily when they are closing their shops and before going to bed, and in the gurudwaras singing the hymn completes the daily program when the scripture is put to rest for the night. Reciting "Kirtan Sohila" signifies a completion or closing and in the funeral context it marks the end of life.

Women in Ritual

In contrast to claims that Sikh women do not enter the cremation ground,[36] many women in Varanasi have taken part in cremation ceremonies and strongly deny their exclusion from this field. Nowadays there are no rules preventing women from participating, even if the accomplishment of a cremation remains anchored in the performance of a male chief mourner. In his sociological analysis of Sikh funerals, Kalsi observes that rituals are instrumental for the transmission of social values and the maintenance of power relations between men and women in the Sikh social structure. In his analysis these rituals confirm a subordination of women and encourage a stigmatization of widows.[37]

The impact of modernization in an urban setting like Varanasi forces a reconsideration of this interpretation. Even if the value of a patriarchal family structure is maintained in Sikh families, the critical power relation is really between the younger and elder generation, since both younger men and women are subordinate to elders. The traditional stigmatization of widows retains little support among Sikhs today. For instance, the ritual *chadar pauna,* in which a widow is remarried to the brother of her husband, is considered an old-fashioned custom no longer practiced in Varanasi. If widows or widowers want to remarry, they go through the ordinary marriage ceremony. Similarly, the custom of giving a turban to the male chief mourner at the death of his father, symbolizing the succession of paternal authority, is no longer practiced. Women's participation at the cremation ground must be seen in light of these changing attitudes toward gender roles. The fact that the cremation ceremony centers on a male mourner and that women often do not participate is explained by the enduring influence of the traditional gender roles in the Hindu majority society. Cremations in Varanasi remain ultimately a Hindu ritual that has been overlaid with Sikh meaning.

Responsible for the household, women have many functions and duties to perform in the house after the corpse has left. They often follow the mourning party to the gurudwara, where they ritually wash themselves and pay respect to the guru. On their return to the house they take a bath, dress in new clothes, and start to clean the rooms. Belongings of the dead, like clothes, mattresses, and bedsheets are collected and given to sweepers or poor people. In some families women follow a practice of reciting *Japji* in the gurudwara during the cremation. Others invite female friends and relatives to their house for readings of *Sukhmani* in the evening of the cremation day, sometimes hosting these readings for several days. Especially on the fourth day after death, families in Varanasi assemble women for *Sukhmani* readings, and if the death was natural and at an old age sweet sugar cakes are served.

Immersing the Flowers

When the pyre has burned down, the remaining bones of the cremated body, the "flowers" (*phul*), are collected in a ceremony referred to as *chauta,* "the fourth" day after cremation. On this day the chief mourner picks up the bones from the cremation place, washes them in milk, ties them in white cloth, and consigns them to a river. Due to the constant stream of cremations in Varanasi this ceremony is often simplified. The bones are either collected immediately after cremation or just washed into the river Ganga when the body has burned down.

The Sikhs in Varanasi are acquainted with the custom of bringing "flowers" to Kiratpur in Punjab and many have themselves brought bones there in pots, but for most Sikhs Varanasi is a more convenient choice to immerse the bones in Ganga. Drawing a parallel to the immersion of images of deities and sacred books, Jonathan Parry proposes that the Ganga operates as an "agent of desacrilisation" by neutralizing sacred things, even persons.[38] In a recently developed cremation ceremony for Guru Granth in Punjab, the disposing of ashes from scriptures is analogous to Parry's suggestion.[39] Most Sikhs do not attach importance to any particular river, but sometimes the last will of a departed family member specifies a place for the immersion. When the mother of a wealthy Sikh family died, for instance, her "flowers" were taken to Allahabad under car escort to be immersed in the confluence (*prayag*) of the rivers Yamuna and Ganga. Social status is often a motivating factor in choosing a significant place for immersion, and the use of modern transportation makes these more exceptional actions feasible.

Not only is the place of immersion often of little consequence, but the religious dimension also seems to be missing when it comes to human remains, except for the bones of gurmukhs. A thirty-eight-year-old woman told the following story:

> My great-grandfather's brother was a very religious man. He was doing *puja-path* [worship-reading] all the time. When he died and they were picking up his bones they found *Ik Omkar* [the opening syllables of Guru Granth] written on his forehead at three places. When they were cleaning them [the bones] they were getting darker. It looked like someone had carved it on his forehead.

Having the opening syllables of Guru Granth inscribed in the remains is the ultimate evidence of a gurmukh. It is believed that they devoted themselves so much to the divine words that the first characters of the scripture will mark their bones in the end. Other Sikhs tell similar stories of how people want to get an auspicious sight (*darshan*) of the bones of gurmukhs. But these legendary stories are exceptions to the ordinary life of most people, who treat the disposal of remains more pragmatically. The brisk business of cremations in Varanasi makes many Sikhs suspicious of the handling of dead bodies. A man who had just performed the last ritual for his mother said:

> They do not let it [the body] get fully burned before they throw it in Ganga. It is like an abuse of dead bodies. You can see corpses of dead people floating in Ganga. Therefore we decided to stay until the body was burned down and washed away the ashes and bones in the river.

Though the bones of ordinary people are not treated reverently like those of the gurmurkhs, most Sikhs think the ashes and bones should be treated respectfully, even if they are just washed away.

Condolence and the Last Prayer

In the year 2002, when a highly respected member of the Sikh community and esteemed citizen of Varanasi passed away, a local Hindi newspaper dedicated a supplement to his life and service to society. No less than twenty-one obituary notices, sponsored by the temple committee and private businesses, filled the edition. While expressing condolences in statements like "We deeply mourn the sad demise of our beloved, may his soul get a place at the feet of the Guru," the companies also used the notices to advertise cookies, ice cream, undergarments, and other products. In Varanasi it is uncommon to find advertisements such as these combined with obituaries; they usually occur in connection with the death of a public figure. The Sikhs have a different tradition of expressing sympathy in the death of a family member or friend.

A major ceremony after the cremation is the arranging of an unbroken and complete reading of Guru Granth, akhand path. A couple of days in advance of the reading, the family will put up an announcement on a blackboard in the temple inviting community members. The akhand path should preferably start on the eleventh day after death and be completed on the thirteenth day, but the family usually tries to arrange the completion to happen on a Sunday, when shops are closed and most people are free from work. The reading can be arranged in the house of the deceased or in the gurudwara, which employs a team of professional readers for these readings. Akhand path should be continuous for forty-eight hours, and the readers usually take turns, performing two hours each to avoid errors from exhaustion.

The completion of this reading (bhog) signifies the end of a mourning period when all relatives and friends are invited to the gurudwara on the afternoon of the same day for a last prayer, Antim Ardas, in the name of the deceased. On this occasion, people express their condolences by dressing up in white clothes and turbans and participating in the prayer.

The family places a photograph of the deceased on the floor in front of Guru Granth, a lower position than the scripture, and present offerings to the temple, such as money, food, blankets, mattresses, and even wedding gifts of the departed, which are placed before the scripture. Musicians perform a special kind of devotional music called *vairagi,* literally "one free from worldly desire," to create an atmosphere for meditation. At the end of the program the granthi performs the last Sikh prayer, in which he pleads for peace for the departed soul. All the mourners then line up in rows, men and women separately, at the entrance of the gurudwara and community members express their sympathy by greeting the mourners. Afterward all are invited to share food in the communal kitchen.

Ancestors in Memory

Though the mourning period has now officially ended, families members continue to honor the dead through offerings and scripture readings. On the thirteenth day or shortly thereafter, the family arranges an ancestor ceremony by inviting five people from the gurudwara for a meal. Families say they feed panj pyare, "the five beloved" of Gobind Singh. Before the meal, family and guests jointly perform an Ardas in the name of the departed. Many say that this ceremony is for the peace of the dead person's soul or represents selfless service (seva). One granthi, often invited for these occasions, gave the following explanation:

> They think that our feet came into their houses. If I will invite five people to my house for selfless service, it is like inviting Brahmins for food. They want to do service for the servants as much as they can do, service for the guru's house.

The five beloved represent the community of Sikhs and the gurudwara, and feeding them is a meritorious act. It is noteworthy that even though it has become associated with death, Sikhs also arrange this ceremony on the occasion of birth and marriage.

On the seventeenth day after a death the family goes to the gurudwara and offers food in the name of the deceased. Depending on status and means, the offering may consist of food, fruit, or money for the communal kitchen. The offerings are brought forth while the family or the granthi perform Ardas in front of Guru Granth. Similarly, one month and six months after a death the family will again present offerings in the gurudwara, but this time only dry food, such as flour, rice, and sugar. Regardless of the divergent views on death pollution, most families will not participate in any kind of festivities until they have arranged an additional unbroken reading of Guru Granth either in their house or in the gurudwara. In general, this is done between the third and the sixth month following the death.

Barsi, the anniversary of a death, marks the completion of a year and again the family may summon people from the gurudwara to feed them or may give donations to the communal kitchen in memory of the departed family member. On this day many arrange selfless service outside their community by offering food and blankets to poor or homeless people in Varanasi. In addition, another reading of the scripture called *Salana path,* "the annual reading," should be completed on the anniversary of the death. If the deceased was closely related to the family members, they will continue to complete a reading on this day over the years to come. Usually this annual reading is either an unbroken akhand path or a *khulla path,* an open reading spread over time according to choice, but the auspicious completion (bhog) should always fall on the day of the anniversary of the death. Many Sikh families invite relatives and friends for food and arrange devotional music programs when the reading has come to an end.

IN A WESTERN SIKH DIASPORA

The Sikhs in Sweden constitute a small community of about a thousand individuals. Most came in the 1970s and 1980s as politically or economically motivated immigrants directly from India or through other European countries. Today the majority reside in and around big cities, where they have organized local Sikh associations. By voluntary work and donations, the first Swedish Sikh temple, Gurudwara Sangat Sahib, was inaugurated in Stockholm in 1997. Five years later the Sikhs in Gothenburg, on the west coast, completed Gurudwara Guru Singh Sabha. The establishment of registered communities and temples has created an institutional representation in Sweden. Regularly Sikhs host other Swedes in study visits to their temples, and they actively engage in interfaith dialogues.

The Sikh community in Sweden today is composed of families of varied social backgrounds. Despite this diversity, life cycle rituals and communal rites practiced in different regions are strikingly uniform. The present normative code of conduct, *Sikh Kahit Maryayda,* exerts a great deal of influence on the communal religious life and even frames the life cycle rituals of Sikhs who do not strictly follow the khalsa ideal.

When Sikhs come together in a new social context, they tend to keep the basic structure of funeral rituals described above, while other features are adjusted to the rules and customs of the majority society. This relationship with the host country has created a reciprocal effect: Swedish funeral specialists adjust funeral procedures for the newcomers, and Sikhs adopt new cultural attitudes and customs from the surrounding society. From this social interaction, ritual practices do become modified, with new meanings created.

Funerals in Sweden

In the year 2000 the Lutheran Church of Sweden and the Swedish government separated from a close relation that began in the sixteenth century. Previously the Swedish Parliament regulated all affairs of the Church of Sweden. This event redefined the position of the Church of Sweden, which shifted from being the national church to being only one religious community among others. However, in connection with this divorce, the government appointed the Church of Sweden to be the responsible authority for funeral activities in the country, since it was considered the most appropriate public institution to meet the terms of the funeral law, which was revised in 1999. In 2000, when the funeral law came into force, a handbook on funeral customs was issued to guide personnel in churches, municipalities, hospitals, and other administrative divisions.[40] The handbook reflects that within the last decades of the twentieth century Sweden became a multireligious society. Today funeral specialists need to be acquainted with numerous ways of managing death formalities, including Sikh practices.

All Swedish taxpayers are obliged to pay a funeral fee. In exchange, the local governments have a financial responsibility for funerals for all people registered within a municipality, while the church works as the executive institution, guaranteeing burial or cremation and a room devoid of Christian symbols for death ceremonies. The Swedish strategy to avoid a complete privatization of funeral activities has not undermined the interests of funeral directors. Private or cooperative undertakers are usually contacted immediately after a death. They help the family members with the mandatory death certificate, transportation, coffin, and other arrangements, and educate them about the rules and standard procedures. In many cities funeral directors have built up a local clientele among immigrants, based on trust and recommendations from community members. Though funeral directors play a prominent role in arranging funerals, the Swedish model presupposes that a funeral is a citizen's right with governmental bodies as the liable parties.

Even though many of these directors still work mainly from a Christian perspective, the legal statute requires that they respect the religious tradition of the deceased. Many Sikhs see death as an occasion when they can meet representatives of the majority society in mutual respect. Christian priests, for example, are not obligated to be present at Sikh funerals but sometimes attend out of curiosity.

Adjusting Funeral Rites

In Sweden today most deaths occur in hospitals, forcing changes in funeral rites. Sikhs usually perform death rituals in the hospital and from there transport the body directly to the crematorium. In practice, both funeral directors and nursing staff at the hospital leave the performance of religious rituals to the mourners. Within a couple of days, the immediate family gathers in the hospital to bathe the deceased body and dress it in new clothes in a washing room adjacent to the morgue. The body is placed in a coffin and those gathered may read hymns suitable for the occasion. In one case when a child died in Stockholm, about fifty community members met in a hospital ward to read the text *Sukhmani.* Because the Swedish Sikh communities do not have full-time granthis, the presidents of Sikh associations or elder community members are sometimes invited to arrange for prayers at the hospital. In this way the rituals of the last bath, readings, and the prayer for the deceased, which in India take place in the private home, have been transferred to public institutions in Sweden.

Sewa Singh Kalsi reports that Sikh immigrants in England were at first shocked when a funeral director arranged a coffin instead of a bier for a funeral. They believed that the soul got trapped inside the coffin.[41] Nowadays Sikhs in Western countries are familiar with the use of coffins, and in Sweden many Sikhs have come to see it as a reverential custom. They are, however, concerned with the details of how coffins should look. For instance, they allow coffins jointed by screws or plugs but not nails, since nailing a coffin is considered to be like nailing the body. The newly introduced "environmental coffin" in Sweden, a casket designed to reduce air pollution from crematoriums, meets these religious demands. Some Sikhs see a coffin as equivalent to the thick wooden bier used in India for cremation. In this manner Sikhs have attached new meanings to a foreign custom they are obliged to follow.

Kalsi also informs us that the custom of bringing the dead to the gurudwara for a last visit before the cremation has become an integral part of Sikh funerals in England. The coffin is brought into the main hall of the gurudwara where the granthi performs an Ardas before the hearse is taken to the crematorium.[42] Bringing the coffin to the gurudwara is a way of adjusting the tradition of bringing the dead for a last visit at the guru's place in India to a new social context. The Sikhs in Sweden disapprove of this custom, even if some have participated in similar practices among Sikhs in neighboring countries. Their strong reaction is related to the architectural design of gurudwaras in the new countries.

Unlike gurudwaras in India, where Sikhs can easily place the bier outside the inner sanctum, the European gurudwaras are often built in ordinary houses and do not have space for temple courts as in India. To be able to offer the deceased a last attendance, the coffin must therefore be brought all the way into the main service hall where Guru Granth is installed, considered a pure area.

The use of coffins in crematoriums has transformed the funeral ceremony, which is held in a chapel connecting to the crematorium. In the presence of a funeral director, the chief mourner usually opens the coffin. Instead of smearing the whole body with clarified butter, the mourner puts it in the nose of the dead and sometimes places flowers and money in the coffin. One officiator and the gathered mourners of the assembly recite the compositions *Japji* or *Kirtan Sohila,* perform devotional music, and read the Ardas before the coffin is moved from the chapel to the furnace room. Among Sikhs in the southern part of Sweden, women are often invited to perform these readings, since they are often more educated than their husbands and know the religious texts better. Even though the traditional gender division in funerals has become more relaxed in Sweden, it is still the eldest son or some other male who symbolically offers the fire by opening the furnace door or pressing the button of the crematory.

The Swedish rules regarding cremation practices have caused some challenges for Sikhs. Swedish funeral directors are aware that Sikhs prefer to cremate the body in an open coffin so that the soul can easily leave the body, but security regulations prevent compliance with their wishes. For the same reason the lid of the coffin must be screwed down as it is deposited in the oven and usually only a few persons are allowed to be present. Unlike outdoor cremations in India, Swedish crematoriums do not permit a view of the full burning procedure by mourners. Crematorium assistants may allow them to remain in the hall and sometimes let them observe from an inspection window, but it is the crematorium staff who will supervise the body and the remains.

In cities that have gurudwaras the mourning family and participants usually go to the temple after a cremation to read Baba Sundar's hymn "The Call of Death." To give the mourners relief, other families help them in preparing food for forty-eight hours following the death. Most families do a khulla path, an open reading of Guru Granth, which should be completed between the seventh and thirteenth day after death. Just as in India, the mourning family invites all community members for the last prayer when the reading is completed. They place a picture of the deceased in front of Guru Granth and may perform recitations of different hymns related to the occasion of death. In the end all share a communal meal provided by the family of the deceased. At places where the community does not have a permanent gurudwara, the mourning family invites friends and relatives to their house for a reading of either *Sukhmani* or *Kirtan Sohila* and an Ardas, followed by a meal.

Since crematoriums grind the bones to ashes by machine and store them in urns until disposal, the ceremony of collecting bones is precluded. Relatives must sign for ashes within a year, and by permission from the County Administrative Board they are allowed to spread them anywhere outside burial grounds or take them to India for immersion. In the latter case, the crematorium seals the ashes in an airtight container and the Indian Embassy assists the family in preparing a certificate for the customs authorities in India. As many Swedish Sikhs maintain contact with their homeland by traveling annually to India, they usually bring the ashes of a deceased person for immersion at Kiratpur in Punjab.

CONCLUSION

As this chapter has shown, the ritual use of Sikh religious texts, such as recitation and singing of hymns, came to play a central role in the Sikh funeral rites at an early stage of the Sikh tradition. After the declaration of khalsa and the recasting of the Sikh scripture, Guru Granth, as Guru, written manuals of the Sikh code of conduct evolved in the eighteenth century and codified the ritual practices of Sikh funeral ceremonies. Readings from the scripture and offerings of food to the community became significant components of the prescribed funeral rites. Following the tradition of written manuals, the modern *Sikh Kahit* stipulates recitations of the scripture and the Sikh prayer Ardas for funeral ceremonies. As a normative manual, it exerts a major influence on the way Sikhs practice rituals worldwide.

With Guru Granth as the core of their religion, Sikhs have developed sophisticated methods for using the scripture in times of illness, dying, and death. Through the examples of the Sikh communities in Varanasi and Sweden, we have seen that text recitations, together with community service and readings of the Sikh prayer, remain the essential elements of Sikh funeral rites in two very different cultural contexts. Given the authority of Guru Granth in the Sikh tradition, the ritual use of texts in Sikh death ceremonies seems to have a conservative force that has enabled these three central elements to persist in the face of radical social changes in contemporary societies. In a Western country like Sweden, Sikhs have maintained the structure of funeral rites while adjusting some rituals in order to conform to the hosting country's regulations and customs. Though some outward changes have been necessary, the important point is that Swedish Sikhs continue to recite the same texts as Sikhs in India even though the conditions are different.

The diasporic situation, in which Sikhs are brought up in another culture and often required to define their religion for the majority society, has highlighted a need to differentiate the religious elements in their tradition from inherited cultural customs. In other words, Sikhs are forced to identify what is essential to the tradition and to reconsider what elements of the tradition can be adapted to their new context. In an article on the Sikhs in the United States, Gurinder Singh Mann writes:

> The large-scale move away from the Punjab has created a situation in which Sikhs must draw clearer lines between the religious and cultural elements of their identity. In my view, this process will bear significantly not only on the future of the Sikh community in the United States, but on the tradition in general.[43]

Mann raises three issues currently being debated within Sikh communities in the United States as part of this process: gender, the religious education of Sikh youth in the diaspora, and linguistic barriers to understanding the Sikh religious texts. While these issues affect the Sikh tradition in general, they are particularly relevant to ritual practices and will no doubt have a significant impact on how Sikhs in Western societies and also in India will practice their funeral rites in the coming years.

Sikhism promotes equality between all people, and Sikh women play an active role in Sikh religious life, both in private and public spheres. Women can do recitations from the scripture and community service in the gurudwara just like men. As we have seen in this chapter, however, the cremation ceremony is still a male business, centered on the performance of a chief male mourner. Traditionally, if there is no son then an uncle or some other more distant male family member will act as the chief mourner. Due to the impact of modernization, these attitudes are in the process of changing, allowing women a greater role in death rituals, even in a traditional society like Varanasi. Cremations in Sweden still remain centered on the male chief mourner, but in some parts of Sweden women have already taken over the intermediary role of a granthi by reciting religious texts and the prayer at funeral ceremonies.

Sikhs are aware of the contradiction of stating that their religion promotes equality and at the same time practicing rituals that support gender segregation. In India this contradiction is justified by reference to local cultural traditions, which Sikhs are obliged to follow. The distinction between what is essential to the religion and what is cultural overlay is often made in this way, at least on the intellectual level. Because most young Sikh men and women of the second generation in Sweden today are investing in higher education and social integration in the new country, while keeping their religious identity and retaining contact with their homeland, more changes in the gender division in rituals can be expected in the future. The influence of attitudes from the surrounding Western culture, higher education of women, and the age and generational composition of the diasporic communities will almost certainly lead to the relaxation of traditional gender divisions in funeral rituals.

A major challenge for the diasporic communities, which has been a topic of debate for several years, is what to do about the new generations who do not have sufficient knowledge to speak their home language, Punjabi, or read the gurmukhi script of their religious texts. Since text recitation is fundamental to Sikh funeral rites, the linguistic issues will have major implications on future funeral ceremonies. Sikhs in the diaspora will probably either use translations of their religious texts, employ professional readers to recite texts that the majority do not fully understand, or adopt a combination of the two methods.

The modern conduct manual, *Sikh Kahit,* must be seen as one attempt to distill Sikh religious rituals from cultural customs, and in the future Sikh funerals rites may be even more directed by the normative code of conduct in practice. But even if Sikhs make a greater distinction between religious and culturally inherited elements of rituals, one would expect that new cultural customs in the hosting countries will also be integrated into their practices. The use of coffins in Sikh funeral rites in Sweden is one example of how Sikhs have adapted a foreign custom they are obliged to follow. In the interplay between a religious tradition and the social context, religious practices are always in the process of being reconstructed with new meanings created, while fundamental religious elements tend to persist.

NOTES

I am greatly indebted to Professor Gurinder Singh Mann at the University of California, Santa Barbara, for his valuable suggestions and comments on this chapter. Thanks are due to Professor Tord Olsson and my colleagues at the seminar of History and Anthropology of Religion, Lunds University, for comments on an earlier draft. The fieldwork in India was supported by a grant from the Crafoord Foundation. Funding for studying the historical sources used in this chapter at the University of California, Santa Barbara, was provided by the Swedish Foundation for International Cooperation in Research and Higher Education (STINT).

1. Fieldwork was conducted in Varanasi (India) from October 1999 to December 1999 and from August 2000 to April 2001. I have used an anthropological method with participatory observations, conversations, and interviews with people working for gurudwaras and laity. The data for the section on Sikh funerals in Sweden was collected in Malmo, Stockholm, and Gothenburg during the spring of 2003.
2. Gurinder Singh Mann, *Sikhism* (Upper Saddle River, NJ: Prentice Hall, 2003).
3. Guru Granth (GG), 21, 75, 906, 1014, 1026, 1090. Standard Version.
4. GG, 1035.
5. GG, 64, 156, 489, 939, 1238.
6. GG, 222, 437, 689, 955, 1014.
7. GG, 1067, 1344.
8. GG, 686, 942, 1029, 1040, 1343.
9. Louis E. Fenech, *Martyrdom in the Sikh Tradition: Playing the Game of Love* (New Delhi: Oxford University Press, 2000), 67.
10. Fenech, *Martyrdom in the Sikh Tradition*, 69.
11. Guru Granth Sahib (GGS), 578–579.
12. GG, 182, 259, 278, 298.
13. GG, 358.
14. GG, 128, 986.
15. GG, 229.
16. Bhai Gurdas (1558–1637), a Sikh scribe who interpreted the Sikhs' beliefs and practices, tells that Nanak's compositions *Japu ji*, *Sodar*, and *Arati* were recited in Kartarpur. Jodh Singh, *Varan Bhai Gurdas* (Patiala and New Delhi: Vision and Venture, 1998), 68.
17. Singh, *Varan Bhai Gurdas*, 154.
18. GGS, 12–13.
19. GG, 648.The word used for "well" is *hasan*, which also may signify the "tower of silence" where the Zoroastrians expose their dead. Surinder Singh Kohli, *Dictionary of Mythological References in Guru Granth Sahib* (Amritsar: Singh Brothers, 1999), 63.
20. GG, 609.
21. GG, 223, 62.
22. GGS, 923–924.
23. Gurinder Singh Mann, *Sikhism*, 78.
24. Catherine Bell, "Ritualization of Texts and Textualization of Ritual in the Codification of Taoist Liturgy," *History of Religions* 27, no. 4 (1988): 366–392.
25. Bell, "Ritualization of Texts," 390–392.
26. W.H. McLeod, *The Chaupa Singh Rahit-Nama* (Dunedin: University of Otago Press, 1987), 57–138.
27. *Sikh Rahit Maryada* (Amritsar: Shiromani Gurdwara Parbandhak Committee, 1994), Article XIX.
28. Diane Eck, *Banaras: City of Light* (New York: Knopf, 1982); Jonathan Parry, *Death in Benares* (Cambridge: Cambridge University Press, 1994); Christopher Justice, *Dying the Good Death* (New York: State University of New York Press, 1997).

29. Jonathan Parry renders another oral version of this story of how the wealthy Punjabi Khatri and trader Lala Kashmiri Mal purchased the platform in the eighteenth century. When funeral attendants at Harishchandra ghat demanded an exorbitant amount of money for cremating Lala Kashmiri Mal's dead mother, he bought land at Manikarnika by covering a part of the ghat where his mother was cremated with gold coins. Parry, *Death in Benares*, 44–45.

30. Indera P. Singh, "A Sikh Village," in *Traditional India: Structure and Change*, ed. Milton Singer (Philadelphia: American Folklore Society, 1959), 277–278; Sewa Singh Kalsi, "Change and Continuity in the Funeral Rituals of Sikhs in Britain," in *Contemporary Issues in the Sociology of Death, Dying and Disposal*, ed. Glennys Howarth and Peter C. Jupp (New York: St. Martin's Press, 1996), 41.

31. GG, 74, 144, 662, 876, 1091.

32. GG, 1426–1430.

33. Kalsi, "Change and Continuity," 33.

34. GG, 62.

35. Kalsi, "Change and Continuity," 34.

36. Kalsi, "Change and Continuity," 34; Hew McLeod, *Sikhism* (London: Penguin Books, 1997), 148.

37. Kalsi, "Change and Continuity," 30–43.

38. Parry, *Death in Benares*, 188.

39. Kristina Myrvold, "Värdigt slut för gudomliga ord," *Sydasien*, no. 4 (2002): 20–23.

40. Bengt Erman and Gunnar Nordgren, *Begravningsskick* (Stockholm: Verbum förlag, 2000).

41. Kalsi, "Change and Continuity," 39.

42. Kalsi, "Change and Continuity," 40.

43. Gurinder Singh Mann, "Sikhism in the United States of America," in *The South Asian Religious Diaspora in Britain, Canada, and the United States*, ed. Howard G. Coward, John R. Hinnells, and Raymond Brady Williams (Albany: State University of New York Press, 2000), 272.

II

DEATH IN CONTEMPORARY SOCIETIES

CHAPTER 9

Contemporary American Funerals

Personalizing Tradition

KATHLEEN GARCES-FOLEY AND JUSTIN S. HOLCOMB

Mark Jerrison died in a car accident one week after getting married. He was thirty years old. While his death was a tragedy by all accounts, his funeral service was intentionally a celebration of his life. It was held on a Tuesday afternoon at a funeral home chapel. The service was overflowing with hundreds of family friends dressed in the traditional black of mourners and the casual clothes of Californian youth. Though a Protestant minister opened and closed the funeral with a brief prayer, the hour-long service was filled with stories of Mark told by close friends and family. No scripture was read and no sermon given, but it was clear from their words that Mark was a committed Christian now resting in peace with God and reunited in Heaven with departed family members and friends. As family members placed a flower wreath on Mark's closed casket, a rock song played over the loudspeaker.[1]

Mark Jerrison's funeral had many elements of what Americans think of as a traditional funeral: a funeral home, casket, minister, prayer, music, eulogy, flowers, and tears. It also exhibits many nontraditional elements, such as the spontaneous, shared eulogy, the negligible role of the minister, the use of popular music, and the celebratory theme. Furthermore, though a great deal of Mark's funeral spoke of Christian beliefs, it did not adhere to any prescribed religious liturgy. Amid the formality of the funeral home and tears of grief, this contemporary funeral allowed for humor and the spontaneous participation of the bereaved. Despite the recognizably traditional elements of this American funeral, the inclusion of many nontraditional elements points to the rather radical changes taking place in funeral practices in the United States. Some commentators on American culture view these changes as a sign of decline. What they see in Mark's funeral is the loss of religious belief, the diminished authority of clergy, and the triumph of individualism. Presbyterian minister and death educator Thomas G. Long identifies these changes as the erosion of sacred space, sacred community, and sacred story.[2] In this light, the funeral is one among many sacred American traditions that is failing in an age of secularism and radical individualism. Underlying this gloomy appraisal is the very real concern that without a connection to place, community, and religion people are left bereft of the resources to face death effectively. Their feeble attempts to patch together death rites without the depth of tradition are shallow, fragile, and inadequate in the face of death.[3]

Compelling as this narrative of secularization and decline is, the changes afoot in American funeral practices can also be interpreted as a sign of religious renewal or, at the very least, a continuation of religious sensibilities in new forms. The rapidly expanding options that families have in responding to death, from showing a video biography at the funeral to wearing jewelry made from ashes, are evidence of a good deal of inventive energy being put into the creation of death rites that are personally meaningful. Seen in this light, the contemporary funeral is a constructive reaction against the impersonal, cookie-cutter, ostentatious, theologically focused, tradition-determined, somber funeral practices of the twentieth century. Though stories of frozen bodies and space burials grab headlines, much more common today are funeral services in which mourners adapt traditional forms to create a personalized, family-led ceremony. Personalized funerals, which contain many familiar funeral elements, are increasingly preferred by Americans as more "authentic" rituals than the traditional funeral practices of the twentieth century. The popular appeal of personalized funerals suggests that this new funeral style is better suited to contemporary social changes, like religious pluralism, declining community ties, and spiritual seeking, that characterize contemporary American society. This chapter explores contemporary funerary practices in the United States with particular attention to these emerging trends and a critical eye to oversimplified appraisals of this rapidly changing social phenomenon.

Much of the current literature on American funerals focuses on the disposal of the body, the mortuary cosmetology practices associated with preparing a body, the casket, the business aspects of funeral homes, and the rising number of cremations. There has been surprisingly little reflection on what we normally associate with funerals: a religiously based service held in a house of worship, in a funeral home chapel, or at the gravesite. Reflecting on this strange absence in the literature, religion scholar Ronald Grimes writes, "The omission of the funeral liturgy is consonant with the assertion that American attitudes toward death are not shaped primarily by religious institutions, that is, by organized, denominational religion."[4] Like Grimes, we find this omission startling since funeral liturgies are widely held in the United States, and they continue to be shaped in both form and content by denominational religion despite the strong influence of the funeral industry. In an effort to better understand what role religion plays in American death, this chapter focuses on the funeral service itself, as well as the ritual activities surrounding the disposal of the remains and the establishment of a memorial, which together we refer to as "funeral practices." While these public and private rituals continue to be largely shaped by traditional religious institutions, we contend that Americans are increasingly constructing funeral practices out of the plethora of religious idioms available to them, which are neither tied to nor controlled by organized, denominational religion.

FROM TRADITIONAL TO POSTMODERN

Like all the chapters in this anthology, this chapter highlights the tensions between tradition and change in the contemporary social context. One difficulty in talking about this tension with regard to funeral practices in the United States is defining what we mean by the traditional American funeral. The narrative of decline would have us believe that until recently a single, "traditional" funeral form was uniformly practiced. To the contrary, even during periods characterized by considerable uniformity in death practices, there has always been diversity along religious, class, and ethnoracial lines. In order to identify trends, however, we do need to be able to generalize on the basis of widely shared patterns. Sociologist Tony Walter's description of three different kinds of deaths—the traditional, modern, and postmodern—is a helpful typology for differentiating these social patterns.[5] These three ways of responding to death are ideal types, meaning that they are abstract ideas, which are useful for describing the dominant patterns in funeral practices at different periods of American history. They help us understand how funerals have changed historically in response to social changes and how contemporary funerals are both continuous and discontinuous with previous funeral practices.

A "traditional" death, as Walter describes it, is one that is guided by religious tradition. The clergyperson is the authority figure in the traditional funeral. Theological discourse is used to interpret death, prayer is the method of coping with the loss of a loved one or community member, and the focus of the funeral ritual is on the soul as it travels to the afterlife. Long's use of the term "village funeral" to describe this form points to the importance of the local community as the context for the traditional death.[6] By contrast, the "modern" death rests on the authority of medical and funeral professionals. Families rely on these death experts rather than traditional knowledge of how to respond to death, which was the purview of the clergy and local community. Technological advances in embalming, cosmetic reconstruction, and casket materials are given precedence over religious concern for the journey of the soul, and the family relinquishes control of the body to the funeral home. Cultural historian Gary Laderman identifies the viewing of the dead, after the body has been made to look serenely asleep, as the focal point of the modern funeral.[7] The "Postmodern" death is a reaction against the authority of both religious tradition and medical and funeral experts in order to have an authentic experience of death and farewell.[8] In the postmodern death, authority rests with the individual, or the family on behalf of the individual, and personal choice drives ritual planning. Psychological discourse dominates the postmodern response to death and the primary method for coping with death is therapeutic, to express feelings. Rather than focus on the journey of the soul or the preserved body of the deceased, the personality of the dead is memorialized. The social context for the postmodern funeral is once again the family and friends, but professionals like clergy and funeral directors play a supportive role as the bearers of symbolic resources and guides through legal bureaucracy.

Though traditional and modern funeral forms have dominated in earlier periods of American history, aspects of traditional, modern, and, increasingly, postmodern death have often been woven together in the twentieth century. Contemporary funerals exhibit to varying degrees elements of all three. Too much emphasis on what is innovative in funeral trends can give the false impression that sacred place, sacred story, and sacred community have disappeared completely. Though rare, it is still possible to find a traditional, religious funeral that does not rely on the support of the funeral industry. The modern funeral style, complete with embalming, viewing, a church service, and burial, is still the norm in the southern and eastern United States. Postmodern funerals, which eschew prescribed religious tradition, are increasingly common among professional, middle-class Anglo-Americans, but even those unaffiliated with a religious congregation are likely to turn to a clergyperson to conduct the funeral. Given the ways in which traditional, modern, and postmodern styles are combined today, it is clear that there is no single, uniform pattern for contemporary funerals; however, it is the emphasis on personalization that best characterizes the current trends in American funeral practices. Above all, contemporary funerals display a wide array of ritual possibilities reflecting the diverse religious expressions of Americans.

Before we turn to the contemporary scene, it is helpful to look briefly at the history of funeral practices in the United States to understand how we got here. In the next few sections we trace the development from traditional to modern to postmodern funeral forms and examine how these forms respond to changes in the social context. We also include a section on the more unorthodox postmodern practices, such as space burials and Internet memorials, which are suggestive of the seemingly limitless potential for further innovation in American funeral forms. Finally, we tackle the question of what these changes mean for understanding American religious life today. Throughout this chapter we argue that American funeral practices are undergoing a period of transition in which the traditional, modern, and postmodern approaches to death are being renegotiated between the family, the funeral industry, and religious authorities in the context of secularism and individualism. Though the authors lean in different directions, we find ample evidence in contemporary funerals of both decline and renewal, narcissism and community, shallowness and substance, the bizarre and the innovative. Even in an era marked by mobility, nuclear and fragmented families, diminished community ties, religious pluralism, and individualism, funerals still serve the important social function that sociologist Émile Durkheim noted ninety years ago: gathering a community together in the face of loss for mutual support and reaffirmation of community bonds.[9] Contemporary funerals also serve a new function: the opportunity for individual self-expression on the part of both the deceased and the mourners. While this "personalization" trend is a cause for alarm to some, we argue that it is an adaptive strategy in an age of depersonalization that can also serve to reinforce community bonds.

THE TRADITIONAL PURITAN WAY OF DEATH

The Puritans brought with them to their new home in America funerals and grieving practices that were quite simple. As historian David Stannard has described the typical Puritan funeral, it began with the washing and dressing of the body in the home by family members.[10] Visitors would come to the home or the church of which the deceased was a member to see the body laid out, and prayers would be said during the viewing of the body. These prayers were for the consolation of the living and not for the soul of the deceased, whose fate was already determined, according to Puritan theology. Within two to four days the body would be buried and the mourners, family and close friends, would go to the home of the deceased for food, prayers, and condolences. As in the prayers said during the viewing, the focus of the postburial activities was the grieving survivors.[11]

Though Puritan funerals and burials started as simple affairs with unelaborate rituals and ceremonies, by the end of the seventeenth century they had become much more formal. Mourning gloves and scarves were worn, funeral verses were inscribed on coffins, and elegant mourning rings were given to those who attended the funeral procession. Many Puritans collected these artifacts of death as the form of Puritan funeral practices gravitated toward the elaborate and extravagant.[12] David Moller argues that the appearance of ornate rituals is understandable since the "aggrandizement of funeral ceremonies helped the Puritan to live with the overwhelming fear of death."[13]

As the simple funerals of the Puritans gave way to more elaborate funerary forms in the centuries that followed, evolving social forces undermined the cohesion that accompanied the community rituals of the Puritan way of life and death. Commenting on the legacy of the Puritan way of death and the rise of individualism, Stannard writes: "It was into this sort of world that there emerged an attitude towards death and dying that was characterized by self-indulgence, sentimentalization and ostentation—a world diversifying and compartmentalizing the cohesiveness of Puritan culture: a meaningful and functioning sense of community."[14] The nineteenth century brought images of death that not only avoided the focus on terror and separation from loved ones but also romanticized and beautified death as a peaceful deliverance from the suffering of earthly existence. Elegant cemeteries were built, tombstones were dramatically etched and decorated, mourning time extended from a few days to a year or more, dying became accentuated by elaborate rituals, and death was characterized as life's most edifying experience.[15] This lavish response to death and increasing sentimentalization has been interpreted as a response to the rise of individualism and declining sense of community.[16]

THE RISE OF THE AMERICAN FUNERAL INDUSTRY

The emergence of the modern funeral in the late 1800s was closely tied to the development of a funeral industry. Early American undertaking had reflected the simplicity of the traditional funeral. Through the eighteenth century, local tradespeople provided both goods and services for the funeral, burial, and mourning, but the extended family prepared and buried the body. Over time the undertaker began to emerge as a professional involved solely with the disposal of the body. Carpenters became coffin makers and then expanded their business to include renting out funeral hearses or carriages and providing labor service at the gravesite.

It cannot be overstated how significant the introduction of embalming was to the development of the modern funeral. Gary Laderman notes that embalming was not a widespread practice during the late 1700s and 1800s, but it began to gain public approval during the Civil War.[17] As thousands of soldiers died far from home, families wanted their remains preserved during the journey back to their towns for burial, and embalming allowed them this option.[18] The successful embalming of President Lincoln and the preservation of his body displayed in a funeral procession around the country contributed to the respectability and public acceptance of the new practice.

> The president's paraded body added to the viability of embalming as a fundamental, utilitarian, and specialized technical service for the dead. It is certainly what the people wanted. In their own experience a last gaze and the chance to see the body off was part of the conventional routine when a family member died. The Civil War disturbed that convention by increasing the distance between the dead and the living; Abraham Lincoln's body, through the perceived success of embalming, demonstrated that distance could be overcome and that the living could still view their dead—though a cost would be attached to the art of preservation.[19]

Undertakers originally embalmed the body at the family home. As embalming techniques progressed in the late 1800s and early 1900s, however, it became necessary to embalm in specialized facilities, which led to the creation of the modern funeral home.[20] With the development of legislation regulating embalming practices, the undertaker emerged as a professional specialist in the care and handling of the dead, supplanting the role of the family and local community. When preparation of the corpse moved from the home to specialized facilities, the attendant practices of viewing and mourning followed, and the undertaker took on the all-encompassing role of the funeral director.

Some representatives of the emerging death industry began to market their commodities with the aim of attracting disoriented and confused customers who were no longer sure of how to handle the death of their loved ones.[21] The activities, products, and services associated with death were gradually modified by the demands of a consumer-oriented market that located the dead within this market and turned the embalmed corpse and the funeral surrounding it into a commodity. Americans came to believe that the well-trained, professional "funeral directors" had the necessary expertise to guide them in offering a fitting farewell. Through industrious efforts to disseminate ideas about proper preparation, display, and disposal of the corpse, as well as the pattern of mourning, funeral directors established authority over the funeral by the early twentieth century.[22] As funeral homes were built in large and small towns, people expected the body to be taken from the family home to the funeral home, where it was prepared, embalmed, viewed, prayed for, and mourned over. The funeral director arranged and managed all the details of the funeral for the family, whose only role now was to grieve. The smooth efficiency and assured propriety of the modern funeral came, of course, at a price.

THE MODERN FUNERAL

When people speak today of the demise of the traditional funeral, they are not referring to the severe simplicity of the Puritan funeral but to the much more elaborate modern funeral orchestrated by a funeral home—what religious historian Stephen

Prothero refers to as the embalm-and-bury regime.[23] Though talk of the traditional funeral often masks the diversity that has always existed in American ritual practices, the funeral industry was able to wield considerable power in defining the "acceptable" form of modern funerals by the mid-twentieth century. When anthropologists Richard Huntington and Peter Metcalf surveyed American death practices in the 1970s, expecting to find diversity reflecting that of the American population, they found instead considerable uniformity:

> Given the myriad variety of death rites throughout the world, and the cultural heterogeneity of American society, the expectation is that funeral practices will vary widely from one region, or social class, or ethnic group, to another. The odd fact is that they do not. The overall form of funerals is remarkably uniform from coast to coast. Its general features include: rapid removal of the corpse to funeral parlor, embalming, institutionalized "viewing," and disposal by burial.[24]

What Huntington and Metcalf describe as the typical American funeral was, in fact, the typical Christian funeral, since Jewish families practiced burial without embalming as quickly as possible and often may rely on Jewish burial societies to make this happen. Also, it is interesting to note that while Huntington and Metcalf mention the viewing, which was often held the day before the funeral service, they omit entirely the significance of religious rituals. While Huntington and Metcalf stress the features controlled by the funeral industry, it is useful to imagine how the modern Christian funeral, including the religious rituals at the center of this death rite, unfolded from the perspective of the bereaved in order to understand what the postmodern funeral is reacting against.

By the mid-twentieth century, death occurred increasingly in hospitals and nursing homes and preparation for the funeral and disposition were firmly ensconced as the purview of the funeral director.[25] When death occurred, the funeral home of the family's choice was called to retrieve the body and assume the role of organizing the practical aspects of the funeral, preparing the body for viewing, and managing the entire process of disposition.[26] The body was quickly removed to the funeral home where it waited in a refrigerator storage unit. In many communities the funeral home was a local fixture with which the family was already familiar. In preparation for the viewing, the body was embalmed and made to look lifelike through facial reconstruction and makeup. The family contacted its clergyman to make arrangements for the religious aspects, namely the viewing and the funeral, which were held in a church or, for greater convenience and less expense, in the funeral home chapel. These preparations and the distance family members had to travel to attend the funeral made it necessary to delay the service for several days or even a week.

One of the major decisions for the modern funeral was the type of casket to be used. The family was taken to the "selection room" at the funeral home to choose from caskets ranging from pressed wood and cloth to various metals to elegantly finished hardwood. The prices ranged from several hundred dollars to near $10,000. If they had not already done so, the family selected and paid for a plot and headstone, either before or after the burial, a that met the strict regulations of the cemetery. In addition to these basic decisions, there were numerous smaller, but no less significant, questions to be answered. What would the obituary say? What type of clothes should the deceased wear? Who would be the pallbearers? Who would ride in the limo? What would be the inscription on the tombstone? Who would give the eulogy? The funeral director guided the family through all the many details that had to be quickly taken care of, from filling out legal forms and ordering floral arrangements to contacting the extended family and friends.

The day before the funeral, guests arrived at the funeral home for the viewing and signed the guest book. They came to pay their last respects and to offer condolences to the family members. A rosary or other prayers might be said and guests spent time in quiet prayer or talked in small groups. Emotions were restrained, platitudes were exchanged, and it was customary to comment on how peaceful the deceased looked and how well the family was holding up. On the day of the burial, family members and friends gathered once again at the funeral home or at their house of worship for the funeral service led by the clergy. This service was theologically focused and included traditional religious words of consolation and commendation. It might include a brief eulogy; however, the focus of the service was not on the deceased but on a religious narrative of death and immortality. As Thomas Long explains it, "When the sacred community gathered in the sacred space for a funeral, it was in order to re-enact a commonly held sacred story, an underlying conviction about the nature of life and death. Funerals . . . were religious dramas played out in the public theater of worship."[27] The solemn service was followed by a slow motor procession to the local cemetery, where more prayers were said by the clergy, and the deceased was buried among family and friends who had gone before. Afterward, the community of family and friends gathered at the family home for food and remembering.

The modern American funeral was dramatically different from the traditional funeral of the first colonizers of the New World. Technological progress, professionalization of the funeral industry, mobility, the nuclear family, and urbanization all played a role in the creation of this new social ritual. Over time, the simplicity of the traditional Puritan funeral was exchanged for the complexity and expense of the modern funeral. The funeral home guided families through an intricate set of expected rites, many of which were created and promoted by the funeral industry. Still, the modern funeral, like the traditional funeral, rested on a strong connection to a particular place, a community of family and friends, and, for the vast majority of Americans, a shared belief in Christianity. Many elements of the modern funeral are still quite common today. Embalming, viewing, religious funeral services, and burial are still practiced by most Americans, but these "traditional" funerary rites are no longer the only way to give a proper farewell to the dead.

THE CRITIQUE OF THE FUNERAL INDUSTRY

Though the funeral industry had been criticized since its inception, by the 1950s the commercialism associated with modern funerals was drawing increasing negative attention. In 1959, LeRoy Bowman, documenting these excesses in *The American Funeral: A Study in Guilt, Extravagance, and Sublimity,* claimed that modern funerals had lost their fundamental meaning and dignity.[28] In his view, the American funeral had become "an anachronism, an elaboration of early customs rather than the adaptation to modern needs."[29] Bowman portrayed funeral directors as salesmen who often sold unnecessary products, and he believed that consumers could avoid this type of exploitation by becoming aware of the essential functions of funeral rites. The function of the funeral director, claimed Bowman, should be to help the family fulfill its own wishes, which would require greater flexibility in funeral services.[30]

In 1963, Jessica Mitford's *The American Way of Death* brought considerable public attention to the American funeral industry. Like Bowman, Mitford criticized the materialism of the modern funeral and laid the blame on the funeral industry. The opening paragraph of *The American Way of Death* begins: "O Death, where is thy sting? O grave, where is thy victory? Where, indeed. Many badly stung survivors, faced with the aftermath of some relative's funeral, have ruefully concluded that the victory has been won hands down by a funeral establishment—in disastrously unequal battle."[31] Mitford's critique drew attention to the commercialism and exploitation she saw driving the funeral industry, such as misrepresenting embalming as legally required. She singled out embalming, the very heart and soul of the funeral industry, as particularly outrageous.[32] Embalming, according to Mitford, is a bizarre and grotesque practice. She also took issue with the language the funeral industry used to soften the reality of death: coffins had become "caskets," hearses had become "coaches," flowers were turned into "floral tributes," ashes became "cremains," and the corpse now waited peacefully for burial in the "slumber room."[33] Mitford's critique echoed concerns of many in the 1960s that the religious and social traditions of the funeral had become pompous formalities that lacked authenticity and benefited the funeral industry much more than the bereaved.

In response to criticisms and legislation, the funeral industry began to make substantial changes in the 1980s. Regulations of the Federal Trade Commission required funeral service providers to give consumers detailed information about prices and forbade misrepresentations of legal requirements for the disposition of human remains.[34] More importantly, the changing tastes and religious mores of the consumer forced the industry to offer greater flexibility in the kinds of services available, including the option of cremation, which it had greatly resisted. The demand for more personalized and simple funerals should be seen in light of much larger cultural changes that began in the 1960s with the coming of age of the baby boomer generation. As religion scholar Wade Clark Roof notes, baby boomers, with their strong value for inner authenticity and self-understanding, were the vanguard of an ongoing cultural transformation.[35] He argues that the boomers' turn to "spiritual seeking" within and beyond traditional religious walls was not a sign of secularization but the emergence of a new kind of religious script. The reaction against the authority of religious tradition and the funeral industry in the 1960s also tapped into what Paul Irion calls the "American ambivalence toward ritual," due to the association of ceremonial formality with class structure and rote, compulsory behavior.[36] Rather than reject death rituals altogether, baby boomers have insisted on more control over the ways they ritualize death in order to insure an authentic and personally meaningful farewell to loved ones.

THE POSTMODERN FUNERAL

The postmodern funeral is characterized by personalization, informality, and participation, which together create what is experienced as a more authentic and thus satisfying farewell than the somber, standardized, and theologically focused funerals of the past. The postmodern funeral is ultimately about choice, allowing for considerable more autonomy than either the traditional or modern funeral forms. Increasingly, Americans want the freedom to create a funeral experience that will speak to them and about them. For many, the embalm-and-bury regime with a clergy-led religious service does that well. A national survey in 2003 found that approximately 60 percent of Americans would choose this type of funeral for themselves.[37] What about the other 40 percent? For those who do not opt for the so-called traditional funeral, the options available are astounding. The first decision that will need to be made is whether to dispose of the body through cremation or burial. Cremation rates in the United States increased from 5 percent in 1963 to 28.6 percent in 2003, but in California and Hawaii the figure is 52 percent and 61 percent, respectively.[38] Though this increase is substantial, it is interesting to note that cremation rates in most Western societies have been considerably higher for several decades: 70 percent in Great Britain, 47 percent in Canada, and 55 percent in Australia.[39] U.S. cremation rates are catching up and are projected to rise to 35 percent by 2010 and to 43 percent by 2025. Such a significant shift in funeral practices has serious implications for the funeral industry and religious institutions.

Just as embalming ushered in the modern funeral, cremation has opened the door to innovative new death practices that are quickly becoming institutionalized through death-related industries and religious communities. When cremation became the countercultural alternative to the embalm-and-bury regime in the 1960s, it was performed without any ritual and thus perceived, as it had been for centuries in the West, as antireligious. The fact that Americans with religious affiliations are much more likely today to choose burial suggests that cremation is still perceived as less religiously appropriate.[40] Still, due to public demand, cremation has become widely accepted by the funeral industry and many faith communities. Today only a handful of American religious groups, such as Muslims, the Church of Jesus Christ of Latter-day Saints, and Orthodox Jews, forbid cremation. Far from being an antireligious choice, cremation has prompted the development of entirely new rituals surrounding the actual cremation of the body, the disposal of the ashes, and the designation of a memorial. Since the 1980s, many faith communities have adapted their funeral liturgies to the absence of a body and burial and devised new liturgical forms appropriate for cases of cremation. Grieving family and friends have also created rituals surrounding cremation, such as scattering ashes at sea or installing a plaque on a park bench, and new industries have formed to facilitate these rituals.

The question of cremation versus burial is only the first of many that families will be faced with in the immediate aftermath of a death if no prearrangements were made.[41] Along with the practical issues of disposal of the remains and selection of a casket or urn and monument marker, there are religious and aesthetic issues of ritual-creation that families must address if the funeral is to be experienced as meaningful. Who should lead the service, who should be invited to participate, what readings and songs would be in keeping with the deceased's life, and what aspects of her or his life should be shared in the eulogy? How can the service be a source of healing for the mourners? Families with a religious affiliation—somewhere around two-thirds of the American public—will discuss these questions with their clergyperson, and their religious tradition will provide the basic script of the service, with varying degrees of room for personalization depending on the denomination. For those unaffiliated with a congregation, the funeral director or a hired, unknown minister will most likely fill this role as ritual expert, but the unaffiliated family can also create a service without the assistance of professionals.

As part of a much broader liturgical renewal, many American religious institutions released revised funeral rites in the 1980s and 1990s that draw on sociological and psychological understandings of grief in order to be more pastorally sensitive to the needs of the bereaved, including their need to personalize the service.[42] These accommodations to the therapeutic role of the postmodern funeral have their limits. Even though personalization is now accepted and expected within many religious communities, the focus on the deceased is not supposed to overshadow the religious message of the service. Ideally, the personal story of the deceased is framed within the sacred story of the religious community.

Another issue on which Muslim, Orthodox Jewish, and some Christian groups have stood their ground is the centrality of the body in the funeral rite and the importance of burial. This focus on the body in the Abrahamic faith traditions stems from its essential role in a future resurrection. Muslims in the United States do not practice cremation and, while some Reform and Conservative Jews do, the preference of both Muslims and Jews is to bury the body within twenty-four hours so as to return it quickly to the earth. For some religious leaders, having the body present at the funeral is an important rejection of the death-denying tendencies of the West.[43] As Lizette Larson-Miller explains in her discussion of Anglican Christians in an earlier chapter, the presence of the body and the physical placing of the body into the earth are seen as vital steps to accepting the reality of death.

Though most Christian denominations allow cremation, members of many mainline Christian churches are encouraged, or in the case of Catholicism expected, to wait until after the body has been viewed and prayed over as part of a funeral liturgy before holding the cremation. Viewing the body is encouraged as a necessary step in the acknowledgement of the reality of death. While the traditional acts of viewing and having the body present at the funeral may have theological value, they are also quite costly to the family. For example, any kind of public viewing or delay in burial will necessitate that the body be embalmed. While not a legal requirement, it is a funeral home practice to insist on embalming except in cases of immediate burial to avoid the unpleasant and challenging problems of handling a rapidly decaying corpse. Another added expense is the cost of the casket. While some kind of a casket container must by law be purchased to enclose the body during cremation, many families feel compelled to buy a more attractive casket if it is to be seen at a funeral service. Since cost savings is a common reason people give for choosing cremation, it is not surprising that there is some resistance to paying the added cost for embalming and a casket in order to hold a traditional viewing and funeral prior to cremation.[44] To accommodate families who proceed with cremation before the funeral liturgy, the Catholic church officially allowed for this exception in 1996.[45]

Families that are unaffiliated with a religious congregation have no limitations on the funeral service beyond their own sense of propriety. In the face of so many options, this freedom of choice can be quite a burden for a newly bereaved family that must make decisions very quickly. Unlike the pioneers of the postmodern funeral in the 1960s, however, unaffiliated families now have numerous resources to turn to in the form of books, Web sites, clergy-for-hire, and funeral directors. Their tastes and choices are also informed by their own experience of attending postmodern funerals or observing fictionalized versions on television or in the movies. Books and Web sites provide access to death practices from around the world, which may appeal to the spiritual seeker more than the all-too-familiar Christian or Jewish rituals. For example, one can easily choose "exotic" practices borrowed and adapted from Buddhism or Hinduism or scientific and therapeutic-oriented practices of New Age religion and the bereavement movement.[46] The more innovative postmodern funerals are often a bricolage of religious beliefs and rituals.[47] While the publication of funeral guides is a growing business, it is doubtful that many Americans have the initiative to thoroughly research and construct an original death ritual. Even though one-fourth of Americans make formal funeral plans with a funeral home, few people plan their own funeral service in advance, leaving that job to their grieving family in the immediate aftermath of their death. Funeral directors have stepped in to fill the gap between the grievers' desire for a personalized service and their lack of resources, expertise, and energy to create such a service.

In response to the demand for new and different kinds of death rituals, the American funeral industry underwent a drastic transformation in the last decades of the twentieth century. As Laderman explains, "The new watchword on the lips of many within the industry was 'adapt,' and the subsequent rise of unconventional, stylized funerals represented a democratization of the consumer marketplace, where individuals can, in the words of the ubiquitous contemporary fast-food slogan, 'Have it your way.'"[48] Recognizing that few consumers really wanted to "seize control" from the industry and do things entirely on their own, the industry reinvented itself as the premier guide and resource for creating meaningful and therapeutic death rituals. Central to this shift was the promotion of the idea that the primary function of funerals is grief facilitation and that the funeral director is best suited to serve the grieving family as the grief facilitator. Since the 1960s the field of psychology of death has developed extensive literature on grief therapy,[49] and the funeral industry has been able to use these ideas, popularized through grief support groups, to further legitimate its essential role in the so-called grief process. In an increasingly secularized society, funeral directors see their pastoral sensitivity and guidance at the time of grief as a crucial public service that counteracts the "denial of death" in American culture. Among other therapeutic benefits, funeral directors insist that the funeral service, particularly when coordinated by those experienced in the profession, continues to serve the important function of gathering a community to support the bereaved.[50]

While the industry has learned it must offer an array of options to satisfy the contemporary consumer, it has vigorously fought deritualization by insisting that "memorialization" activities are an essential part of the grief process. According to a Cremation Association of North American brochure, "Direct disposal of cremated remains without funerals or memorialization of any kind can cause serious traumatic problems for survivors."[51] The "traditional" funeral, complete with embalming, viewing, and burial, is now promoted not because it shows proper respect to the deceased but because it best facilitates grief and closure for the survivors. Funeral directors strongly encourage those who insist on cremation to hold a memorial service and to purchase a plot for the ashes or some other kind of permanent memorial marker, claiming that the communal ritual and physical space in which to remember the dead are vital to the mourners' psychological health. Such memorialization activities obviously have a financial payoff for the funeral industry, since the funeral home can charge for the use of the chapel space, the container, the plot or vault for the ashes, and the monument marker, as well as receive a commission for referrals to related businesses such as those that provide for scattering of the ashes at sea. It is important to note, however, that the profits to be made from such services are quite small in comparison to those derived from the embalm-and-bury services. Gradually death-related industries are developing more extensive memorialization services, like video tributes and artwork made from ashes, which will help to make up this loss in revenue as more consumers choose alternatives to the embalm-and-bury funeral.

PERSONALIZING TRADITION

Rather than create an entirely new kind of death ritual, most families prefer to personalize the funeral traditions they are already familiar with. For the nearly 80 percent of Americans who identify as Christian, this means that the funeral service will follow a standard model: opening words, prayer, reading, eulogy, sermon, music, and closing prayer. Even among families unaffiliated with a faith community or tradition, this format is quite common.[52] Postmodern funerals may also include additional ritual elements, such as a floral tribute in which participants place flowers on top of the casket or a candle-lighting ceremony in which individual candles are lit from a central one, symbolizing the continuation of life. The easiest way for families to be involved in the service is in selecting and perhaps leading the readings, music, and eulogy. Except for those few who want to create an entirely unique ritual, families will look to their clergy or funeral director for guidance in planning the service, depending on their connection to organized religion. Funeral homes usually offer selections of hundreds of scripture readings and religious and secular poems, as well as popular taped music, from traditional hymns to contemporary songs. It is somewhat surprising, given the choices families have in planning a funeral, that the same readings and songs are so often used. The frequent use of certain pieces, such as Psalm 23 and "Amazing Grace," reenforces their preferred status, since many find their familiarity comforting.

By far the easiest way to personalize a funeral is to focus on the life of the deceased. The eulogy has long been a part of American funerals, but it has become the central focus of the postmodern funeral. It is possible to have a service that consists almost entirely of storytelling, as was the case at Mark Jerrison's funeral. A shared eulogy, in which everyone is invited to speak, is increasingly common and may be combined with a preplanned eulogy delivered by a clergyperson or a family member. While the shared eulogy allows for widespread participation and can be the most memorable part of the service, it is also the most potentially detrimental, since the informality of the open microphone opens up the opportunity for someone to say something inappropriate. Some clergy are critical of the eulogy-focused funeral because it turns the funeral into a wake and deflects attention from the religious message of the funeral. On the other hand, for those concerned that a theologically focused funeral will exclude and alienate some of the mourners or offend the values of the deceased, this is exactly what appeals about the eulogy-focused funeral. Religious beliefs can certainly still be expressed in a highly personalized funeral, as they were in the case of Mark Jerrison's funeral, but these beliefs belong to the individuals who share them and are not presented as the shared sacred story of the entire gathering. Focusing on the life of the deceased has become a practical means of creating an inclusive funeral service in a religiously pluralistic society.

Though the postmodern funeral has wide boundaries for what is considered an acceptable farewell, there are some new trends that are commonly viewed as beyond the pale. Not surprisingly, these unorthodox options receive much media attention. Here we will describe four that the reader most likely has heard of: home funerals, online funerals, space burial, and cryonics. Even though only a handful of Americans choose these options each year, these unorthodox death practices appeal to the same widely shared desire to create a farewell that is personally meaningful and expressive of the unique life of the deceased.

Do-it-Yourself or Home Funerals

Although most funerals continue to be arranged by funeral directors, a small number of Americans have fought to regain control of the body from the funeral industry. Most Americans assume that undertakers must be involved in a funeral, but in very few states is this required.[53] While this assumption is financially lucrative for the funeral industry, the do-it-yourself trend has successfully carved out the legal and practical dimensions of the family-directed home funeral. The decision to have a home funeral is typically based on ecological and religious values, economic limitations, and social needs. More important than the cost savings, minimizing reliance on the funeral industry allows families to be more intimately involved in the funerary process. There is no single model for a home funeral. Those arranging a home funeral need to be able to prepare the body for disposal and navigate the regulations and paperwork that accompany this process. There are now dozens of books and organizations that can guide families through the challenge of the home funeral, from dealing with bureaucracy and pushy funeral directors to choosing the best materials for caskets.[54] With these helpful aids, friends and family can create an atmosphere that reflects cultural and personal beliefs, including ritual, storytelling, and artistic expression.

In a home funeral, family and friends begin by washing and dressing the body. The hardest situation to deal with in holding a home funeral is the practical matter of the decomposition of the body, which begins almost immediately after death. To help preserve the corpse, ice or dry ice can be placed beneath it while it lies in honor on a bed or in a casket, or the body can be taken to a funeral home for a brief period of refrigeration while the family prepares for the home funeral and burial.[55] If willing to play this subordinate role, the funeral industry's support allows the family to have a home funeral that is compatible with the contemporary context, in which it may take several days for family and friends to gather for a farewell ceremony. Along the same lines, the family can purchase a casket, urn, or plaque from the funeral industry, whether at the local funeral home or over the Internet, without feeling pressure to relinquish control of the body or the process. More likely, though, those who choose to do a home funeral will take pride in constructing their own casket and memorial marker and will prefer to bury the body or ashes of the deceased on their own land or in some other personally significant place rather than a cemetery.

Another option for the do-it-yourself crowd, which has become institutionalized in Britain since the 1990s and has recently been introduced in the United States, is direct burial with no embalming or casket in a natural setting. Called "green burial" or "woodland burial," this form of disposal is only beginning to make headway in the United States with the opening of the third "natural cemetery" in 2003.[56] Instead of the embalm-and-bury regime, green burials entail wrapping the body in a shroud or easily biodegradable material so it can quickly return to the earth. Usually no tombstone is permitted in green burial sites, but some kind of natural marker like a tree may be allowed. With a little help from the cemetery staff, families can deliver their loved one directly into the earth and ritually mark the event however they please.

Online Funerals

Even though the funeral industry has traditionally functioned as a face-to-face service, it is increasingly going online. It is now possible not only to buy caskets and urns online but also to order flowers, obituaries, memorial cards, and grief support books all from one site. E-commerce offers many more options than any single funeral home could, making it easier for customers to personalize their farewell and avoid pressure from salespeople. In addition to the proliferation of death-related materials that can be purchased online, there are a growing number of online services for memorializing the dead, such as webcast funerals and cyber tributes. These online services provide opportunities for those who may be too geographically distant or disabled to take part in the community of the bereaved. In addition, some funeral homes are now equipped with "cremation cams" that allow people to witness the cremation either for religious reasons or for assurance that nothing improper occurs with the remains. This practice is still quite rare, but webcasting of the funeral service is beginning to take root in the industry.

Consider the following example of a webcast funeral described in a *New York Times* article. A week after Barbara Anne Frederiksen Pingree died of lung cancer, family and friends gathered for a memorial service, some in person and some online. More than fifty people logged on to the mortuary's Web site, typed in a private password, and watched the funeral on their computers. Some had martinis and cocktails in hand as they watched Ms. Pingree's great-grandson sing a Danish lullaby in her honor. Despite the unorthodox circumstances, family members unable to attend were thrilled to be a part of the service via the Web.[57] Either through real-time live coverage or stored video that is accessed through a password-protected site, online funeral services allow those unable to attend a way to be present.[58] Once a funeral home has made the investment to install recording equipment, it is also easy to offer for sale a recording of the service as a keepsake.

Virtual memorials not only transcend distance in a transient world, but also present new opportunities for participation and, to use the language of the funeral industry, grief facilitation. For example, instead of just one obituary and one funeral photograph, an online memorial allows mourners to post their own obituary, watch a video of the memorial service, light a virtual memorial candle, add their own pictures and video clips, and, most importantly, their own eulogies. It can also include an archive for a biography, family memories, and photographs, which can be preserved for future generations. Virtual memorials are not meant to replace the memorial service but to supplement it and, most importantly, allow those who could not attend to still be part of the community of grievers. A virtual memorial extends the typical one-hour service indefinitely so that anyone who wants to speak can speak, and what people wish to share may change considerably over time. If the funeral service is an important step in the healing process, the ongoing conversation facilitated by a virtual memorial can play this role even more effectively. Although online funerals and memorials may seem too artificial or removed for some grievers, as Americans get increasingly online this will be the arena of cutting-edge developments in the funeral industry.

Space Burials

Technology has also given rise to an even more unorthodox death ritual, the space burial. In its current form, a space burial consists of the "cremains" of about twenty-five bodies being packed into a capsule that is loaded on a rocket and launched. The capsule is released in space and orbits the earth. After a few weeks the capsule descends into the earth's atmosphere and burns, at which time it can be seen from earth in the early evening and morning. In 2005, a space burial cost only $995 for one gram or $5,300 for seven grams of cremated remains.[59] The Houston-based venture Space Services, Inc. has already conducted four launches, sending the ashes of one hundred people, including thirteen Japanese, into orbit around the earth. In addition to the space burial, the company holds a pre-launch memorial service and posts a dedicated virtual memorial on its Web site for each launch, with pictures and biographies of those on board the launch. Each family is provided with a personalized video of the launch event and memorial ceremony.[60]

A variation of the space burial is the transportation of ashes to the moon. This was first done in January 1998, when the ashes of Dr. Eugene Shoemaker were sent to the moon aboard the Lunar Prospector, a small spacecraft designed to survey the moon for eighteen months before crashing into the surface. This moon burial was a tribute arranged by the students of Dr. Shoemaker, a leading astronomer and researcher of lunar craters who had always wished to visit the moon.[61] Today, Space Services, Inc. offers a lunar service in which one gram of cremated remains are launched into the lunar orbit for $12,500.[62]

Cryonics

Cryonics is best described as an experimental medical technology. This label may seem strange to those unfamiliar with the goals of cryonics, since all persons in cryonic suspension have been declared legally dead. According to the Alcor Life Extension Foundation, the only American company that offers this service, cryonics is not a new way of storing dead bodies; it is a new method of saving lives. Cryogenic suspension involves preserving a body by freezing it, immediately after death is declared, to the temperature of solid carbon dioxide and keeping it frozen until some future time when medical science will be sophisticated enough to allow for resuscitation of the body and continued life. Cryonics made headlines in 2002 when it was reported that the frozen body of deceased baseball great Ted Williams was being kept in a sleeping bag and suspended in a titanium steel cylinder of liquid nitrogen in the Alcor Life Extension Foundation facility in Arizona.[63]

Alcor claims that nearly one hundred individuals have been frozen since the first cryonic suspension in 1967 and that over a thousand people worldwide have made arrangements to be suspended should they become terminally ill or injured.[64] Those who choose this route are hoping that one day medical technology will have the resources to cure the illness or treat the injury that took their lives. While the Alcor corporation would reject our including cryonics as a funerary practice, we do so because it is one of the options Americans have when they consider what should be done with their body, or that of a loved one, after death. The practice is still quite rare, not only because it involves lofty expectations in medical progress but because the cost is prohibitive. Cryogenic suspension of the entire body currently costs $120,000 and for the brain alone the cost is $50,000. Most recent Alcor customers have arranged for neuropreservation, which preserves only the brain, because it uses a more advanced and potentially more successful technology than freezing called vitrification, which is not yet available for preserving the entire body.[65]

CULTURAL SIGNIFICANCE OF EMERGING TRENDS

What does it mean that Americans want funeral and memorial options that allow them to create a personally meaningful farewell? Some would see in these new trends an alarming erosion of religion and community. This fear is not new. Forty years ago Peter Berger warned about the demise of the "sacred canopy" that would leave us alone in the cosmos.[66] Religious pluralism and the loss of what Thomas Long refers to as our "commonly held sacred story" through which to interpret death are undeniable facts of contemporary American culture.[67] But pluralism and the rise of spiritual seeking have not led to the demise of religion, rituals in general, or funeral rites in particular. The vast majority of Americans still choose to mark death within a religious framework, a point that is often overlooked by those who have a narrow definition of what qualifies as religious. The expanding array of new kinds of funeral rituals, from scattering ashes to posting online memorials, combined with the continued use of traditional funeral practices, such as clergy-led services, is a sign of the ongoing vitality of religious life in America. The postmodern trends do not signal a rejection of religion but an expression of new religious sensibilities. Wade Clark Roof calls this new religious style "questing spirituality," as it is marked by the search for authentic religious expression.[68] Rather than face death without tradition, a growing number of Americans face death without a prescribed tradition in the absence of which they are free to choose from many traditional practices and to invent new ones.[69]

The new trends in contemporary funerals strike some observers as superficial and narcissistic. Personalization is understood as yet another example of the "expressive individualism" that sociologist Robert Bellah warned twenty years ago was replacing community bonds and religious commitments.[70] Long makes an impassioned critique of the cult of individualism overtaking funeral rites:

> What may appear on the surface to be a refreshing and healthy trend in funerals—personalization, namely the amount of time and energy focused on the personality and life of the deceased—may in fact be a desperate attempt to fill the aching void left by the collapse of a creed we once believed. When the larger story of God and humanity loses its power over our religious imaginations, then we tell the only holy narrative left to tell—the biography of the deceased.[71]

The danger Long and others fear is that without a comprehensive faith narrative the "shallow well" of the new funeral cannot quench the thirst of the mourner. Further study may well reveal serious limitations to the spiritual, psychological, and social benefits of the postmodern funeral. However, at present the high demand for personalized, informal, and participatory funeral services indicates that this new funeral form is meeting the needs of Americans who, for a variety of reasons, do not find solace in the traditional, theologically focused funeral.

Postmodern funerals, like earlier forms of American death rituals, are still very much a social event. They are not created by isolated, autonomous individuals working in a vacuum but are constructed out of complex negotiations between mourners, funeral experts, and faith communities. Personalized funerals have by now existed long enough that they have begun to develop their own "tradition" in the sense of frequently used elements like the celebration of life theme, shared eulogy, and incorporation of pictures of the deceased. Even the most innovative death rituals are not invented ex nihilo but are influenced by what the planners have seen, read, and heard.[72] The funeral planning process is almost always a communal one, as family members and friends join with the funeral director or clergyperson to create a service that honors the deceased.

Postmodern funerals have a strong communal function not only in the planning stages, but also in their execution. These services invite participation from friends and family and through shared eulogizing create a sense of community among the bereaved. The opportunity for self-expression is not only therapeutic; it also serves to bind together the grievers, some of whom may be strangers, into a temporary community in a society where it is difficult to form intimate bonds. This community is rarely bound by a shared belief system, but the shared love of the deceased and concern for the mourners is enough to provide at least a temporary experience of community, or, as Victor Turner calls it, *communitas.*[73] New technologies like the Internet and video streaming aid this process of forming connections by enabling alternative forms of community unbound by time and space. Though these temporary experiences of community are a far cry from the stable, homogeneous community that the Puritans knew, for a brief period of time people do find solace in the shared support of those gathered voluntarily to remember the deceased.

Perhaps the most important benefit of the postmodern funeral is that the personalization of the service counters a sense of anonymity in this highly bureaucratic society. The funeral may be the last chance for people to really get to know the deceased, and many families consider the funeral not only an opportunity to honor loved ones but an obligation to do so. This strong desire for the world to know the deceased—to know this person as an individual with strengths and foibles and idiosyncrasies and admirable traits—can also be seen in the very intimate interviews families give on television after losing a loved one in a tragedy. Critics may find it a great diminishment that postmodern funerals focus on the story of one little life, but to many Americans the real tragedy would be for that story never to be told.

NOTES

The authors wish to thank Tony Walter, Robert Kastenbaum, Larry Michael, and Gary Laderman for their insightful comments on earlier drafts.

1. This description is taken from field research Kathleen Garces-Foley conducted in 2000 and published as "Funerals of the Unaffiliated," *Omega* 46, no. 4 (2002–2003): 287–302.

2. Thomas G. Long, "The American Funeral Today: Trends and Issues," *Director* 69, no. 10 (October 1997): 10, 12, 14, and 16.

3. Chris Shilling and Phillip A. Mellor, "Modernity, Self-identity and the Sequestration of Death," *Sociology* 27 (1993): 411–443.

4. Ronald Grimes, *Deeply into the Bone* (Berkeley: University of California Press, 2000), 261.

5. Tony Walter, "Facing Death without Tradition," in *Contemporary Issues in the Sociology of Death, Dying and Disposal,* ed. Glennys Howarth and Peter C. Jupp, 193–204 (New York: St. Martin's Press, 1996).

6. Long, "American Funeral Today," 10.

7. Gary Laderman, *The Sacred Remains* (New Haven: Yale University Press, 1996), 164–175.

8. Walter, "Facing Death without Tradition," 197–198.

9. Émile Durkheim, *The Elementary Forms of Religious Life* (New York: Free Press, 1965), 420–427 and 445–446.

10. David E. Stannard, *The Puritan Way of Death: A Study in Religion, Culture, and Social Change* (Oxford: Oxford University Press, 1977).

11. Ibid., 110–113.

12. Ibid., 108–122; Charles Corr, Clyde Nabe, and Donna Corr, *Death and Dying, Life and Living* (Belmont, CA: Wadsworth/Thomson Learning, 2003), 63–64.

13. David Wendell Moller, *Confronting Death: Values, Institutions and Human Mortality* (New York: Oxford University Press, 1996), 14–15.

14. Stannard, *Puritan Way of Death*, 171.

15. Moller, *Confronting Death*, 15.

16. Ibid., 15.

17. Laderman, *Sacred Remains*, 113–116, 167, and 174.

18. Ibid., 157–163.

19. Ibid., 163

20. Gary Laderman, *Rest in Peace: A Cultural History of Death and the Funeral Home in Twentieth-Century America* (New York: Oxford University Press, 2003), 1–44.

21. Laderman, *Sacred Remains*, 166.

22. Ibid., 167.

23. See Stephen R. Prothero, *Purified by Fire: A History of Cremation in America* (Berkeley: University of California Press, 2001).

24. Richard Huntington and Peter Metcalf, eds., *Celebrations of Death: The Anthropology of Mortuary Ritual*, 2nd ed. (New York: Cambridge University Press, 1991), 193–194.

25. See Moller, *Confronting Death*, 83–84.

26. This pattern was not followed by minority religious groups like Jews, who did not have public viewings and, in the case of Orthodox Jews, relied on their own burial societies to prepare the body for immediate burial.

27. Long, "American Funeral Today," 12.

28. See LeRoy Bowman, *The American Funeral: A Study in Guilt, Extravagance, and Sublimity* (Washington, DC: Public Affairs Press, 1959).

29. Quoted in Lynne DeSpelder and Albert Strickland, *The Last Dance: Encountering Death and Dying* (Mountain View, CA: Mayfield, 1999), 276.

30. Ibid.

31. Jessica Mitford, *The American Way of Death* (New York: Simon & Schuster, 1963), 1.

32. Laderman, *Rest in Peace*, xxi–xxii.

33. DeSpelder and Strickland, *Last Dance*, 277.

34. Federal Trade Commission, *Compliance Guidelines: Trade Regulation Rule on Funeral Industry Practices* (Washington, DC: Federal Trade Commission, 1984).

35. Wade Clark Roof, *Spiritual Marketplace: Baby Boomers and the Remaking of American Religion* (Princeton: Princeton University Press, 1998).

36. Paul Irion, "Changing Patterns of Ritual Response to Death," Omega 22, no. 1 (1990–1991): 161.

37. *Consumer Memorialization Preferences* (Cold Spring, MN: Cold Spring Granite, 2003): "African American respondents and those with religious affiliations overwhelmingly preferred a traditional funeral. . . . People with no religious affiliation and incomes over $100,000 preferred cremation" (11f).

38. Cremation Association of North America, www.cremationassociation.org/docs/WebPrelim.pdf; National Funeral Directors Association, "U.S. Cremation Statistics," www.nfda.org/page.php?pID=78.

39. Cremation Society of Great Britain, "International Cremation Statistics," www.srgw.demon.co.uk/CremSoc5/Stats/Interntl/2000/ToStatsI.html; Cremation Association of North America, "Canadian Cremation Figures," www.cremationassociation.org/docs/WebCanFigures.pdf; Death—The last taboo, "Australia," www.deathonline.net/disposal/cremation/australia.cfm.

40. According to the 2003 Consumer Memorialization Preferences survey, 80 percent of Baptists, 62 percent of Roman Catholics, 62 percent of Lutherans, and 55 percent of Methodists prefer burial to cremation.

41. While the majority of Americans plan to prearrange their own funeral, only one-fourth have done so. See "Executive Summary of the Funeral and Memorial Information Counsel Study of American

Attitudes Toward Ritualization and Memorialization: 1999 Update," Cremation Association of North America, www.cremationassociation.org/docs/attitude.pdf.

42. Irion, "Changing Patterns," 166.

43. Ibid., 167. See also Lizette Larson-Miller's discussion of memorial services in chapter 5.

44. According to the "2005 Wirthlin Report: A Study of American Attitudes Toward Ritualization and Memorialization," the main reasons for choosing cremation are saves money (30 percent) and saves land (13 percent); see www.cremationassociation.org/html/pressrelease2.html. According to the latest Consumer Report study, the median cost of immediate cremation (without a service or ceremony) is $1,100, embalming is $750, and a viewing or service is $775, while a complete, traditional funeral with burial starts at $3,000, "How to Buy a Funeral," www.consumerreports.org.

45. Prothero, *Purified by Fire*, 191.

46. Ibid., 206. See also Tony Walter, "Death in the New Age," *Religion* 23, no. 2 (1993), on the close relationship between the bereavement movement and New Age beliefs.

47. For example, *The Natural Death Handbook* (London: Natural Death Centre, 2003) provides examples of good dying, good burial practices, and healthy grieving from many cultures that the Western consumer can pick from in devising a unique funeral service.

48. Laderman, *Rest in Peace*, 147.

49. Ibid., 84, 100.

50. Ibid., 100–109.

51. Cremation Association of North America, "Cremation Is Not the End," www.cremationassociation.org.

52. For a more elaborate discussion of these elements, see Garces-Foley, "Funerals of the Unaffiliated."

53. End of Life: Do It Yourself Funerals, www.npr.org/programs/death/971208.death.html.

54. A popular example of this literature is Lisa Carlson's *Caring for the Dead: Your Final Act of Love* (Hinesburg, VT: Upper Access, 1998).

55. "A Quiet Funeral: Do It Yourself," http://members.lycos.co.uk/funeral/do_it_yourself_funeral.htm.

56. Bob Jackson, "Burial: Rest in Green Peace," *Newsweek*, November 17, 2003.

57. Edward Wong, "Coffins, Urns and Webcast Funerals," *New York Times*, October 5, 2000.

58. On-line Funeral, www.online-funeral.com.

59. Space Services, Inc. "Service Options," www.memorialspaceflights.com/options.asp.

60. Space Services, Inc., www.memorialspaceflights.com.

61. David Whitehouse, "Moon Burial for Geologist." *BBC News Online*, http://news.bbc.co.uk/1/hi/sci/tech/405944.stm.

62. Space Services, Inc., www.memorialspaceflights.com/options.asp.

63. *New York Times*, "Fight Over Williams May End," September 26, 2002; *CNN Sports Illustrated*, "Williams' Eldest Daughter Asks Judge to Keep Jurisdiction," August 13, 2002; *New York Times*, "They've Seen the Future and Intend to Live It," July 16, 2002; *U.S. News & World Report*, "Cold Comfort," July 22, 2002; *Contra Costa Times*, "Techies Go for Ice-Cold Afterlife," August 4, 2002; *New York Times*, "Even for the Last .400 Hitter, Cryonics Is the Longest Shot," July 9, 2002.

64. Alcor Life Extension Foundation, "About Cryonics," www.alcor.org/AboutCryonics.

65. Ibid., "Neuropreservation FAQ," www.alcor.org/Library/html/neuropreservationfaq.html.

66. Peter Berger, *The Sacred Canopy: Elements of a Sociological Theory of Religion* (New York: Doubleday, 1967).

67. Long, "American Funeral Today," 14.

68. Roof, *Spiritual Marketplace.*

69. Walter, "Facing Death without Tradition," 199–202.

70. Robert Bellah, *Habits of the Heart: Individualism and Commitment in American Life* (Berkeley: University of California Press, 1985).

71. Long, "American Funeral Today," 14.

72. Walter, "Facing Death without Tradition," 204

73. Victor Turner, *The Forest of Symbols: Aspects of Ndembu Ritual* (Ithaca, NY: Cornell University Press, 1967).

CHAPTER 10

Forms of Disposal

DOUGLAS J. DAVIES

The way contemporary Western societies treat their dead expresses the value that the living place upon shared past experiences of life more than the value placed upon some future eternal realm. Funeral services emphasize both the personal qualities and achievements of the deceased and the loss and grief of surviving family and friends more than any future afterlife destiny. And all such memory and loss take place in cultures where consumerism and personal choice foster ever-increasing personalization of funeral rites, with the variety of options for how to dispose of the dead increasing each year.

The main traditional forms of human disposal are earth and water burial, cremation, exposure of the corpse to natural elements, sometimes called "sky burial," and preservation, whether in ancient forms of mummification or contemporary cryogenics, in which the dead are frozen. These acts of disposal are usually carried out in the context of ritual activity that not only expresses a society's beliefs about the meaning of life and its ultimate destiny but also engages with complex issues of identity. The way the dead are disposed of thus reflects not only their previous status in life but also how they will continue to relate to the living after having left this world. Here we will often use the word *destiny* to refer to this future and ultimate view of the dead, not least because it is a word that neither accepts nor rejects any specific idea of some eternal heaven or paradise, and because it can equally apply to a place in the memory of the living and the history of a people. It is curious that we often speak of human beings "disposing" of their dead, because while "disposal" seems to indicate the uselessness of the matter dispensed with, the way the dead are treated is usually related to some further purpose and some ultimate concern. In retaining the word *disposal* in this chapter, we realize that the word comes laden with values and intentions; we do not intend it as a negative or debasing term.

THEORIES AND DESCRIPTIONS

In this chapter we seek to understand the significance of different forms of disposing of the dead. To achieve this understanding we will draw heavily upon theories and descriptions relating to death. It is worth emphasizing that theories and descriptions play a central part in the complex process of scholarly interpretation of social phenomena. Interpretation is sometimes called by the rather technical term *hermeneutics* (or even *cultural hermeneutics*) in an attempt to emphasize the formal, rather abstract task that scholars set for themselves. This chapter is, in this sense, an exercise in the hermeneutics of death rites focused upon bodily disposal. However, by drawing upon specific historical examples, it attempts to bring interpretations of death rites out of the abstract and into the concrete in order to illustrate the importance of history in changing attitudes toward human life and death.

Theories are abstract formulations of ideas used to think about the possible explanations for things. They sometimes emerge from a large amount of evidence and become a shorthand way of referring to it, but they can also emerge as an idea, almost spontaneously, which can then be tested by means of many actual cases. It is always worth remembering that theories are, to a greater or lesser extent, provisional and open to change and development over time. They should not be pressed beyond their actual capacity to explain events. This proviso is important because sometimes a theory is treated as an absolute fact and can thus be used inappropriately.

Descriptions also play an important part in seeking to understand human life and the place of death. Description can be either an end in itself, or a first stage leading to the second stage of explicit theoretical interpretation. Description is not easy, especially when we look at things within our own social world and take them for granted. We tend to ignore what visitors would see as quite striking.

Identity

No study of human disposal is possible without using the idea of human identity, the notion of who we are. Identity has two major and interlinked components: the psychological and the social. Our psychological identity develops throughout life and is deeply influenced by how we are brought up by our families and the communities within which we learn, live, and work. It is also much affected by our genetic inheritance and our bodily appearance as well as by such things as our place in our family. As we learn something about what people expect of us and how they regard us, the social element of our identity begins its influence. The values of our culture, forged through history and the effect of influential leaders, become part of our own awareness. We exist as a kind of center of a network of identity in which our deepest biological characteristics interlink with the most distant person or place that we have experienced.

A significant part of our identity is related to death. This relationship begins with the sense of the difference between living and dead things that is deeply ingrained even in young children and develops as we encounter death in persons whom we cherish. Human identity is composed of experiences of personal encounter; in a sense, part of each one of us is made up of "parts" of others. This means that when someone within our network of identity dies, the whole network is affected and adjustments must be made. Grief can be interpreted as the reaction to a loss of part of our identity-network. The disposal of the dead reflects how we wish to make that adjustment. Many theories about grief have their origin in what is called attachment theory, which accounts for the bonds existing between individuals and those with whom they live. This theory is particularly important for any discussion of dead bodies because their disposal is intimately associated with processes of detachment. Historically speaking, for many societies disposal has also meant a relocation of the dead—placing them somewhere else in the identity-network of the living and giving them a new place within their own restructured identity-network. This is where the theoretical idea of rites of passage becomes important.

Rites of Passage

The term *rites of passage* is both a description and a theory. As a description, rites of passage refer to many different sorts of ritual events through which an individual is given a new status within his or her society. Boys become men and girls women. They may pass from being single to being married and then to being parents. They may be initiated into various societies and a few may become priests through rites of ordination, just as students undergo a graduation ceremony. Many other rites also occur to mark the change from an old to a new place in society.

Rites of passage as a theory was first proposed by the Dutch anthropologist Arnold van Gennep (1873–1957), who argued that all rites of status change involve a threefold process that is best described in terms of its middle or liminal phase, framed by pre- and postliminal elements. *Liminal* comes from the Latin word *limen,* "threshold," that which we must pass over or under as we move from one space to another.[1] Indeed, van Gennep spoke of rites of passage as resembling a move from one room within a house to another, as one would move over a threshold or through a corridor. The liminal stage is often one of learning and of being together with others in a period of shared hardship. These three stages are also sometimes described as separation, transition, and incorporation. Van Gennep emphasized that, depending upon the ultimate goal of a ritual, one of these three elements will be stressed at the expense of the others.

Disposing of the dead regularly takes the form of a rite of passage. The element that is stressed depends, to a degree, on the "person" undergoing the major change; in most traditional societies, the spotlight falls on the dead person. While separation from the living plays an important part in the passage, it is the goal of incorporation into the land of the dead that plays the major role. However, in developed societies—where belief in an afterlife is very low or not central—funerals now tend to focus on the element of separation, the separation of the dead from the life once lived and also of the bereaved from their dead relative or friend.

Separation and disposal are, in practice, intimately related to each other. Separation from the identity held in life may begin before death, as when a sick person is placed in a location signaling the onset of death, such as a special hut, hospital or hospice, or temple. Prayer rites may be used to help the dying separate from this life and engage in the next stage of their journey. Prayers can also be a means of preparing the relatives for what is to come, as well as indicating to the dying that life is now coming to an end.

When the dying are pronounced dead, they enter into an intermediate stage in which they are both in this world and yet are not of it. Their body is prepared, usually by being washed and dressed in particular clothing, and they may be visited by various kin and friends, all part of their network of identity, who pay their respects to the dead and sympathize with the living. There then occurs a distinct ceremony in which the living take leave of the dead body through the locally established mode of disposal. At one level that completes the rites of passage of death, but further rites may occur at set periods after the disposal to honor the dead or mark some phase in the journey the dead are believed to be taking. These rites may also mark a planned scheme of reentry of the key bereaved individuals back into ordinary life. These considerations show that van Gennep's scheme of rites of passage is still of some considerable use in contemporary life.

Double Burial

Van Gennep's contemporary, the French anthropologist Robert Hertz (1882–1915) proposed a theory of double burial.[2] He described numerous cases of human disposal—especially from Indonesia—that involved an initial burial or placement in large pots allowing for bodily decay. This first step was followed by a subsequent rite, a "second burial," in which the bones were given separate ritual treatment. Hertz spoke of these as the "wet" and "dry" phases of funerary rites and interpreted them as a separation from ordinary human life and incorporation into the life of the ancestors, or an afterlife. The single act of cremation, he argued, was seldom accomplished as an end in itself, but seemed to demand a further ritual in which the cremated remains were given their own final rites.

To these descriptions Hertz added a significant theory in which he argued that society seemed to express itself through the life of its individual members. It is as though "society" becomes invested in each person. This is, of course, a very abstract way of speaking, but Hertz was trying to show why the process of disposal of human bodies was so very important. It was because the very idea of society, itself vital for community life, for sharing values and beliefs, and for survival itself, was in some way grasped in and through each individual person. So when someone died it was a moment of potential danger, as though society itself was being threatened in the death of one of its representatives. Working on that assumption, we could argue that the disposal of human bodies is done with care in order to ensure that society itself is preserved. This is a good example of a theory of funerals and reflects a period in anthropology when several influential French and Dutch anthropologists were seeking general theories to provide clear explanations for the hundreds of apparently different schemes of human behavior. Hertz's theory of double burial is of real use today when interpreting what people do with the cremated remains of their loved ones.

Conquest of Death

More recent anthropological work has sought to show how human culture takes death and begins to use it for its own advantage. Maurice Bloch's anthropological work on what he calls "rebounding conquest" showed that the human process of birth/life/death has been developed through many rituals, especially rituals of initiation, in such a way that a ritual "death" is always followed by a ritual "rebirth."[3] In other words, the normal facts of life are turned on their head as society recognizes the power of death but then argues though ritual and symbol that society triumphs over death. This is an argument I have developed further in terms of the rhetoric of funerary rites in which "words against death" are pronounced ritually, architecturally and symbolically.[4] As we shall see in this chapter, many of the contemporary trends in disposal, with their emphasis on celebrating and memorializing the life of the deceased, can be understood in light of this theory.

FORMS OF DISPOSAL AND PLACES OF MEMORY

These theoretical issues can now help us interpret contemporary forms of disposal as ways of changing the identities of both the dead and the living and of preserving the integrity of society.

Many people regard it as a sign of respect for the dead that they be given an expensive funeral; it is also one means of displaying the family's wealth to their neighbors at large. In Victorian England, for example, many poor, working-class people sought to save enough money to pay for a respectable funeral so they would not have to be buried as paupers through the charity of their local parish. In some contemporary societies, however, where death is, in many respects, marginalized, people do not wish to spend large sums of money on funerals as they often do on weddings. This is partly because funerals tend to be restricted to the family and are not shared by a large number of friends and the wider social world.

Burial: Disposal

Burial takes various forms. Ordinary inhumation, as that word indicates, involves placing the body in the earth. Normally this involves wrapping the body in materials or a shroud and placing it in a specially made coffin or casket, or the body may be covered with a kind of small roof within the grave. The grave itself may be a simple hole in the ground or it may be stone-lined to form a distinct chamber, as in some very ancient Mediterranean graves, or formed out of concrete, as in some parts of the contemporary United States. The actual act of placing the body in the earth is often accompanied by a rite. The long-established Christian form of inhumation has adapted the words God speaks to Adam in the Genesis creation myth: "You are dust, and to dust you shall return" (Genesis 3:19). Echoing this line, the priest now says "Earth to earth, ashes to ashes, dust to dust" as the body is buried. At the same time, people may throw a handful of soil into the grave and onto the coffin. These words and this act symbolize the change that is now coming about as the corpse passes from the world of the living, characterized by speech, into the world of the dead, characterized by the silent earth. The grave is filled with soil, sometimes by the male relatives of the dead, as in some West Indian traditions. After some months, once the soil has settled, a headstone or gravestone may be added to complete the grave, containing the name of the dead, dates of birth and death, and possibly information about relatives or some message or religious text expressing loss, hope, or faith.

Burial may also take the form of tomb burial, in which the dead are placed not in a hole in relatively close contact with the earth, but in tombs. These may be specially constructed, elaborate pieces of architecture, such as those found in cemeteries of the nineteenth and twentieth centuries, which expressed the wealth or importance of particular families. Burial tombs reflect the earlier custom of burying people within churches and are a form of asserting high status. Royalty were often buried in tombs within great churches, as were others that a society wished to honor. Churches such as London's St. Paul's Cathedral and Westminster Abbey serve as such memorial sites for the honored dead. Westminster Abbey, for example, is the final home for great Britons, those who have marked the life of the nation through their contribution to science, art, and literature. Today it is not bodies but the cremated remains of such people that are placed there. In many other cities, the cemetery takes the form of a necropolis, a city of the dead. As a reflection of ordinary cities, these often contain specific areas where elaborate vaults are constructed, while other areas contain the less elaborate tombs of ordinary citizens or the graves where the very poor are buried with no memorial stone at all. There have even been periods in history, especially in the nineteenth century during periods of epidemic sickness, when mass graves received many poor people's corpses.

Particularly in the Mediterranean, tombs have also been made out of caves, as was famously the case in the biblical account of the burial of Jesus. At the time of Christ, the Jews frequently practiced double burial: first, the body was specially washed and wrapped and placed in a cave; once decayed, the bones were collected and placed in an ossuary box which was itself located in the cave tomb or elsewhere. Many such boxes have been found and they provide an interesting window upon the world of their day through the decorations and inscriptions placed on them. To this day double burial is still practiced by many Greek Orthodox communities in the Mediterranean.[5] The body is placed in a grave and covered with soil. Some years later it is exhumed and the bones are cleaned and placed in the local ossuary, a special cemetery room kept for that purpose.

One highly significant fear in relation to burial concerns the premature disposal of one's own body. The development of medical science in advanced societies has sought to keep the sick alive as long as possible, with death being a final step to be avoided at all costs. Within the medicalized world of hospitals, death is registered both mechanically and clinically: both machines and doctors at the bedside mark an individual's death. This means that contemporary funerals are seldom associated with any fear that the dead are not dead. But in nineteenth-century Europe and the United States, this was not always the case: the worry over being buried alive was real. Many cases were known, and often described in magazines and professional journals in the most gruesome detail, of how some hapless man or woman was buried alive and only when the coffin was exhumed or uncovered for some reason did the state of the now-dead inmate become apparent. Stories were even told of how a pregnant woman gave birth within her coffin.[6] One of the reasons that the living, in the past, sat up with the dead for some days prior to burial was to ensure that the corpse was, indeed, dead. Today in Britain there remains a small minority of people who express a degree of anxiety about being buried alive; interestingly, not so many fear being cremated alive. This may be because the one case would lead to a potentially long period of suffering, and the other, a very rapid death, indeed.[7]

Burial: Memory

While ossuaries, vaults, tombs, or graves may serve as places of final disposal for the dead, they continue to be places of memorial and memory for the living. So although disposal carries with it an idea of finality, such sites usually become triggers for memory. Human imagination comes into play as the dead are given their memorial site. Burial is common in contemporary Western societies. In the United States it almost always involves the embalming and cosmetic presentation of the dead, which gives the impression that they are more alive than dead. This may well help the living to think of death as some kind of sleep in which the deceased can be remembered "as they were," a thought that comforts relatives who believe they have done their best for the deceased, just as they would have helped them when they were alive. In fact, however, the embalming is likely to be partial and very short-lived, and the corpse has to decay within the narrow confines of a solid casket and reinforced grave without the advantage of direct contact with the soil, which would allow decay to quickly take its natural course. If ever exhumation is required under these circumstances, it is far from pleasant for the people undertaking the task to encounter so much bodily corruption contained within such an enclosed and contained space. But what takes precedence is the relationship between the family and the funeral directors and the kind of discussion that is likely to stay on the acceptable level of how the dead will be made to look, how they are dressed, and how they can be "made comfortable" in their casket and "protected" in their grave. Human memory wishes to stop at that level and not to become engrossed with the rotting of the flesh and the natural interplay of organisms in the decay process.

Cremation: Disposal

Cremation presents another kind of possibility for disposal and memory altogether. Cremation has become extremely popular in many parts of Europe and the English-speaking world, except in the United States, where, until the close of the twentieth century, it remained a minority practice. The last decade of the twentieth and the opening years of the twenty-first centuries, however, witnessed an acceleration in the use of cremation both in the United States and in several European countries with a strong Catholic cultural history.

While personal choice, economics, and the availability of a variety of funeral services characterize modern democracy and consumerism, there are social and political contexts in which disposal of human bodies comes under the control of the state. It was only in the opening years of the twentieth century that some European countries allowed people the option of cremation, and it was nearly a century later before a few allowed families the freedom to take cremated remains for personal use. In contrast, cremation was a practice much encouraged in the Soviet Union, where the Communist government tried to wean Russian Orthodox believers away from the practice of burial, which they were deeply committed to. Communist political control elsewhere also sought to change funeral practice from burial to cremation, which would be conducted using new rituals tied to the new political ideology. From the 1950s to the 1980s, for example, the Communist Party of the People's Republic of China sought actively to replace traditional forms of burial and rites focused on the ancestors with modern forms of cremation. The cremation of leading political figures such as Zhou Enlai, whose ashes were widely spread across the country in 1976, reinforced this desire to change cultural practice.

The contemporary use of cremation cannot, in fact, be separated from this historical background. It was in the 1860s and 1870s that the question of using cremation in modern life began. Italy was particularly important in leading these debates and was rapidly joined by numerous other European countries, Australia, and the United States. It was in Great Britain, however, that the theoretical interest grew most rapidly into a public use of this form of disposal. There were three major factors surrounding this issue: the first medical and scientific; the second, philosophical and religious; and the third, technical and engineering-related.

Medicine and science argued that many cemeteries, especially those in towns that had grown rapidly under the influence of the Industrial Revolution, had become overly full and insufficiently deep to prevent health hazards associated with decaying bodies. Social welfare encouraged the idea of cremation as a cleaner and much more sanitary way of dealing with the dead. From the philosophical and religious side came a variety of different arguments, with many freethinking people supporting cremation as an alternative to church-controlled death rites. Some of these arguments were opposed by church leaders who favored the tradition of burial, which linked the idea of Christ's burial and resurrection with those of believers. In particular, church leaders reacted against those who opposed the churches for their own reasons and saw in cremation an opportunity to free funerals from church control. This was especially true in Italy for those whose freethinking took shape within the movement of the Freemasons. Accordingly, the Roman Catholic Church set itself against cremation, forbidding it for Catholic priests and laity until the ban was lifted in 1963.

Since then, traditional Catholic countries have still been relatively slow in taking up the practice. It is quite likely, however, that as the twenty-first century advances, countries like Spain, France, and Ireland will increasingly adopt cremation even if they do not approach the levels seen in places like Great Britain and Sweden. The kind of arguments that took place in the late nineteenth century also emerged at the turn of the twenty-first century in Greece, where the strongly traditional Orthodox Church opposed cremation in debates in which political factors interlinked with religious commitments. It may be that cremation becomes one sign of secularization as the Greek Orthodox Church resists those seeking change.

The technical-engineering aspect of nineteenth-century discussions over cremation was very important in an age when the Industrial Revolution had established itself as a driving force in social change. The construction of special incinerators and their testing with various animals proved the viability of cremation in Western societies. It should be remembered that cremation was already well known as a practice in India and that from about 1870 to 1910, when cremation was established in the West, India was already firmly part of the British Empire. Indeed, in Britain and elsewhere, there were occasional events when very special permission was given for foreign dignitaries to be cremated. But, in general terms, the Eastern custom of cremating people on open funeral pyres was not accepted in Western countries because of a sense of the dignity of the dead that might be denied in watching a body burn. The history of Western culture had also tended to link the burning of bodies with those of heretics or traitors. In India, the British had forbidden the custom of *sati*, the burning of a living woman upon the cremation pyre of her dead husband, regarding it as morally wrong.

Many of these arguments and possibilities took a slightly different turn after the World War I (1914–1918) and were reinforced throughout World War II (1939–1945). In particular, millions of people, especially men in the military, had been killed and buried far away from their home; their villages and towns had no graves for them. In this sense these wars forced a break in tradition. Women did not have to follow the husband into his grave, as custom would probably have otherwise ensured. Now, for the first time in cultural memory, people had a choice over what might happen to them when they died.

Cremation: Memory

The possibilities of memorializing the dead after cremation only began to emerge with time. When cremation was first introduced, there was a general assumption that the ashes produced by cremating a corpse would be buried in a grave or placed in some traditional memorial site. These very ashes came, in the United States, to be given the name *cremains,* a compound noun abbreviating and uniting the expression *cremated remains.* In most other countries, this word is not used and in this chapter we stay with the fuller term cremated remains or, indeed, with the very descriptive *ashes.* Just as the new product prompted a new word, so, too, did the remains prompt new forms of disposal. One innovation lay in columbaria. A columbarium is a specially designed building with shelves or niches for containers of cremated remains. The word derives from *columba,* the Latin for "dove," because when used in ancient times such places looked like a dovecote with its individual compartments for the birds. Modern columbaria, like the extensive one built at London's Golders Green Crematorium, expressed the seriousness of this new form of disposal of human remains while also echoing ancient, classical culture. They also provided historical and cultural validation for what was to become a significant cultural innovation. The columbarium as an expression of continuity did not, however, remain dominant, and its use declined in the later twentieth century.

In many parts of the world cremated remains are buried in cemeteries, in preexisting graves of buried family members, in small graves of their own, or in special areas set aside for this new form of human remains. Cremated remains are not always actually interred but are also scattered across lawns or memorial gardens. Sometimes there is a clear identification of where ashes have fallen but, more often than not, only a general area of dispersal or deposit is known. Families feeling a need for a distinct memorial can often purchase a stone marker or curb that lines areas of these memorial gardens. They can also pay for a tree or shrub that carries a memorial record of their dead relative. Other forms of memorial markers include wall plaques fixed to curbs, walls, or monuments set amid large areas of memorial lawns. Occasionally remains are buried or strewn in areas of woodland adjoining crematoriums or preexisting cemeteries.

A major development in memorialization takes the form of memorial books. These specially prepared volumes are made to last for centuries and even involve methods borrowed from historical crafts used by monks employing velum and leather. The names of the dead along with particular messages requested by relatives can be inscribed in the books using traditional forms of calligraphy and illuminated artwork. This approach was much fostered in Great Britain, where practically every crematorium possesses a specially designated chapel or room containing the book of remembrance. Each day the book is opened to the page that lists cremations performed on that day in earlier years. The book thus marks the anniversary of each cremation. If relatives visit on other days, the crematorium staff is happy to turn the book to the appropriate page. Relatives can also have a copy of the book entry to keep at home. With the beginning of the twenty-first century, it is also possible for kinsfolk to access these memorials through computer and Web networks.

But the memorializing of the cremated dead does not stop there. Here we can take Great Britain as an example of what is beginning to take place in other parts of the world regarding the private use of cremated remains beyond traditional cemeteries. While many people were content with the burial of ashes in graves or the scattering of ashes in cemetery areas, there remains—probably for a significant minority—a degree of unease over these methods of disposal. In part this unease developed from a sense that cremation services resembled an industrial production line. This was especially true in Britain in the 1960s when cremation came to dominate over burial as the major form of disposal. The result was that many cremation services had to take place in a relatively limited number of crematoriums. This meant that each event could last only twenty or thirty minutes as one family after another was rushed through the process. This sense of being in a queue fostered the image of a conveyor belt in a production line. It is an interesting fact that, in Britain, it became almost conventional for people to speak in very concrete terms of the process of cremation as a conveyor belt. People described the coffin as being placed on a conveyor belt and passing into the flames when, in actual fact, very few crematoriums actually possessed a conveyor belt and those that did never used it to take the coffin into the flame but only out of the crematorium chapel. The important fact is that people felt caught up in a pressurized event. In cultural terms, this awareness differed a great deal from the emotions aroused by traditional burial services conducted in local parish churches, where there was always enough time to conduct ritual in time honored ways.

This sense of being "processed" sometimes goes hand in hand with a corresponding awareness of depersonalization. It is as though the dead are being rendered into a product in as fast a time as possible and are then simply scattered on a purpose-made lawn. In Britain, from about the mid-1970s, one response to this was a growing custom of families taking away the remains of their cremated kin in order to do what they wanted with the ashes. Family members or a single individual often take cremated remains to a spot that holds strong memories of special significance either for the dead person or, more likely, for both the survivor and the deceased—for example, where they took holidays together, engaged in leisure pursuits, or spent their honeymoon. A fisherman's ashes might be placed in a favorite river or a soccer fan's ashes at a sports ground.

This practice marked a period of invention of tradition at an individual and group level. It may, of course, seem contradictory to speak of invention of tradition when dealing with individuals, since "traditions" tend to be widely shared activities. What came to be shared was simply the overall act of taking the remains and doing something personal with them. Thus the content of the action would, indeed, be personal, if not highly idiosyncratic.

One way of interpreting this development of private, personalized rituals of disposal is to contrast them with traditional Christian forms of burial as an expression of the fulfillment of human identity. Traditional Christianity taught that it was through the resurrection—after people were accepted into heaven—that they would finally fulfill their destiny in the presence of God. In the technical language of theology, this was an eschatological goal: it belonged to the last things of earth and the entry into God's eternity. In the New Testament, Paul taught that in this life we see as "through a glass darkly" but "then face to face" with God (1 Corinthians 13:12), which was why Christians placed such stress upon burial "in sure and certain hope of the resurrection." Death rites thus took place under the control of the churches whose ministers and priests conducted funerals and represented the doctrines relating to eternity. Cremation, however, offered the possibility of changing this scheme in quite a dramatic fashion, precisely because individuals could now control the ultimate treatment of ashes even though priests might conduct the primary memorial service. Some of these private rites can be interpreted not as the eschatological fulfillment of identity but as what might be called either the retrospective or the contemporary fulfillment of identity. It is retrospective when relatives take remains to places where the dead was once happy or experienced fulfillment in this life. By placing the ashes in a favorite river, on a hill, or in a garden, the living are placing a good deal of significance on the past life of that individual. Similarly, they may place the ashes in a spot of deep significance for both the dead and the living; it may be a place that marks their relationship. In this context the site becomes filled with double significance as it draws powerfully upon the memory of the one remembering what took place there.

In some countries, as in parts of Holland, for example, cremated remains are made into ornaments or even placed in pieces of personal jewelry that a relative can wear every day. This is a contemporary development of the well-established tradition of memento mori, or remembrance of death, through some object that reminded the living of the dead and, indeed, of death itself. In the nineteenth century these objects took the form of photographs, a lock of the hair of the dead made into a piece of jewelry, or a locket to wear around the neck. Once more, cremation has allowed this long-standing custom to become even more personal in that through the ashes the living can have a very direct sense of contact with the deceased person.

Another possibility opened up by cremated remains was that they could simply be retained by an individual or family for future use. So, for example, an elderly widow might keep her husband's ashes and ask that she be cremated upon death and that her ashes be mixed with those of her husband and buried or scattered somewhere together. Such requests for togetherness indicate the symbolic power of cremated remains that is not possible even if two people are buried together in the same grave. In a world where people are increasingly mobile, families and especially some expatriate groups have divided cremated remains and sent some portion to family members in their homeland. While these options and possibilities of memorializing the dead afford new opportunities, they can also cause difficulties, as when families are divided over deciding what to do with remains.

In contemporary societies such as South Korea, by contrast, cremation is a more public event, with much less attention paid to privacy and personalization. The great crematorium at Seoul has the capacity to cremate a dozen or more persons at any one time, each in a separate crematory, with a small prayer space for each family to spend in religious activities while the body burns. Many families thus express their own personal grief, but in a long, shared hallway where others are also mourning the loss of their relative as the body is being cremated. The remains are then retained in special buildings and can be accessed for later rites.

Woodland Burial: Disposal

Yet another form of disposal of the dead that is emerging in Western societies is a variety of burial very different from the traditional form of burial already described and interpreted above. Woodland burial involves burying someone in the environment of a woodland, in clearings, or—more usually—in an area where a tree can be planted over the grave. This trend, which belongs to the 1990s and the new century, may develop quite extensively. It is important to note that these burials are not in cemeteries or churchyards with rows of graves; rather, the dominant visual landscape is of trees, plants, and grass. There is no place in this setting for explicit religious symbolism, but each grave may be marked in some relatively small way, either with a marker, on a map, or in computerized form. People buried in such places are not buried in traditional coffins or caskets, but in some wrapping material or in a coffin made of wickerwork or some other easily decaying material. There is a marked difference between burial in a solid casket and reinforced grave and burial in a shroud exposed to the soil. The intention of woodland burials is expressed in another term used for them, namely "green burials," where "green" suggests the ecological values related to a concern with the natural environment.

The issue of identity resurfaces in green burials, as the people seeking this kind of burial do so quite intentionally, out of a love of nature and a desire to be part of it after death. This desire can be taken at a simple, aesthetic level or as a more philosophical and scientific concern with ecology. This ecological value has, increasingly, become important enough to some contemporary Westerners to lead to the development and institutionalization of an entirely new burial practice.

There are several innovative methods of disposal of the body in developed societies that are, however, extremely costly. To have one's cremated remains sent into space by rocket—one way of expressing the boundless nature of human life that is far removed from traditional religion—is very expensive. So, too, is cryogenics, or the practice of freezing a deceased person (or even just the head of the deceased) in the hope that through future scientific discoveries the cause of death may be counteracted and the dead revivified to take up life again on earth. In this case it is, of course, contradictory to talk about the "disposal" of the body, which is most certainly removed from the ongoing social world but kept in readiness for the future rather than discarded.

For growing numbers of people, the future of the world is part of their own worldview. The problems of global warming, depletion of the ozone layer, and pollution of the atmosphere lead them to question cremation and the gases produced by it. The sustainability of human life comes to be linked with the depletion of tropical forests and the overuse of various sorts of wood. At the same time, most developed societies have begun to promote the recycling of products within a strongly consumerist world. When individuals and families are engaged in recycling their domestic waste as part of everyday life, it is not strange for them to raise basic questions over the disposal of the human body. Green burials or woodland burials bring together many of these concerns: trees are planted, not destroyed; a body is given back to the earth as a kind of recycling; and gases are not produced through combustion, as in the process of cremation.

Woodland burials provide an alternative means of achieving ritual authenticity, itself a topic of real importance in societies characterized by increased individualization. In many modern societies, especially in Europe, there are significant minorities who do not believe in life after death in the traditional Christian sense. For them, funeral ceremonies conducted by priests or religious functionaries can involve many ideas and doctrines that do not harmonize with their own values. Although many people go along with these rites simply because they are customary, there are clear trends appearing in Australia and elsewhere, for example, that funeral services ought to reflect the actual views of participants. In what are sometimes called "life-centered" funerals, the celebrant dwells upon the life and relationships of the deceased. Favorite music might be played and favorite poems read, and there is no sense of having to focus on religious dogma. In other words, the death rites reflect life rather than confront the bereaved with beliefs they may not hold. When deathstyle matches lifestyle, participants are likely to gain a greater sense of integrity and authenticity. When environmental concerns occupy a strongly positive place within someone's lifestyle, ecology can function to some degree as a religious or ethical ideology. This makes it particularly valuable as a frame surrounding death ritual and may explain why woodland burials have had such a growing appeal. Within secularized groups, then, new forms of death rites may be becoming more directly relevant to people than religious rites have been.

This is not to say that woodland burial may not also appeal to actively Christian people who wish to be buried both in an ecologically friendly way and with full Christian rites. There is no formal theological reason why people cannot be buried in such places and in ways that bring them into intimate contact with the soil; indeed, the "earth to earth" motif of biblical texts is perfect for such occasions. The only potential problem is that, unlike traditional Christian graveyards, new woodlands would most likely not be consecrated—a technical term which in some countries involves issues of law—even if individual graves might be blessed (but not consecrated).

Another ecological method of dealing with the body when rendered into cremated remains is to place the ashes into artificial coral reef–like structures that become grown over with submarine plants and animals. Such remains form a "natural" domain similar to that of the woodland burial. While it is hardly possible for mourners to pay anything like a casual visit to the dead as they might in a woodland, they would still have the knowledge that their deceased relative had become part of the natural order.

Woodland Burial: Memory

Many British woodland burial sites start as a simple bare field that is intended to develop into a large woodland, and it is in that very growth that memory is intended to flourish. Growth is, intrinsically, part of the rationale of an ecologically related funeral and it is in that growth that mourners are to see the transformation of their deceased kin. This contrasts with the fixed memorials and statues of traditional cemeteries, whose future is more likely to involve lack of attention and potential vandalism. In parts of western and northern Europe, the relatively rapid increase of focus upon individuals and individualism rather than upon tightly bonded extended families means that some people will probably have no kin available to care for their grave in the future. This likelihood has led some to seek cremation and the scattering of their remains so as to avoid the problem entirely. Woodland burial might also appeal to such single people who can see their postmortem identity in terms of nature and its ongoing life, which will make no demands upon any friend or relative.

One other aspect of this contemporary trend that may reinforce woodland burial as an opportunity for memorializing the dead in the context of nature is the rising numbers of people who follow the wide variety of practices that are earth- or nature-based, often associated with New Age spirituality. It is more than likely that when current generations of such practitioners die, if they do not choose cremation, they will prefer some form of burial in natural surroundings rather than in traditional cemeteries.

Woodlands can also serve a very positive purpose in fostering a more corporate sense of memory. One individual, for example, was visiting Arlington Cemetery—the major military memorial cemetery in the United States—and was prompted by that very traditional and nonwoodland cemetery to establish the National Memorial Arboretum in England, the first trees for which were planted in 1997. It is intended as a memorial to civilians who died in or endured the wars of the twentieth century. Trees symbolize a great variety of ideas in many cultures, and it is perfectly understandable that, in a British context, they should express gratitude toward generations that underwent many privations, suffering, and death, even though those individuals are not actually buried there. The cultural significance of woodlands as part of a national heritage, as expressed in the great landscaped estates of the eighteenth century, provides a symbolic basis for memorializing the past in terms of the currently significant values of ecology.

Exposure

Quite another form of disposal that, on the surface, could be viewed as in alignment with natural processes is exposure of the body to the natural elements and to carrion birds. Such exposure of the corpse is customary among the Parsees, an Indian religious group whose origin lies in the Zoroastrians of ancient Persia and their much persecuted and depleted descendants in contemporary Iran. The Parsees build what are often called "towers of silence," enclosed spaces with high walls and an internal paved area, at the center of which is a pit. Bodies are placed in these enclosures so that vultures might come and strip away the flesh before the bones are deposited within the central pit. We have already intimated that this practice might be viewed as "natural" given the role of the birds, but, in fact, any interpretation of these rites has to take into account the religious beliefs behind them, in particular the Zoroastrian attitude toward both earth and fire. Fire, in particular, is held in high regard and takes center stage in the fire-temples and fire-rites that lie at the heart of worship as a symbol of ultimate power and deity. As is often the case with key symbols of any culture's identity, fire is deemed ritually pure and should not be rendered impure by any inappropriate act. Like the earth, it needs respectful treatment. For that reason, both cremation and burial are regarded as polluting key symbols of reality. These beliefs turn what might have seemed the "natural" practice of exposure into a strongly cultural act of preventing ritual impurity.

Such towers of silence are not, however, acceptable in many of today's societies. Since Parsees have tended to be strongly itinerant, traveling widely as business people and establishing communities far from India or the Middle East, they have had to adapt to local forms of cultural acceptability. The major shift that has taken place in their pattern of disposal lies in the acceptance of cremation, a change that would seem extreme given their deeply respectful attitude toward fire. Parsees have largely solved the intellectual and religious problem by accepting cremation if it takes place in electrically operated crematoriums and not in gas- or oil-powered ovens. The argument is that electric crematories simply heat the cremation chamber to such a temperature that, once the body is introduced, it, as it were, self-combusts. It does not come into contact with fire as it would in gas and oil chambers where actual flames are produced to engulf and consume the body. Such ritual accommodation has also been necessary, for example, in places where vultures have found more accessible food sources, as has occurred in some Indian cities.

Exposure of the dead continues to be practiced in some parts of Tibet, where the human body is cut into portions before being devoured by carrion birds or animals. Not only does the origin of this practice reflect economic and ecological realities, such as the unavailability of suitable sites and conditions for burial or wood for cremation, but it also reflects a religious attitude that is much more concerned with the ongoing journey of the soul after death than with the future condition of the body. It is a stark expression of the transience of earthly life.

The Ongoing Relationship Between the Living and the Dead

Relatives are often concerned that the deceased's wishes as to disposal have been carried out. While most would explain this concern as a respect for the dead, it is also possible that fear plays its own part. In many traditional societies, patterns of disposal followed custom and convention not only to ensure the correct transfer of the dead from the realm of the living to that of the ancestors, but also so that the living might be left in peace. The widespread idea of souls or some kind of life force associated with the deceased has often made the living alert to the possibility of an influence from beyond the grave—for example, that the immoral behavior of the survivors might be punished by the ancestors. This belief should not be seen as belonging only to the past or to undeveloped societies.

A significant element of bereavement is that the survivors often dream of the dead and also have a sense of the presence of the dead sometime after the funeral. These "visits" from the dead can give to the living strong impressions about how they are currently living their life, as well as about their relationship with the dead. This relationship may be one of powerful authority or one that is very relaxed. In traditional hierarchical societies, where the old play a highly significant part in ordering the lives of the young and where descendants have to take on the power passed to them, it can be expected that the period of transition following death may be fraught with anxiety. Rites of disposal have a major part to play in this transition of power and responsibility.

Disposal is seldom complete and final. Although the body decays or is burned, psychological relationships with the person whose body it once was often continue. Descendants may see aspects of their deceased relatives' lives reflected in their own behavior. For example, a woman may become aware of using particular expressions or sayings of her dead mother and, in using them, feel a certain renewed kinship. Similarly, a man might see in the way he writes or walks the very way his father wrote or walked; once more a link between them is activated. It is only with increasing age that this phenomenon tends to emerge, since the living need to attain the age that their parents were when they did these things. So, while the disposal of the body of the parent is clearly achieved through burial or cremation, there is a sense in which not everything is "disposed of" in a clear-cut fashion. These examples show that memories are not simply thoughts or ideas that may arise in dreams, but that they may actually become embodied in the conscious life and daily existence of the living.

The continuing psychological relationship between the living and the dead is often most strongly evoked by visits to the place of disposal, whether the grave or the place where cremated remains were deposited. In many countries certain religious festivals or public holidays become the occasion for affirming links with the dead, as may, at a more individual level, moments of crisis in someone's life. Memorial Day in the United States is one such occasion when families visit cemeteries and the graves of family members.

One of the best-known communal festivals is the Day of the Dead in Mexico. This celebration is a version of the Christian feasts of All Saints and All Souls, held at the beginning of November each year in most countries of Catholic tradition. In Mexico there is great festivity, with many special displays of skulls and skeletons that recall the theme of death and also the dead relatives of particular families. These displays may include contemporary images alongside more traditional ones. Families set up altars containing pictures of the dead and offerings of food. The dead are invited to come and join with the living in an extensive festival in the home and in public, just as the living visit graves to decorate them and make offerings.[8]

Ghosts, Vampires

Such festivities of reunion reflect a positive attitude toward disposal, but not all deaths and subsequent disposals of bodies are so positive. Sometimes there is what might be called "problematic disposal," the living believe that the dead have not properly taken their path out of this world. Beliefs about unsuccessful disposal often include the idea that the dead may appear as a ghost, a partial, disembodied presence of the dead in the land of the living. Ghosts may disturb or even terrify the living, especially if the living have not done all they could to ensure the proper disposal of the dead and their passage to the afterlife. In such circumstances all is not lost, however, because, depending upon people's beliefs, it is possible to conduct further rites that will grant peace to the dead person. Such rites may take the form of an exorcism, a ceremony in which a malevolent ghost is commanded by a priest or someone with appropriate authority to leave that place and go to its own proper home in eternity.

In some current contexts, ghosts are treated in a therapeutic fashion more than in a religiously imperious way; such ghosts are regarded as wandering and lost and in need of help and direction. This kind of contact with the dead after their apparent disposal is not the same as the intentional desire to contact the dead that led to the rise of spiritualism. This movement was rooted in the nineteenth-century United States, but it caught on in Europe, especially after World War I, when bereaved parents or lovers sought some sense of contact with or message from the dead through séances.

The folk beliefs of many cultures have dwelled upon the idea of the restless dead who, for some reason of circumstance or malice, prey upon the living. The notion of a vampire is moderately widespread. In parts of the Himalayas it was thought possible that if a family that was too poor to buy the wood necessary for cremation buried the body instead, then the deceased might became a kind of vampire. European myth has conjured up the image of Dracula, often associated with Transylvania and popularly promulgated by film and television to become a figure of fear who exists in a state between death and life, in need of the blood of living people for his own survival. It may well be that the increased level of unfamiliarity with dead bodies in the later twentieth-century world of developed societies has fostered a degree of fear about death and the dead and encouraged a wistful anxiety that emerges in Dracula films or television serials, popular with contemporary American teenagers, featuring vampire slayings.

CONCLUSION

Far from being a simple process, the disposal of human remains in the contemporary West has come to involve numerous complex issues of human psychology, social relationships, and the organization of space. The death of any individual demands a reorganization of the identity of the mourners and the society of which the deceased was an integral part.

We have been assisted to a great degree in writing this chapter by the theoretical ideas of identity and social networks, as well as the idea that society comes to a form of expression through the bodies of its members. It is precisely because each human body is a condensed cluster of values that its disposal has to be accomplished with care; the changing value systems of contemporary cultures display this concern, whether through increased focus on individualism, ecological interests, or even an exploration of disposal outside of traditional "religious" terms. Because all of these human relationships have taken place within particular places, and because that spatial element of human life continues in the various ways grieving people think of the dead and of the life that lies in the future, the mourning of the dead and various kinds of ongoing relationships with them are afforded value-laden spaces in which to occur.

NOTES

1. Arnold van Gennep, *The Rites of Passage* (Chicago: University of Chicago Press, 1960, orig. ed. 1909).

2. Robert Hertz, *Death and the Right Hand,* trans. Rodney and Claudia Needham (London: Cohen and West, orig. ed. 1970).

3. Maurice Bloch, *Prey into Hunter* (Cambridge: Cambridge University Press, 1992).

4. Douglas J. Davies, *Death, Ritual and Belief,* 2nd rev. ed. (London: Continuum, 2002).

5. L.M. Danforth, *The Death Rituals of Rural Greece* (Princeton, NJ: Princeton University Press, 1982).

6. Jan Bondeson, *Buried Alive* (New York: W.W. Norton, 2001).

7. Douglas J. Davies, and Alastair Shaw, *Reusing Old Graves: A Report on Popular British Attitudes* (Crayford, Kent: Shaw and Sons, 1995).

8. Elizabeth Carmichael and Chloe Sayer, *The Skeleton at the Feast: The Day of the Dead in Mexico* (London: British Museum Press, 1991).

CHAPTER 11

Spontaneous Shrines and Public Memorialization

SYLVIA GRIDER

The spontaneous shrine phenomenon burst into the international public consciousness with the saturation TV coverage of the aftermath of the death of Princess Diana in the summer of 1997.[1] Cameras panned relentlessly across the acres and acres of grief offerings—flowers, photographs, candles, balloons, teddy bears—that cascaded across the London landscape, turning parts of the city into vast shrines dedicated to the dead princess. Some spectators likened the scene to sea-waves of flowers breaking against the palace fence. The fascination with these shrines was so intense that the BBC aired an hour-long program simply titled "The Shrine," which visually surveyed the offerings with a minimum of verbal commentary. The resources of cut flower providers throughout Europe were almost totally depleted by the demand for flowers for the princess, a phenomenon that a news reporter dubbed the "Floral Revolution."[2]

This public outpouring of grief seemed without precedent, not only in its suddenness and spontaneity but also in sheer magnitude. News commentators consistently and solemnly intoned that the world had never seen such a tangible response to tragedy. Scholars, however, were quick to point out that there were indeed precedents, though on a smaller scale: most notably, in England, the public response to the catastrophic crushing of fans against the security fence at Sheffield's Hillsborough soccer stadium on April 15, 1989. In the United States, the 1995 bombing of the Alfred P. Murrah Federal Building in Oklahoma City was the scene of a huge spontaneous shrine that covered the security fence surrounding the site. An even earlier significant precedent was the leaving of thousands and thousands of personal and idiosyncratic mementos along the base of the Vietnam Veterans Memorial, which was dedicated in 1982. Other parallels in the expression of public grief that scholars noted included the roadside crosses that mark the sites of fatal car wrecks in the United States and elsewhere and the public grief offerings left at various sites associated with dead celebrities, such as the Graceland estate of Elvis Presley

(d. August 16, 1977), the Dakota Apartments in New York City where John Lennon was murdered (d. December 8, 1980), and the tombstone of rocker Jim Morrison at the Père Lachaise Cemetery in Paris (d. July 3, 1971). Although the creation of spontaneous shrines at sites of disaster and tragedy is now practically worldwide, the phenomenon is identified primarily with England and the United States.

In contemporary American and western European society, tributes by the living to the memory of the dead vary considerably in complexity and degree of official or institutional involvement. At the official level, communities, municipalities, and nations create official memorials that are usually sculptural or architectural and often memorialize national heroes and wars. From the Tomb of the Unknown Soldier to the Lincoln Memorial, all are expensive and all are intended to be permanent. But even these massive and impressive structures assume a temporary vernacular quality when visitors leave a transient bouquet of flowers at their base. At the same time, many families no longer feel that the traditional space for private grief—the cemetery—is an adequate space to express their grief.

Temporary memorials have become common as highway shoulders, sidewalks, fences, walls, and disaster sites are unofficially set aside by mourners as temporary, liminal sites where the living engage in ritual communication with the dead and their fellow "public" mourners. In this chapter I will provide an overview of key aspects of this emerging contemporary grief ritual, using the growing body of recent scholarly literature, from a variety of disciplines, including folklore, sociology, art history, and communications theory, that researchers have published in response to this dramatic phenomenon. Though there is no firm consensus on the terms used to describe this new form of public memorialization, this chapter will attempt to define the various forms and show their interconnection, beginning with the development of the spontaneous shrine phenomenon and then turning to its relationship to "cybershrines," roadside crosses, and public memorials such as the AIDS quilt and urban murals.

SPONTANEOUS SHRINES AS SACRED SPACE

Spontaneous shrines, while not necessarily religious, are treated as sacred space for the duration of the time that they are in place. Sacred spaces are sites that are set apart and distinguished from the surrounding area in such a way as to focus the attention of visitors on their very separateness. According to one authority, "To designate a place as sacred imposes no limit on its form or its meaning. It implies no particular aesthetic or religious response. But if sacred spaces lack a common content, they have a common role. To call a place sacred asserts that a place, its structure, and its symbols express fundamental cultural values and principles."[3]

Shrines are one type of deliberately created and defined sacred space. Basically, shrines are distinctive structures that are sanctioned by religious authorities and designed to house holy or special artifacts. Some shrines are believed to have special healing qualities and thus are visited by the sick and injured, who not only take away special tokens, such as vials of water, but also often leave behind mementos of their visit, such as flowers, written messages, or lighted candles. Shrines function as sites of devotion where visitors offer prayers and have a sense of access to a sacred realm. Different religions throughout the world erect and honor shrines with various degrees of devotion. As Paul Courtright points out in *The Encyclopedia of Religion,* "Shrines form one of the most enduring influences within a religious tradition. Fixed in space, preserved in tradition, looking back to events that took place at the beginning of the universe or at paradigmatic moments in the traditions of religious history, shrines serve to protect and engender the vitality of the religious traditions to which they bear witness."[4]

One reason that spontaneous shrines constitute a separate shrine subcategory is that they are vernacular, unofficial constructs and thus outside the control or sanction of any particular religion. Most spontaneous shrines are communally and anonymously created at previously unmarked, even profane, places close to the site of catastrophes and disasters resulting in multiple violent deaths. Usually people begin leaving memorabilia at the death scene as soon as the site is accessible. Mourners choose where to put their grief offerings without consulting first with authorities—they just do it. The general pattern is that as soon as a few artifacts are placed at the site, other mourners put their offerings there with them. Thus the shrines grow by accretion. Sometimes these temporary shrines are created in response to especially wrenching and disturbing individual murders, accidents, or fatal kidnappings. One function of spontaneous shrines is to draw attention to the previously ordinary place where some violent event occurred. The most distinguishing characteristics of spontaneous shrines are their proximity to the precipitating event and the extraordinary range of idiosyncratic mementos from which the shrines are created. The shrines are spontaneous because they are erected in response to sudden, unpredictable tragic events. These artifact assemblages are sacred by virtue of the actions and intentions of the people who create and tend to them.

The spontaneous shrine phenomenon draws on and syncretizes a combination of traditional or vernacular death practices, many of which have Christian roots. For example, the Catholic belief in the sanctity of the ground where a person's last breath was drawn has generalized into a widespread folk belief among non-Catholics, especially when violent and unexpected death is involved. The proximity of spontaneous shrines to sites of violent death is based on this precedent. Pilgrimages to sacred sites, including shrines, are part of the sacred worldview of nearly all of the world's major religions, including Christianity, Islam, Hinduism, and Buddhism. One consistent feature of sacred pilgrimage is for pilgrims to leave tokens and mementos at the sites they have visited. Similarly, spontaneous shrines are composed entirely of the associated grief offerings placed by mourners, without which there would be nothing to distinguish any particular site from the rest of the adjacent area. For example, the bare security fences that authorities erect around crime and disaster sites are not sanctified until mourners begin to place artifacts on them. Home altars, usually created and tended by women, are also a significant component of both folk Catholicism and nonsectarian spirituality. The variety of often unusual artifacts or offerings enshrined in home altars is echoed in the idiosyncrasy of the items that constitute spontaneous shrines. Many of the items, such as beer bottles or war medals, have meaning only for the person who places them on the altar or in the shrine.

Elaborate, colorful grave decorations are another common devotional feature in many Christian cultures, especially for Hispanic Catholics during the festive Mexican Day of the Dead (October 31), when feasts and special decorations, especially flowers and candles, are set out in cemeteries and families gather to eat together and honor their loved ones. Visually, spontaneous shrines—with their riot of flowers, candles, balloons, and photographs—closely resemble such colorful decorated graves, especially when the spontaneous shrines contain crosses and other Christian symbols.

The urge in the United States to remember the dead with idiosyncratic assemblages of popular culture artifacts and vernacular artworks has begun to extend beyond the distinctive cemeteries of Hispanics and various other ethnic groups. Cemetery personnel report a growing trend toward elaborate grave decoration in mainstream, nonethnic cemeteries, including seasonal assemblages for Halloween, Thanksgiving, Christmas, and other holidays.[5] At this point it is difficult to determine the exact relationship between spontaneous shrines erected by strangers to people they have never met and decorating the graves of one's friends and relatives, but both phenomena are the tactile, vernacular expression of love, compassion, and grief for the passing of a fellow human being.

TERMINOLOGY AND CHARACTERISTICS

Although there is general scholarly agreement on the term "spontaneous shrine," most journalists and some scholars frequently refer to spontaneous shrines as "memorials."[6] Of course, the shrines do memorialize the dead and situate a temporary place of remembrance for the deceased. However, memorials in general are not necessarily sacred nor are they always linked to a particular place. Memorials can also honor events, heroes, and even abstract concepts such as peace and war. For example, in his study *Sacred Ground: Americans and Their Battlefields,* Edward Linenthal elaborates on the memorial urge in American culture:

> Dominating the patriotic landscape are various places that memorialize war. Beyond memorial halls, auditoriums, and veterans hospitals, this martial landscape consists of street names, memorial highways—Monument Drive in Richmond, Virginia, being one obvious example—memorial parks, military cemeteries, war museums, and monuments ranging from whole memorial complexes—the Indiana War Memorial Plaza in Indianapolis, for example—to thousands of statues in cities and towns throughout the nation. Martial pilgrimage sites represent some of the most popular attractions in the country: for example, the Tomb of the Unknown Soldier in Arlington National Cemetery, the Marine Corps War Memorial (popularly known as the Iwo Jima Memorial) and the Vietnam Veterans Memorial in Washington, D.C. and Valley Forge.[7]

Further complicating the confusion of terminology, the media and some scholars seem to prefer the term "makeshift memorial." For example, many of the articles describing shrines that were created in New York City after 9/11 used this new term.[8] The problem is not so much with the noun "memorial" as with the adjective "makeshift." The location of these grief assemblages is specific and deliberate, referencing the site of some catastrophic or traumatic death by being placed as closely as possible or practical to the actual spot where someone died. The presence of a shrine brings a focus of order and purpose to the chaos and destruction created at the site of the catastrophe. Furthermore, artifacts are not placed at shrines in a random or "makeshift" way. Some mourners spend a great deal of time preparing their offerings, such as artworks, in advance and make special pilgrimages to the shrines to place their offerings in them. At the same time, it is true that the actions of other mourners are literally spontaneous—they leave at the shrine whatever they happen to have with them—hats, clothes, jewelry, name tags, key rings, driver's licenses, and so forth. Even in this case, though, pilgrims generally are careful to select a location for their offerings, based on consideration of others, individual preferences, or aesthetic tastes. To cite one example, the various T-shirts, caps, posters, flowers, candles, stuffed animals, and school paraphernalia that were placed at the site of the fatal collapse of the Texas A&M University student bonfire in 1999 were carefully arranged along the vertical plane of the security fence surrounding the site. Most items were deliberately placed so that they did not overlap and obscure other offerings. Separate groupings of closely related artifacts were laid carefully on the ground in front of the fence or grouped together where there was space on the fence. This same pattern of careful, deliberate placement is evident in other documented shrines, such as those at the site of the bombing of the Federal Building in Oklahoma City, at firehouses throughout New York City after 9/11, and on the campus and parking lots of Columbine High School.

Another distinguishing characteristic of spontaneous shrines is their vernacular quality, that is, the lack of any official sanction or direction regarding where the shrines develop or what is placed in them. Official, bureaucratic involvement with the shrines generally occurs only when a municipal or government agency determines that it is necessary to remove the shrine, usually because it interferes with vehicular or foot traffic. Such was the case with the shrine covering the sidewalk at the entrance to the TriBeCa apartment of John F. Kennedy Jr. following his death on July 16, 1999. This shrine spilled over from the steps of the building onto the sidewalk and then flowed down the block in both directions. When pedestrian traffic was blocked by the cascade of artifacts and people stopping to view them, authorities had the shrine removed. Often, however, the people who erected and tend to a shrine or the people who live in the neighborhood will decide when and by whom it is to be dismantled. Most people are relieved when tattered and dilapidated shrines are removed. Eyesores do not honor the memory of the dead.[9] What becomes of the artifacts in the shrines is usually a matter of local discretion, and often family members of the deceased are given their pick of the artifacts before the shrines are dismantled. Sometimes mourners will take responsibility for temporary upkeep of shrines by removing and replacing wilted flowers or straightening up the artifact assemblage after a windstorm or a downpour. Because of the fragile quality of most of the artifacts from which they are created, spontaneous shrines are temporary. Within a few days or weeks, the natural forces of weather and direct sunlight rapidly damage and ultimately destroy these artifacts, especially paper and artworks that were never intended to remain out of doors. Visitors rarely vandalize shrines or indiscriminately take items away from them.

There is a growing desire to preserve the artifacts from spontaneous shrines, perhaps fueled by the widespread knowledge of the archiving of the artifacts from the Vietnam Veterans Memorial, which will be discussed in detail below. In addition to the Vietnam Veterans Memorial collection, professionally archived and managed collections have been established to preserve the artifacts from the shrines at Oklahoma City, Columbine, and the Texas A&M University bonfire, and there may be other smaller collections that are not as widely known. In December 2001, Congress designated the Museum of American History at the Smithsonian Institution as the official repository of materials related to the 9/11 attacks. A commemorative traveling exhibit, September 11: Bearing Witness to History, contains selected artifacts from 9/11, including not only items from spontaneous shrines but also relics recovered from the rubble, such as a crushed filing cabinet.[10]

HISTORY OF SPONTANEOUS SHRINES

Scholars generally agree that the catalyst that led to the currently pervasive spontaneous shrine phenomenon is the widespread public gesture of leaving idiosyncratic offerings at the base of the Vietnam Veterans Memorial in Washington, DC. From its very inception in 1982, the Vietnam Veterans Memorial has been the center of controversy, mirroring the fractious role of this war in public memory. Paradoxically, it is the most frequently visited memorial in the capital. Almost as soon as it was dedicated and open to the public, visitors began leaving mementos at its base. As a site for a spontaneous shrine, the granite memorial with the names of the dead inscribed on its reflective face is an apt surrogate for the jungles of Vietnam where these Americans died and where most citizens can never visit. Primarily because of the reverent way visitors act in its presence, the memorial itself functions as a shrine. The flood of grief offerings left at the base of the memorial was totally unexpected, and a management policy had to be developed in order to deal with this outpouring of the American spirit. The Wall has been the subject of a flood of articles and books written by both journalists and scholars; historian Kristin Hass has written the most thorough study of the memorabilia, *Carried to the Wall: American Memory and the Vietnam Veterans Memorial.*[11] In this book, she not only explains the role these artifacts play in documenting the nation's tormented memories of the war, but also provides extensive lists of the artifacts which have been left at the Wall.

Currently, the National Park Service administers the site and is responsible for collecting the memorabilia daily. All the items are then taken to the Museum of Archaeological Regional Storage warehouse in Maryland, where they are cataloged and archived. Items from this unmediated collection are not given to family members, as is the case with some artifacts at the Oklahoma City memorial and elsewhere. Instead, everything left at the Wall is accessioned, except flowers and redundant items such as small American flags with no writing or associated items.

The phenomenon of leaving mementos at the base of the Vietnam Veterans Memorial has received constant, extensive media coverage, and in the process the significance of the memorial has continued to grow in the public consciousness. So has the awareness of placing personal memorabilia there. At some undefined point within the last twenty years or so, public awareness of leaving memorabilia at the Wall apparently generalized into leaving memorabilia at any site of publicly expressed grief, whether the site is contested or not, and spontaneous shrines have been the result. An exhibit of selected artifacts at the Smithsonian was so popular that it is now installed as a permanent exhibit in the Museum of American History. In part as a result of the popularity of this exhibit, over time the curators of the Vietnam memorial collection have noticed a significant change: many people now attach notes to their offerings in which they give or withhold permission to put the items on display.

No known inventory exists of all the spontaneous shrine sites—there must be thousands—but here I will survey the major shrines that have had a significant impact on the overall history and development of this contemporary grief ritual. One of the earliest spontaneous shrines developed on August 16, 1977, when Elvis Presley died at his Graceland estate in Memphis, Tennessee. Grieving, hysterical fans flocked to the site by the thousands or perhaps tens of thousands. They left behind their candles, flowers, and other mementos along the base of the wall in front of the estate. Media coverage, however, focused more on the mourners themselves than on what they brought with them and what they left behind. Visitors to Graceland today continue to bring and send floral arrangements and other memorabilia to be placed on Presley's grave on the estate grounds, and other shrines dedicated to Presley have been established by private individuals throughout the country. Fans reacted similarly when John Lennon was murdered outside his New York City apartment nearly sixteen months later, on December 8, 1980.

On April 15, 1989, a horrendous catastrophe at the Hillsborough soccer stadium in Sheffield, England, resulted in the creation of an extraordinary and dramatic spontaneous shrine.[12] This catastrophe is regarded by many scholars as the precedent that foreshadowed the shrines for Princess Diana. At Hillsborough, police control of the rival crowds at the semifinal soccer match between Liverpool and Nottingham Forest broke down and fans flooded toward the infield, where nearly a hundred were crushed to death against the security fence, in full view of the television audience, the teams on the field, and the other spectators. Fans and officials did all that they could to rescue the injured and dying, including many children, from the mass of wreckage.

That evening, a requiem mass at Liverpool's Roman Catholic cathedral attracted so many mourners that another mass was set up outside to accommodate the thousands of mourners who could not get into the cathedral. The spontaneous response of the mourners was remarkable and unprecedented. According to one description:

> Inside the cathedral, a large Liverpool FC [Football Club] banner—made the night before by a nun on the cathedral staff—hung by the altar. Before the mass began, one lad haltingly darted to the front and laid an item of football regalia at the foot of the banner; one or two others followed. At the end of the service, there was a large queue to lay regalia at the altar. One lad left his shirt there, and went home bare chested.
>
> Outside, without any knowledge of what was going on inside, the same was happening. A Liverpool banner left at the altar before the service was used as an altar-cloth. A man hesitatingly placed a bunch of flowers on the altar; then came a tiny teddy bear draped in the

> red favours of Liverpool FC, followed by a blue and white bear placed on the altar by an Everton fan. There followed a flood of fans, especially children, bringing up scarves, shirts, rosettes, flowers.[13]

Another public response in the aftermath of the catastrophe was to turn the soccer field into a huge spontaneous shrine composed primarily of flowers and team scarves.[14] An estimated 1 million people visited the shrine, most of whom left mementos. Media coverage of the memorial service and the shrines made a huge impression on viewers, locally and worldwide, apparently establishing in their minds that one simple, appropriate response to tragedy and disaster is the creation of an idiosyncratic shrine at the site.

On the morning of April 19, 1995, Timothy McVeigh walked away from his explosive-packed rental truck parked at the Fifth Street entrance to the Alfred P. Murrah Federal Building in Oklahoma City. Moments later the truck exploded, blowing away the entire face of the nine-story building and killing 168 people, including 19 children. People throughout the world were horrified by this vicious terrorist attack in America's heartland. Relief and rescue efforts got under way immediately and television crews from throughout the country converged on the site, providing constant coverage for millions of viewers worldwide. Within hours after the rescue efforts began, workers created a shrine to the victims in the bomb crater. Later, when the entire site was enclosed by a security fence, mourners tucked flowers and other mementos into the mesh of the fence. Ultimately, close to a million items covered that fence, a section of which is temporarily incorporated into the permanent memorial. The designers of the Oklahoma City National Memorial intended for memorabilia to be left at the 168 individual glass and bronze chairs, each inscribed with the name of one of the victims, which are the symbolic centerpiece of the memorial. This is one of the first examples of institutionalizing the spontaneous shrine phenomenon in an official memorial site. However, because of unexpected problems with the grass covering the "footprint" of the building where the chairs are located, visitors are not yet allowed to walk among the chairs and leave their offerings. The section of fence at one end of the memorial is the temporary solution to the dilemma of where people are supposed to leave their memorabilia.

Two years after Oklahoma City, when Princess Diana and her fiancé, Dodi Fayed, were killed in a grinding car crash in a Paris tunnel during the evening of August 31, 1997, it seemed that the whole world went into shock, followed by grief. The British media termed this reaction "The Week the World Stood Still." Following the precedents set at Hillsborough and Oklahoma City, oral tradition says that within hours of the news of her death, a London cab driver placed a single rose on the fence of Buckingham Palace. That act precipitated the overwhelming outpouring of flowers and memorabilia that followed, blanketing parts of London with acres of flowers, balloons, photographs, and stuffed animals. Media commentators were astonished by the volume of the vernacular, popular response to the death of the princess, especially when that popular response was contrasted with the nonresponse of the royal family. It seemed as though the whole world wanted to leave a grief offering, to do something tangible to express its mourning. As a result, other shrines for the princess developed at such places as the gates of the Spencer family estate at Althorp, the Alma Tunnel in Paris, and British consulates throughout the world. Mohamed el Fayed, the father of Dodi and owner of Harrod's Department Store, set up a shrine to Diana and Dodi in one of the main display windows of the store, which has become a major tourist attraction in London.

After the funeral of the princess, the city of London was faced with cleaning up the acres and acres of deteriorating memorabilia. Armies of volunteers washed and cleaned the stuffed animals, pillows, and quilts, which then were distributed to hospitals, nursing homes, and orphanages. Flowers were composted and the collected books of condolence were turned over to the Spencer family, which has stored them at the family estate, Althorp.

Charles Spencer, brother of the princess, established a museum and memorial to Diana on the grounds of the estate, which is open to the public in the summer.[15] The former stable displays artifacts from the princess's early life as well as some of her famous gowns, including her wedding gown. The princess was buried in a private ceremony on a small island in the middle of a lake on the property, and visitors to the estate can walk the short distance from the magnificent house and adjacent museum to the lake. A small pavilion on the shore of the lake has been turned into a shrine for Diana, where visitors leave their bouquets and other mementos that they have brought for this purpose.

Two years after the death of Princess Diana, two more American tragedies and their associated spontaneous shrines received international news coverage—the school shootings at Columbine High School in Littleton, Colorado (April 20, 1999), where thirteen people were murdered, and the collapse of the bonfire at a student rally at Texas A&M University (November 18, 1999), which killed twelve students. It is instructive to compare the two violent events, although the deaths at Columbine High School were the result of deliberate murder and the bonfire collapse was an unfortunate accident resulting from flawed design and student inexperience. Both events took place on their respective campuses, in totally familiar surroundings, and almost the same number of people died in each event. The shocked and grieved public reaction to both was partially expressed through the creation of spectacular spontaneous shrines. The artifacts left at the shrines—in addition to the expected flowers and candles and religious items—were distinctively adapted for each site. The shrine at Texas A&M University contained a high percentage of university-related items, ranging from Corps of Cadets insignia to football tickets to clothing emblazoned with school logos and colors. The Columbine shrine contained a large number of school-related items also, not only from Columbine but from other area high schools. These two artifact assemblages make it clear that each shrine, although containing predictable items from the general popular culture repertoire, is customized and localized to reflect the specific event and the individuals who were killed. This pattern of distinctiveness emerges over and over as scholars examine the shrine phenomenon and publish lists of the articles contained. For example, the Vietnam Veterans Memorial shrine contains an abundance of military-related items as well as patriotic items such as American flags. The shrine at National Aeronautics and Space Administration following the explosion of the Columbia space shuttle on February 1, 2003, contained toy shuttles as well as Israeli flags in honor of the Israeli astronaut who was killed.

The shrine at the edge of the lake where Susan Smith drowned her two sons on October 25, 1994, was filled primarily with children's toys.[16] On June 30, 2000, eight fans were crushed to death during a Pearl Jam concert in Roskilde, Denmark, when people in the unruly crowd began "surfing" (i.e., being handed from person to person above the heads of the crowd) and the rest of the crowd surged forward, crushing some of those in the "mosh pit" against the stage. The spontaneous shrine that developed in the pit later that night reflected the nature of the event. Beer cans, drug paraphernalia, Pearl Jam T-shirts, flags, blue jeans, and folding chairs were placed among the myriad candles and flowers that had been brought to the site. And yet another example: On February 18, 2001, popular race car driver Dale Earnhardt, "The Intimidator," was killed in a crash during the last lap of the Daytona 500 NASCAR race. Fans throughout the country created spontaneous shrines in his memory, and the main items in these shrines were direct references to Earnhardt, especially pictures and models of his black car with the number 3 clearly visible. The selectivity and care exercised in choosing items to place in these shrines make it clear that these sacred sites may be spontaneous, but they certainly are not makeshift or random.

The most recent and widely publicized spontaneous shrines to date are those that developed at various sites following the terrorist attacks of 9/11. New Yorkers responded to the destruction of the World Trade Center by creating shrines at a variety of sites, ranging from Washington Square and nearby churches to fire stations throughout the city.[17] Visitors to the city came to the shrines and added their mementos to them. U.S. embassies around the world were turned into shrine sites in sympathy and solidarity for what had happened to the United States.

The earliest and most distinctive public response in various locations throughout New York City was the posting of scanned and xeroxed pictures of missing loved ones, which were treated as sacred icons by those who stopped to view them and ended up weeping and praying for people that they had never met. These photocopied snapshots and portraits reinforced the function of spontaneous shrines as sites for communication between the living and the dead.

Shrines at the entrances of fire stations and elsewhere throughout the city helped to symbolically reduce the huge catastrophe site to a more comprehensible scale. The Pentagon and the Flight 93 site near Shanksville, Pennsylvania, on the other hand, were compact enough to attract shrines at a single location near each site. Tourists and mourners constantly visit the Flight 93 site and continue to leave mementos there; this pilgrimage will probably continue for the foreseeable future, just as is the case at Oklahoma City.[18]

ARTIFACTS IN SPONTANEOUS SHRINES

One of the distinguishing characteristics of spontaneous shrines is the extraordinary profusion and variety of items that they contain. Most of these items are drawn from the commonplace inventory of whatever is available from such franchises as WalMart and Target. Examinations of the contents of scores of shrines reveal a fairly consistent repertoire of such items among the almost infinite range of idiosyncratic and one-of-a-kind artifacts.

Candles, both votive and other types as well, are ubiquitous in shrine assemblages, and someone often lights these candles at night and replaces them when they melt away. These candles echo the lighting of votive candles in various churches as well as the candles on altars. Crosses and rosaries, saints' medallions and angel figurines, Bibles and various religious tracts, are common offerings in shrines. Scripture—either by the quoted text or by chapter and verse reference—is included in various messages, ranging from large posters to printed tracts to graffiti.[19] The content of many poems and personal messages to the dead also is grounded in Christian belief in salvation and the hereafter. Photographs of the dead are also common.

Like candles, real and artificial flowers are almost universal among the offerings found in spontaneous shrines. The flowers left in such profusion for Princess Diana were primarily common varieties, such as roses and carnations, bought as prepackaged bouquets from local shops. Of course, when gardens are in season, people leave hand-picked flowers at shrines as well. Single blossoms, often long-stemmed roses, are also common.

We expect religious iconography in response to death. But spontaneous shrines, because they are vernacular and thus outside the social conventions that govern formal religious observances such as funerals, contain infinitely more than flowers, candles, rosaries, and crosses. Mourners bring everything from teddy bears to diplomas to T-shirts to bottles of beer and on and on, leaving these idiosyncratic offerings to bear silent, enigmatic witness to their grief. The collection of artifacts from the Vietnam Veterans Memorial best demonstrates the almost infinite range of shrine artifacts. In that collection among the thousands and thousands of archived artifacts are items such as flags, newspaper clippings, live ammunition, coins and currency, rosaries, Spam, baby pacifiers, unsmoked cigars, wedding rings, bags of dirt, and even a full-size, working motorcycle. To someone viewing the contents of a shrine, these offerings at first may seem random and perhaps inappropriate. Only the person who left the item truly knows why it becomes part of the overall shrine.

Of all the categories of artifacts left at spontaneous shrines, plush toy animals in general and teddy bears in particular have drawn the most attention but, paradoxically, are the least understood offerings. The history of the teddy bear and why the toy is named after President Theodore Roosevelt is well known. Basically, the toy was developed to commemorate Roosevelt's refusal in 1902 to shoot a captive bear cub during one of his western hunting expeditions. The toy has since captured the hearts of millions of children and adults around the world, but especially in the United States and England.

There are probably a variety of reasons why people leave teddy bears in spontaneous shrines. Over the years, the cuddly plush toys have become "emotional comfort food" for both children and many adults, especially in the aftermath of violence and trauma. In the United States, various police units, ambulances, hospitals, and battered women's shelters keep a supply of teddy bears to give to frightened children in order to calm them. When family possessions are wiped out in fires or natural disasters, teddy bears almost invariably are included in the goods donated to families with children. The association with comfort and the innocence of childhood provides one possible explanation for the practice of leaving teddy bears at shrines, especially when children have been killed.[20] As pointed out in an article in the *Quarterly Journal of Speech,* the deaths of children are especially traumatic in our culture:

> [T]here is much in common between public mourning at twentieth-century shrines and the private grief rituals of the nineteenth century. . . . Then, as now, the death of a child was the most unacceptable and disturbing death and provoked an increased need to find active expressions of grief. . . . In the twentieth-century shrines we can see that same lingering hope in the hallowing of the site where the special child crosses over to a heaven that is basically a continuation of earthly life.[21]

There is no way to know when the first teddy bear was left as a grief offering at a spontaneous shrine, but some key events shed light on the phenomenon. After the death of Elvis Presley in 1977, grieving, hysterical fans practically mobbed Graceland in their need to get as close as possible to "The King." Teddy bears were common at the shrine that developed along the base of the wall surrounding the estate.[22] One explanation for the inclusion of the toys might be a symbolic response to Presley's popular 1957 recording, "Just Let Me Be Your Teddy Bear."

When the Alfred P. Murrah Federal Building in Oklahoma City was bombed on April 19, 1995, most of the children in the building's day-care center were killed or injured and the photograph of a fireman tenderly cradling one of the dead toddlers became the iconic image of that terrorist disaster. The deaths of these children tore at the hearts of the citizens of Oklahoma and the rest of the country. Thousands of teddy bears and other children's toys were deposited at the spontaneous shrine at the site to acknowledge the dead children as well as the adults who were killed.[23]

Princess Diana, a patron of many children's hospitals and other benevolent organizations, was frequently photographed comforting ill and injured children. Her association with the world's children is probably the reason why so many teddy bears and other stuffed animals became part of the various shrines erected in her memory. When the Diana shrines were being dismantled, as many of these toys as possible were distributed to children in hospitals and orphanages.

After 9/11, citizens throughout the United States sent teddy bears, often by the crate- and truckload, to to be distributed to "the children of New York," causing problems for the city officials who had to decide what to do with this unexpected avalanche of toys. As many of these toys as possible were distributed throughout the city. In some cases, the teddy bears and other toys were simply stacked up outside emergency centers and such for people to take away.

We can only assume that the extensive media coverage of these high-profile spontaneous shrines supports the association of teddy bears and shrines in the minds of the general public, whether children are the victims being memorialized or not. Now, we expect to see teddy bears and other toys in shrines, as incongruous as they may seem. It is their placement in the shrines that transforms these secular, mundane plush stuffed animals into sacred gifts to the dead.

MEDIA SPIN-OFFS

One sign that spontaneous shrines have become an expected, common response to tragedy in the United States is their appearance in the entertainment media. After 9/11 shrines were featured in such popular venues as the television program's *West Wing* (NBC, September 24, 2003) and *CSI: Miami* (CBS, October 13, 2003). Images of shrines are an effective rhetorical device with which to conclude a dramatic episode involving the violent death of one of the characters. In *West Wing,* the season premier dealt with the kidnapping of the president's daughter. A shrine along the fence of the White House was depicted behind the credits, indicating the probable death of the kidnapped daughter. Likewise, in *CSI: Miami,* the episode concluded with images of a small cross and shrine at a riverbank and characters throwing white roses into the water in memory of another kidnapping victim. Lighted candles in a spontaneous shrine were the focus of the concluding episode of the movie *Pay It Forward,* released in 2000, apparently to put the murder of the young protagonist into a sacrificial, devotional context. Car headlights stretching down the hill toward the town below invoked images of the candlelight vigils and parades that have become such an integral part of the contemporary grieving process in reaction to violence and trauma.

In the news media, roadside crosses and spontaneous shrines frequently serve as backdrops for television reporters who are broadcasting from a scene of violence and death, thus reinforcing the emotional impact of the reporter's commentary. Newspapers and magazines also feature photographs of roadside crosses and spontaneous shrines to illustrate news stories about fatal accidents and other traumatic deaths.

PUBLIC MEMORIALIZATION IN THE CONTEMPORARY WORLD

The human need to memorialize the deaths of both loved ones and strangers extends beyond spontaneous shrines and cemeteries into other venues as well. Some of these forms of public memorialization are quite old and others reflect the latest technological advances. Here I discuss some of the most prevalent and look at their relationship to the spontaneous shrine phenomenon.

Cybermemorials

The ubiquitous nature of the Internet is utilized in the creation of memorial Web sites, which scholars have designated by various names, including "virtual memorial" and "cybermemorial."[24] In addition to using photographs of the deceased and appropriate music, some of these memorial Web sites are interactive so that viewers can "sign" a virtual condolence book, "light" a virtual candle, or, more important, leave a message. The virtual nature of these offerings does not diminish their authenticity. The grief of mourners seated at their computers can be just as heartfelt as that of mourners who visit spontaneous shrines in person, and people are comforted by becoming part of the larger grief process through interaction with cybermemorials. An exhibition review of the Vietnam Veterans Virtual Wall discusses the effectiveness of the cybermemorial, especially the leaving of messages:

> Clearly, people use these sites in ways for which the real wall was not designed. The stories told here are designed for public examination. They are messages *about* the dead and those they left behind, not private letters written *to* or objects left *for* those lost in Vietnam. Virtual walls thus are more conducive to communication and allow users to create and pursue stories that they cannot share at the real wall. The Vietnam Veterans Memorial's physical limitations are at least partially overcome by the cybermemorial's less constricted venue.[25]

Although most of these memorial Web sites are put up by the mourners themselves, some Web entrepreneurs will create them for customers at a nominal fee. A similar entrepreneurial spirit is exhibited by Web sites that offer ready-made crosses for sale to those who want to erect them at car wreck sites but do not want to make the crosses themselves. The online urge to make a financial profit exists in the real world also, as demonstrated by the souvenir kiosks selling WTC kitsch. Such money-making schemes have not been particularly successful, especially those online, and some audiences regard them as offensive.

Roadside Crosses

Roadside crosses that mark the sites of fatal car wrecks are not only the most widely distributed of vernacular shrines, but also the most deeply rooted in history.[26] Roadside crosses are an integral feature of the cultural landscape throughout Central America, Mexico, and the Hispanic southwestern United States. Many scholars trace the widespread contemporary roadside cross tradition to this older Hispanic cultural practice, which is grounded in vernacular Catholicism and the custom of marking with a small cross those places where pallbearers put down the casket and rested on the way to the cemetery.[27] These shrine crosses must be distinguished from other common categories of roadside crosses, namely the evangelizing "Get Right with God" crosses that dot the southern U.S. landscape, the devotional Penitente crosses of New Mexico, fields of crosses that are set up periodically as an antiabortion protest, and other types.[28] The crosses that mark fatal car wrecks are small spontaneous shrines, set up and tended by the families and friends of those who were killed. Few passers-by, other than researchers and photographers, ever stop and look carefully at these small crosses and associated memorabilia. The memorabilia resemble those left at larger spontaneous shrines, although one significant difference is that many roadside shrines contain automobile parts and other references to the fatal accident. Motorists are the main audience for the crosses. State and local authorities throughout the country have differing opinions about the safety and legality of these crosses when placed on state and federal property (i.e., road right-of-ways); some areas try to ban the crosses completely while others offer to put up uniform markers. Some authorities regard the crosses as a warning to the public that the roadway is dangerous, but others regard them as a dangerous distraction to motorists. The public generally ignores any official pronouncements and puts up the crosses as personal sites for mourning and remembrance, thus creating a dialog between the vernacular process and official attempts at control. In some cases, whenever the authorities remove one of these crosses, the mourners put up another in its place. Other crosses have stayed in place for years.

A significant difference between roadside crosses and larger, more elaborate shrines at other sites of tragedy and disaster is that roadside crosses are set up and tended by friends and families of the deceased, whereas the larger spontaneous shrines attract visitors and mourners who have no personal relationship to any of the dead. People can and do feel grief and a sense of personal loss in the aftermath of tragedy and disaster that strike strangers halfway across the globe. The hundreds of thousands of visitors who come to Oklahoma City by the busload and leave behind their memorabilia generally did not know any of the people who were killed or injured in the terrorist bombing of the federal building. Neither did most of the mourners who left memorabilia after the death of Princess Diana know her personally, but they felt a bond with her nevertheless, probably because of the extensive media coverage of practically every aspect of her life. Both grieving pilgrims and tourists flock by the thousands to such shrines as Elvis Presley's Graceland and Princess Diana's family home of Althorp. The grave of cult musician Jim Morrison in Père Lachaise Cemetery in Paris is a pilgrimage destination for fans as well as curiosity seekers.

Project AIDS Memorial Quilt

Public memorials to the dead—both known and unknown—continue to evolve into more and more creative and interactive forms. For example, in order to draw public attention to the AIDS epidemic, as well as memorialize loved ones, the NAMES Project AIDS Memorial Quilt was started in 1987.[29] In a well-coordinated project, friends and families created thousands of grave-sized (three feet by six feet), individualized quilt panels to honor loved ones who died of AIDS. Each panel reflects and celebrates an individual life in idiosyncratic ways, just as the content of spontaneous shrines is customized to reflect the event and/or the individuals being memorialized. When the panels are spread out and exhibited together, they visually proclaim the enormous loss of life that this epidemic has claimed. These assemblages are expressions of communal grief, just as are the spontaneous shrines. The combined panels together have much the same effect on viewers as the pictures placed on "Walls of the Missing" following the 9/11 attacks on the World Trade Center, the engraved names of the thousands of dead on the Vietnam Veterans Memorial, and the room in the Oklahoma City National Memorial museum containing the names and portraits of the 168 victims of the bombing. By 2000, the quilt, to which panels are constantly being added, contained more than 45,000 panels, each representing one beloved individual lost to AIDS.

Urban Murals

Yet another artistic expression of public memorialization is the elaborate murals that are painted on city walls in memory of people who have died, usually from gang-related shootings and other varieties of urban violence.[30] There are also wall murals dedicated to victims of car wrecks, AIDS, and even middle-aged heart attack victims. Generally painted on walls near the spot where the death took place, these dramatic, colorful murals are created in the same ecstatic, free-flowing style as the spray-painted graffiti that festoons subway cars in many cities, especially New York City. Many murals reflect a distinctly Hispanic aesthetic flair. The walls are integral parts of the communities in which they are displayed. According to Martha Cooper and Joseph Sciorra, who have documented the memorial walls of New York City:

> The memorial wall transforms personal grief into shared public sentiment by serving as a vehicle for community affiliation and potential empowerment. Covering the expenses for materials and the artist's labor is often a collective endeavor, with neighborhood residents making contributions in memory of one of their own. The murals create new public spaces for community ceremony. Life is celebrated at the walls with parties marking anniversaries and birthdays. These centers of congregation become rallying points for candlelight processions and demonstrations held by community people who march through the streets in opposition to violence, drugs, or police brutality.[31]

Frequently, memorial wall murals become sites for spontaneous shrines as mourners leave personal memorabilia at the bases of the walls.

CONCLUSION

What does this contemporary, vernacular public memorialization mean? Clearly, spontaneous shrines, roadside crosses, and urban murals express the communal sense of loss and disruption experienced not only by close friends and family but also by strangers who feel a connection with those who have died violently. Because the shrines usually are created at or near the site of the violent deaths, they sanctify or hallow the site and provide a temporary space where the living can feel a sense of communion with those who died there. The disruptive violence in which people died is mediated by the quiet act of placing a memento in the shrine. Paradoxically, by creating shrines, mourners also can silently but eloquently protest and express their outrage or bewilderment at the terrorism and senseless murder taking place in their midst. For example, in his study *Signs of War and Peace: Social Conflict and the Use of Public Symbols in Northern Ireland,* folklorist Jack Santino documented spontaneous shrines in Ireland that "are created by regular, everyday people who feel a need to commemorate the loss of a life, to call attention to how the life was lost, and to consecrate the place where the unthinkable happened."[32] Protest and other conflicting feelings in the midst of grief are most often expressed in the notes and other written messages that mourners leave behind. For example, a study of the "strategies of redemption" contained in messages left at the Vietnam Veterans Memorial reported:

> These messages are not carefully prepared so that other visitors may read them. Often, they are scrawled on notebook paper or the back of a map in the heat of the instant, then dropped

> to the ground. They are introspective, sometimes written as though to a departed friend. At other times they are addressed to no one at all. What they have in common is grief, and the need to visit the Memorial as part of the healing process.[33]

Contemporary spontaneous shrines at sites of tragedy are the most recent development in human death ritual in the West. As we have seen, these spontaneous, public responses to grief are often associated with official government or private memorials. In the case of the Vietnam Veterans Memorial, the official site came first and was later expanded through the spontaneous offerings of mourners. Today spontaneous shrines at disaster sites like the fence at Oklahoma City's Murrah building are the first impulse, and later official planning committees, recognizing the sacrality that the public has invested in these sites, will incorporate them into official memorials. Other forms of public memorialization, such as cybershrines, roadside crosses, wall murals, and moving memorials, exhibit varying degrees of institutional sponsorship and public spontaneity. Rather than maintaining a strict differentiation between the official memorial and the spontaneous shrine, these forms of public memorialization are better understood as dynamically related phenomenona.

Even though many shrines contain distinctive Christian symbols, in general the shrines are the expression of an overriding sacred impulse to acknowledge the dead that transcends any particular denomination. Part of our shared humanity is feeling a sense of loss from the deaths of our fellow humans. We mark the passing of friends, loved ones, and even strangers with heightened action, or ritual. In contemporary American and European society religion is losing much of its dominance and control. As a result, most rituals associated with death that were formerly performed at home or in a religious setting now are closely controlled by hospitals, funeral homes, and other secular authorities. The shrines also provide an opportunity to perform a ritualized action of placing an object, an offering, at the shrine. These mementos are the material, tactile expression of a grief that is too deep for words. Because spontaneous shrines are public, they allow people to express grief and outrage for the passing not only of loved ones but also of strangers. According to sociologist C. Allen Haney and his colleagues:

> Spontaneous memorialization suggests . . . the effort to reinvest ritual with new meaning by moving ritual into the public sphere, by acknowledging the fears and losses felt by the members of the larger community, by reinserting the importance of the individual through emphasizing both individual qualities of the deceased and individual needs of the survivors, by enlarging the definition of those impacted by a death to include previously excluded groups, and by acknowledging the social issues implied in violent deaths through allowing the grieving to be done in public without institutional guidance.[34]

Societies are constantly evolving so we should not be surprised when old rituals change or new ones emerge in order to be consistent with contemporary norms and values. Spontaneous shrines and other forms of public memorialization, such as roadside crosses, cybershrines, the AIDS quilt, and urban wall murals, all help mourners express their grief, outrage, and bewilderment in the presence of violent and unexpected death.

NOTES

1. Among the most significant studies of Princess Diana's death are *Mourning Diana: Nation, Culture and the Performance of Grief,* ed. Adrian Kear and Deborah Steinberg (London: Routledge, 1999); Robert Turnock, *Interpreting Diana: Television Audiences and the Death of a Princess* (London: British Film Institute, 2000); and *The Mourning for Diana,* ed. Tony Walter (Oxford: Berg, 1999).

2. For more information, see Susanne Greennhalgh, "Our Lady of Flowers: The Ambiguous Politics of Diana's Floral Revolution," in *Mourning Diana: Nation, Culture and the Performance of Grief,* ed. Adrian Kear and Deborah Steinberg, 40–59 (London: Routledge, 1999); and Anne Rowbottom, "A Bridge of Flowers," in *The Mourning for Diana,* ed. Tony Walter, 157–172 (Oxford: Berg, 1999).

3. Joel Brereton, "Sacred Space," in *The Encyclopedia of Religion,* ed. Mircea Eliade, 12: 534 (New York: Macmillan, 1987).

4. Paul Courtright, "Shrines," in *The Encyclopedia of Religion,* ed. Mircea Eliade, 13: 302 (New York: Macmillan, 1987).

5. See, for example, Travis Cunningham, "Increase in Grave Items Raises Grounds Maintenance Concerns: Mementos Present Dilemma for Cemeteries," *American Cemetery* 73, no. 3 (March 2001): 22–23; and Grey Gundaker, "Halloween Imagery in Two Southern Settings," in *Halloween and Other Festivals of Death and Life,* ed. Jack Santino, 247–266 (Knoxville: University of Tennessee Press, 1994).

6. Folklorist Jack Santino coined the term "spontaneous shrine" in the catalog for a photo exhibit in Northern Ireland: "'Not an Unimportant Failure': Spontaneous Shrines and Rites of Death and Politics in Northern Ireland," in *Displayed in Mortal Light,* ed. Michael McCaughan (Antrim: Antrim Arts Council, 1992).

7. Edward Linenthal, *Sacred Ground: Americans and Their Battlefields* (Urbana: University of Illinois Press, 1991), 3.

8. Jeffrey Durbin, "Expressions of Mass Grief and Mourning: The Material Culture of Makeshift Memorials," *Material Culture* 35, no. 2 (Fall 2003): 22–43.

9. Petula Dvorak, "Residents Say 'Enough' to Makeshift Shrines," *Washington Post,* November 30, 2002.

10. http://americanhistory.si.edu/september11.

11. Kristin Hass, *Carried to the Wall: American Memory and the Vietnam Veterans Memorial* (Los Angeles: University of California Press, 1998). A dramatic large-format picture book with minimal text depicting memorabilia left at the memorial is Thomas B. Allen, *Offerings at the Wall: Artifacts from the Vietnam Veterans Memorial Collection* (Atlanta: Turner, 1995).

12. See Grace Davie, "'You'll Never Walk Alone': The Ainsfield Pilgrimage," in *Pilgrimage in Popular Culture,* ed. Ian Reader and Tony Walter, 201–219 (New York: Macmillan, 1993); and Tony Walter, "The Mourning After Hillsborough." *Sociological Review* 39, no. 3 (August 1991): 599–625.

13. Walter, "The Mourning After Hillsborough," 616.

14. Davie, "'You'll Never Walk Alone.'"

15. www.althorp.com.

16. For an overview, see George Rekers, *Susan Smith: Victim or Murderer* (Lakewood, CO: Glenbridge, 1996). The Smith shrine is also described in Erika Doss, "Death, Art, and Memory in the Public Sphere: The Visual and Material Culture of Grief in Contemporary America," *Mortality* 7, no. 1 (2002): 63–82.

17. Tony Hendra, ed., *Brotherhood* (New York: American Express, 2001).

18. The Web sites for these two national shrines are www:flight93memorialproject.org/ and www.oklahomacitynationalmemorial.org/.

19. Chris Harris, "Secular Religion and the Public Response to Diana's Death," in *The Mourning for Diana,* ed. Tony Walter, 97–107 (Oxford: Berg, 1999).

20. The most thorough study of teddy bears in contemporary culture is Elizabeth Lawrence, "The Tamed Wild: Symbolic Bears in American Culture," in *Dominant Symbols in Popular Culture,* ed. Ray Browne et al., 140–153 (Bowling Green, OH: Bowling Green University Press, 1990).

21. Cheryl Jorgensen-Earp and Lori Lanzilotti, "Public Memory and Private Grief: The Construction of Shrines at the Sites of Public Tragedy," *Quarterly Journal of Speech* 84 (1998): 164.

22. Among the significant studies of Elvis Presley and popular culture are Sue Bridwell Beckham, "Death, Resurrection, and Transformation: The Religious Folklore in Elvis Presley Shrines and Souvenirs," *International Folklore Review* 5 (1987): 88–95; Erika Doss, *Elvis Culture: Fans, Faith, and Image* (Lawrence: University Press of Kansas, 1999); Karal Ann Marling, *Graceland: Going Home with Elvis* (Cambridge: Harvard University Press, 1996); and George Plasketes, *Images of Elvis Presley in American Culture, 1977–1997* (New York: Harrington Park Press, 1997). A study specifically of Elvis shrines is Bill Yenne, *The Field Guide to Elvis Shrines* (Los Angeles: Renaissance Books, 1999).

23. The most thorough study of the Oklahoma City bombing, including the spontaneous shrine, is Edward Linenthal, *The Unfinished Bombing: Oklahoma City in American Memory* (New York: Oxford, 2001).

24. Kenneth Foote, "Virtual Memorials," in *Violence in America: An Encyclopedia,* ed. Ronald Gottesman and Richard Brown, 2: 356 (New York: Scribner's, 1999). The term "cybershrine" is also moving into general usage, primarily among New Age groups and fan clubs of Gothic-themed musical groups.

25. Ed Martini, "Exhibition Review of The Virtual Wall (www.virtualwall.org)," *Journal of American History* 87:3 (December 2000); online at www.historycooperative.org/journals/jah/87.3/exr_8.html.

26. Studies of the roadside cross phenomenon include Holly Everett, *Crossroads: Roadside Cross Assemblages in Contemporary Memorial Culture* (Denton: University of North Texas Press, 2002); Sylvia Grider, "Roadside Shrines," in *Religion and American Cultures: An Encyclopedia of Traditions, Diversity, and Popular Expressions,* ed. Gary Laderman and Luis Leon, 2: 387–388 (Santa Barbara: ABC/CLIO, 2003).

27. See, for example, Rudolfo Anaya et al., *Descansos: An Interrupted Journey* (Albuquerque: El Norte Publications/University of New Mexico Press, 1995); Estevan Arrelano, "Descansos," *New Mexico Magazine* 64 (February 1986): 42–44; and Cynthia Henzel, "*Cruces* in the Roadside Landscape of Northeastern New Mexico," *Journal of Cultural Geography* 11, no. 2 (1995): 93–106.

28. Martha Carver, "Get Right with God: Harrison Mayes' Roadside Advertising Campaign for the Lord," *Journal of the Society for Commercial Archaeology* 18, no. 2 (Fall 2000): 14–19; Marta Weigle, *Brothers of Light, Brothers of Blood: The Penitentes of the Southwest* (Albuquerque: University of New Mexico Press, 1976); and Dennis Kolinski, "Shrines and Crosses in Rural Central Wisconsin," in *Wisconsin Folklore,* ed. James Leary, 445–456 (Milwaukee: University of Wisconsin Press, 1998).

29. Cleve Jones, *Stitching a Revolution: The Making of an Activist* (San Francisco: HarperSanFrancisco, 2000); Cindy Ruskin, *The Quilt: Stories from the NAMES Project* (New York: Pocket Books, 1988).

30. Martha Cooper, and Joseph Sciorra, *R.I.P.: Memorial Wall Art* (New York: Henry Holt, 1994).

31. Cooper and Sciorra, *R.I.P.,* 14.

32. Jack Santino, *Signs of War and Peace: Social Conflict and the Use of Public Symbols in Northern Ireland* (New York: Palgrave, 2001), 76–77.

33. Cheree Carlson, and John Hocking, "Strategies of Redemption at the Vietnam Veterans Memorial," *Western Journal of Speech Communication* 52 (Summer 1988): 210.

34. C. Allen Haney, ChrisTina Leimer, and Juliann Lowery, "Spontaneous Memorialization: Violent Death and Emerging Mourning Ritual," *Omega: Journal of Death and Dying* 35, no. 2 (1997): 169–170.

CHAPTER 12

Disaster, Modernity, and the Media

TONY WALTER

The dominant sociological wisdom about death is that in the modern world death is present in private but absent in public, sequestered and marginalized into hospitals and funeral parlors, with medicine having taken over from religion as the buffer between humankind and death.[1] In a previous article, my colleagues and I disputed this thesis. We argued that death is very much present in the public arena, but the main vehicle transporting it there is not medicine but the mass media, and we looked in particular at the news media and their focus on the emotions of the bereaved following newsworthy deaths.[2] In this chapter, I will look at disasters, the threats they pose to the sense of security we normally feel in a modern society, and the role of the news media both in highlighting these threats and in relegitimating modernity. I will suggest that the news media take on the traditional role of religion in highlighting human frailty, tackling the problem of suffering, and affirming an overarching worldview.[3] In now rather secular Europe, the media typically play this role instead of the churches; in the much more religious United States, they typically play it alongside the churches.

THE DISASTER SCALE

By *disaster,* I mean the nationally or internationally reported violent deaths of more than a few people who, at the moment of death, had been going about their ordinary, everyday, peacetime business—shopping, traveling, going to school. There is a scale along which media audiences identify with those immediately caught up in a disaster. The more everyday the business, and the more the victims are like me or my family, the greater the chance that the disaster could have happened to me, and the more involved I am. American media audiences, for example, were highly involved emotionally in the bombing of the Murrah building in Oklahoma City (1995), the shooting of children at Columbine High School (1999), and the terrorist attacks of September 11, 2001. Earthquakes, fires, floods, random shootings, and terrorist bombs all make an impact on media audiences. Terrorists understand that terror is greatest when they kill and maim ordinary people going about their ordinary business.

A bit along the scale away from this extreme are disasters arising from activities in which some of us engage, but which are inherently dangerous—certain sports, flying (especially travel in an age of international terrorism), and space travel. Examples include the downing of Pan Am 103 over Lockerbie, Scotland, in 1988, and the loss of the space shuttle *Challenger* in 1984 and *Columbia* in 2003.

Further along the scale are disasters in other countries, and at the far end are disasters in third-world countries that are reported in an entirely different way—the dead are definitely not like me, the risks of famine and civil war they face are not risks I face, and media reporting leads me to identify less with the victims than with the heroic bearers of aid from my own, first-world country.[4]

This chapter is concerned with how disaster threatens our modern way of life and how the media deal with our own fears of mortality. It therefore looks primarily at disasters near to home.

FATEFUL MOMENTS

Disasters threaten not only individual lives, but also key elements of modern culture. They are examples of what Anthony Giddens calls "fateful moments," when people are forced to face concerns that the smooth workings of modernity normally keep well out of consciousness. They threaten what Peter Berger terms the *nomos* or sacred canopy, the moral and social order that is constructed to keep anomie and meaninglessness at bay. We know that each individual member of society must die—a celebrity dying in old age, even a domestic murder or a bank robbery gone wrong, is accountable in terms of everyday reasoning and does not challenge the fundamentals of modernity. Disasters, however, can undermine the *nomos* (namely, the idea that our modern world is essentially safe) that has been socially constructed to make mortality bearable. Considerable repair work has to be done to the sacred canopy; a theodicy must be developed that accounts for suffering. Traditionally, religions did this repair work; today, the media are very much involved in it. "Every human society," Berger says, "is, in the last resort, men banded together in the face of death." One way or another, churches, journalists, television audiences, mayors, and presidents band together in the wake of disasters to produce rhetoric and narratives that put the tangled fabric of modernity back together again.[5]

It is misleading to see all complex modern societies as sheltering under one, overarching sacred canopy. More typically there are more than one. In the United States, by far the most religious of the West's large nations, there are the canopies of individual denominations and religions. Second, there is the canopy of American civil religion, including the image of America as the promised land, offering democracy, safety, and prosperity to all who migrate there and (in the less isolationist phases of its history) undertaking a God-given mission to bring democracy and prosperity to the rest of the world. And third, there is the canopy of modernity. Modernity includes values such as progress, rationality, safety, and human perfectibility that, although formally secular, in their elevation to the status of absolute values partake of much of the character of the sacred. In European societies, which lack the American sense of manifest destiny and which—with the exceptions of Ireland and Poland—are much more secular than the United States, it may be that there is just one overarching canopy: secular modernity. In this chapter, I discuss how disasters can threaten three key tenets of modernity: faith in rationality and technique, faith in progress and the future (symbolized by our children), and faith in human goodness.

THREATS TO TECHNIQUE

Modernity could be defined as the systematic use of what Jacques Ellul terms technique —technology and rational organization—in order to control nature for human purposes. The natural world is rendered predictable, human life is rendered comfortable and convenient, and as a result all manner of personal and communal projects can be attempted. Power stations and the national grid enable me to light and heat my study at the flick of a switch; technical ingenuity and mass production have provided me with the computer on which I am word processing this chapter. Sewage, agricultural, and medical technologies have pushed sickness and death into the background; a couple of centuries ago most people my age would not be writing book chapters, they would be dead. It is perhaps appropriate that Ellul has described technique as the major god of the modern era.[6]

Postmodernity could be defined as a still evolving stage in which the technical control of nature becomes so assured that the work ethic that undergirded it may be relaxed. In this view, what is needed today are not factories full of workers but playful consumers with ever-escalating demands.[7] Alternatively, postmodernity can be seen as the preoccupation not with controlling nature, but with using science to control the side effects of the technologies used to control nature: learning how to combat global warming or finding a way to die that uses the best in modern medicine but avoids the dehumanization of the modern hospital.[8] But in both interpretations of postmodernity, the technical conquest of nature is assured. This assumption is challenged only by the deepest of deep ecologists.

Natural Disasters

This modern and postmodern triumphalism is threatened by two kinds of disaster. One is the natural disaster in which, despite the very best technology, many people die. Earthquakes, volcanoes, cyclones, floods, and droughts reveal that the human conquest of nature is not total. Floods and droughts may, of course, demonstrate not only the violence of nature but also the consequences of overweening technology, inept management, and ecological mismanagement: deforestation in the Himalayas may be the cause of floods in Bangladesh; the high death toll in the 1988 Armenian earthquake was attributed largely to the poor construction of Soviet-era apartment blocks. Nevertheless, earthquakes, volcanoes, and cyclones are genuinely natural events, to which even the best-constructed building or the most ecologically sound environment may still be vulnerable. Pictures of vehicles thrown about like toys when an earthquake hits California or Japan are vivid reminders of the basic vulnerability of inhabiting a geologically active planet. Pictures from tornado-hit Florida carry a similar message. Though the threat of natural disaster is significant in such places, it is minimal in the more benign natural environment of northwest Europe; few Europeans feel threatened by an earthquake in Japan, California, or Armenia.

Technological Failure

The accident at the Ukrainian nuclear plant at Chernobyl in 1986 dramatically illustrated technical and organizational failure, analyzed at length in the media: where would the fallout land and is there another nuclear power station elsewhere that may blow its top even more disastrously? The Three Mile Island accident in 1979 raised similar issues for Americans, and accidents at chemical plants, such as Bhopal, India, where three thousand died in 1984, can also affect the surrounding population. The loss of the space shuttles *Challenger* (1984) and *Columbia* (2003) was dramatic, not least because of live pictures and the presence aboard of representative individuals such as schoolteacher Christa McAuliffe. But industrial disasters that directly threaten the general populace are relatively rare in the West. Far more common are transport disasters: London, for example, saw in 1987 the Kings Cross underground station fire (thirty-one dead) and in 1988 the Clapham train crash (thirty-five dead), while the new year of 1989 began with the crash of a Boeing jet at Kegworth a hundred miles north (forty-seven dead).

Not only are transport disasters relatively common, they also can tap into a typically modern intimation of mortality. While nuclear or ecological Armageddon, or possibly a hospital operation, may for some be ultimately more terrifying, fears associated with travel are more everyday and more immediate. As a young man, I felt immortal. But hints of my mortality, or at least of my body's frailty, would come unbidden when I was traveling—and still do. While driving on the interstate or autobahn, I realize with a start that I have not really been concentrating. Stopping at a roadside café, I may briefly ponder the cars hurtling toward each other in opposite directions; what a few minutes ago had been the routine event of driving at that speed now appears only a knife-edge from disaster. A minute more and I am back in everyday consciousness, ordering my coffee and chatting to my companions. On a ferry going across the Channel from England to France, I enjoy the salt air and the anticipation of the holiday to come, but I also look over the side and see the seething green water fifty feet below and wonder: if I should fall overboard, what would be my chances? And when I take off in a jumbo jet, I feel both elation and fear: elation that so many people can be lifted so effortlessly into the sky, fear that if something should go wrong there is little any of us can do to save our lives. Modern means of transport are an awesome demonstration of modernity, of technology overpowering natural limitation. The average human body can walk four miles per hour, and run and swim for short distances. Modern transport transcends this bodily limitation, yet the very same transport can give us intimations of the body's ultimate frailty. When, therefore, a plane, train, car, or boat does come to grief, there is plenty of potential for news audiences to identify with what they see and read.

Human and Organizational Failure

The investigation that inevitably follows such disasters often reveals not technical failure but human or organizational failure. Modernity consists not just of technological wizardry, but of rational organization that ensures that human frailty does not undermine the technology. Modern organization is expected to be fail-safe, with quality control systems detecting and compensating for human error. It is precisely the failure, or absence, of such fail-safe systems that can lead to disaster. The capsize of the roll-on, roll-off car ferry *The Herald of Free Enterprise* just outside the Belgian port of Zeebrugge in 1987 led to the worst death toll for a British vessel in peacetime since the sinking of the *Titanic* in 1912; the eventual verdict pointed not only to a technical design fault (the vulnerability of a large, undivided car deck to just a few inches of water) but also to a fault in operating procedures (leaving port with the bows doors open). Similarly, the Clapham rail disaster revealed not only a technical fault in the signaling but also the pressure and stress under which signal maintenance staff typically operate. Both the *Challenger* and the *Columbia* space shuttle disasters led to allegations that there were organizational failures in the entire safety culture at the National Aeronautics and Space Administration (NASA). The 1989 Hillsborough disaster, in which ninety-four soccer fans died directly in front of television cameras, resulted from an organizational failure in policing the fans in the soccer stadium and possibly also a human error by the commander in charge that day. (Being crushed to death in a crowd is another situation, like everyday travel, of which one may have forebodings. I have experienced the excitement of being in a dense crowd, only the next moment to realize that a marginal increase in pressure would prevent my lungs from expanding.) More worryingly, Diane Vaughan's account of NASA shows how modern organizations routinely manage risk so that the occasional disaster is inevitable not because of the lack of technique, but *because* of technique.[9]

So whether the technology has failed, whether the organization has failed, or whether technique itself cannot save us from disaster, the threat is the same: technique has failed us. And technique is the very lifeblood of modernity. By contrast, most third-world disasters are portrayed as caused by lack of technique; the situation is then saved by technique, in the form of Western airlifts of supplies and doctors. Rather than threatening modernity, such disasters legitimate it.

THREATS TO CHILDREN

At 9:30 AM on Wednesday, March 13, 1996, in the small and hitherto quiet Scottish town of Dunblane, Thomas Hamilton strode into the elementary school, made his way to the school gym, and killed sixteen five- and six-year olds and their teacher, wounding several more before turning his gun on himself. Dunblane seemed to invoke something new, striking a chord in the British nation, and indeed abroad, that I had not before witnessed.

Previous disasters had led to various forms of memoralization for those directly affected. It has become the norm in Britain for well-wishers to bring flowers to the site of a disaster. After the Hillsborough disaster there were various rituals of remembrance for the citizens of Liverpool and for the soccer community nationwide.[10] After Dunblane, however, there was a memorial across the entire nation. Four days later on Mothering Sunday, at 9:30 AM, a one-minute silence was observed on national radio and television, in churches, at McDonald's, and in several supermarket chains; in some places buses and trains stopped; at London's Heathrow airport planes turned off their engines and motorists stopped. In other places and in some families, the silence was observed later in the day. The mass media were indispensable not only in advertising but also in initiating and organizing this tribute.

After other disasters, national leaders have visited the site and/or survivors a day or two later. The formal response to Dunblane was unprecedented, both in its speed and in its unity. As *The Independent* newspaper recorded on Thursday: "Scottish Secretary Michael Forsyth sat in Dunblane yesterday with his Labour shadow, George Robertson, and frankly admitted: 'I cannot find words to express the horror at what has happened in Dunblane here today.' On this occasion, in his loss for words, he spoke for both of them." The next day, the prime minister and the leader of the opposition visited Dunblane together. The presence together of these political opponents expressed the unity that had gripped the nation, this unity being expressed in their loss for words, just as it was by the silence of millions the following Sunday. Queen Elizabeth visited on Mothering Sunday. This is how the front page of the *Daily Mail* reported it the following day, under the headline THE QUEEN WEEPS FOR THE CHILDREN:

> THE QUEEN wept a mother's tears as she carried the grief of the nation to Dunblane yesterday.
>
> The emotions a sovereign tries to hide spilled out when she met parents of the young massacre victims.
>
> She and the Princess Royal were there in an attempt to ease the despair and sorrow of lives torn apart. Instead they found themselves overwhelmed.
>
> . . . . She has not let her public mask drop so dramatically since she wept with the mothers of Aberfan thirty years ago.

Clearly Dunblane had touched a nerve. It was the same nerve touched in 1966 in the Welsh mining village of Aberfan when an unstable coal tip buried an elementary school and adjacent houses, killing 144, of whom 116 were children.[11] Children are valued highly today; we invest in them with reasonable expectation of their outliving their parents and teachers; we believe they are safe in school. The death of a child, mourned in Victorian Britain less than the death of a grandparent, is now seen as the epitome of tragedy.[12] Whereas traditional societies are symbolized by the elders who represent the authority of tradition, modernity is symbolized by the youth who represent the future and progress. The front-page picture run by several newspapers the day after the Dunblane shooting, depicting individual photos of the teacher and each member of her class with their smiling, hopeful young faces, spoke both of innocence and of the future, a future cut short. David Hope, the archbishop of York, wrote in the *Times:* "Any murder is abhorrent, that of a child doubly so. A child is a symbol of hope, a fresh start, new possibilities, a life uncluttered by the failure and the wounds and the deep resentments we adults carry. It seems so cruelly unfair to extinguish such a source of light."[13] Every parent in the land, and many children, must have been appalled. In Sweden, Dunblane led the early evening television news on the day of the shooting. But, unprecedentedly, the newscaster started by directly addressing the children who would inevitably be watching at that time of day, reassuring them that what happened in Scotland was very unusual, that children in Sweden were safe, and that gunmen did not go around attacking them. In Britain, where death education is not on the national curriculum, teachers in many schools that week discussed Dunblane with their classes.

THREATS TO THE BELIEF IN HUMAN GOODNESS

Dunblane, unlike the other disasters I have discussed, also raised the question of the existence of evil. On Friday, March 15, the school's head teacher was headlined in several newspapers as saying, "Our school was visited by evil. Evil visited us yesterday and we don't know why. And we don't understand it and I guess we never will" (*The Times*). Organizational failures may be traced simply to human carelessness or stupidity; no one suggests that the personnel or systems at fault are evil. Terrorists and assassins, even though their deeds may be headlined as evil and irrational, have their own rationales, even if it is not my rationality, while some will sympathize with their cause. Dunblane was a reminder of an aspect of humanity that has no part in modern discourse, a fateful moment if ever there was one.

Modernity is associated with Enlightenment ideas concerning progress and human perfectibility: criminals can be reformed, madmen can be treated, gurus speak of personal growth, and original sin is consigned to the dustbin of an unenlightened past. In media coverage of Dunblane, the premodern idea of evil was resurrected by the media to explain that which, given the national consensus on the value of children, seemed otherwise inexplicable. Child molesters, along with mass and serial murderers, have also been portrayed by the British media as the incarnation of evil.

The media did discuss whether Dunblane indicates a need for reform of the gun control laws, but—at least in the first few days—these discussions all indicated that, even if reform were introduced, nothing can prevent an evil person going on the rampage. Likewise, media discussions about improving security in schools accepted that no security could keep out a really determined and heavily armed intruder.[14] This somewhat despairing discourse is in marked contrast to that following disasters of all other kinds. These are immediately followed by declarations of determination to find the cause of the disaster so that in the future football grounds or roll-on, roll-off ferries will be safe; or they are followed by politicians affirming that security will be improved and the terrorists will never win. Even after truly natural disasters, there is usually plenty of scope for heroic rescue work over the ensuing days, seeking survivors in the rubble of the earthquake or evacuating people from their flooded homes. But immediately after

Dunblane, political leaders and technical experts were at a loss for words. This also was the case after the sinking of the *Estonia* ferry in 1994, to be discussed later.

Immediately after the 1995 Oklahoma City bombing, the press and much of the American public assumed that the perpetrators must have been Islamic extremists. The arrest, a few days later, of the crew-cut American army veteran Timothy McVeigh and his accomplice raised more threatening issues. For many Americans, he became the embodiment of evil. For others, though, he highlighted the dangers of both permissive gun laws and also right-wing propaganda that not only criticized the federal government but called patriots to raise arms against it. In one view, McVeigh was an unnaturally evil individual threatening a country many Americans like to consider the most perfect on earth; in the other view, he revealed a sickness at the very heart of America. Either way, the problem of evil resurfaced in ways difficult to resolve.[15]

UNITY AND DIVISION

Benedict Anderson has argued that the daily ritual of reading national newspapers, knowing that thousands of our fellow citizens are doing the same, helps us imagine ourselves as belonging to a nation. Watching television news performs the same function. When disaster strikes, this effect of belonging to an imagined community of a nation in mourning is heightened, as Edward Linenthal observes in his study of the response to the Oklahoma City bombing. Indeed, if one were to ask what holds a pluralistic, modern industrial society together, even one with multiple sacred canopies, one would have to look at events such as Dunblane, Columbine, Oklahoma City, and 9/11.[16]

Not all British disasters have Dunblane's effect of unifying the nation. When causes for a disaster can be sought and/or found, they can divide people. After the Hillsborough soccer stadium disaster, various acrimonious statements blamed the disaster on the behavior of the Liverpool fans or police incompetence. After the Clapham rail crash, politically divisive questions about the safety implications of government rail policies were raised. After the denationalization of the railways a few years later, subsequent rail crashes continued to raise political questions. The case of Fred and Rosemary West, who serially killed several young women (including some of their own children) before burying them in their back garden at 25 Cromwell Street in Gloucester, was as shocking as Dunblane but came to light over a number of weeks so there was no one moment of shock that could unite people, though socially divisive questions were raised about why police, social workers, and neighbors had not realized earlier what was going on.

Other profoundly divisive disasters include civil rights and antiwar demonstrations in which citizens are shot by their own security forces, such as the four students shot by the National Guard at Kent State University in 1970 and the thirteen Northern Irish civilians shot by the British army on Bloody Sunday in 1972. Terrorist attacks where there is some sympathy for the terrorists' cause, if not for their methods, can also lead to very mixed reactions. Disasters that *did* unify an entire nation include the buried school at Aberfan in 1966, the sinking of the ferry *Estonia* in 1994, and the explosions of the space shuttles *Challenger* and *Columbia.*

PUTTING MODERNITY BACK TOGETHER AGAIN

The picture I have painted seems pretty bleak: disasters do indeed threaten not only life but modernity and the values and security associated with it. They can also shock a nation's sense of itself. The *Estonia* sinking challenged Sweden's sense of itself as the safest nation on earth; Oklahoma City challenged the American Midwest's sense of peace and security; 9/11 challenged America's sense of itself as invulnerable. Newspapers dwell at length on these threats because shocking stories sell. But, having undermined our sense of security, the media's reporting of disaster then goes on to reconstruct it. As Peter Berger was at pains to point out over thirty years ago, religion is in the business of reconstructing the moral and spiritual order in the face of the threats that death, in its various forms, poses for society. I argue that the news media do the same. So how do they do this?

Technological Fixes

When a disaster has been caused by the failure of technology and/or organization, the news media extensively cover the search for a cause and a technical fix that will prevent similar tragedies in the future. From the very first day of coverage, journalists speculate on the possible causes. After the jetliner crashes, the search is on for the black box, and its recordings are reported as soon as they have been analyzed. After tragedies such as the Hillsborough stadium crush, an official enquiry is set up, giving both an interim and a final report some months later. On February 3, 2003, two days after the *Columbia* space shuttle broke up on reentry, newspapers on both sides of the Atlantic headlined the search for causes: "Search for answers begins" (*USA Today*), "Investigators seek clues" (*International Herald Tribune*), "Grim search for clues after shuttle disaster" (*Daily Telegraph*).

One advantage, of course, of focusing on the cause is that it will be days, or even months, until this is ascertained. In the meantime, speculation will sell yet more newspapers, and when the official verdict is finally delivered, the story of the disaster can be run yet again, followed later still by investigative journalism revealing the complacency of the authorities in light of the findings. Where human failure is confirmed, the subsequent rolling of heads makes for yet more news stories. A good news story erupts suddenly, lasts a week or so, and may be revived subsequently; disasters fit this news cycle perfectly.

There are thus good journalistic reasons for focusing on the technical cause of the tragedy and the technical fix that will hopefully prevent future tragedies. But why is the public interested in all this postdisaster analysis? One reason surely is that we want to be reassured that the next sports stadium, ferry, or airplane we enter will be safe. Our trust in technology and technique has been dented, and we want that trust restored. If Ellul is right that technique is the god of modernity, and if technological and organizational disasters raise questions about the credibility of that god, then postdisaster journalism powerfully restores the god of technique to its place of preeminence. Technique may have failed us, but technique will yet save us.[17] In addition, those whose carelessness has sabotaged the efficient functioning of technique may be ritually punished. We may note here that the media seek relatively simple causes with relatively simply solutions, and if an individual manager's head can roll, so much the better. The news media at this point reflect the interests of politicians who need to be seen as in control.

More complex and intractable problems concerning the management of risk in high-technology organizations are usually skated over in the news.[18] By the turn of the millennium, however, the media began to highlight deep-seated problems in the safety culture of large organizations. In the United Kingdom, this became a theme in the reporting of major rail accidents at Ladbrooke Grove and Potters Bar, while in the United States the *Columbia* shuttle disaster of 2003 led to more probing headlines than had the earlier *Challenger* disaster: "SENT TO THEIR DEATHS: NASA ignored warnings that astronauts' lives were at risk" (*Daily Express,* February 3), "NASA ignored shuttle safety" (*London Times,* February 3), "Hard questions on horizon for NASA following disaster" (*USA Today,* February 4).

In the modern world each death has to have a cause. The medieval idea that human life can be cut down at any time by a capricious God has been rejected, and since the nineteenth century all modern societies have insisted on certification stating the cause of each and every death. One way we come to terms with our mortality is to disaggregate it into nine hundred and ninety-nine specific malfunctions of the body.[19] Where no such malfunction is apparent, a postmortem examination must be conducted. The belief that the physical world is ordered and predictable is a defining element of Western science.[20] The possibility, therefore, that airplanes randomly drop out of the sky or trains crash for no reason entails a return to the unpredictability that was left behind with the Middle Ages. Though it is medicine that has promoted this modern antipathy to causeless death, it is the news media that have publicized the (almost always successful) search for causes. Science and medicine take on theology's function of generating a cosmology, while the news media take on the function of church and priest in assuring the populace that the god of technique is still credible and worthy of their trust.

Ordinary Goodness

How did the media put modernity back together again after Dunblane? Even though an official inquiry was immediately set up and there was much talk of tightening the gun laws, there was little faith in a simple technological or political fix. Even with legal changes and improvements in security, it was recognized that little can stop an infanticidal and suicidal maniac. The control that is so central to modernity, and the desire to protect children that is so central to parenthood, could not be guaranteed.

What the tabloid newspapers in fact suggested would save the people of Dunblane from despair was its children. On its front page on Saturday, March 23, the *Daily Mirror* had a full-page picture of a child smiling from her hospital bed with the caption DUNBLANE AMY'S SMILE OF HOPE: "On the day pals returned to school after last week's slaughter, survivor Amy Hutchison grins cheekily in hospital. It was a smile that gave hope for the future. See pages 2, 3, 12, & 13." On page 2, an article headlined FIRST STEPS begins: "Three survivors of the Dunblane massacre showed yesterday that the courage of little children can fight off memories of past evil and bring hope for the future." The story goes on to tell of the courage of the children in hospital, including one who has just left to go home. On page 12, under the headline EVIL HAS LEFT MY SCHOOL, the paper reported:

> As hundreds of pupils streamed back to their desks—some confident, some serious—head teacher Ron Taylor said: "This has been a long, dark week full of tears, and Dunblane is still in mourning.
>
> However, the evil that came last week has gone.
>
> *Strength.* This morning I was walking round the school and came across a group of children laughing and joking together. I went around another corner and found a couple of kids arguing. Normality is returning. . . .
>
> . . . . This marks the beginning of our recovery. And, mark my words, we will recover—I promise you that."

The *Daily Mail* (Saturday, March 16) had already found hope in a young child. It describes five-year-old Rachael Hally (a classmate who survived because she had been home sick the day of the massacre) pleading with her parents to let her visit the hospital where her friends lay sick: "The normally bubbly little girl was subdued. . . . Too young to fully understand what happened, she was aware something was terribly wrong." The article continues: "But the resilience of youth can never be underestimated. Within a few minutes Rachael and her friends were once again playing together, exploring the colorful collection of toys in Ward 17."

The *Daily Express* (Monday, March 18) ran a color picture of the queen wiping away her tears during her visit to Dunblane, with the caption: "But after the tears came hope for the future, when [she] travelled to hospital to meet young survivors." The formula is clear: the only thing that can stanch such terrible evil is the innocence, optimism, laughter, and sheer ordinariness of childhood.[21]

Clive Seale has demonstrated this same formula in reporting on children with cancer, in which children's ordinary heroism is the main source of hope in the face of a dread disease. Indeed, this theme emerges throughout the media's handling of health issues. We live increasingly in a culture of manufactured fear, especially fear of health problems. The media offers not just technical advances in medicine to alleviate our fears but also the ordinary goodness and the ordinary heroism of individuals as the main source of comfort.[22] It appears then that media coverage of disaster and of health problems relies on the same formula for fixing modernity—technical fixes plus ordinary goodness.

After many disasters, the media affirm the ordinary, and sometimes extraordinary, goodness of the local community. Stories of the heroism of rescue workers, notably after the Oklahoma City bombing and 9/11, abound. There are also stories and photos of acts of kindness from strangers and of communities that come together to help the afflicted across ethnic, class, and religious divisions. Such stories, which were as prevalent in the media coverage after 9/11 as stories of the victims' pain, constitute what Linenthal terms "the progressive narrative" in which the goodness of ordinary citizens shines through in the bleakest of hours. It is this narrative of hope that news editors assume their audiences want to hear, rather than "the toxic narrative" of wounds that never heal.[23]

Many disaster stories and pictures depict traditional images of comfort, such as strong male figures comforting women and children, who in turn collapse in tears. Male authority figures such as policemen, firemen, and head teachers stand firm and dry-eyed, supporting the distraught. Women do the emotional labor on behalf of courageous men.[24] After the 2001 Selby rail crash, the main regional paper ran a picture with the caption, "COMFORT: An emergency worker hugs the train driver's widow, Mary Dunn, as she in turn comforts one of her sons at the site of the crash." On another page, a story runs, "Nine-year-old James Dunn, the son of freight train driver Stephen Dunn, 39, who lost his life, held tightly onto the hand of Superintendent Tony Thompson of British Transport Police."[25] There is always someone strong enough to hold us, and there is always someone vulnerable enough to cry for us, and these characters in the story reflect traditional hierarchies of age, status, and gender. In third-world disasters, the script primarily depicts first-world relief teams rushing to the aid of helpless victims, thus reinforcing conventional notions of Western supremacy and benevolence and third-world dependency.[26] Through such traditional images and narratives of strength the modern world is put back together—in the media images, if not for the survivors and victims themselves.

The Construction of Mindlessness

That an individual such as Thomas Hamilton, acting entirely on his own, can gun down innocent children is something few will ever understand. Its meaninglessness is a threat to an otherwise ordered world. But there are other violent acts for which their perpetrators have perfectly clear rationales, but which the mainstream press choose not to explicate. During the Cold War, in which the dominant narrative was the clash between two ideologies, terrorism by groups that could not easily be accommodated within this narrative was typically condemned by political leaders as "senseless," "mindless," and "meaningless," condemnations dutifully reported by the mass media. Such politically motivated constructions of specific types of acts as mindless function, I argue in this section, to protect certain key values.[27]

Prior to 1989 the media reporting of terrorist acts also confirmed them as mindless. First, the perpetrators were termed terrorists, rather than guerrilla fighters or freedom fighters. To label someone a terrorist is to define that person in terms of the consequences of their actions, terror, and who but a madman would want to create terror for its own sake? To label someone a freedom fighter is to define that person in terms of a cause—freedom—that is at the heart of modernity.

Second, terrorist acts were depicted as isolated incidents, out of context, with emphasis on the consequences (how many dead, pictures of destroyed property) rather than on the historical antecedents to the incident and its underlying causes. These issues were discussed much later in documentary pieces. The result was that the consequences—terror—were portrayed as fact, while causes were relegated to mere "opinion."

Third, members of terrorist groups were rarely interviewed. During the troubles in Northern Ireland, there was a ban on members of the Irish Republican Army (IRA) and other paramilitary groups being interviewed on UK television and radio; the majority of interviewees were English politicians, all of whom joined to condemn the latest bombing as "pointless."

Much terrorism seems to be rooted, ultimately, in the inherent contradictions of democracy. Democracy allows 51 percent of the population to dominate the other 49 percent, and in Northern Ireland for much of the twentieth century this permanently excluded the considerable Catholic minority from political power. Toward the end of the century, many subregions within nation states discovered that democratic self-determination is fine for an entire nation state but not for subregions within it. Such were the powerful sources of terrorist activity by, for example, the IRA and ETA (Euskadi Ta Askatasuna). The logic of their cause pointed directly to contradictions within the structures of democracy. The media's characterization of their acts as "mindless" was much less threatening to the core value of democracy than would be a serious consideration of terrorism's causes. The Cold War was being fought in the name of democracy, so democracy had to be kept on its pedestal. Anyone who attacked the West and was not a Soviet ally must be mad.

Since 1989, however, the news media seem to me to have given considerable airtime and column inches to the underlying causes of terrorism.[28] In addition, the Internet now makes it much easier to find such background information. When on June 7, 2003, I typed *Al Qaeda* into the Google search engine, the top two items were highly informative articles about Al Qaeda, including interviews with its supporters. Certainly after 9/11, much media attention was paid to the possible motives of the attackers, with many stories addressing the question many Americans were asking: "Why do they hate us so?" There was doubtless much disinformation about the attackers' motives, but the main narrative in the American media—a sustained assault by a nexus of evil upon American values and democracy—was very different from narratives about the "mindless" Cold War terrorist. Indeed, the Cold War has now been replaced by a war on terrorism, terrorism being defined as unannounced attacks on Americans, American interests, and American allies.

Theodicy

In most disasters, the news media relegitimate modernity by declaring that rationality and technique will win out in the end. Following mass murders and certain other atrocities, attempts to restore faith and trust are more symbolic than practical, with pictures of smiling children and strong policemen rather than talk of public inquiries. After terrorist attacks, the declarations are made by a government that is resolutely determined to root out the terrorists. Like churches that preach hellfire and damnation, the media first scare us to death and then offer salvation and comfort.[29] This formula has traditionally been the terrain of religion, and just as its use can reinforce the power of religion so it is effective in selling newspapers.

I am speaking here about comfort for the media audience as a whole. There is considerable evidence that media reporting of disasters can exacerbate the suffering of individual victims, survivors, and mourners. Some may feel pride that their loved ones are publicly acknowledged but hurt that their words have been manipulated to create a story that will sell. Or the media may drop the story when it is still very much on the mind of those suffering personally, who feel that society has gawked at their suffering and then abandoned them. Then, later, when they are trying to forget the tragedy and get on with their lives, the disaster becomes front-page news again because of some new finding or because the official enquiry is published. What may comfort the population at large may totally fail to comfort those directly involved in the disaster.[30]

Just as the prevalence of suffering poses a tricky problem for religions that posit the existence of one loving God,[31] so disasters that threaten children and that raise the specter of unadulterated evil raise tricky problems for modernity. Indeed, as I understand it, this is the challenge presented in Zygmunt Bauman's book *Modernity and the Holocaust,* in which he argues that the evil of the Final Solution was no aberration but the very epitome of rational and technical organization.[32] The realization that rational organization can be used for evil purposes poses a major problem for modernism as a belief system premised on progress and optimism about human nature. The continued existence of evil is an unresolved contradiction in modernity, just as suffering is unresolved in Christian theology.

Discourses about evil in the American media and by American leaders are more explicit, and more hopeful, than in the United Kingdom. In the United States, as noted at the beginning of this chapter, the sacred canopies of American civil religion and of fundamentalism both offer a useful narrative of evil and redemption. After 9/11, President Bush used this discourse to initiate a holy war against evil around the world, a theme readily taken up by the American media. Indeed, the American media paid little attention to those who thought differently, knowing that most Americans wanted to hear this message of renewed vigor in the nation, hope for the future, and assurance of a military fix. Christianity's solution to the problem of evil is to locate it within the human race, so that sin and its conquest lie at the heart of Christian theology. And by extension, they lie at the heart of the vision of America as the promised land. President Bush was able to draw on this double symbolism in his rhetoric of the "war against terrorism." Lacking such symbolism, many Europeans and their newspapers opposed the war, fearing that George Bush would become more of a threat to world peace than Al Qaeda.

Though faith traditions in the United States retain greater authority to mediate disasters, even in secular Europe the media are not entirely alone in repairing the holes that disasters rip in the sacred canopy of modernity. Religious institutions are still important sources of solace and reordering if they can articulate the feelings of the local community, as was, for example, the case in Liverpool after the Hillsborough disaster and in Dunblane. A significant role for the churches is possible when many or all of the dead come from the same community, when there is a significant religious presence in that community, and when there is a religious building such as a cathedral that symbolizes not only faith but also the town or city itself. All three of these factors were present in Liverpool and in Dunblane. Televised relays of church services, and press reports of them, can also function to bring in a wider audience: fourteen days after the 1988 crash of Pam Am 103 over the Scottish town of Lockerbie, BBC television abandoned its scheduled program to relay live the memorial service in Lockerbie's parish church. So the media and formal religion can work together to repair the canopy.

There are very rare occasions when journalists and political leaders cannot respond adequately to disasters and the traditional role of formal religion is restored. Dunblane and Hillsborough came close to this,[33] but a clearer example occurred in Sweden in 1994 immediately following the sinking of the *Estonia* ferry with the loss of 852 lives. Radio and television newscasters were at a loss for words and/or overcome by tears, and they turned for comment not to technical experts but to church leaders. In secular Sweden, where technique is so efficient that Swedes cherish their country as the safest on earth, the shock was so great that, for a while at least, both journalists, and many citizens relied on the Church of Sweden for comfort. The one group of authority figures who remained calm and were not shown crying were priests, bishops, and archbishops. One scholar remarked on the regained status of the church by stating: "Sweden, what is that? At 5 pm on this Wednesday, Sweden is an electronic crisis group under Archbishop Gunnar Weman's gentle chairmanship. Unbelievers as well as believers are equally welcome."[34]

In Europe, with its state churches, religion used to provide the Durkheimian function of articulating the *conscience collectif* of an entire society, but with the extension of democracy this has been supplanted by politics—leaving religion to articulate personal rather than public belief. But where democracy breaks down and/or where groups feel they have no adequate political representation (Northern Ireland, Poland under Russian domination, or, to a much lesser extent, the Scots under English domination), religion can remain a powerful articulator of group identity. My argument in this chapter is similar. The mass media have generally taken over from religion the task of theodicy, the task of interpreting the meaning of death and suffering. But when the media are not up to the task, notably when the tragedy is so huge or so evil, that even television newscasters cannot cope and remain composed, then churches and church leaders may return to fill the vacuum.

In the United States, despite the separation of church and state, the president is much more likely than European political leaders to use religious language in a wide range of speeches, and not least after disaster. After the 2003 *Columbia* shuttle disaster, President Bush paid tribute to the crew's courage and after quoting from the Bible added: "The same creator who names the stars also knows the names of the seven souls who died. We can pray that all are safely home."[35] In the United States, the theodicies purveyed by political leaders, mass media, and churches routinely merge into one another.

CONCLUSION

This chapter has assumed that modernity may be seen as a secular religion.[36] I have used Giddens's notion of the fateful moment to explore how disaster threatens modernity, and Berger's work on religion and world-maintenance to explore how the news media have taken on the classic religious function of repairing these rents in modernity's fabric. I have argued that in reporting disaster the media first threaten, then reassure, often in the same story or report. Berger has argued that "legitimations of the reality of the social world in the face of death are decisive requirements in any society";[37] this article demonstrates how this requirement is now performed in large part by the news media. In this respect, the evidence does not support those scholars, such as Giddens and Mellor and Shilling, who assert that death has been banished from public discourse.

In a remarkable book, Gail Holst-Warhaft writes, "Grief makes us vulnerable, but it may also empower. It tears us apart, but it may reassemble us in ways that astonish."[38] In Durkheim's and Berger's analysis, death threatens to tear a community apart, and the community responds by ritually reaffirming its values.[39] In Holst-Warhaft's analysis, however, the passions of grief are so powerful that they can change society; governments, frightened of where these passions may lead, typically attempt to dull grief and its rituals so that the status quo may be reestablished. Occasionally, as with 9/11 and the subsequent "war on terrorism," a government may keep those passions alive for its own ends. But at other times, the passion of grief may be used by mourners themselves to subvert established authority and to change society. Holst-Warhaft gives as examples the mothers of the disappeared in Argentina, and the way in which the gay community eventually used AIDS to challenge society's views both of the disease and of homosexuality. This more radical channeling of the power of grief, however, rarely makes headlines. It typically comes from the grassroots, from groups with limited access to the media, and it typically bears fruit years after the initial deaths, long after they have ceased to be hot news. Since this chapter has focused on national mass media and their headlines, pictures, and stories in the period immediately following disasters, examples of socially transforming responses form little part of the analysis. At least on the national level, we find that the Durkheim/Berger analysis fits.

This chapter has focused on news reports rather than the other components of media messages, namely the process by which the report is produced and how the audience interprets the report and/or changes its behavior in the light of it. The news report itself is by far the easiest to study, and it constitutes the focus of most media research. To collect data, researchers need only switch on the video recorder or visit newspaper archives on the Internet. Researching the first phase—how the message was produced, what its creators thought they were up to—is more difficult, since it requires access to and information from the creators of the message. Likewise, researching the final stage is also difficult, as the researcher has to ask the audience what it thought of the message or text; finding out how the message may have influenced the audience's behavior (such as investigating whether violence on television makes some viewers more violent) is very difficult indeed.

The temptation for media researchers is to analyze the text or image and then to speculate as to what its meaning is for both its producers and its audience. I have focused on the reports themselves, but on occasion I have strayed into speculation about how audiences respond to them, and such speculations should be treated with caution. Most problematically, I have suggested that reconstituting society is a latent function of media reporting of disaster. I use the word *function* to refer to the sociological consequences—quite possibly unintended—of disaster reporting. I do not know whether journalists intend these consequences, nor whether media audiences perceive them. Until this latter is established, my thesis, like many functionalist theories, not least in the area of religion, remains no more than a hypothesis. So, this chapter is suggestive rather than definitive. Though its argument about function may be hard to prove or falsify, it does raise many empirical questions that media research often addresses but has yet to address in the case of death and disaster. To what extent does media reporting of disaster replace religious mediations, and to what extent does it amplify or extend religious mediations beyond the local community to the national level? To what extent do the media's postdisaster legitimations shape audiences' feelings about mortality and modernity, and to what extent do media reports reflect these feelings? To what extent do audiences report feeling disturbed or reassured by postdisaster reporting? Does the "first terrify, then console" formula fit either the intensions of journalists or the perceptions of their audiences? How were disasters reported in the days before radio and television, when there were only newspapers, and when religious theodicies were more acceptable? Given the ongoing need of humans to make sense of their own mortality, and the expanding reach and power of the media, such questions are of more than just academic interest.

NOTES

I thank Andrew Buck, Grace Davie, Kathleen Garces-Foley, Ken Robertson, and Bill Thompson for their comments on earlier drafts, and Sophie Gilliatt and Per Pettersson for originally stimulating me to write this piece.

1. Robert Blauner, "Death and Social Structure," *Psychiatry* 29 (1966): 378–394; Norbert Elias, *The Loneliness of the Dying* (Oxford: Blackwell, 1985); Anthony Giddens, *Modernity and Self-Identity* (Oxford: Polity, 1991); Ivan Illich, *Limits to Medicine* (London: Marion Boyars, 1976); Philip Mellor and Chris Shilling, "Modernity, Self-Identity and the Sequestration of Death," *Sociology* 27 (1993): 411–432.

2. Tony Walter, Michael Pickering, and Jane Littlewood, "Death in the News: The Public Invigilation of Private Emotion," *Sociology* 29 (1995): 579–596. A useful collection of articles may be found in the virtual themed issue "Death and the Media," *Mortality* (2003), www.tandf.co.uk/journals/archive/deathandthemedia.asp.

3. Other social scientists who have suggested that the modern news media play an implicitly religious, or ritual, function include Karin Becker, "Media and the Ritual Process," *Media, Culture & Society* 17 (1995): 629–646; Daniel Dayan and Elihu Katz, *Media Events* (Cambridge, MA: Harvard University Press, 1992); John Langer, *Tabloid Television: Popular Journalism and the 'Other News'* (London: Routledge, 1998).

4. Jonathan Benthall, *Disasters, Relief and the Media* (London: I.B. Tauris, 1993).

5. Giddens, *Modernity and Self-Identity;* Peter L. Berger *The Sacred Canopy* (New York: Doubleday, 1969): quote from p. 52 of the UK edition, *The Social Reality of Religion* (London: Faber, 1969).

6. Jacques Ellul, *The Technological Society* (London: Cape, 1965), and *The New Demons* (New York: Seabury Press, 1973).

7. Nicholas Abercrombie et al., eds., *The Authority of the Consumer* (London: Routledge, 1993).

8. Ulrich Beck, *Risk Society: Towards a New Modernity* (London: Sage, 1992).

9. Diane Vaughan, *The Challenger Launch Decision* (Chicago: Chicago University Press, 1996). See also Charles Perrow, *Normal Accidents: Living with High-Risk Technologies* (Princeton: Princeton University Press, 1999).

10. Tony Walter, "The Mourning After Hillsborough," *Sociological Review* 39 (1991): 599–625. For the media's role in the subsequent history of memorial silences in the UK, see Tony Walter, "From Cathedral to Supermarket: Mourning, Silence and Solidarity," *Sociological Review* 49 (2001): 494–511.

11. Joan Miller, *Aberfan: A Disaster and Its Aftermath* (London: Constable, 1974).

12. Philippe Ariès, *The Hour of Our Death* (London: Allen Lane, 1981); Neil Postman, *The Disappearance of Childhood* (New York: Vintage, 1994). On Victorian mourning, see John Morley, *Death, Heaven and the Victorians* (London: Studio Vista, 1971).

13. *Times* (London), March 16, 1996.

14. As the weeks passed and the judicial enquiry began (May 1996), the gun control issue took over as the main news story. In November 1997, it became illegal in Britain to own, sell, or buy any handgun.

15. Edward T. Linenthall, *The Unfinished Bombing: Oklahoma City in American Memory* (New York: Oxford University Press, 2001).

16. Benedict Anderson, *Imagined Communities: Reflections on the Origin and Spread of Nationalism* (London: Verso, 1991); Linenthall, *Unfinished Bombing.* See also Dayan and Katz, *Media Events.*

17. My argument here is comparable to Beck's in *Risk Society* (1992). Disasters, like ecological problems, seem at first to undermine trust in science and technology, but in the end serve to bolster that trust—for it is science that will diagnose the exact nature of the problem and fix it.

18. Vaughan, *Challenger Launch Decision;* Perrow, *Normal Accidents.*

19. Zygmunt Bauman, *Mortality, Immortality and Other Life Strategies* (Oxford: Polity, 1992); Lindsay Prior and Michael Bloor, "Why People Die: Social Representations of Death and Its Causes," *Science as Culture* 3 (1992): 346–374.

20. Robin Horton, "African Traditional Thought and Western Science," *Africa* 37 (1967): 50–71.

21. For an analysis of how the media attempted to shore up the idea of childhood innocence following the murder of two-year-old James Bulger by two ten-year-old boys in 1993, see Chris Jenks, *Childhood* (London: Routledge, 1996), chapter 5.

22. Clive Seale, *Media and Health* (Thousand Oaks, CA: Sage, 2003); Frank Furedi, *Culture of Fear* (New York: Cassell, 1997).

23. Linenthal, *Unfinished Bombing.*

24. On emotional labor, see Arlie Hochschild, *The Managed Heart* (Berkeley: University of California Press, 1983).

25. *Yorkshire Evening Post,* March 5, 2001.

26. Benthall, *Disasters, Relief and the Media.*

27. Glasgow Media Group, *Bad News* (London: Routledge, 1976); J.A. Walter, *Sacred Cows* (Grand Rapids: Zondervan, 1980), chapter 8.

28. This statement clearly needs to be tested by content analysis of news reports during, and after, the Cold War.

29. Seale, *Media and Health,* shows how the "first scare, then reassure" formula also characterizes media panics about health.

30. "One Year On: The Terrible Legacy of Oklahoma," *Guardian* (Manchester), April 18, 1996.

31. Berger, *Sacred Canopy,* chapter 3.

32. (Oxford: Polity, 1989).

33. Grace Davie, "You'll Never Walk Alone: The Anfield Pilgrimage," in *Pilgrimage in Popular Culture,* ed. Ian Reader and Tony Walter, 201–219 (New York: St. Martin's Press, 1993).

34. Per Pettersson, "Implicit Religion Turned Explicit: A Case Study of the Estonia Disaster," paper presented to the Denton Conference on Implicit Religion, Denton, Yorkshire, England, May 1996, 29.

35. *Independent* (London), February 2, 2003.

36. For elaboration of this idea, see Ellul, *New Demons;* Walter, *Sacred Cows.*

37. Berger, *Social Reality of Religion,* 43–44.

38. *The Cue for Passion: Grief and Its Political Uses* (Cambridge, MA: Harvard University Press, 2000), 19.

39. Émile Durkheim, *The Elementary Forms of the Religious Life* (New York: Collier Macmillan, 1961); Berger, *Sacred Canopy.*

CHAPTER 13

Grief, Religion, and Spirituality

DENNIS KLASS

Although there is no consensus among scholars about what evolutionary function it serves, grief seems to be an instinctual response that is hardwired into the human psyche. It is part of our evolutionary heritage. A simple definition of grief is that it is the response to the loss, or threatened loss, of an attachment. If we are not attached to someone, we do not grieve when he or she dies. Attachment is just scholarly jargon for what we call love in common language. Grief, then, is the price we pay for love. Love, of course, is a complex phenomenon. Love is not an emotion—we feel a lot of emotions intensely in our relationship with those we love: joy, anger, jealousy, to name just a few. Grief has as many intense emotions as love. The opposite of love is not hate. Perhaps we can hate no one more than we can hate someone we love. The opposite of love is indifference. If we do not care, we do not grieve. We can, of course, love someone we do not personally know: a media personality, a musician, a political leader. We can also love things other than people: a special place or object that symbolizes something important to us. We can grieve for whatever we love.

It is not easy to define religion because all religions are complex phenomena that touch every area of human individual and social life. A useful definition of religion includes three elements. First, encounter or merger with transcendent reality, that is, the sense that there is something beyond our mundane existence which we can, at least for moments, experience as an inner reality. Second, a worldview, that is, a higher intelligence, purpose, or order that gives meaning to the events and relationships in our lives. Third, a community in which transcendent reality and worldview are validated. We can see this triune structure in many religious traditions. In Islam, for example, Allah is the God who can be found but who cannot be understood by human intelligence, the Prophet Muhammad was given the revelation to which humans should conform their lives, and the Ummah is the community of all those who submit to Allah. Buddhism has the three refuges: the Buddha, the Dharma, and the Sangha. Christianity affirms the trinity of God the father, who is unknowable in Himself, God the son, who is in human form, and God the holy spirit, who is the giver of understanding and the undergirder of the church. In Chinese religion, which is an amalgam of Taoism and Confucianism, Heaven or Ti is the unnameable reality; Tao is the ordering principle in nature, and Li is the ordering principle by which humans can find harmony within society. In each of these traditions, the sense of the transcendent, finding purpose, and membership in community are all necessary elements of religious or spiritual life.

In this chapter we will focus on religion and grief. Both are universal human experiences, found in all cultures at all historical periods. People everywhere turn to religion for solace in their grief, but how religious beliefs and practices provide comfort to the grieving has received little scholarly attention. Here we will try to unravel this complex relationship through a close examination of parental grief after a child has died. After looking at the parent-child bond in biological and cultural-religious contexts, we will listen to the experience of parents in a self-help group to try to understand more clearly the religious dynamics of their grief.

Clearly the parent-child bond has been formed by evolutionary needs. Mortality rates for children until the advent of modern medicine were as high as they are now for very old people. In parts of the world today, a significant percent of the children die from diseases, infections, and accidents. Because human children are so helpless for their first decade, the goal of parenting must be to keep the children safe and well. Survival of the species depends on enough children surviving. The grief of parents after a child has died, then, is the interaction of two basic instincts, parenting and grief.

In humans, there is something in the parent's bond with the child and the child's bond with the parent that is akin to the bond we feel with the larger invisible realities. When we think about how humankind has tried to describe the spiritual life, from the time of the earliest cultural artifacts to the present, we find parenting as the most common symbol of the connection between humans and their gods. From stone-age Europe we find images of women with large stomachs, hips, and breasts. These were the Great Mother. Early agricultural religions associated bearing children and plentiful harvests. The same dynamic governed human fertility and the fertility of the land. About ten thousand years ago permanent cities were built. Society was organized by male hierarchies. The mother goddesses were repressed and male father gods, incarnate in warrior kings, took the world stage, but the parent-child symbol remained. In Egypt the sun god was Ra. The earthly ruler was Pharaoh, the son of Ra. About two thousand years ago, Jesus, who was called the Son of God, taught a prayer to his followers that began, "Our Father who art in heaven." On another part of the planet, Confucius taught that the benevolence of the father and the pious obedience of the son were the ethics that could protect civilization against chaos. In some places the goddess retained her power. In a Kali temple in India I was looking at a painting of a decapitated male body from which fountains of blood poured out. My hostess came behind me and said softly, "Kali is like your mother. Her anger can be strong, but when she is angry at you it is because she loves you." As we shall see, when children die, the parents' grief is deeply intertwined with their relationship to the transcendent.

BIOLOGY AND CULTURE

The biological basis of grief seems well established. We recognize vocalizations, facial expressions, and body postures of grieving people from cultures very different from our own. Still, we always experience and express our instincts within cultural forms. We can think of instincts as a script or narrative through which we interpret our environment and act in ways appropriate to our interpretation. If we perceive a threat, for example, we can fight or run away. That is an instinct. What we perceive as a threat and how we construe that threat and whether we fight or run away from this particular threat is a cultural matter.

The grief response, then, will be triggered by different kinds of deaths and those deaths are construed differently depending on the cultural narrative in which the instinct is experienced. For example, in one culture a death might be construed as the result of witchcraft while in another it might be construed as an indication of God's anger, and in another it might be construed as the result of a disease that could have been prevented with better medical treatment. In addition to the sadness that seems characteristic of all grief, we might then experience fear of witchcraft, guilt under God's anger, or our own anger at poor medical treatment. Depending on the circumstances, the feelings can be quite complex. For example, if the death could have been prevented with better medical treatment, we might feel shame or remorse that we did not demand that the person get to the physician earlier. But if the person tried to get to the physician and was stopped at a roadblock of an army that is occupying our country, then our grief becomes part of a political narrative that may motivate us to join the resistance forces or perhaps to work for peace so no one else need ever experience what we did.

Sorrow expressed by crying and withdrawal seems to be one side of the core individual instinctual responses. The other side of the core instinctual responses seems to be reaching out to others to share feelings and to engage in communal rituals. Those two sides work together to create the intersubjective space in which grief, as we will show later, is expressed and resolved. Crying elicits a similar response from others. When we are near someone who is crying, we often begin to cry ourselves, even if we do not know the person. Grieving people's emotional or physical withdrawal often elicits a hug or other comforting gesture from those around them, thus inviting them back into communion with others.

How or even whether we express this instinctual response depends on our culture. Many cultural demands and prohibitions can influence personal and social behavior. For example, some cultures have rules against crying, or against crying in public. Scholars have developed little good cross-cultural theory of grief, but it appears that where there are rules against crying, they are more likely to apply to men than to women. But how grief is expressed is a great deal more complicated than just gender difference. Norwegian anthropologist Unni Wikan compared how families, especially mothers, in two Muslim cultures are expected to act after a child dies. In Egypt family members "cry as if pouring their hearts out. Females will scream, yell, beat their breasts, collapse in each other's arms and be quite beyond themselves for days, even weeks on end."[1] The mother is expected to go into a catatonic-like state for months or even years. In Bali, on the other hand, the family members, including the mother, try to restrain their emotions. They "strive to act with calm and composure, especially beyond the circle of closest family and closest friends. But even among intimates, their reactions will be moderate, and laughter, joking and cheerfulness mingle with mutely expressed sadness."[2]

Both cultures are Muslim and share the same belief system. But, as Wikan points out, the official theology of a religion does not determine how sorrow is expressed in different cultures. In both cultures, the official Muslim teaching is that each death has been predetermined, but predestination can be interpreted differently. In Egypt, emotions are to be expressed, because to hold in the emotions is bad for a person's mental health.

> The God in whose power they place themselves is one whose name they invoke time and again every day, beseeching him to help them through the miseries they see as inescapably grounded in their own human lot. Truly more than they can bear, they call on him to bear witness to their trials and tribulations, rewarding the just, punishing the unjust, making tomorrow a better day. True life is fated, but not immune to human effort; God helps only her who helps herself. Theirs is a very close and present God, compassionate, just, and forgiving. Should not God understand that sadness is one thing, subjugation to his will is another?[3]

In Bali, sad or negative emotions are not to be expressed because the emotions will spill from the individual to the community and thus cause negative feelings in the community. Those negative feelings would weaken the spirit of the individual and of the individuals in the community. In their weakened state, people in the community would be vulnerable to black magic, which causes up to 50 percent of deaths. To express sorrow not only affects others, but also affects the dead. "If we cry and are unhappy, the soul will be unhappy too, not free to go to the God. We must contain our sadness that the soul will be liberated to go to heaven."[4]

In modern, Western culture, cultural demands and prohibitions are filtered through social scientific theory. Psychologists, psychiatrists, and counselors define what is good behavior and what is bad, what is good mental health and what is unhealthy. In this sense, social science and mental health professionals have the same authority to prescribe behaviors in contemporary Western culture as religious tradition and clerics do in traditional societies. Two very different theories about grief have existed side by side in modern Western culture. In terms of grief, *modern* means beginning in 1914, when the sheer scale of death in World War I could not be assimilated into the Victorian era's romantic grief narrative and demanded new understandings of grief.

The first theory, sometimes called the "grief work" model, was articulated by Sigmund Freud in his essay "Mourning and Melancholia,"[5] which was first published during the war, in 1917, and was used by counselors and advisers, including many clergy. In this theory the purpose of grief, often called grief work, is to reconstruct an autonomous individual. That is, death is the end of life, so the task of the griever is to sever the attachment with the person who has died and to form new attachments that serve the griever's needs in the present. Thus, if a widow remarries or begins to date, counselors say that she is "moving on." Grief in this theory, then, is largely an inner, psychological process. According to some psychiatrists, grief is a preprogrammed sequence of stages put in motion by an environmental situation, much as birds have nest building or migration programmed into their brains. The process of grief occurs by working through and resolving feelings. People are encouraged to cry and feel bad, because, the theory goes, grief is a series of feelings that must be expressed or else they will be bottled up and cause psychic harm. This theory was the dominant cultural narrative of grief for most of the twentieth century.

We can call the second theory of grief "the continuing bonds" model.[6] In this theory, death ends a life; it does not end a relationship. Grief, then, is the process of rewriting our life story in light of the death. According to this theory, grieving people have two different tasks. First, they must learn to live in a world that is different. It is different because the person who died is no longer there. If a man's wife dies, he is now single and whatever he did with her, he must now do alone or with someone else. Second, grieving people discover that the dead person still plays important roles in their lives, even though the roles might not be the same as the person played when alive. So, in this theory, the successful resolution of grief requires the mourners to construct a durable life story that enables them to integrate memory and continuing interaction with the deceased into their ongoing lives. In this theory, grief is not just a psychological issue. Grief is intersubjective, that is, grief is about the relationship between the survivors and the person who died, and it is also about the relationships among the survivors. In traditional societies, the process of grief is largely ritualized as religious myths and doctrine are used to understand and bring meaning to the experience of death. In the contemporary world, we no longer belong to tightly knit communities in which religious rituals provide the main vehicle for grieving. Many of us are unsure about the efficacy of such rituals or find that they simply do not provide enough solace, so we turn to friends or family or even strangers in a grief group with whom we can share our grief.

As the twenty-first century began, the continuing bonds model was adopted by most counselors, although the grief work model continues to have a great deal of influence on popular culture, as frequent references to "closure" and "moving on" indicate. In this chapter we will use the continuing bonds model because to some extent this model grew out of my own research with bereaved parents.[7] Most of the personal stories I use in this chapter are from that research (though I have changed names and some details to protect anonymity).

PARENTS' CONTINUING BOND WITH THEIR DECEASED CHILDREN

We can best understand grief after a child dies if we listen closely to bereaved parents themselves. The following material is drawn from a two-decade ethnographic study I conducted in my role as professional adviser to a local chapter of Bereaved Parents of the USA, a self-help group. As I observed the group over the years, it became clear that it functions much as religious communities have always functioned in grief, helping people to manage their connection with transcendent reality, finding meaning in the child's death and their own grief, and being a member of a community in which their pain as well as their bond with their dead child is honored and shared. It seems to me, then, that just as in our times social science provides the definitions of healthy thinking, feeling, and behaving that religious authority used to provide, the self-help group provides the kind of close-knit community in which grief can be successfully resolved that was provided by the religious community in traditional societies.

We are not sure if the parental bond was as strong when children were important in a family's economic success because they provided much of the labor. But we know that in contemporary Western culture, the parent-child bond is a major exception to the individualistic, self-chosen bonds that characterize modernity. The child is an extension of the parent's self. Parents feel pride at their children's successes and shame or guilt at their children's failures. When a child dies, a part of the self is cut off. Bereaved parents learn to accept or resign themselves to the reality that their child is dead. They learn to invest themselves in other tasks and other relationships. Still, they report, there is a sense of loss that cannot be healed. Many bereaved parents find the comparison with amputation useful. One father said, "It is like I lost my right arm, but I'm learning to live as a one-armed man." Like amputation, parental bereavement is a permanent condition. The hopes, dreams, and expectations incarnate in the child are now gone.

Bereaved parents no longer have a physical relationship with the child. Instead, they maintain the child as an inner and a social reality that they can call on in difficult times, that comforts them in their sorrow, and that provides a means by which they can access their better self in their new and poorer world. The bonds with the child are not simply a mental construction; that is, they are not just an idea or a feeling. Rather the bonds include all levels and modalities of experience: "Representations of people always include visceral, proprioceptive, sensorimotor, perceptual, eidetic, and conceptual components."[8]

We get some sense of the bond with the child in a report from a father. When he began running for exercise, his seventeen-year-old daughter encouraged him to keep it up. She was killed in an accident two weeks before they were to run a five-kilometer race together. He thought about quitting running but did not because he thought she would have been disappointed to think she had caused him to abandon running in general and the race in particular. Instead of quitting, he ran wearing her number. After that, she became his running partner, in whose presence he evaluates his life. Running became a symbol for his journey "toward the light," the place where his daughter's presence often becomes real.

> Every time I ran, I took a few minutes to think about Dorothy and how I was dealing with her death. I was alone with no distractions but the pounding of my feet, and I could focus on her and my feelings. I tried to coach myself a bit, inch myself toward the light. That done, I often moved on to report silently to her about what I'd been doing lately, about what I thought of the weather, how my conditioning was going, what her younger brothers were up to. Frequently, I sensed she was nearby, cruising at my elbow, listening.

WORLDVIEWS: MAKING SENSE OF DEATH AND OF LIFE

Bereaved parents find resolution to their grief in the sense that they learn to live in their new world. That is, they construct a durable life story that enables them to integrate their memories and continuing interaction with their dead child. In this sense, they "re-solve" the matter of how to be themselves in their family and community in a way that makes life meaningful. They learn to grow in those parts of themselves that did not die with the child. One mother wrote, "Being a bereaved parent will always be a part of our lives—it just won't be the most important or only part." But somewhere inside themselves, they report, there is a sense of loss that remains. A bereaved father wrote in a newsletter:

> If grief is resolved, why do we still feel a sense of loss on anniversaries and holidays and even when we least expect it? Why do we feel a lump in the throat even six years after the loss? It is because healing does not mean forgetting and because moving on with life does not mean that we don't take a part of our lost love with us.

One of the parts of the self that many parents lose when their child dies is the spiritual sense that they are linked to a larger transcendent reality. A woman whose two babies died said:

> There's lots of people who go around thinking if they are good then bad things can't happen to them. I just tell them, "It has to happen to somebody." I don't pray in church anymore. I go because you are supposed to. How can I tell the children to go to church if I don't? But I don't pray. I just do my grocery list. I think I used to pray and feel close to God. But not any more. I don't feel anything there.

She does not find the presence of God in her solitude as she once did. But she insists that her living children go to church, for that is a rule, and if she is to enforce the rule, she too must follow it. God still reigns supreme in her superego and in her family system, because there is still a need to maintain external order in the world. But for now, in her soul, God is dead.

After the death of their child, parents often are beset by depression, anger, resentment, shame, envy, humiliation, and self-doubt. The world no longer makes sense to them. They were supposed to protect their child, but they were powerless to do so. One of the challenges bereaved parents face, then, is to find meaning in the child's death, meaning in their lives now that the child is dead, and meaning in the child's life even though the life was not what the parents expected when the child was born. The parents know death in a new way. This new reality tests the parents' worldview, the set of beliefs and assumptions, sometimes conscious but usually unconscious, about how the universe functions and about how much and what kind of power humans can exercise in the universe. Sometimes the worldview the parents had before the child died is adequate. Often, however, the worldview must be revised.

When bereaved parents talk about their "faith," they talk about their basic assumptions about the world and their power.[9] Those assumptions include their sense of connection with transcendent reality. "I know that not everyone can say this," said a woman in the group, "but I am so thankful that I never lost my faith." By "faith" she does not mean theology or belief. She means the feeling she has when she prays that God is close and protective. It is, she said, an inner sense she can remember having as a child when she went to church with her grandmother. At a meeting, a mother said, "After Melody died I lost my faith. I never got it back, but I got a new one." The new faith is not simply a different set of beliefs; it is a new connection with transcendent reality.

At the beginning of this chapter we discussed grief in terms of instincts that are part of our evolutionary heritage. We said then that instincts are never found in their purely biological form, but rather instincts are expressed in cultural forms. When we talk about what social scientists call instincts, we are talking about what religious scholars call worldviews, because worldviews are the cultural forms in which instincts are experienced and expressed. We are talking about the meaning people make of their lives, because instincts and worldviews are the basis of perception. A worldview is a cultural way of perceiving reality, a set of patterns by which we respond to reality. In the computer metaphor, instincts and worldviews operate in real time. When we observe parents reshaping their worldviews and their bonds with their children, then, we are observing the very intricate interaction between grief and parenting instincts within one cultural expression of both. Even to the outside observer it seems an overwhelming task. We should not be surprised, then, that the resolution of parental bereavement is measured in years, rather than in weeks or months.

A NEW KIND OF RELIGIOUS COMMUNITY

We noted above that grief is intersubjective, that the process of grieving unfolds in conversation. In intimate interactions with others, bereaved people rewrite their life story, their biography, and the story of the person who has died. In Bereaved Parents of the USA, the continuing bond with their children is an important element in the bonds that form between members of the group. What are the parents to do with the love they gave to their child and that the child gave to them? The parents' social identity is ambiguous at best and marginal at worst. Parents report that friends and family do not know what to say, so they say nothing. Parents find that they make others uncomfortable, so people avoid them. Many contemporary communities, then, seem to be inadequately equipped either to help parents in their grief or to integrate the deaths of children into their community narrative. In the self-help group, members say, they share the love their children gave them. Through the opportunity to share this continuing bond, they form a close-knit community with each other and even form bonds with each other's children. Though they may be marginalized in the larger culture, the self-help group can create a new community based in shared pain, a shared search for meaning, and the shared memories of their children. The Bereaved Parents "Credo" describes what happens in the group:

> We share our fears, confusion, anger, guilt, frustrations, emptiness and feelings of hopelessness so that hope can be found anew. As we accept, support, comfort and encourage each

> other, we demonstrate to each other that survival is possible. Together we celebrate the lives of our children, share the joys and triumphs as well as the love that will never fade. Together we learn how little it matters where we live, what our color or our affluence is or what faith we uphold as we confront the tragedies of our children's deaths. Together, strengthened by the bonds we forge at our gatherings, we offer what we have learned to each other and to every more recently bereaved family.[10]

In the Bereaved Parents group we find, then, a community made up of people whose connection with each other is not the biological bonds of extended family, nor the geographic and economic bonds of the village and neighborhood that form the basis of community in traditional cultures. The group explicitly eschews social class, ethnic heritage, and religious tradition as a basis for membership. In doing so, it offers members an identity that is based on voluntary association and on the perception that others are like themselves. They have a new kind of community in which to work out the religious problem of re-forming a worldview. It is based not on a shared faith, but rather on shared pain and on a willingness to help each other come to terms with the death of children. The self-help group provides the opportunity for intimate conversation through which grief is resolved.

Bereaved parents' experiences of transcendent reality, establishing or maintaining a worldview, and affiliating with a healing community are all intimately intertwined with the parents' continuing bond with their dead child. As I tried to understand what was happening in the group, it became apparent that the best lens I could use was how the continuing bond parents maintained with their dead child was used and transformed within the group process. Rituals and symbols that evoke the bond with the child play a central role in this process and in creating bonds among members of the group. One example is the opening ritual of each group meeting. The same ritual begins each meeting, whether it be the regular monthly meeting, the quarterly business meeting, or the national board meeting. Around the circle each parent mentions his or her name and then the child's name, something about the child's death, usually the child's age and death date, and often something special about the child. At many monthly meetings, parents light a candle and place it in front of them to commemorate a child's birthday or the anniversary of the death. If traditional religious rituals begin by evoking the name of the gods or God, this community begins its interactions by evoking the names of dead children. Everything that follows the ritual opening of the meeting is done in the context of the evocation of these sacred dead. At the end of the ritual, all those names and all that pain create a deep quiet, punctuated by the soft sobs of people new to the group. At one of the chapter's monthly meetings, as members rise from their chairs after ninety minutes of sharing, the leader raises her hand and says in a strong voice, "I am Sean's mom!" Members respond with the same affirmation: "I'm Tiffany's dad!" "I'm Lisa's mom!" "I am Jason's dad!" Then they have coffee and donuts.

The largest gathering of the year in the local chapter is the holiday candlelight service. Early in the life of the group, parents discovered that many had a hard time at Christmas because it is a child's celebration, and their families were uncomfortable with having the dead child as part of the festivities. One woman reported that she was furious at a family

Thanksgiving dinner when no one mentioned her son's name even though he had died only a few months earlier. When she confronted one of her brothers, he told her that the family members had discussed the question and had decided not to bring up her son's name because they thought it would make her sad to remember it. She was aghast. Did they not know that her son was on her mind every moment? If they acted that way at Thanksgiving, how would they act at Christmas? So the group members decided that if their families did not publicly remember, they would. Thus began the tradition of opening the winter holidays with the candlelight memorial service. One parent is chosen to speak. The speaker usually shares his or her narrative: the meaning of the child's life, the meaning of the death, and the meaning of the parent's life now. The service is interspersed with songs that express the parents' thoughts and feelings. At the highlight of the service, the name of each child whose parents are present is read and the child's photograph is projected onto a screen. As their child's name is read, parents, often accompanied by the child's siblings, grandparents, aunts, uncles, and friends, rise and light a candle. One year, as the parents stood holding their lighted candles, a children's choir sang the Muppet song "Rainbow Connection." One of the meetings of the chapter takes place in an old river town. The memorial service centers on the use of candles and roses. The candles are lit in a building by the river. At the end of the service, everyone goes to the river, where a rose for each child is put into the current. Most parents take the candle home and make it part of their family celebrations by lighting it during dinner or as the family's holiday presents are opened.

A significant portion of national and regional meetings is devoted to ritual, such as the creation of bulletin boards with pictures of the dead children. The boards line both sides of a long hallway or fill one large room in the hotel. Some parents just pin their child's pictures on the board, but many prepare quite elaborate displays that communicate the child's personality or character. The picture boards area is a popular gathering place during the meetings. Conversations often begin between strangers. "This is your child? My son had a car he loved too. He was killed in that car so I feel pretty ambivalent about all the pictures he took of it. But he did love it and he was never so happy as when he was working on it. How did your son die?" They bond with each other as they share memories and they feel comfort in sharing their child with others.

Rituals also play an important role in affirming that the parents' bonds with the dead children are a social reality, not just an internal reality. One meeting of our local chapter consists of a cemetery tour so members can "get to know the children better." People sign up the week before so a route can be mapped out. The coordinator secures a large van so everyone can ride together. At each grave, the parent of the child buried there introduces the child, tells favorite stories, and perhaps displays pictures, tapes of songs, or artwork. After each presentation, the group lingers at the grave before moving on to the next. In the middle of the day, the parents stop at a restaurant for lunch, then resume the tour until all the children have been visited. The day ends with many hugs and thanks for a wonderful day. At a business meeting when the first tour was reported, there was long laughter at the description of the waitress's befuddled look when the tour members answered her innocent question about why they were having lunch together. The group laughed because everyone there knew that being bereaved parents puts them outside the normal world of consumer culture, yet they have learned within the group that they are all right. If the culture provides them with few rituals by which they can be in touch with their dead child, they can invent the rituals themselves and identify themselves as a member of the group that shares the bonds with the children.

The ritual of the annual picnic is another important opportunity to affirm these bonds. In the announcement for the picnic, we can get a sense of how bonds with the dead child also form bonds between the parents in the group:

> Our children lost are the heart and soul of our picnic. It is for and because of them that we have come, and it is for them that we have our cherished balloon released [sic], a time set aside in our day to remember and include our special children.
>
> Helium filled balloons are passed out, along with markers, giving us all one more chance to tell our children the things we most long to say—mostly "I Love You." And then, oblivious to the world around us, we stand as one, but each involved in his own thoughts, prayers, and emotions as we release hundreds of balloons to the sky and they disappear to a destiny we are certain they will reach.

The children are the heart and soul of the group, because the shared bonds with the dead children bond the members to each other. The children are in the midst of the group, not simply within each of the individual parents. Yet the children are also wherever balloon messages are carried. The ritual provides a means by which the parent can both reach out to the dead child and feel the presence of the child within. They "stand as one, but each involved in his own thoughts, prayers and emotions." Because the bond with the child is shared within the group, the parents can be in touch privately with their child. Because the group shares in the strong bond with the child, there is tremendous strength within the group. Because there is such strength within the group, the bond with the child feels surer. One balloon sent into the sky would seem a lonely and fragile message. Hundreds of balloons, each addressed to an individual child, are sure to get through.

Some rituals that bereaved parents create are more personal. Many years after his daughter's death, a father reported about his own holiday, "Ellen's Day." He said that George Washington, Christopher Columbus, Abraham Lincoln, and Martin Luther King were all very special people and that as a way of recognizing them, people set aside a day and named it after them to honor their lives and their memories. Following this tradition, a few years after Ellen's death, he decided that he would set aside a day each year to honor her life and memory. As the years went by, a new tradition built up. He does not go to work that day. In the morning he visits her grave. He tells her what he has been doing with his life over the past year, what has happened in the lives of other people who were important to her, how the world has changed since she died, and what things endure. After his time at the grave, he does something special for the day. Each year he thinks about what the activity should be, because it should be something that Ellen would have liked, something that they might have done together, or something that brings out the part of the father that feels connected to Ellen. He was divorced when Ellen died, so it was a holiday for one. When he remarried, his new wife joined in the holiday rituals even though she had not known Ellen. Ellen is a part of her new family so she is a full participant in the rituals. The father said, "I don't expect the world to join in this celebration, but neither will I let the year be complete without this special day being included in the calendar of hearts."

In forming a self-help group, the parents have opted to find the resolution of their grief in the resources of the bond they had with their living child. The bond that forms between bereaved parents in the self-help group is not unlike the bonds with ancestors or local saints that are a vital element in community and family membership in traditional cultures. When Ellen's father remarried, for example, his new wife bonded to Ellen much as the wife in a traditional Japanese household bonds to the ancestors of the family into which she has married. The lighted candles at the holiday memorial service seem very much like the lighted lanterns of *bon* (the summer festival when the dead return for a three-day visit) in Japan. The photographs on the bulletin boards at regional and national meetings seem very much like the photographs on the *butsudan* (buddha altar) in a traditional Japanese home. Visiting graves together seems very much like the family's ritual cleaning of graves in China or the Memorial Day observances of late nineteenth-century America.

The problem of the bereaved in the twentieth century was that they were surrounded by people who felt bad *for* them, but did not feel bad *with* them. Because the bereaved did not have close-knit communities that actively maintained bonds with the dead, they were forced to carry on these bonds alone or relinquish them. The contemporary self-help group provides a new form of religious community in which members find a new "family" of sorts who will feel bad with them. In making the bond with the dead children the core of their bond with each other, they make grief into an interpersonal experience, not merely a psychological experience. The process begins, they say, when they share each other's pain, when grief becomes an intersubjective reality. "My child has died" becomes "Our children have died."

THE SOCIAL REALITY OF CONTINUING BONDS

Interactions within the continuing bond with the dead child have the character of both outer and inner reality that we find in many other kinds of religious experience. The interaction is not simply an objective presence; the meaning of the experience is strongly personal. Neither can it be said to be simply subjective. Many parents argue strongly against reducing the experience to a psychic reality, or as one person said, "Don't tell me that this is just in my head." At the same time parents are usually able to grant that the meaning of the child's presence is very personal and may not necessarily be the same meaning that a dead child has in other parents' lives. They usually understand that other parents may find different meanings in interactions with their own child. Just as in other religious experience, the message and meaning in the interaction with their dead child are self-evident to the bereaved parents. Their child appears, acts, speaks, and influences. The intense experiences they feel within the bond with their child, like religious beliefs, do not depend on rational proof or disproof.

As parents learn to manage their continuing bond with the child in the self-help group, many learn to include the child within families and other social systems. Many parents consciously work to maintain the bond with the child in their own lives and in the communities that are important to them. Several families do this by including a picture of the dead child in family portraits made after the child's death. Others do it by consciously evoking the memory of the child on significant occasions. As the child becomes stabilized in the family and community, the child can in turn become a stabilizing presence in the parents' life. One mother reported:

> I am just now learning to include my son into my life in a way that comforts me. Emily goes with me to the cemetery, and we talk about life and death. At four, she is curious about her little brother. . . . She surprised me with her fiercely protective reactions. As she grows, Jason becomes more real to her. As he becomes more real to her, he becomes more precious and more real to us all.

Like angels, saints, and bodhisattvas in religious traditions, the spirits of dead children bridge the gap between transcendent reality and everyday reality because they participate in both realms. Like ancestors and saints, dead children become guides to right living. One of the most obvious functions of religion for individuals is to control impulses. In psychoanalytic terms, God and the dead are often part of the superego. They are on the side of internalized social regulation. The society does not have to police each individual at every moment because the guidelines for good behavior have been appropriated into each individual psyche in the form of conscience and moral guidance. The dead are part of that internal guidance system. One member of the group was an alcoholic who had stopped drinking three years before his fifteen-year-old daughter, Andrea, was shot when she was a bystander during a holdup. He was having trouble maintaining his sobriety in the months after her death. From her childhood, Andrea had been the one in the family who "could tell me off when I was being stupid. She would just say, 'Dad, cut the crap.' She loved me and didn't back off like the boys did. When she told me to stop it, I did." About six months after her death, he was standing at the grave when he heard a voice say, "Dad, why are you acting this way? This is what you were like when you were drinking." Within a week Andrea was his constant inner companion, helping him control his rage and maintain his hard-won sobriety.

SOLACE: COMFORT AMID HOPELESSNESS, DESPAIR, AND SORROW

Immortality means transcending death. Central to the spiritual reality of parental grief is the loss of one of the parent's hopes for immortality. Although we are confronted with the undeniable fact that each of us will die, one of the ways parents can be certain to live on is in their children. Parents hope that their child will live out each parent's best self, that the child will fulfill their dreams and, in doing so, carry on the parents' life after they have died. When a child is born, the father and mother take their place in the genealogical succession. In some cultures, genealogical immortality is the most important kind of life after death, so child rearing and ancestor veneration go hand in hand. Lineage and pedigree are less important in modernity, where marriage has become primarily an emotional bond with a self-chosen mate. Today the parent-child bond often becomes the only relationship that endures as divorcing parents make new couplings that meet their individual economic and intimacy needs.

The loss of a child not only devastates the parents' hopes for the future but, as we said earlier, greatly challenges their entire worldview. Because the parental bond with children is so intimately connected with their relationship to the transcendent, when a child dies, the parents may feel that they have lost that sacred connection. One of the spiritual tasks faced by bereaved parents as they re-create their worldview is to either reestablish the connection or create a new one. One of the ways parents are able to find some solace in this connection is by maintaining their bonds with their dead children. Before looking more closely at how parents do this, it is helpful to consider briefly how the connection with the transcendent is understood in various religious traditions.

In the Asian religious traditions, the experience of transcendent reality is most often conceived as "nondual." In the nondual there is no other. Indeed, at the highest levels of awareness in Hinduism, the true self (*atman*) is understood to be a part of the universal spirit (*brahman*), and in Buddhism, the real self (*atman*) is understood to be an illusion (*anatman*). True perception does not discriminate between thisness and thatness. In Zen, I learn that my hearing and the bell are not distinct from each other, but rather that reality is the hearing experience. The goal in meditation (if it can be said to have a goal) is to know that my conception of my self is an illusion, that I make a false distinction between "me" inside the skin bag and "not me" outside the skin bag. I am an interaction that is happening in the now.

In Western spiritual traditions, the experience of transcendent reality is most often conceived as an encounter with what Rudolf Otto calls the "Wholly Other." Scholars of comparative religion have found Otto's distillation of Western religious experience useful. Otto says that what makes an experience religious is the "peculiar difference of *quality* in the mental attitude and emotional content of the religious life itself."[11] Otto names that quality the "holy" or the "sacred." We know the holy, he says, in a mental state that is irreducible to any other. At the core of the holy is the *mysterium tremendum et facinans,* a mystery that is overpowering and fascinating. Before the mystery, he says, we feel awe—which literally means that we are speechless. The mystery, he says, overpowers us so we behold the majesty of the divine who is "Wholly Other." Yet, he says, even as we are overpowered, we know we are creatures in the presence of our creator.

In grief, the experience of the nondual or the experience of the holy becomes the experience of solace. Solace, or consolation, is a basic experience in religion, though not one that has been much discussed by scholars of comparative religions. Comforting, after all, is one of the chief functions of religions, though scholars have seldom written about the theoretical basis for such comforting. The defining characteristic of solace is the sense of soothing. Solace means pleasure, enjoyment, or delight in the face of hopelessness, despair, and sorrow. Solace comes into the heart of the pain but does not remove the pain. As lexicographer Samuel Johnson says, "Consolation, or comfort, signify some alleviation to that pain to which it is not in our power to afford the proper and adequate remedy; they imply rather an augmentation of the power of bearing, than a diminution of the burden."[12]

Solace is found within the sense of being connected to a reality that transcends the self. That is, within the pain, hopeless, or despair, we feel in touch with something that transcends our immediate condition. For bereaved parents, solace comes in the sense of transcendent reality experienced in the midst of devastation. This transcendental reality can take many forms, but the most common forms are connected with the parents' continued interaction with their dead child. Their child is dead. That is a fact. But in another sense, their child lives on and connects them with other transcendent realities in their lives. Life has shown them that their child was all too mortal, but as they continue their bond with the child, the child connects them with that which transcends death. In this sense, their child is immortal. As we noted above, the child takes on functions similar to those of the saints and angels in the Western traditions and the gods, buddhas, and bodhisattvas in the Eastern traditions. The spirit of their child bridges the gap between the worlds of the living and the dead because the child has dual citizenship and belongs to both heaven and earth.

Paths to Solace

When we examine the data from bereaved parents, we can identify four common ways that parents interact with their dead child that bring them solace: linking objects, religious rituals, memories, and identification. Each of these four is used in religions as ways to interact with other sacred realities.

The first way parents find solace is in linking objects—that is, objects that seem to contain the child's presence, such as the child's possessions, favorite songs, or playmates. Linking objects are like relics of the saints that we find in many religions. When, for example, Buddhists make a pilgrimage to a stupa that contains a fragment of the Buddha's body, they feel as if they are in the presence of the Buddha himself. In the same way, Japanese people feel the presence of those who have died when they pray at their household buddha altar where the memorial tablets are displayed. The parents' relationship to linking objects develops over the first few years of grief. It is common for parents to gradually rely less on the exterior presence of the linking object because they develop a more interior sense of their child's presence. In the months after her child died, one mother reported, a stuffed animal "was like a crutch for me. I felt that as long as it was near me as I went to sleep each night, so I could reach out and touch it, or smell it, that Barry's death was not so final." One day as she cleaned, she put the stuffed animal in another room and found she did not miss it: "By then the memories of Barry were ingrained into my mind so well I didn't need to look at a symbol of his life to remember him by."

The presence of a linking object is a self-validating truth to the parents that, although they know full well that their child is dead, yet, in a sense, the child lives. One mother had many memories of being at the beach on Padre Island, off the coast of Texas, with her son. They would look for sand dollars that the boy saved. She remembered those times as mystical experiences in which her bond with nature and her bond with the child were intertwined. In a newsletter article, she wrote that the child "was especially awed by the setting sun and as we walked the beaches, always he would stop and watch the sun go down—I did too! I was so happy with him." In the late winter after the boy's death, she went to Padre Island and, acutely feeling her son's absence, walked the beach alone, "just the sand, the sea, a beautiful setting sun, the screeching gulls, God and me." She talked to God and begged Him for a sign that her son still lived. She asked God, "Please send me a sand dollar." She knew it was the wrong season for sand dollars. The local people had told her that they had seen no sand dollars since the summer.

> But I only wanted just one sand dollar—just one! Watching the fading sunset and listening to the roar of the waves, darkness began to fall, so I turned to go back when there by my feet, the waves pushed up one lone sand dollar—a small but perfect sand dollar!
>
> That is exactly the way it happened and I cannot begin to tell you the feelings I had. My prayer had been answered.

The answer to her prayer for a sign that the child still lived was the linking object of the sand dollar. It renewed her link to her son, to God, to the past she shared with the child, and to a place that had always seemed eternal to her. The sand dollar, coming out of the sea and onto the land beneath her feet, crossed the boundary between the living and the dead, between timelessness and change. She had at that moment a sense of the uncanny, a feeling often associated with religious belief and practice. Sand dollars were out of season, yet one washed up at her feet. Although the sand dollar's appearance was a rare statistical probability, no natural laws were violated. But it was a miracle for her, no matter what her scientific mind might have known. After this intense experience of finding the sand dollar, the memory of this experience also can serve as a linking object.

Some linking objects can be quite long-lasting. In many cultures, graves remain a place where the living can feel the presence of the dead. In contemporary Western culture, each person is put in a separate grave, which is often not in the same plot as the family's other dead. When people who personally remember the dead person die, the sense of presence at the grave fades. In many cultures, however, the grave is for the whole family. The presence of the dead at the grave, then, can endure for many generations, since those who have died recently are in the same place as the ancestors who died many years ago. Sometimes graves can be a linking object for people who never knew the deceased or who are not part of the family. For example, I was overwhelmed at Wounded Knee as I stood at the mass grave of the Native Americans massacred there in 1890.

The second way that bereaved parents find solace is in traditional religious ideas and devotion. In their prayers and religious rituals some parents find that their sense of the presence of God and their sense of their child's presence merge. One mother wrote a letter to her dead daughters describing what she experiences when she attends Catholic Mass:

> Every time I attend the sacrifice of the Mass, at the part where our Blessed Lord comes into our hearts, I feel so close to your angelic presence. What a divine experience! The only problem is that it doesn't last long enough. If only the others could share these feelings.

For Catholics, the most sacred moment in the Mass occurs when the bread and wine are transubstantiated, actually becoming the body and blood of Jesus. So when Jesus becomes fully present on the altar and then becomes part of her as she eats and drinks, her daughters are part of that reality.

A mother experiencing the presence of her dead daughters at the moment the risen Son of God is made present is well within orthodox religion. Many parents have developed religious ideas and a sense of transcendent presence in devotion that are outside the orthodoxy of churches or theological doctrine. Before her child's death, one mother had already developed a pantheistic spirituality in which God seemed to her to be everywhere. Her dead daughter could now have the same omnipresence. On the girl's birthday her mother wrote a letter as if from the child.

> I would have been twenty today, bound by earthly constraints. Do not cry, Mom. I am forever, I am eternal, I am ageless. I am in the blowing wind, the first blades of grass in the spring, the haunting cry of the owl, the shriek of the hawk, the silent soaring of the turkey vulture. I am in the tears of those in mourning, the laughter of little children, the pain of the dying, the hopelessness of the homeless. I am the weightless, floating feeling when you close your eyes at night; I am the heaviness of a broken heart. . . . Like an invisible cocoon I surround you. I am in the moonlight, the sunbeams, the dew at dawn. . . . Do not cry. Remember me with love and laughter and yes, with pain. For I was, I am, and I will always be. Once Amy, now nameless and free.

The third way parents find solace is in memory. The bond between the living and the dead continues in memory. Unconflicted and peaceful memory often comes only at the end of a difficult process. At first memories can be very painful, because they are reminders of the death. In cases where the death is very traumatic, parents may show symptoms of post-traumatic stress disorder (PTSD), in which the memory of the event is suppressed, but at unpredictable points floods the mind in flashbacks that feel as if the trauma is happening all over again. But even when parents do not have PTSD, they remember the pain of the cancer or the disfigured body after the accident. Memories are also reminders of the loss. When parents remember the child, their first thought is that the child is gone. It takes time and many retellings of the story before the bad memories of the death give way to memories of the child's whole life. Some people think that all they have left of the child is their pain, so if they lose the memory of the pain, they will lose their child. One mother reflected on the discovery that letting go of the pain did not also mean letting go of the child.

> You know, I remember being afraid that someday I would wake up and my feeling of being bonded to Kelly wouldn't be there. I thought that when the pain left, she would be gone too. But now I find that I hope the memories will come. The times in the hospital are not what I

> remember. I remember the good times, when she was well. Sometimes I just look at her pictures and remember when we took them. I never know when I will look at the pictures, but I feel better afterwards.

As the details of memories fade, the bond remains. Twenty years after her daughter died, a mother's memory of the girl's ballet recital still brings the feelings back.

> I can't remember the details of that afternoon. . . . But I remember the feeling, somewhere between laughter and tears. I remember loving that small, beautiful person, my child. I remember my sense of admiration for her, and a fittingly stifled flood of pride. . . . I have forgotten so many things, but I remember the feeling. Always the feeling.

Memories are individual, but more important, memories are communal and play an important role in both religious communities and families. After the Prophet Muhammad died, for example, his followers systematically collected all the memories people had of him. That collection of memories, called the hadith, is second only to the Qur'an in helping Muslims decide what is right. For Jews, the collective memory of the exodus from Egypt, the destruction of the Temple in Jerusalem, the diaspora, and the Holocaust creates the Jewish religion, just as the hadith is important for maintaining the continuity in Islam. Another example is war memorials, which do not honor the war itself, but rather the collective memory of those who died in the war. Remembering together, then, is one of the core intersubjective activities of grieving. The rituals of the self-help group—the holiday candlelight service, the balloon release, the picture boards—are all rituals of collective memory. The shared memory of ancestors is a central basis of family bonds in all cultures, but we have seen how the inability of family members to talk openly about their deceased children is a major strain on family unity in modern, Western cultures.

The fourth way parents find solace is in identification, that is, making their inner representation of the child a part of their self-representation. This kind of solace has a somewhat different character than the three forms described above. It is found in a sense of reinvigorated life, in renewed feelings of competence. One mother wrote a poem in which she says that her child's life story has been cut short. She wonders what the story would have been if the child had lived. She resolves the question by deciding that the child only lived the prologue of a story and that she would live out the meaning that the child's life began. The meanings of her child's story are love, devotion, joy, and knowledge. If she can live so those values are real in her life, then her dead child's life story will have been completed. She writes about this commitment with these words:

> These truths will speak
> through my pages,
> Making your prologue—
> forever mine.

Often, identifying with the child means deciding to live fully in spite of the death. One parent wrote, "I came to the decision that I was to try to use my gift of life to the utmost as my son had used his." The child often represents the parent's best self. Children seldom consciously represent darker parts of the parent's self. The parents' image of the dead child often reverts to an ideal, just as saints, angels, and bodhisattvas personify the ideal values that the whole community should live by. The child, then, can be a model by which the parent and the community can live more authentic lives. The idealization of the child provides another way in which the child serves as a connector between heaven and earth, between perfection and reality.

These primary ways parents find solace in their continuing bond with their child are not exclusive, because the experience of transcendent reality is multidimensional. Bereaved parents may retain the linking objects from early in their grief while at the same time finding the presence of the child within religious practices. They can memorialize the child at the same time they incorporate the child into their identity, their own sense of selfhood.

Negative Solace: Revenge and Retribution

The world would be a simpler place if continuing bonds with the dead always led to peace and harmony. We only need to watch the nightly news, however, to see that grief and continuing bonds with the dead play an integral role in long and bitter wars. We see funerals with the bodies covered with national flags and the mourners vowing to revenge these deaths by killing members of the enemy tribe, ethnic group, or nation. War and violence between peoples are a complex phenomenon that cannot be reduced to individual or family grief, but perhaps if we understand grief and continuing bonds better, we can see at least one aspect of the spirituality that expresses itself in revenge.

Fantasies of revenge or retribution are a negative kind of solace. In cases of wrongful deaths, especially murders, some bereaved parents take comfort in thoughts of the perpetrators suffering. For example, a woman whose son had been murdered by his girlfriend and her new lover said she could not sleep because when she closed her eyes she kept seeing her son's battered body. She said that in order to fall asleep she imagined in great detail the two murderers being subjected to medieval-like torture. Those images were comforting to her, much as the sense of the child's presence gives comfort to other bereaved parents. Such thoughts are normal. Everyone can identify with the hope that the one who hurt us will suffer for it, even if we cannot inflict the suffering ourselves. When we have no power to right the wrong, we look outside for retribution to bring justice and thus to show that the world is orderly. Justice can come in this life or in the next. We hope for justice from the criminal courts or from divine intervention. We hope there is a power greater than ours—God, the state, or a superhero like in the movies—that can put the world aright. That is, the fantasies put us in touch with at least the hope of transcendent reality, the hope that there is a being with greater power than we have to bring justice in a world gone wrong.

Revenge is an aspect of grief in some of the most gripping human dramas. When Hamlet meets his father's ghost on the battlement, it is not to receive comfort in his grief. Rather, Hamlet is commissioned to seek justice for his father's death, and the revenge tragedy is set in motion. From ancient times until quite recently, ghosts often came back to request or demand justice for their wrongful deaths. I do not know why, but I have never heard from bereaved parents that their dead child supported them in their revenge fantasies. It may be that the duty to seek justice in wrongful deaths has passed from the family to the state. Because the family no longer has the power to extract revenge, the spirits of the dead do not ask. Revenge can remain a fantasy in societies where the rule of law is well established. Where the rule of law is not established, revenge may move from fantasy to action.

The solace of revenge or retribution fantasies, like actions of revenge or retribution, seldom grows into positive resolution. Instead, parents find that it "eats you up." At a meeting of another self-help group, Parents of Murdered Children, several parents who had just begun attending vented the rage they felt toward their children's killers, voicing their desire to have the killers suffer as badly as their children had suffered. A woman whose son had been murdered ten years earlier by killers who were never found said, "After a while I just had to give that up. One day I just said to myself that they had taken enough from me and they were not going to take any more." As time passes, virtually all the parents in the group find that hopes of revenge are a dead end, and they let them go. Many, however, do not leave their revenge fantasies completely behind. After telling me about how he decided that the hate was "killing me while it wasn't doing a damn thing to them," a father whose daughter had been gang-raped and then murdered ended the conversation by saying, "Still, if I ever found myself where I could do it, I know I would kill those sonsofbitches and never give it a thought."

Revenge for a child's death can, in some times and places, take on political significance, since bonds with ancestors are an important element in family and even national bonds. Patriotic celebrations often take the form of memorials for those who have died that the nation might live. Ethnic, racial, or political membership is often infused with spiritual feelings. Indeed, for many people, God and country feel as one. A shared religious sense of the bond with the dead child can get merged with the sense of transcendent reality they feel in their ethnic, racial, or national membership. Among the symbols that bind a nation together are the images of its young who died so that the nation could gain or keep its land, freedom, king, religion, form of government, or economic power. All peoples encourage a strong bond with their dead heroes or martyrs.

Fantasies of revenge that identify the dead with the nation or tribe become very destructive when they are acted out politically. The perpetrators of genocidal movements and protracted ethnic conflict in this century have justified their actions to themselves as the restoration of the sacred honor of their dead that had been taken from them in defeat generations or even centuries ago. In cultural narratives in which blood must be answered by blood, the legal system may be responsible for extracting punishment. If the legal system is not adequate, God can be responsible for justice in the next world, or perhaps humans must act on God's behalf to bring about the justice for which these dead cry out. In those times, the fantasies of revenge and retribution that most people feel in their grief at what seems a wrongful death can be acted out in reality. In the name of those fallen for the cause, other people's children may be killed with impunity. It is difficult to stop a cycle of violence when each side merges the solace of the inner representations of the dead children with a spiritual feeling of peoplehood and a drive for revenge that feels as if it has divine sanction.

CONCLUSION

When we begin to understand how grief and continuing bonds with the dead function in the lives of the survivors, we see that continued bonds with the dead are not a separate category of bonds that transcend the limitations imposed by physical life. Continuing bonds with the dead are intertwined with the bonds we maintain with other unseen and transcendent realities. Elaine Pagels, one of the leading contemporary scholars in religious studies, found that her continuing bond with her dead husband gave her a deeper understanding of spiritual life in the ancient world:

> In 1988, when my husband of twenty years died in a hiking accident, I became aware that, like many people who grieve, I was living in the presence of an invisible being—living, that is, with a vivid sense of someone who had died. . . . In the ancient Western world, of which I am a historian, many—perhaps most—people assumed that the universe was inhabited by invisible beings whose presence impinged upon the visible world and its human inhabitants.[13]

In many cultures the lines between the ancestors, the saints, the gods, or, in monotheism, God, are blurred. The family ancestors, the tribal deities, the martyrs for the faith, and the Lord of Hosts can all be aspects of sacred reality that individuals and communities experience. When we understand interactions with the dead in the lives of bereaved people, such as the parents I have described in this chapter, we can understand a great deal about the religious lives of people everywhere. We can understand something of the way biological instincts are expressed in cultural forms. We can understand how the religious experience of connection to transcendent reality brings solace in the midst of pain. We can understand how a community that shares pain and shares bonds with the dead is a religious or spiritual community. We can understand how individuals and communities find and use beings that are intermediaries between the sacred and the profane, between the living and the dead. We can understand how relics, religious rituals, memories, and identification are all ways we bond to the dead and to other spiritual beings. Finally, perhaps we can understand something of the drive for justice and the need for revenge that motivates much of humankind's ethnic and religious strife. Grief and religion are both universal aspects of the human experience. We should not be surprised, then, that they are interwoven at so many points.

NOTES

1. Unni Wikan, "Bereavement and Loss in Two Muslim Communities: Egypt and Bali Compared," *Social Sciences and Medicine* 27, no. 5 (1988): 452.
2. Ibid.

3. Ibid., 459.

4. Ibid., 458.

5. Sigmund Freud, "Mourning and Melancholia," in *The Standard Edition of the Complete Psychological Works of Sigmund Freud,* ed. and trans. James Strachey, 14: 243–258 (London: Hogarth Press, 1961; original work published 1917).

6. Dennis Klass, Phyllis R. Silverman, and Steven L. Nickman, eds., *Continuing Bonds: New Understandings of Grief* (Washington, DC: Taylor and Francis, 1996); Tony Walter, *On Bereavement: The Culture of Grief* (Buckingham: Open University Press, 1999); Robert A. Neimeyer, *Meaning Reconstruction and the Experience of Loss* (Washington, DC: American Psychological Association, 2001).

7. Dennis Klass, *The Spiritual Lives of Bereaved Parents* (Philadelphia: Brunner/Mazel, 1999).

8. Anna-Maria Rizzuto, "The Father and the Child's Representation of God: A Developmental Approach," in *Father and Child: Developmental and Clinical Perspectives,* ed. Stanley H. Cath, Alan R. Gurwitt, and John M. Ross, 357–607 (Boston: Little, Brown, 1982), 359.

9. Ronnie Janoff-Bulman, "Assumptive Worlds and the Stress of Traumatic Events: Applications of the Schema Construct," *Social Cognition* 7, no. 2 (1989): 113–136.

10. "Credo," Bereaved Parents of the USA.

11. Rudolf Otto, *The Idea of the Holy: An Inquiry into the Non-rational Factor in the Idea of the Divine and Its Relation to the Rational,* trans. John W. Harvey (New York: Oxford University Press, 1923), 3.

12. Quoted in *Webster's Unabridged Dictionary,* 1913.

13. Elaine Pagels, *The Origin of Satan* (New York: Random House, 1995), xv.

Epilogue

Evan Berry

In considering contemporary religious systems as they are practiced, it would be easy to view the rapid rates at which cremation is replacing burial as evidence of the declining importance of religion. It would be easy to interpret the growing use of therapeutic language in funerary services as a sign that religious community is being usurped by individualism. It would be easy to consider the incorporation of teddy bears and sports memorabilia into religious rituals as an example of commodification. In other words, it would be convenient to see the changes in the religious landscape of modernity as simply the encroachment of market forces, bureaucratization, and secularism. But such a view misses the important ways in which religious traditions exist in creative tension with the surrounding world. The authors in this volume resist oversimplified explanations, preferring the challenge and rich complexity of a descriptive method. They seek in different ways to illustrate the dynamic interaction between religion and forces of social change in the contemporary world.

This study of religious responses to death centers on the relationship between religious traditions and the sociocultural environment of modernity. While the contributors have deployed a range of theories and interpretations to describe the interaction of religion and modernity, throughout the volume there emerges a shared skepticism toward models of conflict between modernity and religious tradition. It is clear from the preceding studies that religion, rather than fading away as irrelevant, continues to play a vital role in the lives of individuals and communities.[1] In this concluding chapter, I focus our attention on the contribution these studies make to our understanding of the complex relationships between religion and its social context in modernity. The first half of this chapter analyzes three fields of social change where modernity and religion enter into dynamic relation: (1) technological change; (2) therapy culture, individualism, and market forces; (3) globalization, diaspora, and politics. The second half systematizes the various ways in which the authors of this volume have incorporated these challenges into their understanding of religion.

SPACES OF SOCIAL CHANGE: TECHNOLOGY

There are at least three ways in which the technological changes integral to modernity affect the shape and content of religious activity surrounding death. The first regards the growth of institutionalized systems of mechanized cremation in many Western nations. Throughout this volume we have seen religious traditions wrestling with cremation, in each case settling upon a unique negotiation. In some cases, concern about the wholeness of the human body mandates an outright rejection of cremation as an appropriate means of disposal, as with Orthodox Judaism. In other cases, cremation poses a challenge to established liturgical practices that rely on the language of burial and interment, prompting a renewed theological discussion of the images and symbols deployed in funerary ritual. This is evidenced by the flexibility of the 1979 Episcopalian *Book of Common Prayer*, which gives priests the option to change the phrase "we commit his body to the ground" to either "we commit his body to the deep" or "to the elements" (Larson-Miller). Cremation is a challenge not only for traditionally religious persons. For members of the modern establishment who might describe themselves as "spiritual, but not religious," cremation merits ritualization outside the funerary script of traditional religion. Taken as generative religious forces, secular anxieties about the anonymity of cremation and concerns about the authenticity of new memorialization rituals might contribute to our understanding of the variety of consumer choices surrounding cremation and the treatment of ashes. Whether through orthodox rejection of cremation, liturgical adaptation to changing disposal preferences, or innovative practices by "spiritual seekers," the spread of crematory technology fuels religious revision and the rearticulation of themes and symbols.

The second way in which technological change profoundly affects religion is the near ubiquity of modern medicine. One immediate consequence of this ubiquity is that death is removed from the domestic sphere and relocated in a market-oriented, bureaucratic, medical space. Certainly the religious needs of the dying and their loved ones shape the institutional channels through which death is regulated, but these needs often find themselves in conflict with the procedures of rationally organized medical systems. For instance, Rebecca Golbert argues that modern medicine perpetrates a "conspiracy of silence" through which doctors attempt only to cure illness, often at the expense of addressing the inevitability of death. Alternatively, medical professionals often are unsympathetic to the specificities of religious deathways, such as the desire of many Hindus to die on the ground, rather than in a hospital bed. Whether rejecting the powerful mythos of medical know-how, as Christian Scientists have done, or embracing lifesaving technologies as products of God's gift of reason, religious traditions are forced to reckon with changes wrought by modern medicine.

A third type of change to influence religious traditions is the growth of media technologies. Modernity is in part characterized by technological advances like the printing press and the camera, which have both radically altered the way in which religious themes and ideas are transmitted. Premodern religious symbols were much less likely to move across space and time than modern ones, which are now embedded within a vast matrix of reproducibility and manipulability. But the technologization of religious symbols is not necessarily detrimental; Mark Elmore points us to the twofold change that photography has brought about in Hindu ancestor veneration. First, photographs have changed the material construction of spaces for ancestor veneration. Second, photographs have actually altered the way in which ancestors are remembered: they work to individualize ancestors, keeping their faces fresh in the memory of the living. The same process can be seen in the rearticulation of myths and ideas in new media, like the retelling of the story of Nangak Prakanong in a recent Thai movie (Goss and Klass). On a broader scale, Tony Walter describes the profound ramifications of mass media coverage of disasters and mass death. In his view, the mass media have taken up some of the functions traditionally ascribed to religious institutions. Coverage of national disasters like the 1995 bombing of the Murrah building in Oklahoma City or the 1999 shooting at Columbine High School is designed to systematically destroy and then rebuild our "sense of security" thus serving to interpret "the meaning of death and suffering" to a mass audience. Walter's analysis points beyond the conclusion that media usurpation of religious functions is a sign of secularization. The media are here described as a kind of modern religious authority that reinforces the mythos of technology, offering a promise of methodical progress against danger and disease.

SPACES OF SOCIAL CHANGE: THERAPY, INDIVIDUALISM, AND THE MARKET

If cremation, medicine, and the media form a series of technological changes for religious traditions to respond to, then psychotherapy, individualism, and market forces represent the interrelated challenges of being situated in a so-called secular culture. Much as mass media serve as an interpretive lens through which modern societies understand and relate to death, the language of psychology and "therapy culture" also serves as the predominant interpretative framework for modern perceptions of death and dying. Sylvia Grider argues in her study of spontaneous shrines that the function of spontaneous memorialization is to respond to tragic deaths with a personally meaningful and carefully managed gesture of memory that allows survivors to "express their grief, outrage, and bewilderment in the presence of violent and unexpected death." Several contributors to this volume have invoked Ann Swidler's notion of the "cultural toolkit,"[2] arguing that religious traditions serve as symbolic reservoirs on which people draw at times of heightened meaning and that the language of therapy (grief, healing, "moving on," etc.) functions in much the same way. In addition to serving as a source of meaningful language, therapy can also provide a structure for communities of shared meaning, as with the support groups for the parents of deceased children described by Dennis Klass.

For many scholars of religion, individualism is a dirty word, synonymous with selfishness and antithetical to religious ethics and community.[3] For many such scholars, individualism refers to the process by which religious authority and community are replaced by impersonal market relations and consumer choice. That funerary practices exist in a market system where the demands of individuals are met by a variety of service providers is troubling to some clergy members, such as the Protestant pastors interviewed by Glenn Lucke. The concern of such religious actors about the "ongoing tension" between "the personal and the theological" dimensions of modern funerary rites points to deeper worries about the devolution of religious authority from institutions to individuals (Lucke and Gilbert). But this line of criticism misses the religious features of individualism: those who are skeptical about "expressive individualism" fail to see the innovative forms of pastiche and symbolic recombination at the heart of personalized funerary practices.[4] To dismiss the inclusion of country and western songs in a Protestant funeral as mere "personalization" indicates a theological commitment to what ought to be included in a funeral. The inclusion of new symbols and practices is less a sign of religious decline than a signal of new modes of religious appropriation of cultural objects or, as Kathleen Garces-Foley and Justin Holcomb phrase it, "a continuation of religious sensibilities in new forms."

These forms of religious improvisation and innovation permeate the fluid boundary between religiosity and capitalism. As Douglas Davies succinctly puts it: "deathstyle matches lifestyle." Like individualism, the marketplace presents religious traditions with both a challenge and an opportunity. On the one hand, markets demand that religions work to protect symbols from the profane forces of commodification, and, on the other hand, markets extend these symbols beyond their ordinary contexts, making them accessible across socioreligious boundaries. The movement of religious symbols across time and space through a symbolic marketplace points to the importance of the third arena of social change: globalization, immigration, and diaspora.

SPACES OF SOCIAL CHANGE: GLOBALIZATION, DIASPORA, AND CONTEMPORARY POLITICS

The numerous religious concepts and behaviors regarding death described in this volume exist in a marketplace of ideas and services, and they also reflect the complexity and exchange of a globalized world. Religious texts, practices, and practitioners are moving across the globe. Several contributors to this anthology take up the issue of religion in diaspora, reporting how immigrants negotiate between the demands of their religious traditions and the demands of the host culture. The challenges of diaspora include the absence of religious leaders, distance from important sacred sites, and a poor understanding of nonnative religions by the dominant host culture, all of which are evidenced in Mark Elmore's description of Hindu funerals in the United Kingdom. This is not to say, however, that immigration works as a destructive force on religious tradition. As Kristina Myrvold shows, the experience of diaspora both encourages conformity with the dominant host culture and heightens the desire for the maintenance of tradition. Not only does the diaspora community change in the face of a hegemonic culture, the dominant culture is also necessarily affected by the presence of the diaspora, sometimes creating social spaces for, and even an understanding of, diaspora religion.

Diaspora is but one space where religion engages with the changes of a globalized world. The constantly changing landscape of political organization and power directly affects lived religious practice. The Chinese occupation of Tibet has severely curtailed the ability of Tibetans to practice Buddhism as they formerly did and has prompted the emigration of thousands of Tibetan monks to India, the United States, and elsewhere. The Tibetan plight has spurred a sympathetic following of Western Tibetan Buddhists, such as those Robert Goss and Dennis Klass encountered in Colorado. Juan Campo describes the way in which war and terror have narrowed the possibilities for mourning in Iraq: the unmarked mass graves of Saddam Husayn's murderous rule present a serious challenge to completing a proper Islamic burial, and the dangers of the American occupation and the insurgent resistance offer little safety for public religious practice.

THEORETICAL CONTRIBUTIONS

If this collection represents a weaving together of scholarly descriptions of religion and death in a changing world, the cloth is formed by the union of an empirical and historical warp with a rich theoretical woof. Three theoretical contributions can be delineated in the preceding pages, in addition to a number of rhetorical and metaphorical tools useful in interpreting religious systems. These theoretical orientations crystallize around a series of dynamic dualisms: prescribed/performed, religion/culture, and authentic/inauthentic. In utilizing and challenging the neat boundaries of these dualisms, the authors also offer several fresh ideas about how to describe the continuing vitality of religion in modernity.

A number of authors in this volume employ the tension between prescribed and performed religious activity in order to capture the complexity of continually shifting forms of religious approaches toward death. This dualism is most explicit in Juan Campo's chapter about the frequency with which Islamic expectations for proper mourning are transgressed. His archetypal example is that of the fourteenth-century Muslim scholar Abu Hayyan, who grieved for his daughter far beyond the sanctified limits of mourning. Yet Abu Hayyan's mourning was more than just transgressive; it served as a productive force, taking up potent Islamic symbols and reconfiguring them in verse to communicate a deeply religious sentiment to future generations. Campo elucidates how this tension works as a generative force in religious tradition:

> The prescribed consists of formalized rules governing belief and practice constructed, maintained, and implemented by religious authorities. . . . The performed dimension of religion, on the other hand, tends to be suppler, giving people the freedom not only to express religious and cultural norms, but also to appropriate, contest, adapt, and change them.

Looking back on three examples from this anthology, we can see how a dialectic relationship between the prescribed and the performed provides a more nuanced understanding of religious dynamics. First, this framework allows us to better understand the struggle between individualism and religious authority in modern death rites. Religious authorities prescribe spaces in which religious sentiments are to be expressed, thus defining the limits of religious thought and action. These spaces can be sufficiently ample to house the ideas, emotions, and actions of religious communities, but they do not always leave enough room for maneuvering. Thus, elements that may seem inappropriate to clergy members are woven into funerary ritual at the behest of individuals. Garces-Foley and

Holcomb go further. They suggest that American religion is built around a skepticism of rote compulsory behavior and that the American ambivalence toward ritual represents a discomfort with the notion that religious traditions exist primarily as mediated, regulated patterns of behavior. Such discomfort and ambivalence about scripted religious ritual is a driving force in the development of individualized, personalized rituals. Second, we see the same dynamic in Lizette Larson-Miller's description of a Catholic funeral for a teenage girl. In covering the coffin with kisses while wearing the deceased's favorite lipstick, the teenager's friends improvised within an officially sanctioned ritual space. From this perspective, it might even be said that religion (the prescribed) exists largely as a set of authoritative regulations within which religiosity (the performed) is carried out. Third, we see in Sylvia Grider's chapter that the flourishing of public memorials, especially as spontaneous shrines, is an important new form of ritualizing death. Though such activity draws upon Christian tradition, it does so in a striking way, often working outside the boundaries of officially sanctioned ritual space. The limitations of prescribed places for grief and mourning have led many people to seek new locations for memorial altogether: soccer stadiums, roadsides, sidewalks, public squares, and the Internet.

A second theoretical premise advanced by many of the authors in this volume is the reciprocal exchange of symbols and actions between religious and cultural systems. This exchange comes clearly to light in the essays that deal with diaspora and globalization, as for instance in Goss and Klass's account of the exiled Tibetan Buddhist community that forms the core of Naropa University in Boulder, Colorado. The interaction between Tibetan monks living in the United States and Americans curious about Buddhist thought and practice has created a unique environment where Tibetan Buddhism both influences and is influenced by American culture. Such reciprocity is predicated on the notion that religion and culture do not constitute mutually exclusive spheres of human life. This exchange is found also in Kristina Myrvold's discussion of Sikhs in Sweden who employ both modern medicine and prayer in the attempt to heal the sick. With regard to healing in particular, and religion in general, it is important to remember that the interplay of traditional and modern social systems does not represent a zero-sum trade-off. As Myrvold explains, "instead, secular and religious remedies are intertwined and complement each other." This reciprocity between religious and cultural systems is fundamental to understanding religion not only in the context of modernity, but throughout the historical developments of religious traditions. Along the axis of religion in premodernity, Larson-Miller provides us with the example of the simultaneous "Christianization" of Roman culture and "Romanization" of Christianity. Along the axis of religion in modernity, we see the symbolic dialogue between religious activity and material culture in Grider's analysis of spontaneous memorialization. The items that constitute such memorials are often idiosyncratic, unscripted, and highly personal. Through the vernacular utilization of everyday objects, memorials disrupt the boundary between the sacred and profane as decidedly religious items, like rosaries and crosses, are placed together with less obviously sacred symbols, like teddy bears, beer bottles, and letters.

A third area of theoretical unity offered in this volume surrounds the question of religious "authenticity." Much of the history of the academic study of religion has been dominated by the theological description and comparison of religious traditions. This privileging of belief over practice has fostered a language of reified religious forms, and it is precisely this privileging with which Dennis Kelley takes issue. Positing that a religion can be portrayed in terms of what its adherents believe suggests that religious traditions can be captured solely as a set of ideas. This emphasis on theology is troubling in its attempt to reduce thriving, evolving religious communities to a fixed set of principles or practices, especially when this work is carried out by anthropologists of European descent. This method essentializes religion and thus denies communities the capacity for dynamism. Kelley argues that this process of essentialization has led to the dismissal of contemporary Native American religious practices as "inauthentic" and that such a dismissal is not only linked to a history of colonial domination, but also misses the vitality of indigenous religions. What binds many of the essays in this volume together is the attempt to avoid reifying religious traditions by considering them in perpetual dialogue with their sociocultural environments.

The studies presented here offer a series of robust models for scholarship on religion in modernity. The attempt to understand and describe the vitality of religious systems grows from a desire to describe religion as more than static beliefs, and the fruit of this project is a nuanced vocabulary of religious dynamism. Let us consider a few examples. Kelley's quest to wrest the interpretation of Native American traditions from the hands of those who are prone to approach it as a static, historical phenomenon has led him to offer a valuable rhetorical device useful to the scholar of religion. His metaphor applies the musical concept of *reprise* to the same question about religious innovation. The dichotomy between modern and traditional societies is a constructed distinction that rests heavily upon the idea that modernity is only that which is innovative, and tradition is only that which is static and unchanging. But innovation is impossible without a theme on which to vary—hence Kelley's deployment of the symphonic reprise. Another essay that proffers two significant metaphors for religious dynamism is Larson-Miller's analysis of pre-Reformation Christian traditions. She describes the layering process of religious rituals surrounding death: officially sanctioned rituals provide a basis for all ritual activity (e.g., a funeral performed by a priest using traditional texts), upon which popular religious practices are layered (e.g., a preference for all black attire at funerals), to which secular traditions are added (e.g., obituaries in the local paper). Larson-Miller's vocabulary of layering is rendered stronger by her second metaphor, that of religious narrative. The three layers of ritual practice are conjoined together precisely because they share a narrative about the meaning of human life and death. But "narrative" here is not reducible to some core belief that constitutes religion, rather, narrative becomes a tool for scholars to understand religious change: the work of interpretation and reinterpretation only functions in regard to a central narrative.

CONCLUSION

In considering the engagement between religion and modernity, the scholars included here offer specific descriptions of religious postures toward death. Much of the theoretical focus implicit in these analyses centers on questions of secularization and religious transformation. Such religious transformation is often implicated as the source for the increase of persons who identify themselves as "spiritual, but not religious," but little has been said about the deathways of such people. A future challenge for students of religion and death regards the relationship of nontraditional religious systems to death and dying. What kinds of rituals are enacted by atheists? What constitutes a good death for someone who is spiritual, but not religious? Reaching deeper into the structures of modernity, what kinds of social repercussions do scientific conceptualizations of death have? If the changing social context of the modern world finds reciprocal changes in religious traditions, then perhaps those changes also work to alter our very understanding of death itself. Does the universality of death make it a "fact" universal among all religions and societies? How could scholars of religion consider and describe the ways in which societies and religions mediate experiences of death? As an attempt to ask about religion and death in a changing world, the scholarship presented here represents a point of departure for such inquiries.

Though diverse in their approaches and particularist in their projects, the essays gathered here offer more than just a fresh look at "the world's religions" and more than just an engaging compendium of religious responses to death and dying. These essays offer an alternative to the staid interpretation of religion that depicts it as in conflict with modernity, the usual narrative of unchanging religions in a changing world. Instead, we see here a variety of ways in which religion is embedded in a modern context and constantly in dialogue with its changing social context. Religion, these authors argue, is a dynamic social enterprise, well-suited to engage with the challenges and the changes of modernity.

NOTES

1. Sociologists of religion including Auguste Comte and Émile Durkheim have advanced the argument that religion is an archaic form of meaning-making that will disappear in the face of growing scientific certainty. Since these arguments have largely failed to explain the importance and staying power of religious traditions in the United States and elsewhere, the theory of secularization has been adapted in various ways. Some scholars, like Stephen Bruce, argue simply that church attendance is decreasing, while others argue that religion is becoming merely a social force among others, unimportant in daily life, as in the work of David Yamane and R. Steven Warner. These perspectives are countered by scholars who assert that religion continues to inform modern social life, both in traditional forms and in forms hitherto unrecognized (e.g., "science as salvation," environmentalism, Marxism). Such arguments are made by sociologists and intellectual historians such as Mary Midgley and José Cassanova.

2. This argument is well expressed in Ann Swidler's "Culture in Action: Symbols and Strategies," *American Sociological Review* 51 (April 1986): 273–286.

3. Such concern about the forces of individualism and their effects on religious communities has been classically expressed by sociologists Peter Berger and Robert Bellah.

4. The attempt to articulate the ways that modern individuals balance their religious lives between individualistic bricolage and institutional affiliation is well formulated in Wade Clark Roof's *Spiritual Marketplace: Baby Boomers and the Remaking of American Religion* (Princeton, NJ: Princeton University Press, 1999). For a discussion of "expressive individualism," a term first employed by Robert Bellah, see especially chapter five.

About the Contributors

Ronald K. Barrett is a professor of psychology at Loyola Marymount University in Los Angeles, where he created and teaches Psychology of Death and Dying (with an accompanying lab). He is an internationally recognized specialist on the study of cross-cultural differences in death, dying, and funeral rites and has published widely on African American funeral practices and multicultural perspectives.

Evan Berry is a PhD candidate in religious studies at the University of California at Santa Barbara. His scholarship focuses on ideas of nature in modernity as they raise questions about religion, science, spirituality, and secularization. He is a contributor to the *Encyclopedia of Religion and Nature* (2005).

Juan Eduardo Campo, associate professor of Islamic studies and the history of religions at the University of California at Santa Barbara and codirector of the UCSB Center for Middle East Studies, is currently editor of the Facts on File *Encyclopedia of Islam* (2005) and writing a book on Muslim, Hindu, and Christian pilgrimages in modernity. He is also studying religious beliefs and practices relating to food in Middle Eastern cultures. His book *The Other Sides of Paradise: Explorations into the Religious Meanings of Domestic Space in Islam* received the American Academy of Religion's Award for Excellence (1991).

Douglas J. Davies is a professor in the study of religion at the University of Durham, England. He holds the degrees of Litt M, and Litt D, from Oxford University and an Honorary Theol D from the University of Uppsala in Sweden. His research in the anthropology and sociology of belief, ritual, and symbolism is reflected in *Death, Ritual and Belief* (2002), *Anthropology and Theology* (2002), *An Introduction to Mormonism* (2003), and *The Mormon Culture of Salvation* (2000). He is currently preparing for publication *The Encyclopedia of Cremation* and undertaking a major study of the transmission of religious values across generations.

Mark Elmore is an assistant professor at the University of North Florida. He is currently working on a book that examines the relationship between religion and state in Himachal Pradesh, India. He is also working on a documentary film entitled *Pratibimba* that examines controversies surrounding ritual killing in this same region.

Kathleen Garces-Foley received her doctorate in religious studies, specializing in religion in America, from the University of California at Santa Barbara and currently teaches at California State University, Northridge. She has published articles on the hospice movement and funeral practices of those unaffiliated with religious institutions. Her other research interests include immigrant religious communities and the growth of multiethnic congregations in the United States.

Richard B. Gilbert is a hospital chaplain, Anglican priest, certified thanatologist, and executive director of the World Pastoral Care Center. He received his PhD in pastoral psychology from the Graduate Theological Foundation and Rewley House in Oxford. He has published numerous books and articles on the subject of thanatology, including *Finding Your Way After Your Parent Dies: Hope for Grieving Adults* (1999) and, as editor, *Healthcare and Spirituality: Listening, Assessing, Caring* (2001).

Rebecca Golbert received her D Phil in social anthropology from the University of Oxford. She has taught at the University of Maryland, College Park, and is currently completing a book manuscript based on her doctoral research on Ukranian Jewish youth culture and identity in post–Soviet Ukraine. Her postdoctoral research, funded by fellowships from the U.S. Holocaust Memorial Museum and the National Council for Eurasian and East European Research, focuses on the intersections of memory and history in constructions of the Holocaust in Ukraine.

Robert E. Goss is a theologian and clergy within the Universal Fellowship of Metropolitan Community Churches. He has a doctorate in Comparative Religion from Harvard University, specializing in Christianity and Indo-Tibetan Buddhism. He is the author of *Jesus ACTED UP: A Gay and Lesbian Manifesto* (1993) and *Queering Christ: Beyond Jesus ACTED UP* (2002). This book was named a finalist for the Lambda Literary Awards. The Center for Theology and Natural Sciences in Berkeley, California, named Goss a 2000 Templeton Foundation winner in the international course competition in science and religion for his course, The Problem of Evil: Theodicies from the Natural Sciences, the Social Sciences, and Comparative Religions.

Sylvia Grider is an associate professor of anthropology at Texas A&M University, where she teaches courses in folklore, professional ethics, and material culture. As principal investigator of the Bonfire Memorabilia Project, she oversees the conservation and management of the artifacts collected from the spontaneous shrine that developed on the A&M campus following the fatal collapse of the student bonfire in 1999.

Justin S. Holcomb is a postdoctoral fellow at the Center on Religion and Democracy at the University of Virginia. He is currently editing *Theologies of Scripture and the Politics of Interpretation,* which explores the issues of authority and knowledge in Christian traditions. He has taught death and dying courses at Emory University and the University of Virginia.

Dennis F. Kelley is a visiting lecturer in the Department of Religious Studies at the University of Missouri–Columbia. His research interests are in myth, symbol, and ritual theory as well as indigenous religious traditions and practices in the modern world. He is coeditor of *American Indian Religious Traditions: An Encyclopedia* (2004).

Dennis Klass is a professor at Webster University, St. Louis, Missouri. His long-term ethnographic study of a local chapter of a self-help group of bereaved parents is reported in *The Spiritual Lives of Bereaved Parents* (1999). He is also coeditor of *Continuing Bonds: New Understandings of Grief* (1996). His current research is on grief and continuing bonds with the dead across cultures.

Lizette Larson-Miller is an associate professor of liturgy and dean of the chapel at the Church Divinity School of the Pacific/Graduate Theological Union. Her research areas are historical liturgy and sacramental theology. She was a Luce Fellow in 2002–2003, researching a project titled "Holy Ground: Sacred Space in Public Places." Her book, *Anointing of the Sick,* was published in 2005.

Glenn Lucke is a dissertation fellow at the Institute for Advanced Studies in Culture at the University of Virginia. His research interests include sociology of culture and religion, and his dissertation examines the resource capital of various American religious communities and their relative cultural power.

Kristina Myrvold is a PhD candidate in religious studies specializing in Sikh studies at Lund University, Sweden. Her doctoral thesis focuses on religious practices and textual use among the Sikhs in Varanasi, India, where she has conducted fieldwork for several years. She has published several articles on Sikh religious practices, including the adjustment of Sikh communities in Sweden, in Swedish books and journals.

Tony Walter is a reader in sociology at the University of Reading, UK, where he set up and ran an innovative MA program in Death and Society. He has written and lectured widely on death in modern society. His books in this area include *On Bereavement: The Culture of Grief* (1999), *The Mourning for Diana* (1999), *The Revival of Death* (1994), *Pilgrimage in Popular Culture* (1993; with Ian Reader), and *Funerals and How to Improve Them* (1990). He has also written on the sociology of religion, tourism, landscape, work, and unemployment.

Index